Odd Affinities

T0385630

∴

Odd Affinities

∵

VIRGINIA WOOLF'S SHADOW
GENEALOGIES

Elizabeth Abel

THE UNIVERSITY OF CHICAGO PRESS
CHICAGO AND LONDON

The University of Chicago Press, Chicago 60637
The University of Chicago Press, Ltd., London
© 2024 by The University of Chicago
All rights reserved. No part of this book may be used or reproduced in any
manner whatsoever without written permission, except in the case of brief
quotations in critical articles and reviews. For more information, contact the
University of Chicago Press, 1427 East 60th Street, Chicago, IL 60637.
Published 2024
Printed and bound by CPI Group (UK) Ltd, Croydon, CR0 4YY

33 32 31 30 29 28 27 26 25 24   1 2 3 4 5

ISBN-13: 978-0-226-82569-4 (cloth)
ISBN-13: 978-0-226-83267-8 (paper)
ISBN-13: 978-0-226-83268-5 (e-book)
DOI: https://doi.org/10.7208/chicago/9780226832685.001.0001

The University of Chicago Press gratefully acknowledges the
generous support of the University of California, Berkeley,
toward the publication of this book.

Library of Congress Cataloging-in-Publication Data

Names: Abel, Elizabeth, 1945– author.
Title: Odd affinities : Virginia Woolf's shadow genealogies / Elizabeth Abel.
Description: Chicago : The University of Chicago, 2024. | Includes
    bibliographical references and index.
Identifiers: LCCN 2023034966 | ISBN 9780226825694 (cloth) |
    ISBN 9780226832678 (paperback) | ISBN 9780226832685 (ebook)
Subjects: LCSH: Woolf, Virginia, 1882–1941—Criticism and interpretation.
Classification: LCC PR6045.O72 Z533 2024 | DDC 823/.912—dc23/
    eng/20230807
LC record available at https://lccn.loc.gov/2023034966

♾ This paper meets the requirements of ANSI/NISO Z39.48-1992
(Permanence of Paper).

For Christian
&
In Memory of Richard

The book grew day by day, week by week, without any plan at all, except that which was dictated each morning in the act of writing. The other way, to make a house and then inhabit it, to develop a theory and then apply it, as Words-worth did and Coleridge, is, it need not be said, equally good and much more philosophic. But in the present case it was necessary to write the book first and to invent a theory afterwards.

Virginia Woolf, "Introduction," *Mrs. Dalloway*

If you look for things that are like the things that you have looked for before, then, obviously, they'll connect up. But they'll only connect up in an obvious sort of way, which actually isn't, in terms of writing something new, very productive. So you have to take heterogeneous materials in order to get your mind to do something it hasn't done before.

W. G. Sebald, in Joseph Cuomo, "A Conversation with W. G. Sebald"

What I've learned in these past few years, is that when we make something, whether it's a painting, a letter, a connection with someone, or even just a memory, we don't yet know what the legacy of that creation will be—we don't know what it might come to mean to ourselves or to someone else in the future.

Kabe Wilson, *Looking for Virginia: An Artist's Journey through 100 Archives*

Contents

Contents

List of Figures

Acknowledgments

I am deeply grateful to the manuscript readers for the University of Chicago Press, whose exceptionally detailed, incisive, and generative comments salvaged a sprawling manuscript. I am also very grateful for the support and guidance of the Press's editorial staff, especially Alan Thomas, who shepherded this project deftly through the stages of the review process, and Randolph Petilos and the Press's manuscript editing, design, production, and marketing staff, who assisted in the production and publication process from the first day of copyediting to the published book.

I thank the Department of English at the University of California, Berkeley, for its intellectual support and compassionate leave policy, including a family caregiving leave at a critical moment in my life. I am especially grateful to two colleagues, Susan Schweik and Steven Goldsmith, for their insightful comments on the manuscript and emotional support throughout its composition. Thanks also to staff members Linda Fitzgerald, Solomon Lefler, John McChesney-Young, Joemari Cedro, and Grace de Guzman for their problem-solving expertise and encouragement. I am honored to hold the John F. Hotchkis Chair, which has generously supported the research on which this project rests. I am especially grateful for the support of my resourceful research assistants: Eliot D'Silva, Gabrielle Elias, Sylvie Thode, and Irene Yoon. I also thank the curators and staff of the James Baldwin Papers at the Schomburg Center for Research in Black Culture, Manuscripts, Archives, and Rare Books Division of the New York Public Library; the Virginia Woolf Collection at the Henry W. and Albert A. Berg Collection of English and American Literature, New York Public Library; the Irita Taylor Van Doren Papers at the Library of Congress; and the Walter O. Evans Collection, the James Weldon Johnson Collection, and the Dorothy Peterson Collection at the Beinecke Rare Book and Manuscript Library, Yale University.

Many thanks to the France-Berkeley Fund at the University of California, Berkeley, for supporting colloquia at Berkeley and the Sorbonne Nouvelle, at which excerpts from this project were delivered and debated. These colloquia initiated enduring conversations with an exceptional group of French Woolf scholars: Anne Besnault, Claire Davison Marie Laniel, Catherine Lanone, Caroline Pollentier, Floriane Reviron-Piégay, and Anne-Marie Smith-Di Biasio.

I am also grateful for audience responses to portions of this book that were presented at the Modern Language Association annual convention, the Psychoanalytic Institute of Northern California, the Modernist Studies Association, the Berkeley Psychoanalytic Society, the International Conference on Virginia Woolf, L'Institut du Monde Anglophone, and the Oxford Research Centre in the Humanities.

For more general support of this and many other projects, I thank Maryl Gearhart, Marianne Hirsch, Dorothy Kaufmann, Georgina Kleege, Suzanne Lacke, Judith Meyer, Marta Peixoto, Geoffrey Saxe, and Beth Shamgar. To Andrea Walt I offer special thanks for embodying the art of listening. I am grateful to Arwed Messmer for permission to reproduce his photograph of a butterfly collection in the Zoological Museum in St. Petersburg, and to Kabe Wilson for sharing his video about a quest for Woolf that links our projects through their odd affinities.

My parents, Marion Buchman Abel and Reuben Abel, died before this book began, but their nurturance made it possible to begin. My brother, Richard Abel, consistently affirmed his interest in this project while tactfully refraining from questioning its progress. My son, Benjamin Abel Meyer, brought a touch of sweetness to every day.

My husband, Richard Meyer, was boundlessly supportive, attentive, and encouraging. I could not have written this or anything else without him. Although he did not live to see this book come out into the world, his presence enabled and lives in every turn along its long path to completion.

My companion, Christian Marouby, brought his compassionate intelligence to bear on every word and led me gently step by step into a world beyond the ending.

Woolf Tracks

> She waved her hand, going up Shaftesbury Avenue. She was all that. So that,
> to know her, or any one, one must seek out the people who completed them;
> even the places. Odd affinities she had with people she had never spoke to,
> some women in the street, some man behind a counter—even trees, or barns.
> It ended in a transcendental theory which, with her horror of death, allowed
> her to believe, or say that she believed (for all her scepticism), that since our
> apparitions, the part of us which appears, are so momentary compared with
> the other, the unseen part of us, which spreads wide, the unseen might sur-
> vive, be recovered somehow attached to this person or that, or even haunting
> certain places, after death . . . Perhaps—perhaps.
>
> Virginia Woolf, *Mrs. Dalloway*

Walking across London, Clarissa Dalloway ponders the odd affinities with
people and places that might enable an invisible part of herself to persist in
new forms after her death. In an odd reversal, physical bodies become mere
"apparitions" by virtue of their visibility, while an unseen essence gains
shifting but embodied afterlives. This path of self-extension is not direct:
it wends through the ebb and flow of words and air to diffuse into what
Clarissa elsewhere describes as "a mist between the people she knew best,
who lifted her on their branches as she had seen the trees lift the mist but
it spread ever so far, her life, herself."[1] If something of Clarissa survives her
mortal body, it will not follow the lines of biological descent, but the wayward paths of odd affinities.

I begin with Clarissa's musing in this talismanic modernist text—the
Woolfian novel that has most clearly survived its author's death to assume
diverse afterlives across a century and several continents—to pose my
central questions.[2] How does Woolf's own essential "life, herself" survive
beyond the covers of her books in writing that "completes" without acknowledging her? How has she served as one of the "invisible presences" in
the unfolding of diverse American and European literatures?[3] Rather than a
study of Woolf's ever more visible global images and lineages, this is a book
about the odd affinities that constitute her spectral afterlives: the mist between the branches of her acknowledged genealogies, the ripples beneath
the surface of her literary wake.

The four writers on whom I focus—Nella Larsen, James Baldwin, Roland Barthes, and W. G. Sebald—are (with the partial exception of Larsen) themselves major figures whose stature hardly rests on their tenuous relationships to Woolf. What makes those relationships worth uncovering is the light they cast on texts and lineages that have been defined in other terms. Traversing national, racial, and gender boundaries, these writers share little obvious common ground, although the two pairs into which they divide have some internal affinities that Woolf's imprint brings into sharper and more complex relief. By following surprising echoes in accordance with Woolf's own recommendation for "reading at random" without concern for "fixed labels and settled hierarchies," I discover odd affinities that stray beyond her acknowledged paths of literary influence.[4] These wayward genealogies yield new ways of reading the arc of "long modernism" and of displacing Woolf from her perch as cultural icon while revealing less conspicuous traces of her presence.

Invisible Presences

As Susan Stanford Friedman claims and charts impressively, Woolf's legacy derives primarily from her position as "a 'woman writer' . . . , as the writer gendered female, and often, as the writer linked with feminism."[5] Some of my motivating questions, therefore, are how else, in what other guises, where, and to whom Woolf may have traveled less visibly, and how these uncharted routes might alter our maps of twentieth-century literary geography. Three of my four authors are male, two are African American: both unexpected and illuminating lines of Woolfian transmission, the second so much so that it trumped an earlier intention to focus exclusively on Woolf's male heirs. In addition to the formal and rhetorical links that are the subject of this study, these writers are affiliated by reticence. Woolf goes unnamed (with a couple of brief exceptions) in the essays, letters, and interviews in which three of my writers were prolific. Her transmission, as in Clarissa's transcendental theory, is tentative and understated, easily overlooked and unannounced by textual or paratextual declarations. Formal echoes whose inherently abstract character makes them ideal vehicles of anonymous transmission become especially elusive when they circulate unmarked through different narrative and social settings.

When not blatantly proclaimed, as by the title and characters of Michael Cunningham's *The Hours*, echoes of Woolf's novels can be hard to discern. Even the few pointed verbal gestures—such as the echo of *Mrs. Dalloway*'s Hugh Whitbread in *Passing*'s Hugh Wentworth—are uncertain and oblique:

quite different from Monica Ali's decision to name the invisible and inaccessible employer of Bangladeshi immigrants in *Brick Lane* Mr. Dalloway.[6] In contrast to the dizzying production of adoring and abhorring "versionings" that have accompanied Woolf's accession to stardom as the signal female modernist and popular cultural heroine and monster—from the wholesale novelistic, cinematic, theatrical, musical, and choreographic adaptations of her novels to the cherry-picked phrases and images that decorate calendars, t-shirts and coffee mugs—odd affinities constitute an ambiguous and ambivalent terrain: neither mimicry nor mockery but resonances whose discretion reflects partial and provisional allegiances and whose discernment requires attunement to fine-grained verbal and narrative textures.[7]

To map this terrain, I draw from several theories of literary inheritance and influence: an extensive body of work whose most relevant versions map discontinuous, dispersed, and semiconscious processes of transmission. I adapt Foucault's understanding of genealogy as both the practice and the object of an inquiry into the relationships and discontinuities among submerged lines of descent and seemingly disparate modes of writing.[8] Since my inquiry falls within a literary field characterized by intertextual echoes and absorptions rather than homologous structures of thought, however, I also draw from Bakhtin's notion of an "unintentional, unconscious" intertextuality that, in this instance, is less unconscious of its Woolfian sources than indifferent to their cultural capital.[9] Most helpful has been Wai Chee Dimock's conception of a wayward, unpredictable, time-traveling literary resonance that unravels static notions of textual and authorial integrity and enables us to discover the surprising connections that Sebald heralds in the epigraph to this book.[10] Unexpectedness is key to *Odd Affinities*: the subtle reemergence of unstressed features of Woolf's work in texts that share little obvious common ground with it. Like the stray airs that invade and threaten to dismantle the Ramsay's house in the "Time Passes" section of *To the Lighthouse*, the echoes that disseminate Woolf's words over time undermine stable categories of genre, period, and national tradition, but also advance an alternative conception of dispersed, communal authorship that Woolf embraced overtly toward the end of her career but held dear throughout it.

Woolf called this her "philosophy of anonymity." The phrase occurs in the context of her speculation, prompted by a negative review of *Flush* in *The Granta*, about "how tremendously important unconsciousness is when one writes."[11] More than simply withholding one's name, anonymity for Woolf entails shedding identity. Her privileged figure of authorship is a fisherwoman who drops her line into the "pools, the depths, the dark places" of a common imaginative reservoir.[12] To claim ownership of one's own thoughts, or by extension those of others, short-circuits creativity. In her short story "The Fascination of the Pool," Woolf expands upon the image of deterritorialized authorship:

> Many, many people must have come there alone, from time to time, from age to age, dropping their thoughts into the water. . . . Perhaps that was the reason of its fascination—that it held in its waters all kinds of fancies, complaints, confidences, not printed or spoken aloud, but in a liquid state, floating one on top of another, almost disembodied. . . . The charm of the pool was that thoughts had been left there by people who had gone away and without their bodies their thoughts wandered in and out freely, friendly and communicative, in the common pool.[13]

In addition to revising the narcissistic figure of the reflecting pool, the figure of the common pool anticipates the most recent evolution of the ecocritical framework that has displaced the postmodern rhetoric of "versioning" as the dominant discourse for theorizing Woolf's cultural circulation. The focus on an ecology of remixing and recycling Woolf initially gained prominence at a 2019 conference at the Université de Lorraine titled *Recycling Woolf*, whose featured event was the presentation by the keynote speaker, the multimedia British artist Kabe Wilson.[14] In *Of One Woman or So* by Olivia N'Gowfri, anagrams for *A Room of One's Own* and Virginia Woolf, respectively, Wilson recycles Woolf's famous lecture by cutting up and remixing all (and only) its words in the frequency with which they appear in the original. In a tour de force that rewrites the text as the narrative of an African woman student's adversarial but ultimately revisionary engagement with *A Room of One's Own* at Cambridge, Wilson dramatically repurposes Woolf's text without entirely effacing its original author, whose identity is preserved in encrypted form.[15] In his more recent work, however, Wilson has gravitated toward Woolf's conception of a collective repository of cultural memory and production. After a transition through the discourse of composting, a more radical dismantling of authorship than recycling, he arrives in *Looking for Virginia: An Artist's Journey through 100 Archives* (2023) at a wide-ranging exploration of the conscious and unconscious associations that join disparate memories, dreams, images, and archives.[16] Centered on the proximity of water and of lighthouses that signal unexpected junctures, *Looking for Virginia* enacts Woolf's vision of a fluid intersubjective cultural memory tapped into by a dreaming fisherwoman/artist.

Wilson's description of his project on "Dalloway Day" (June 15, 2022) as discovering "the times she [Woolf] appears in history and culture where we don't expect her to be there" aligns most closely with *Odd Affinities*, which seeks out unexpected and fleeting writerly engagements with Woolf's oeuvre.[17] Although the writers in this study don't declare their affinities with Woolf for a variety of ultimately unknowable reasons—embarrassment, anxiety, shame, indifference, diffidence—as much as from a commitment to anonymity, they produce an underacknowledged alternative to the culture of celebrity. By mapping this shadowy genealogy, I seek to elicit a submerged narrative thread without doing violence to the diversity and complexity of the texts and traditions at hand a project that requires attending to the ways that Woolfian resonances engage with traditions more explicitly at work within these texts. This uncovering inevitably involves a paradox, for even if the endeavor originates, as this one did, in a critical version of the fisherwoman's musing, it becomes an intentional recovery project that endangers the values it seeks to recover. Although this paradox cannot be resolved, I hope it corresponds to Woolf's recognition that the printing press that murdered Anon also enabled her survival in another form, as well as to Woolf's mission of rescuing women writers from a culturally imposed anonymity that denied them recognition.[18] Since anonymity is always at risk of shading into invisibility, it must be placed in a dialectical relation to its opposite. Between the anonymous fish in the friendly common pool and the thoughts encircled within the "band of famous names" inscribed around the "huge bald forehead" of the British Museum reading room, there must be some mediation.[19]

My mediation recruits several terms that modulate *anonymous*. The first is *minor*, traditionally a term of disparagement aimed particularly at women's writing, but recently revalued as an intentional effect of decentering.[20] By reclaiming it from Woolf's detractors, prone in the past to dismissing interest in her work as "an embarrassingly minor aesthetic passion," I seek to identify genealogies in which she plays a subsidiary role: not as a determining force but as a subtle imprint or resonance that enters into dialogue with other textual influences as one voice in a cosmopolitan mix of cultural interlocutors whose assemblage stages an encounter that alters all the participants.[21] Depriving Woolf of her status as the sovereign term places her in an association in which, as Wai Chee Dimock argues, it is "an open question what is primary, what is determinative, what counts as the center, and what counts as the margins."[22] In this way, *Odd Affinities* diverges from a singular focus on the Anglo-American "commemorative novels" produced by an array of "woolfalators" whose primary claim to our attention is the ingenuity of their strategies for updating Woolf.[23]

To (re)minoritize Woolf in the anti-identitarian terms of her position rather than her gender is to reconceive her role as a flash point in canon formation. The prevailing narrative of her ascent is that the intervention of second-wave feminism in the 1970s transported her from her position as a "minor" figure preoccupied with "minor" events in an ambitiously internationalist white male modernist movement to a major figure in a feminist counter canon that propelled her in turn to global stardom within an international hypercanon.[24] But rather than this linear (if somewhat circuitous) trajectory, I propose a more dynamic model that positions Woolf simultaneously in all three of the domains that David Damrosch designates as the *hypercanon*, the *counter canon*, and the *shadow canon*.[25] Critical attention has focused primarily on Woolf's increasingly vexed yet remarkably tenacious position in a culturally, racially, and nationally diversifying feminist counter canon in which, despite the antagonism provoked by her persistence as an "old dead girl" who has outlived her usefulness and overstayed her welcome, she has endured for better and for worse as the white modernist precursor who presides over women's textual production as no other woman writer ever has.[26] What began as a prescient anticipation by Black women writers who were instrumental in envisioning Woolf as a feminist foremother and adapting her formulations to different circumstances—consider Toni Morrison's pathbreaking master's thesis, "Virginia Woolf's and William Faulkner's Treatment of the Alienated" (Cornell University, 1955) or Alice Walker's "In Search of Our Mothers' Gardens" (1974) and "One Child of One's Own" (1979)—soured with the rise of alternative canons of color in relation to which Woolf's class and racial entitlements became increasingly conspicuous and offensive. For contemporary women writers of color, Woolf has arguably become a female counterpart to Milton's bogey, yet her obstructive visibility also makes her a ready cultural reference point, a shorthand for self-positioning: whether as the "she-one" of Pamela Mordecai's "Angel in the House" or the "room of one's own" that writers of color must "forget" in Gloria Anzaldúa's "Speaking in Tongues."[27] Less adversarially, brief allusions can import a cultural universe into a revisionary context, as when Chimamanda Ngozi Adichie begins her short story "The Arrangements" by revising the opening sentence of *Mrs. Dalloway* ("Melania Trump said she would buy the flowers herself"), establishing in one deft stroke her own literary authority and the cultural pretensions of the soon-to-be "first" lady.[28]

The fault lines of this expanding counter canon have been well mapped, but their consequences for Woolf's status within the hypercanon and its ancillary shadow canon haven't been adequately explored. In Damrosch's account, concerned to assuage the apprehension that major writers could be displaced by emerging minor ones, most established hypercanonical writers survive or even find their status enhanced by the ascendance to their ranks of a few anointed members of the counter canon. Only the peripheral figures within the hypercanon will find themselves demoted by the new arrivals to a "shadow" canon of minoritized figures. But what about the fate of counter-canonical writers within the hypercanon? Rather than shedding her position in the counter canon, like a butterfly ascending from a chrysalis (a trope we will have occasion to revisit), Woolf carries her counter-canonical legacy with her into the hypercanon. As a consequence, rather than crowding peripheral figures into a shadow canon, she paradoxically comes to occupy a place in that canon as well. Having moved from a minor to a major figure only after and as a result of her star role in a feminine counter canon, she wears an imaginary "hands-off" sign as the literary property of the canon she helped to inaugurate, sequestered as a special case within the hypercanon. Her trajectory from minor to major writer transports her as well into a strangely illuminated shadow canon within the hypercanon, where she remains both minor and major, overexposed and invisible (as she is in Damrosch's essay).

Woolf's overdetermined position within these diverse canons informs her literary genealogies. For many contemporary women of color, her ascent to the hypercanon rebuts any claim to counter canonicity, although her prominence continues to elicit commentary even as a negative example. For most of their white female counterparts, by contrast, Woolf's dual status is a mutually enhancing source of inspiration that continues to incite revisions, elaborations, adaptations, and biofictions.[29] Woolf's masculine successors confront a different configuration in which national rather than racial differences inflect gender. Among the Anglo-American writers for whom the obstacle Woolf's celebrity presents to their own ascension to a relatively narrow national hypercanon outweighs the restraining influence of her place in the counter canon, one strategy has been to dramatize her presence in a maternally inflected version of the oedipal agon that Harold Bloom envisions between "strong" male writers.[30] In this context (as well as elsewhere) Woolf has remained hypervisible, as in the case of Michael Cunningham's *The Hours*, which stages her suicide as its narrative preamble and arguably its precondition, as if the outsize maternal precursor to whom he claims he "lost his virginity" and from whom he draws his title and inspiration must be dispatched for her literary successor to claim his full authority.[31] Ian McEwan displaces a subtler version of the failure of this struggle onto the narrator of *Atonement*, Briony Tallis, whose attempt to publish her manuscript "Two Figures by a Fountain" is short-circuited by the judgment of the fictional editor Cyril Connolly that it "owes a little too much to the techniques of Mrs. Woolf."[32]

To locate the opposite approach, in which Woolf assumes a minor role in a shadow genealogy, we need to go beyond the constraints of a single, crowded, and thus hotly contested cultural tradition. For although no one would now dispute that Woolf has become what the editors of the recent *Edinburgh Companion to Virginia Woolf and Contemporary Global Literature* call "a global icon, a transnational symbol," she remains most conspicuous on Anglo-American turf.[33] Following the transnational turn in Woolf studies represented quite spectacularly by that and other recent collections of essays, a turn that presupposes and builds upon Woolf's own newly appreciated cosmopolitanism, I track her legacy in some unexpected places as an implication or resonance in a shadowy genealogy reconceived as a vein of literary transmission rather than an artifact of canon formation.[34]

To bring Woolf out of the shadows while retaining her status *as* a shadow, I supplement *anonymous* and *minor* with the critical purchase of *queer*. The *transverse* relation implied by Eve Kosofsky Sedgwick's famous derivation of *queer* from "the Indo-European root—*twerkw*, which also yields the German *quer* (transverse), Latin *torquere* (to twist), English *athwart . . . across genders, across sexualities, across genres, across 'perversions'*"—maps well onto Woolf's wayward genealogies.[35] This book could have been titled *Queer Affinities*, especially in view of the explicit queerness of Baldwin and Barthes and the implicit queerness of texts by Larsen and Sebald, but I have chosen to work instead with Woolf's own more capacious, old-fashioned, and British-inflected *odd*.

The cluster of loosely affiliated critical terms—*odd, anonymous, minor, queer, transverse*—have in common a sense of deficiency or deviance that brings a subtly oppositional pressure to bear on the construction of linear genealogies. This pressure also generates a distinctive version of the "long modernism" that, in response to the recent expansion of modernism's historical and geographic boundaries, has become a prevailing narrative of twentieth-century Anglophone and European literature.[36] While sharing this narrative's basic two-part structure, each part of which in this case is subdivided into two chapters, the two halves of *Odd Affinities* are located in off-centers of high and late twentieth-century modernism: Harlem (and its expatriate extension to "Paris Noir") in the early and middle decades of the century and a cluster of European cities (Prague, Antwerp, Paris, London) toward the century's end.[37] The affinities between and within these two portions diverge from the lines of transmission that typically unfold according to shared (albeit sometimes adversarial) cultural or ideological assumptions: Woolf to McEwan, Conrad to Achebe, Faulkner to Morrison, and so on. *Odd Affinities* seeks to navigate a path between the implicit straightness of studies of long modernism, premised on continuities, and the perspective of queer theory, which seeks their disruption.

Long Modernisms

Odd Affinities offers a new twist on the critical consensus that, rather than being displaced by postmodernism, modernism went dormant during the middle decades of the twentieth century and underwent a revival toward the century's end. According to some of these accounts, the increasingly evident aesthetic and ethical limitations of postmodernism actually engendered modernism's second life.[38] With a certain irony, the promotion of traditional modernist virtues (aesthetic and ethical seriousness, formal integrity, psychological depth) by old-guard critics has been tacitly redeemed by some of the new modernist approaches that critique, diverge from, and yet build on their foundation as a platform for restoring modernism's authority after the postmodernist vogue.

That there has been a return to modernism in much late twentieth- and early twenty-first-century fiction seems indisputable.[39] Critical accounts of this return typically divide between a section on high modernism and a section on its later twentieth- and early twenty-first-century manifestations (variously denominated as neomodernism, late modernism, remodernism, metamodernism, new postmodernism, and post-Modernism).[40] Conceptualized according to a variety of formal and thematic rubrics, these studies share the fundamental premise that rather than being exhausted by the middle of the century, modernist forms solicit (in Michaela Bronstein's words) "a variety of possible futures," even that they "chase" the future.[41] According to these critics, it is modernism's own recalcitrance, its internal tensions and conflicting allegiances, that invite its redeployment in the present. Bronstein's underlying argument that modernist forms function as "empty vessels" that direct our attention toward "the variety of possible substances the container might hold" works well for Woolf (who is strangely excluded from this study) and is broadly shared.[42] As the editors of the series in which Bronstein's book appears declare, "What travels, then, is not content but forms."[43] An alternative approach focused less on novelistic form than on modernist "outsider" figures also finds fertile ground in Woolf.[44]

Odd Affinities takes an additional step by reading the formal modulations of long modernism through the optic of Woolf's oeuvre. It maps modernism's long *durée* through two mutually traversing trajectories: the arc of Woolf's career as it intersects a twentieth-century genealogy constituted by her tacit and shifting presence. Reading long modernism through its odd Woolfian affinities reveals some of the ways that narrative forms and their representative tropes soften, waver, and break under the weight of an increasingly melancholic history. Form is central, even in its unraveling, because its dual status as "transhistorical, portable, abstract" and as "material, situated, political" makes it a fine-tuned instrument for reading long modernism's intersections with Woolf's own evolution.[45] The first half of this study examines how the carefully crafted narrative form of *Mrs. Dalloway*, whose fulfillment exacts the death of Septimus Warren Smith, offered a strain of African American modernism in the first half of the century a supple tool for calibrating the relative claims of aesthetic and social forms. As *To the Lighthouse* opened more space for personal and historical rupture, only provisionally remediated at the end by Lily Briscoe's painting, it anticipates both the more profound challenges to social and aesthetic integration inflicted by the Second World War and the emerging association of unassuageable grief with the more modest claims of visual mediums and oral narratives that prioritize intimate processes over totalizing forms. After starting with a high modernist embrace of impersonal form designed in part as a bulwark against mortality, which World War I had brought to heightened consciousness in the 1920s, the second half of *Odd Affinities* turns to some European engagements with the more profound and private forms of mourning unleashed with special force by World War II. In this section, Woolf's formal aspirations and elegiac modes are subjected to greater pressure by the resistant melancholy and uncanny twists of history, but her work is transported across the watershed of the Second World War into some kindred projects of the late twentieth century. The crisscrossing arcs of long modernism and Woolf's literary career ultimately converge from opposite sides of the Second World War. Their course begins, however, with the surprising refuge Woolf's high modernist form offered a strain of African American modernism.

Woolf's Room in African American Modernism

African American modernism is not an obvious site at which to uncover the legacy of a writer who has been conspicuously absent from recent attempts to bring Black and white modernisms into closer proximity. If Woolf is referenced at all in these attempts, it is usually as a negative example of class and racial privilege, a locus of racial insensitivity, or a problematic case of the wrong kind of modernism: the "good" (elite, discrete, and insular) variety rather than "bad" (critical, outspoken, and radical) one.[46]

Traditionally, Anglo-American and African American modernisms have been aligned (if at all) through shared aesthetic strategies that, while not overtly gendered, are implicitly masculine. Houston A. Baker Jr. frames even his most recent call to expand the chronological and geographic

boundaries of the Harlem Renaissance in terms of a vernacular, experimental blues geography that continues to define the common ground of a
transracial modernism as a predilection for social and aesthetic transgression.[47] Consequently, James Joyce has been claimed as a precursor by an
experimental Black modernist lineage running from Bruce Nugent to Ish-
mael Reed, whereas Woolf's lyrical cadences, hypotactic syntax, elevated
diction, and resonant sonorities have barred her from a blues geography
defined by its vernacular idiom and syncopated rhythms.

The scant attempts to connect Woolf with the Harlem Renaissance typically proceed via a negative juxtaposition to her more verbally and socially
transgressive contemporary Zora Neale Hurston, since, as Kristin Czarnecki puts it, "both were at the vanguard of their artistic coteries" and consequently bear comparison despite fundamental aesthetic differences.[48]
Rather than succumbing to the assumptions that Ann du Cille dubs "Hur-
stonism," which confers authenticity on a certain folk perspective and vernacular idiom compatible with the blues aesthetic, however, I turn to Nella
Larsen's *Passing* for a comparison with Woolf and a point of departure for
a recessive strain of African American modernism that embraces a poetics of psychological and social interiority and the narrative strategies they
entail.[49]

There is a tradition within African American letters that validates private
space despite the manifest obstacles imposed on people whose foundational
legal status was as property rather than as property owners. The precarity
and rarity of "a room of one's own" and the internal world it shelters should
not blind us to their value as supplements to a literary tradition shaped
primarily by the imperatives of economic and political struggle. From the
enforced enclosure of the fugitive slave's hideout, the attic "loophole of
retreat" in which Harriet Jacobs guarded her interiority for seven years in
Incidents in the Life of a Slave Girl, to spaces of ironic retreat and political resistance such as the invisible man's underground hole, variations on a room
of one's own have served as loci of self-preservation, self-exploration, and
social critique for African American writers.[50]

The trope of the room, I contend, transported a version of English modernism from *Jacob's Room* (1922) to *Giovanni's Room* (1956), with key stops
along the way at *Mrs. Dalloway* (1925), *Passing* (1929), and *A Room of One's
Own* (1929). Like the train compartment in Woolf's essay "Mr. Bennett
and Mrs. Brown" (1924) that transports the English novel from Edwardian to Georgian iterations, the room transports the modernist novel from
London to Harlem via the feminized figure and forms of novelistic interiority that are represented by the character Mrs. Brown. Rather than a sealed
and static foil to Hurston's autobiographical *Dust Tracks on a Road* (1942),

the room and the aesthetic it represents were vehicles of literary *movement* across cultural, sexual, and racial differences.

One key stop was Nella Larsen's *Passing*, published the same year as *A Room of One's Own*, which begins in Irene Redfield's private writing room and unfolds through a series of middle-class domestic spaces. The trope of the room had an earlier iteration in Woolf's *Jacob's Room* (1922), however, the breakthrough text that occasioned the critique by Arnold Bennett that in turn provoked "Mr. Bennett and Mrs. Brown." Less obviously, *Jacob's Room* also launched a vein of literary transmission that—crossing both racial and gender boundaries—linked Baldwin both to Woolf and (through her) to Larsen. In *Giovanni's Room*, Baldwin reworks Woolf's anti-Bildungsroman and reroutes it from the elite precincts of Cambridge and Bloomsbury to the sordid underbelly of Paris in the aftermath of World War II.

Baldwin's engagement with Woolf also extends to *Mrs. Dalloway*, especially to Woolf's newly discovered technique of "dig[ging] out beautiful caves" of memory behind her characters rather than recounting events chronologically.[51] Taking the plunge she resisted in *Jacob's Room*, Woolf developed a narrative method that freed her from the tyranny of plot through a spatialization of temporality that conjoins narrative method, the trope of spatial containment, and the formal ideal of a work that is "complete in itself; it is self-contained."[52] It is this breakthrough of Woolfian modernism, the moment at which her narrative discourse assumes decisive authority over the stories she recounts, that both Larsen and Baldwin adapted for their own purposes.

Beyond the intrinsic pleasures of formal mastery, what did the aesthetic of a bounded interior offer African American modernists inescapably aware of, and under mounting pressure to engage with, the relentless encroachments of a social exterior? A refuge, perhaps, from the demands of the political, and a method and sanction for inscribing their works in the field of the literary, resisting the pressure, felt acutely by Baldwin, to write social protest rather than literary fiction and to identify first and foremost as a racial representative. It enabled, that is, the relief from context that is a classic affordance of the modernist aesthetic that has rarely been afforded to African American writers.

But if the aesthetic of the "whole and entire" text—a phrase that circulates between Woolf's essays and Baldwin's (as we will see)—provided some reprieve from the demands of social context, the converse is also true. Larsen's and Baldwin's reprisals of *Mrs. Dalloway*'s narrative strategies call attention to the social costs of formal self-enclosure. By adapting one of Woolf's key narrative turning points, *Passing* and *Giovanni's Room* convert it into a pressure point, foregrounding what has been foreclosed by the seamlessness of closure. Their primary agent for this task is the outlier character Septimus Warren Smith, Clarissa Dalloway's "mad," expendable alter ego.[53] Septimus stands at the interface between Woolf's aesthetic design, which requires his expulsion, and her social vision, which requires his inclusion. He is the locus of the conflict between novelistic structure and "life" that Woolf describes in general terms in *A Room of One's Own*: "Life conflicts with something that is not life," and therefore a beloved character must die "because the shape of the book requires it" (71). As the signal manifestation of Woolf's outsider status, moreover, Septimus afforded a point of entry for African American readers and writers. His inclusion made Woolf a more palatable bearer of a high modernist aesthetic for writers who found an instrument and ally in this dissident, derided, prophetic figure. Toni Morrison makes this explicit in her master's thesis, in which Septimus stars as a locus of dissent, and in her reimagining of Septimus as Shadrack in *Sula*.[54] Larsen and Baldwin trained their gazes less on the character of Septimus per se than on the closural strategies to which he is recruited. Replaying the abjection of a disruptive figure of exoticized or degraded otherness—Clare in *Passing*, Giovanni in *Giovanni's Room*—they put pressure on the arc of an expulsion as a strategy for resolving the tensions between the formal and the social.

Their attunement to narrative tensions may have enabled these African American modernists to respond to Woolf in ways that were less available to their white counterparts. Rather than tracking their response across the century, however, I will follow Woolf's modernist mandate of "tampering with the expected sequence" and swerve across the Atlantic Ocean to another continent, culture, medium, and moment (*AROO*, 80). This rupture takes us beyond *Jacob's Room* and *Mrs. Dalloway* to the novel in which Woolf inserts a radical break that enabled her to grapple, in a way not previously available, with the ravages of time and grief.

Time Passes

Through their blend of formal innovation and urban location, Woolf's first two modernist novels were good fits for a strain of African American modernism. It was *To the Lighthouse*, however, that traveled most resonantly to Europe later in the century and that consequently affords a pivot to part 2 of *Odd Affinities*. Rather than the canonical division of Woolf's career between the high modernist decade of the 1920s (culminating in the publication of *The Waves* in 1931) and the more politically grounded, aesthetically realist 1930s (culminating in the publication of *The Years* in 1937 and *Three Guineas* in 1938), *Odd Affinities* expands on the division drawn by the break between the two narrative portions of *To the Lighthouse*, taking off from the rupture at the novel's center in an effort to reenvision the shape of Woolf's career and the long modernist trajectory it anticipates.

The design of *To the Lighthouse* famously separates "The Window" from "The Lighthouse" with a lyrical evocation of time's passage rendered through the indifferent forces of waves and wind that erode the foundations of the Ramsays' world. Interweaving the deaths of Mrs. Ramsay and her two oldest children with allusions to the carnage of World War I, "Time Passes" inscribes a historical rupture between the maternal aura of the Victorian era and a starker but more spacious modernity. Taking advantage of the invitation issued under the sign of "time passes," *Odd Affinities* advances this break historically to the passage of time between the two world wars, an interval often marked by the apprehension that an imperfectly resolved conclusion to the First World War would result in the outbreak of a second one.[55]

The rupture Woolf rendered as "Time Passes" both mimics and masks the smaller interval between *Mrs. Dalloway* and *To the Lighthouse*, a sequence whose seemingly smooth progression along the rails of an evolving modernist aesthetic obscures an affective shift that parallels the changed responses to the two world wars. *Mrs. Dalloway* captures a moment of modernist self-confidence that seeks to hold at bay the massive losses of the First World War, perhaps to deflect anxiety about their potential recurrence. Introduced early, the "perfectly upright and stoical bearing" with which Lady Bexborough opens a bazaar immediately after hearing of her favorite son's death at war could stand as a figure of the novel's, as well as the protagonist's, bearing (*MD*, 9–10). From Clarissa's perspective, the war is "over, Thank Heaven—over," and despite the figures of grief sprinkled through the novel—the "well of tears," the dripping fountains and faucets— the prevailing attitude is resolutely upbeat (*MD*, 5, 9). Woolf's exhilaration at having found her method carries over into the affective tone of the novel, which refuses to dwell long on loss. Although the novel registers skepticism about the official commemorations of World War I through the perspective of Peter Walsh, it does not reflect on the homology between the aesthetic and civic binding of grief.

The turn from *Mrs. Dalloway*'s self-consciously modern form and urban setting on a warm June day when the war is emphatically over to the rural, elegiac *To the Lighthouse*, set with a sense of foreboding on an island on a late September evening, marks a step both backward and forward. With the admixture of personal grief to the impersonal mourning for the war dead, something breaks loose, some space is opened—the space of "Time

Passes"—for the affect suppressed by the perfectly upright bearing. Public memorials yield to a "purplish stain upon the bland surface of the sea as if something had boiled and bled, invisibly, beneath."[56] Swollen by the impact of Mrs. Ramsay's death, the carefully contained well of tears for the anonymous dead morphs into the waves eroding the foundation of the island and threatening to rend the novel in half. Aesthetic consolation and material collapse coexist in a tension whose resolution in Lily Briscoe's painting does not negate the damage to human habitation rendered in the near collapse of the Ramsays' home. The frailty of the human dwelling stands against the completion of Lily's artwork. The symbolic implications of these metaphors become central to the second part of this study, as painting becomes an object of Barthes's critique, and architecture an object of Sebald's desire and despair.

To the Lighthouse offers entrée to a strand of late European modernism that struggles with the increasingly fraught tension between formal resolution and historical dissolution as time (both private and public) breaks free of aesthetic order. Although Woolf's incorporation of maternal death into the heart of war-inflicted losses was a narrative contrivance (her mother actually died in 1895) that affords a certain affective and formal logic, its opening of space for personal as well as social grief also presaged a shift in modes of mourning triggered by a war that not only impacted England far more directly than its predecessor had, but that also called into question the very bedrock of civilization in ways that had been previously unimaginable. Unlike the slaughter of the First World War, which could be ascribed to the folly of self-serving heads of state, World War II appeared to crack open the fundamental pact that grounds our collective humanity.

Changes in the forms of mourning after World War II were overdetermined by a complex of cultural shifts. As a number of cultural theorists and historians have observed, mourning emerged as a problem of the private sphere as one facet of a growing cultural validation of personal experience that was evidenced in the literary field by the rise of the memoir and the emergence of confessional poetry in the United States.[57] This broader context fostered the recognition that painful private forms of mourning had been disregarded, even devalued, by an emphasis on public ceremonials. Although Freud's landmark "Mourning and Melancholia" (1917) was written during World War I, it gained broader currency as a theoretical model only after World War II afforded greater traction for the concept of melancholia. Germany presented a particular opening for the explanatory power of melancholia to account for what Alexander and Margarete Mitscherlich described in *The Inability to Mourn* (published in German in 1967) as a widespread German failure to mourn the demolition of the Nazi cultural universe and the downfall of the authoritarian leader who had served as a national father figure. Concurrently, in the opposite context of post–World War II Britain, Geoffrey Gorer's *Death, Grief, and Mourning in Contemporary Britain* (1965) opened up for inquiry less a collective failure to mourn than a pervasive bafflement about *how* to do so for painful intimate losses not sanctioned by religious rituals or social practices. From this primarily sociological perspective, melancholia is an effect of blocked mourning rather than its cause.

During the following decade in France, Roland Barthes was instrumental in disseminating and valorizing Freud's concept of melancholia (under a different name) in *La chambre claire* (1980, trans. *Camera Lucida* 1981), his meditation on photography, infused with his grief over his mother's death, as a medium that could register the past only as an incurable wound. Barthes's inquiry was galvanized by the co-emergence of psychoanalytic theories of mourning and photography theory in France in the late 1970s. Although translated into French by Marie Bonaparte and Anna Berneau in 1936 as "Deuil et mélancolie" and gradually taken up within psychoanalytic circles by Jacques Lacan, Nicholas Abraham, and Maria Torok, Freud's germinal text received broader cultural attention only in the context of the discourse on photography that was evolving contemporaneously.[58] A critical locus unfolded across six special issues of *Le nouvel observateur* devoted to photography (June 1977–June 1979). The series included French translations of excerpts from classic essays such as Walter Benjamin's "Short History of Photography" (1931) and Susan Sontag's "Photography in Search of Itself" (1977); the majority of the photographs that Barthes reproduces and discusses in *Camera Lucida*; and the first explicit negotiation of photography with the psychoanalysis of mourning in Robert Castel's "Images and Phantasms," which quotes extensively from "Mourning and Melancholia" to argue that photography affords a "form of mental hygiene" that supplements Freud's model by "allowing the dead to 'live on in the memory,'" thereby helping "the mourner to rationalize death, and to go on living. . . . The horror of decomposition is allayed by a frozen, faded smile."[59] That Barthes was already engaging with "Mourning and Melancholia" is clear from his frequent references in *A Lover's Discourse* (1977), but Castel's attribution of therapeutic value to the pious preservation of a "frozen, faded smile" would have sharpened Barthes's critique of photography's function as a weak similitude of a vanished presence.

Although not always directly related to the Second World War, the decades that followed it in Europe sought to map ambivalent, intimate landscapes of grief untouched (and even rendered shameful) by national rituals of collective mourning. However contingently Mrs. Ramsay's death came to inflect the wounds of World War I, it presaged a shift in the imaginative shapes and practices of mourning. The small chronological steps from the deaths of Septimus and Jacob (both casualties of World War I) to that of Mrs. Ramsay telescope a larger set of shifts that made the death of the mother, rather than that of the soldier—whether monumentalized in marble or humanized in fiction—a central literary trope of the affective toll of the Second World War.[60] Within this minor genealogy—intermittent, oblique, indirect—it was the death of the figure who grounds the private sphere, whether she is idealized (like Mrs. Ramsay and the mother of Roland Barthes) or complicit in historical traumas of which she is also the victim (like Austerlitz's mother in Sebald's final novel), that could most fully render the impact of profoundly destabilizing losses. The bid of *To the Lighthouse*, like that of elegiac modes generally, is that even the most profound and shattering loss can achieve some form of closure, but the closure provided by Lily Briscoe's painting becomes increasingly untenable. As personal losses come to bear the mounting costs of mid-twentieth-century European history, the trajectories of mourning yield to a melancholic dwelling on inconsolable grief, interspersed with spurts of mania: a third term whose emergence in literary form casts new light on its clinical trajectory.

This reorientation has cascading narrative effects. An increasingly melancholic vision of history undermines the high British modernist project of rescripting time as space. Whether in the form of a stubborn past that refuses to be sublated—the insistent *ça a été* of Roland Barthes's melancholic photographic temporality—or of the relentless pileup of catastrophes in the melancholic vision of European history that Sebald borrows from Walter Benjamin, a recalcitrant temporality resists symbolic recovery. What Jesse Matz characterizes as the temporal affordances of modernism—deftly wielded through retrospection in *Mrs. Dalloway* and recuperation in *To the Lighthouse*, which in his view, "more than any other canonical modernist text, pursues temporal stewardship through aesthetic form"—succumb to the increased gravitas of a tenacious history.[61]

Consequently, a crisis of anteriority displaces a crisis of exteriority. As the noncompliant figures whose pressure on the social interior demands their expulsion from the narrative interior give way to a foundational figure whose absence is a precondition of narrative, death migrates from an agent of closure to a feature of foreclosure that establishes the terms of the novelistic world. The potential for a new beginning and remediable social world suggested by the glimmerings of dawn with which *Mrs. Dalloway* and

Giovanni's Room both conclude is diminished from the start of the texts in part 2, in which death precipitates a narrative about the negation of foundations that can be restored only obliquely and in part.

Woolf's Refuge in European Modernism

The story resumes in Paris in the late 1970s at a moment when the waning of poststructuralism opened a door to the theorization of affect in general and of mourning in particular. It opened a door as well to a Woolfian version of modernism that had suffered under the joint hegemony of the "linguistic turn" and an avant-garde poetics that had sidelined Woolf (in contrast to Joyce) as insufficiently inventive with language.[62] The dominant thread of this recovery, most visible in the collaborative work of Giles Deleuze and Felix Guattari, and several essays by Jacques Rancière, focuses on *The Waves* as a reservoir of fluctuating deterritorialized sensations and transpersonal "microsensory events" that constitute the lyrical continuum of "life."[63]

A darker, odder thread of Woolfian affinities—more tentative, obscure, and affectively somber—was catalyzed by Roland Barthes during the era in which he both developed his interest in photography and sought to remake himself as a novelist. Woolf plays a minor role in this refashioning, appearing only peripherally in marginal notes to one of his lectures and in the caption to one of the photographs in *Camera Lucida*. These minimalist gestures, however, call attention to her hovering presence both as a shadow to Marcel Proust, on whom Barthes explicitly modeled his novelistic aspirations, and as a tacit backdrop and counterpoint to his meditation on photography and maternal death.

Yet how could we not hear the resonance between Barthes's light room and Woolf's lighthouse? The light in both titles summons us, as it summons the figures within these texts, to acknowledge the connective potential of an immediate, tactile medium. But although light seems able to reach beneath language to forge an intimate connection, once it is channeled through the photographic apparatus of the "light room" (*la chambre claire*), forced into representational service in the production of an image, it reveals its inability to transport a living presence or afford the fulfillment of the final stroke, "there, in the centre," that completes Lily Briscoe's painting and Woolf's novel (*TTL*, 209). *Camera Lucida* is written against the assumptions that have undergirded Western modes of visual representation since the invention of Albertian perspective. Against photography's claim to have fulfilled the promise of painting to recapture a living presence, even if (as for Lily Briscoe) in an abstract form, Barthes insists on unrecuperability.

He renders this insistence formally as well as thematically in the bipartite structure of *Camera Lucida*, which, unlike the three-part structure of *To the Lighthouse*, refuses to yield resolution.

One thread that traverses the second half of *Odd Affinities* is the migration of the maternal elegy under mounting personal and historical duress. Tracing the subgenre's shifting evocation as it travels through the rhetoric of painting in *To the Lighthouse* to photography in *Camera Lucida* to architecture in *Austerlitz* uncovers new features of Sebald's relationship to Barthes, presumed to run straightforwardly through a shared phototextual form and narrative motif of a son's search for a visual image of his lost mother. In the vastly expanded, permanently darkened, irredeemably melancholic landscape of post–World War II Europe, however, the visual register has lost its hold. Melancholy has spread from a consequence of the photographic apparatus to a constitutive feature of a European history from which the only partial and precarious refuge is literary rather than visual. By shifting the frame of elegy from individual to collective loss and from visual to formal modes of recovery, Sebald develops a less agonistic stance toward elegiac forms and their literary representatives.

Sebald's wide-ranging literary genealogies are frequently and variously enumerated, but in a sign of the blinders still imposed by gender, these lineages never incorporate women. As a perhaps unwitting illustration, Arthur Lubow observes that "Sebald was 'Proustian,' people often said. Since his tone was elegiacal and his sentence structure was serpentine, that pigeonholing arose predictably."[64] The pigeonholing Lubow has in mind involves assumptions about memory, but assumptions about gender are less explicit and self-conscious. That an elegiac tone and serpentine syntax could reflect an affinity with Woolf as plausibly as with Proust has been unimaginable to Sebald critics despite the formal resonances and verbal echoes an attentive ear or eye might discern. Less explicit than many of Sebald's intertexts, these resonances play a distinctive role in offering a contrast to *Austerlitz*'s melancholy European geography, whose roots reprise a long genealogy of philosophical pessimism running from Nietzsche to Freud to Benjamin. Woolf offers a fragile novelistic architecture that contests and is contested by the darker undercurrents of European modernism. As an elegy less for an individual than for British modernism's aesthetic optimism, *Austerlitz* weaves Woolfian tropes and forms through and against a broad spectrum of historical, philosophical, and psychoanalytic discourses that place echoes of her oeuvre in conversation with the practices and discourses of very different European modernisms.

Against a European landscape punctuated by decaying or bombed-out domestic, civic, and religious buildings, Sebald wistfully evokes Woolf's figure of the English country house in *Orlando* (1928), her hyperbolic iteration of English modernism's grandiose temporal designs. But he also directs our attention to the great house's architectural and affective underside, the crypt in which Orlando discovers the melancholy works of Sir Thomas Browne, a literary ancestor to Sebald as well as to Woolf. *Austerlitz* interweaves Browne's extensive discourse on moths with Woolf's deceptively minor story-essay "The Death of the Moth," in which (in Sebald's reading) the moth's stoical acceptance of mortality gestures toward both world wars and thus toward a way to rethink Woolf's legacy in the aftermath of Auschwitz.

The dual capacity of literary forms to be both abstract and historical helps clarify the different approaches to Woolf devised by writers in the two parts of this study. Whereas the abstract narrative design Woolf discovered in *Mrs. Dalloway* afforded contact points with African American modernists concerned with the intersections between formal and social boundaries, the more materially grounded architectural tropes that are latent in *To the Lighthouse* and salient in *Orlando* elicited more skeptical engagements toward the century's end. At once increasingly desired and precarious, the figure of the multichambered novelistic house seemed to offer Sebald a provisional British refuge from the convulsions of European history. Underscoring the national provenance of this metaphor, he counters *Austerlitz*'s European philosophical genealogies with an improvised British cultural assemblage that situates Woolf in a lineage running from Sir Thomas Browne to W. H. Auden and D. W. Winnicott. Reprising from the end of the twentieth century the Anglocentric turn of British modernism during the century's middle decades, Sebald keeps Woolf's national heritage in the foreground while excavating the underground it shares with the darker forces of European history.[65]

Rather than an icon frozen in time, Woolf changed, as did the ways she was received and revised by writers who barely acknowledged her. Both peripheral and central, recessive and generative, she acceded to a changing world and a minor but critical position in the margins, showing up where least expected to defamiliarize traditions and texts we thought we knew how to read.

∴

Part One

WOOLF'S ROOM
IN AFRICAN AMERICAN
MODERNISM

∵

[CHAPTER ONE]

Mrs. Dalloway in Harlem

Passing's Contending Modernisms

> Memory as an inversion of historical time is the essence of interiority.
>
> Emmanuel Levinas, *Totality and Infinity*

> She [Larsen] would have been thinking of Josephine Baker; everyone was.
>
> Amber Medland, "They Roared with Laughter," *London Review of Books*

In a charged scene in Nella Larsen's *Passing* (1929), Irene drops a teacup that she claims had been brought north from a Confederate household in the South "by the subway." Correcting herself, she concedes: "Oh, all right! Be English if you want to and call it the underground."[1] The bizarre and gratuitous slip of the tongue and the even more bizarre association of the underground with England rather than with the Underground Railroad that transported slaves to freedom seem planted to suggest Irene's identification with England rather than with her own racial history. The word "underground" performs its own mode of transport along two disparate routes: one that travels from south to north along the American rails of race and one that travels across the Atlantic along the verbal rails of culture. Interrupting the north/south trajectory, Irene makes a verbal detour to England, as if to escape the long reach of American slavery by imaginatively reversing the direction of the Atlantic slave trade.

What other subterranean detours might this lapsus indicate? This chapter teases out *Passing*'s centrifugal gestures in order to inflect the expansion of the Harlem Renaissance in some new directions. Stretched from a local into a global movement ranging across multiple time frames and sites (among them the Caribbean, Africa, Central America, Moscow, Berlin, London, Mexico City, Havana, and Johannesburg), the boundaries of the Harlem Renaissance have been dramatically remapped in recent decades in tandem with those of modernism. Most scholars would now agree with Cherene Sherrad-Johnson's assertion of a mutually constitutive relationship between modernism and the Harlem Renaissance. But which modernism and which Harlem Renaissance?[2] Some versions have been foreclosed by the tenacious assumption that the possibility of a "mulatto modernism" rests on a shared predilection for social and aesthetic transgression that privileges the oral, vernacular, performative, communal, and improvisational over the formal constraints of "high" literary modernism.[3] But the presumption that this was "a cultural moment when open, transgressive, and multivocal talk became recognized as vital and valuable—as the very mark of being modern" continues to render inaudible more oblique, recessive, muffled forms of intertextual talk.[4]

Heeding Maureen Honey's call for the "close reading of Harlem Renaissance creative texts in ways that illuminate their multifaceted aesthetic," I offer *Passing* as a reticent feminine crux of transnational modernist encounter.[5] Larsen's novel might seem an unlikely site for such an undertaking, since in contrast to her earlier, wider-ranging *Quicksand* (1928), the tightly focused *Passing* is set within the traditional boundaries of Harlem's middle class in the late 1920s. Seemingly more interpersonal than intertextual, *Passing* has recently elicited mostly queer and psychoanalytic readings that complicate the earlier focus on narratives of passing.[6] Yet Larsen's practice of intensive, extensive, and assimilative reading, along with the "habit of inscribing her reading into her writing" that produced the widely recognized "intertextual geography" of *Quicksand*, are also at work in *Passing*, although in a more subtle fashion channeled primarily through Irene Redfield and Clare Kendry, the novel's central female pair.[7] Unlike *Quicksand*, whose intertexts are almost entirely American, *Passing*'s intertextual field is international.

As a foretaste, I propose an unorthodox alignment of cultural centers brought into sharp focus in 1925: the canonical (if contested) year of Harlem's proclamation as the "Culture Capital" of the New Negro movement, the "Mecca of the New Negro," as Alain Locke put it in the special issue of *Survey Graphic* that quickly became the signature Harlem Renaissance anthology, *The New Negro*.[8] That year, another capital also gained a more vivid grasp on the American imagination with the publication of *Mrs. Dalloway*. As one American reviewer put it, "To Mrs. Woolf London exists and to Mrs. Woolf's readers anywhere and at any time London will exist with a reality it can never have for those who merely live there."[9] Nella Larsen was an exceptional American reader who grasped not only the power of Woolf's London, but also the (imperfect) fit between the celebration of a regenerated postwar capital city and the proclamation of a revivified Harlem as the site of a cultural renaissance. At the beginning of part 3 ("Finale") of *Passing*, in the only scene in which we see Irene Redfield walking alone (like Clarissa Dalloway) through the streets of her neighborhood, Larsen evokes and

revises *Mrs. Dalloway*'s signature opening sentence. Tucked into a subordi-
nate clause as if simply another casual afterthought, "Mrs. Dalloway said she
would buy the flowers herself" becomes Irene's recognition that "the morning's aimless wandering through the teeming Harlem streets, *long after she
had ordered the flowers which had been her excuse for setting out*, was but
another effort to tear herself loose" (*P*, 213, emphasis added). *Passing* translates Clarissa's stimulating excursion through a sparkling Westminster on a
brilliant June morning into Irene's aimless ramble through the overcrowded
streets of Harlem on a depressingly warm December afternoon. This is not
the beginning of the narrative but the beginning of its end. Woolf's scene
of renewal after the passage of winter and war has yielded to that moment's
darker underside and aftermath.

Larsen evokes *Mrs. Dalloway* at an oblique intersection between Woolfian modernism and her own cultural turf—so oblique that it has gone unnoticed. Although critics have detected echoes of Hemingway, Fitzgerald,
Wharton, Galsworthy, Conrad, James, and Joyce in Larsen's novels, they
have overlooked Woolf, most strikingly in the case of Larsen's biographer,
Thadious M. Davis, who, after noting that "Larsen chose as models for her
fiction British and American writers in whose works women's friendships
and the conventions of intimacy among women are significantly defined,"
cites only Edith Wharton and Henry James as examples.[10] Larsen's ambivalence toward Harlem, and the consequent lure of other cultural landscapes,
surface in a letter she wrote shortly after moving there in 1927: "Right now
when I look out into the Harlem Streets I feel just like Helga Crane in my
novel [*Quicksand*]. Furious at being cornered [?] with all these niggers."[11]
Yet what drew Larsen to *Mrs. Dalloway* was less the vitality of its external
landscape than the depth of its internal one.

Urban sparkle derives instead in *Passing* from another source and site
of cultural value. Its vehicle is Irene's counterpart, Clare, the dazzling object of the narrative gaze, who after a "long absence in European cities"
streaks through Harlem like a comet, "a flame of red and gold" (*P*, 166, 239).
Although not identified explicitly with a particular European city, Clare's
cosmopolitan flare is associated with the preferred site of Black expatri-
ates, one of whose most celebrated stars, Josephine Baker, left New York
for Paris to stage her landmark debut in the Revue Nègre at the Théâtre
des Champs-Elysées in October 1925: a cultural event whose impact on
French sensibilities rivaled the Ballets Russes' performance of *The Rite
of Spring* in the same theater twelve years earlier.[12] In *Passing*, Josephine
Baker makes a cameo appearance as seemingly gratuitous and as culturally loaded as Irene's reference to the underground. This time, however,
the verbal detour points toward Paris rather than London. In a passage of

reported, one-sided dialogue, Irene professes ignorance of the internationally famous cabaret performer. "Josephine Baker? . . . No, I've never seen her . . . Well, she might have been in *Shuffle Along* when I saw it, but if she was, I don't remember her. . . . Oh, but you're wrong! . . . I do think Ethel Waters is awfully good" (*P*, 219, ellipses in original). Like the reference to the underground, the term spoken under the sign of negation calls attention to what has been disavowed: the English Underground rather than the Underground Railroad and Josephine Baker's transatlantic celebrity rather than Ethel Water's indigenous iconicity.[13] Both scenes gesture beyond Harlem and the New Negro ideology Irene publicly avows. Taking advantage of a common practice of recruiting Baker's image to signal "the modernism of others," *Passing* also locates this other modernism within the diegesis in the attention-grabbing theatrical performances of Clare, whose image Irene attempts futilely to delete from her consciousness as she attempts to erase the memory of Baker.[14] "'I don't remember her [Baker]'" (*P*, 219); "She dropped Clare out of her mind" (*P*, 178). Unlike Irene, however, we will need to keep Josephine Baker in mind.

As a narrative instantiation of Baker's talent for spectacularization, Clare counterbalances the evocation of Woolfian modernism focalized primarily through Irene, whose adherence to a New Negro ideology of racial uplift is a cover for a wayward interiority (as Rebecca Hall's 2021 film of the novel makes clear). This reading gives a literary critical twist to the consensus that the doubling relationship between the novel's "twin" protagonists, variously construed through the lenses of sexuality, psychoanalysis, or character typology (with Irene as the New Negro and Clare as the Tragic Mulatta), is the novel's affective core.[15] By viewing them instead as loci of contending modernisms—an English iteration that brings a tradition of novelistic interiority into the twentieth century and a Black diasporic iteration that brings European, African, and American traditions into a syncretic aesthetic of display—we gain access to a series of opposing terms that constitute *Passing*'s conceptual underlay: interior/exterior, depth/surface, word/image, narrative/spectacle, private room/global stage, and literary form/historical mutability. The constant is a shifting dialogue between contending terms whose resistance to synthesis is a narrative engine and subject that (along with more obvious dissimilarities) differentiates *Passing* from *Mrs. Dalloway*.

Both the excavation of novelistic interiority and the exhibition of theatrical performativity that informs a Black diasporic aesthetic have roots in eighteenth-century London. The city's dramatic expansion during that century made it an exemplar of modern urbanization that paradoxically promoted both a retreat into domestic privacy and a flowering of public

spectacle. The first found expression in the novelistic rendition of a feminized interiority. As a critical tradition from Ian Watt to Nancy Armstrong
has contended, the mutually constitutive rise of the English novel and the
domestic woman produced a "feminine" sensibility that emerges with Samuel Richardson's representation of women's inner lives and culminates in
the modernist transcription of the flow of consciousness. There is a direct
line from what Richardson described in his "Preface" to *Clarissa* as the *"in-
stantaneous* descriptions and reflections" in the epistolary novel to Woolf's
mandate to "record the atoms as they fall upon the mind"; from Richardson's depiction of the "feverish and complicated inner life" transmitted in
Clarissa through letters from "one lonely closet to another" to the little attic
room in which Clarissa Dalloway sequesters her memories of Sally Seton's
kiss; and from Clarissa's attic room to the private sitting room in which
Irene muses about the letter she receives from Clare, her childhood friend.[16]
Making the first part of this lineage explicit, Watt notes that the "closet," or
small private apartment adjoining the bedroom, which had become a signal
feature of the Georgian home, "is an early version of the room of one's own
which Virginia Woolf saw as the prime requisite of woman's emancipation"
(188). What changes over the centuries is the narrative compression that
enables the closet (or such homologous containers as the envelope or the
teacup) to serve as a figure of the modernist novel as well as of its epistolary
origin.

   In contrast to this withdrawal into private space, the increasingly diverse urban population fostered by England's imperial forays, especially
its participation in the Atlantic slave trade that introduced foreign goods
and people of color to London, transformed the city into a cosmopolitan
exhibition stage. Counterpointing the novelistic plunge into interiority was
what Monica L. Miller (whose account I follow closely here) describes as
a "visually obsessed imperial world" catalyzed by exotic appearances and
dazzling surfaces that found expression in theatrical display rather than the
epistolary fiction.[17] As wealth accumulated with mercantile and imperial
expansion, the growing population of enslaved people, often exhibited as
luxury items dressed in extravagant costumes to display their owners' supe-
rior social status, played a salient role in the emergent social spectacle and
on the actual stage. Underlying and reinforcing this culture of display was
an increasingly theatrical, fluid, and spectacular conception of character as
"an experimentation with surface and depth, public and private, self and
other," rather than a stable interiority.[18] In the contestation between visible
character and verbal interiority, Blackness was clearly positioned on the
side of visibility.

   As a consequence of the world stage from which it emerged, Blackness in

eighteenth-century England was constituted through a composite genealogy in which African, Caribbean, European, British, and American cultural
traditions intermixed. For Miller, the theatricalization of a Blackness performed through costume and gesture was crystallized in the figure of the
Black dandy, who became increasingly visible in wealthy households, on the
stage, and in the public square. What started out as the "forced fopperie" of
the dandified Black servant decked out in lavish livery to display his owner's
affluence and cosmopolitan taste evolved among Britain's free Blacks into
a desire for self-styling through ostentatious fashion often borrowed from
European models. Since for Miller Blackness has always already been performed for a white audience and thus is an effect of diaspora, Black dandyism transforms an unwilling display into a deliberate one. Miller's narrative
uncovers the prehistory of a performative, syncretic Black identity that culminates in the theatrical self-displays of the Harlem Renaissance, when (in
Miller's words) "black dandies exploded everywhere and became of actual
and symbolic use and concern to Harlem's intelligentsia" because the Black
dandy's "failure to embody authenticity of race and culture" is what makes
Black modernism modern (*SF*, 22, 180).

As "self-styling subjects who use immaculate clothing, arch wit, and
pointed gesture to announce their often controversial presence," Black
dandies offer a stylistic repertoire through which "black male subjects can
be seen understanding, manipulating, and reimagining the construction of
their images" (*SF*, 1, 5). But why only Black *male* subjects? Although Miller
emphasizes, in accordance with most theorists, that the dandy repudiates
the norms of masculinity by inhabiting "the space between masculine and
feminine, homosexual and heterosexual, seeming and being," she rarely
calls into question the masculinity of her point of departure (*SF*, 5) The one
exception is the failed example of Sara Andrews in W. E. B. Du Bois's *Dark
Princess* (1928), a self-made Chicago woman whose rejection of interiority in favor of a meticulous attention to grooming and clothing prevents
her from actualizing the political potential of African American dandyism.
Clare Kendry, another Chicago-born female dandy conceived the year that
Dark Princess was published, might be seen as Larsen's attempt to reinscribe the feminine within the tradition of the destabilizing Black dandy
who presents (in Miller's words) a "performative text" that is "highly read-
able" without being entirely legible, who displays an "absolutely dogged
sense of self-invention," and who plays with the dialectic between illusion
and reality (*SF*, 16). If the dandy, as Miller argues, is "a modernist sign" that
challenges normative categories, why should that sign be gendered restric-
tively (*SF*, 24)?

Reading Clare Kendry as a feminine iteration of the Black dandy allows

York literary culture in its Sunday "Book Supplement," which became one of the nation's most highly regarded literary weeklies.[32] Under the guidance of the feminist Helen Reid, the wife of the newspaper's president, women were promoted to positions of editorial and literary authority. The most significant appointment was of Irita Van Doren, a leading literary figure and the well-connected wife of the critic Carl Van Doren, as literary editor of the "Book Supplement" in 1926. As part of her mission to solicit articles from distinguished contemporary writers (including Ford Madox Ford, André Gide, Aldous Huxley, Ezra Pound, Rebecca West, and Elinor Wylie), Van Doren reached out to Woolf to contribute to the journal frequently as a visiting critic. Between 1925 and 1931, Woolf contributed twenty reviews and articles to the *New York Herald Tribune* "Book Supplement," which offered the most concentrated and influential sample of her prose nonfiction, from "Character in Fiction" (on August 23 and 30, 1925) and "The Art of Fiction" (under the title "Is fiction art?" on October 16, 1927) to more targeted essays on Fanny Burney, Christina Rossetti, Mary Wollstonecraft, Dorothy Wordsworth, Edmund Gosse, Beau Brummel, and "this man called Hemingway."[33] Her contributions, typically given first billing and printed on the front page of the journal, would have been hard to miss, especially in the October 1927 issues, which she guest-edited and which carried her essays in four consecutive issues. The year that the publication of *To the Lighthouse* clinched Woolf's reputation as a major modernist novelist, she was also emerging for American readers as a signal literary critic.

Woolf's essays would have been especially hard to overlook for Nella Larsen, who in her 1922 application to library school listed the *New York Tribune* (precursor to the *New York Herald Tribune*) as one of the periodicals she regularly read.[34] A committed reader of modern literature and literary journals, she began in the fall of 1927 to work on the novel that evolved into *Passing*. Known as an "extremely well-read" member of an interracial circle of writers and an "avid reader interested in all periods and genres" who had acquired (in Charles S. Johnson's words) "a most extraordinarily wide acquaintance with past and current literature," Larsen was almost certainly aware of Woolf's work.[35] She was a bookworm who lined her living room with "books and more books"; those she couldn't afford to buy she had access to through her various positions from 1921 to 1925 at the 135th Street branch of the New York Public Library.[36] Books unavailable in the U.S. she made a point of requesting from abroad, asking her friend Dorothy Peterson in Paris to bring back "handkerchiefs and a copy of Ulysses if possible and convenient" and, somewhat more cryptically, to "remember Katherine Mansfield."[37] She peppered her letters with references to British protomodernists such as Wilde, Swinburne, and Pater. Lytton Strachey's

Queen Victoria appears somewhat improbably on her list of ten books read in the past two years in response to a question on her 1922 library school application.[38] Her correspondence repeatedly bears witness to her self-identification as a modernist. She was eager to make contact with Gertrude Stein, to whom she wrote to express her admiration for having "so accurately . . . caught the spirit of this race of mine" in "Melanctha," and then to attempt to arrange a meeting in Paris.[39] In a letter to Charles S. Johnson, the editor of *Opportunity*, protesting the magazine's negative review of Walter White's *Flight*, Larsen ironically characterized her perspective as "warped" by her recent reading of "the Europeans and American moderns"—among whom she identifies Huysmans, Conrad, Galsworthy, Proust, and Mann—who had prepared her for stylistic obscurities in *Flight* that could baffle a reader of Edith Wharton or Louis Hémon.[40] Echoing Woolf's distinction between backward-looking Edwardians and forward-looking Georgians, the structure of Larsen's literary identifications is as telling as the substance.

In fact, the two writers came close to meeting in New York between 1927 and 1929. In the course of her correspondence with Woolf, Irita Van Doren invited her to visit New York for a month in the spring of 1927, to write four articles (eventually published the following October), and to meet the writers and critics who congregated in her literary salons. Although the invitation ultimately faltered over negotiations about hotel expenses, Woolf came close to accepting it and, if she had, would have been introduced to the literary society surrounding Van Doren.[41] Nella Larsen was among Van Doren's protégés: "Rita [Irita Van Doren] I have seen several times. One day we had a luncheon engagement at one and finished at four-thirty," she noted in a letter to Carl Van Vechten in 1929.[42] Had Woolf accepted Van Doren's invitation to visit New York, there is a distinct possibility that the English and African American modernists might have met at one of Van Doren's gatherings, dedicated (among other goals) to fostering the interracial literary culture that was a Harlem Renaissance signature. Since the invitation remained a live possibility over the next couple of years, Woolf might even have been among the "distinguished interracial cast of guests" (including Irita Van Doren) who attended the elegant tea party that was given to celebrate the release of *Passing* at the Sherry-Netherland Hotel in April 1929 by Larsen's publishers, Alfred Knopf and his wife, Blanche Knopf, widely considered the most powerful woman publisher in New York.[43] The hypothetical scene of this encounter helps us imagine the unexplored common ground between the literary cultures of Bloomsbury and those of "mongrel Manhattan."[44]

It didn't require a personal meeting for Woolf's writing to travel, of course. Although Larsen never mentions Woolf explicitly, both her novels offer clues to her intimate knowledge of Woolf's fiction. Larsen's first novel, *Quicksand* (1928), as Laura Doyle points out, suggests an awareness of Woolf's debut novel, *The Voyage Out*, through the resonance between the traumatic kiss that Richard Dalloway inflicts on Rachel Vinrace during their journey to South America and a scene in *Quicksand* in which Robert Anderson's uninvited kiss intervenes in the attraction between Helga Crane and Audrey Denney.[45] In *Passing*, the echoes are more diffuse and disparate. Sometimes, they take the form of a sentence, as in the revision of *Mrs. Dalloway*'s opening line. Sometimes they are audible in the choice of a name: Hugh Wentworth, a thinly veiled stand-in for the white Harlem patron Carl Van Vechten (to whom *Passing* is dedicated), is just a shade away from (or has shade thrown on him by) *Mrs. Dalloway*'s very white Hugh Whitbread. Elsewhere, echoes crop up in the setting: Irene's memory of a blazing August day in Chicago "with a brutal staring sun" recalls the mid-June heat wave in London when "the sun became extraordinarily hot" (*P*, 146; *MD*, 15). Echoes can also take the form of paired words, as in the recurrence (with a minor variation) of the adverbial pair "vigorously, violently" that characterizes Septimus Warren Smith's plunge from the window in Clare Kendry's expression of rage "vehemently, violently" at her white racist husband John (Jack) Bellew (*MD*, 149; *P*, 200).

These local echoes are legible in terms of the nineteenth-century practice Daniel Hack has designated "African Americanization": the appropriation and revision of specific features of Victorian texts, including "diction, phrasing, dialogue, description, characterization, and plot."[46] As Hack argues persuasively, these intertextual engagements served multiple functions of cultural positioning, subversive repurposing, recontextualization, and tradition-building that resulted in Victorian literature's enmeshment in African American letters. Hack charts this practice into the early twentieth century, but he retains the Victorian reference point. With the shift in *Passing* to a modernist frame of reference, the focus on specific features of Victorian texts yields to a more holistic transposition of narrative form and mode. Streamlining what they perceived as Victorian clutter was a mainstay of Bloomsbury aesthetics, whether manifested in the art-critical elevation of "significant form" over verisimilitude, the architectural taste for the "visual abstraction" of whitewashed rooms, or the injunction to "Look within" in order to distill "Life" from the "ill-fitting vestments" of the realist novel.[47]

The novelistic allegiance to producing lifelike stories presented special challenges to the mandate of formal overhaul. Woolf addressed these head-on in her critical review of E. M. Forster's *Aspects of the Novel*, which she published under the title "Is Fiction an Art?" (now better known under its British title, "The Art of Fiction") in the *New York Herald Tribune* "Book

Review" on October 16, 1927. Siding with Henry James's "esthetic" view of fiction—that is, with the imposition of patterned forms on formless life— over E. M. Forster's "humane" view, Woolf insists contra Forster that the novel (like a poem or a play) is a work of art rather than a "parasite which draws sustenance from life."[48] Hailing James as the first Anglophone novelist to elevate fiction to the formal criteria for lyric poetry, Woolf advances his example toward the crossover modernist genre sometimes called the "lyrical novel."[49] An individual letter (or the site of its composition or the vehicle of its transmission) can be a figure of aesthetic (as well as psychological) interiority, but its compression differs dramatically from the garrulousness of the epistolary novel. Like the well-wrought urn that has long served as the trope of a bounded lyric whole, or the golden bowl that provides the title of the sole Jamesian novel Woolf cites by title in this essay, the modernist novel is defined more by shape than by story.

Crafting a distinctive form was Woolf's signature desire and achievement in *Mrs. Dalloway*, as her diary entry on June 19, 1923, asserts: "The design is so queer & masterful. I'm always having to wrench my substance to fit it. The design is certainly original, & interests me hugely."[50] Design affords a self-contained narrative and affective world that need not be circumscribed by race. Forms, as Caroline Levine argues, are portable. "They can be picked up and moved to new contexts."[51] And that—with some deliberate deviation—is what Larsen did with the "queer" form of *Mrs. Dalloway*, which functions, with a certain irony, as what Henry Louis Gates Jr. calls a "silent second text," but one that informs the African American text in ways that may be discernible primarily to readers attuned to the dominant canon.[52]

On March 19, 1928, Larsen wrote to Carl Van Vechten that she was having "the most hellish time" with her new novel and had "torn it all up and now face[d] the prospect of starting all over again—if at all."[53] On September 3, 1928, she wrote again: "I have had a very hellish week, but have finished my manuscript."[54] During those intervening five and a half months, she rewrote from scratch the novel she had been working on since the previous summer, producing a streamlined three-part novel, as taut as a three-act play, each part comprised of four chapters and succinctly titled, as if in a play, "Encounter," "Re-encounter," and "Finale." Since the original manuscript of *Passing* (initially titled *Nig*) has disappeared, there is no way of knowing what changes took place, but the result complies well with Woolf's insistence on sacrificing life to pattern. Larsen presents no motive for ripping up her original draft, but I wager that during that interval Larsen read (or reread) *Mrs. Dalloway* and "Is Fiction an Art?" and decided to reshape her novel.

us not only to extend our gaze beyond the confines seemingly imposed by the novel's title—rather than *passing*, the dandy *destabilizes*—but also to open the figure of the Black dandy to other feminine interpretations, including Josephine Baker's, and to place it in conversation with other feminine modernisms. Recuperating the term "mulatto" from Houston Baker's critique of the Harlem Renaissance's solicitation of white patronage, Monica L. Miller positions the (male) dandy as a crossover "figure with both European and American and African origins, a figure who expresses with his performative body and dress the fact that modern identity, *in both black and white*, is necessarily syncretic, or mulatto, but in a liberating rather than constraining way" (*SF*, 178, emphasis added). The masculine dandy toggles between Black and white (masculine) modernisms, aligning them under the sign of a shared syncretic aesthetic. Between what modernisms might the female dandy negotiate? How might we envision a mulatta modernism?

Larsen's version accords with Miller's proposal of the dandy as anti-essentialist antidote to the New Negro's advocacy of racial authenticity. In *Passing*, that advocacy is centered in Irene and manifested through her managerial role for the Negro Welfare League dance. Supplementing Brian Redfield's sarcastic commentary on his wife's social commitment, "Uplifting the brother is no easy job," Larsen offers Clare as a feminine alternative (*P*, 179). This shift in perspective transposes Clare from the well-worn tradition of the tragic mulatta who features in a narrative of passing (including Helga Crane's narrative in Larsen's previous novel *Quicksand*) to the uncharted terrain of the Black female dandy who stars in the theater of mulatta modernism. Unlike the masculine prototype who pivots between Black and white modernisms, Clare does not monopolize this stage but shares it with Irene, whose public advocacy is complemented and complicated by the retreat it provokes from civic life to a disembodied interiority. That Irene experiences loyalty to her race as a suffocating burden as well as a solemn duty becomes clear during her agitation over whether to free herself from Clare by betraying Clare's hankering for Harlem to her racist husband: "She [Irene] was caught between two allegiances, different, yet the same. Herself. Her race. Race! The thing that bound and suffocated her" (*P*, 225). Irene's desire to break her "self" away from her "race" takes the narrative form of an inward turn toward an unracialized space of consciousness whose literary excavation was the mandate of the English epistolary novel.

Irene imagines Clare's voice as "remotely suggesting England" (*P*, 51), but her unsubstantiated characterization more accurately describes her own imaginative world and the verbal fabric through which it is rendered. Echoes of England in *Passing* suggest a modernist twist on a long-standing African American tradition of Anglophilia inspired by (but not limited to)

British abolitionism. According to Elisa Tamarkin, England in nineteenth-century African American discourse signified a lost maternal source of tradition, equality, and civility, a culture in which race was not an inevitable filter of experience.[19] Perhaps such a nostalgia for a deracialized elsewhere accounts for England's remote familiarity in *Passing*, where it constitutes Irene's implicit and less drastic alternative to her husband's longing to emigrate to Brazil, where, according to a widely respected contemporaneous anthropologist, "there is no race problem."[20] "I always did admire the English," Larsen observed in a letter to Carl Van Vechten the year before writing *Passing*, and she weaves her Anglophilia into the text orthographically through a predilection for British spelling, a stylistic tic as politically freighted as it was anomalous during the postwar era of American cultural nationalism.[21] In the 1920s, the desire to recover a national literary tradition by declaring artistic independence from England was funneled through the celebration of "The American Language," as H. L. Mencken called it in the title of his influential 1919 book that defended ordinary American language use against Anglophile purists.[22] It is striking, then, that *Passing* displays some of the features that Mencken identifies as distinctively British English: the spelling of individual words such as *kerb* (rather than *curb*), and a preference for the *re* over the *er* ending in words such as *lustre* and for the *ou* over the simple *o* vowel at the center of words such as *savour* or *candour* or, in an especially charged example, *coloured*, a spelling that differentiates Larsen from most of her African American contemporaries such as Langston Hughes, Zora Neale Hurston, and Jessie Fauset who consistently spelled the word *colored*, as if Larsen were seeking a way to be *coloured* outside the American binary. At a moment when a broad spectrum of white American modernists were rebelling against English linguistic conventions by ventriloquizing a Black vernacular, and when a range of African American as well as Anglo-American modernists professed an allegiance to American cultural nationalism, Larsen was sprinkling *Passing* with Anglicisms.[23]

These Anglicizing inflections are also, of course, a class marker consistent with Larsen's disidentification in her letter to Dorothy Peterson from "all these niggers" in Harlem. Affecting a British enunciation could seem a particularly feminine mode of snobbery, as Langston Hughes charged in the case of Washington, D.C.'s Black high society, which showcased "so many ladies with chests swelled like pouter-pigeons whose mouths uttered formal sentences in frightfully correct English."[24] Beyond class aspirations, however, the desire to disidentify from an imposed racialization without seeming to claim membership in the dominant racial group could find expression in an imaginative transport to a deracialized elsewhere, a transport like that of the Drayton Hotel elevator that wafts Irene "upward on a magic carpet to

In both *Mrs. Dalloway* and *Passing,* narrative form is rendered most distinctively through a recursive temporality derived from the interior lives of the characters: a dramatic departure in both cases from the linear chronology of the novels that immediately preceded them, *Quicksand* and *Jacob's Room,* and one that extends into the twentieth century the inward turn that began with the English epistolary novel.

Caves of Memory

Passing famously begins with a letter, or rather with an envelope. Although not an epistolary novel, it takes off from a classic epistolary scene: in a private room that resembles an eighteenth-century "closet," a letter arrives from the outside world, penetrating the recesses of its recipient's consciousness, reopening a buried past. Diverging from the conventions of epistolarity, however, this envelope is not opened for several pages, and when it is, the letter's "carelessly formed words" and fragmentary phrases, punctuated with ellipses, are scarcely more revealing than the surface of the envelope, to which our attention has been drawn (*P*, 145). Lacking a return address, the "long envelope of thin Italian paper with its almost illegible scrawl seemed out of place and alien," "a thin sly thing" boldly inscribed with Clare Kendry's handwriting in purple ink on "foreign paper of extraordinary size" (*P*, 143). A stand-in for Clare, the vivid and opaque surface of the envelope launches the narrative, but that narrative unfolds within Irene's mind as she reminisces about her childhood friend. Rather than two hearts pouring their feelings into letters (the faux etymology of "cor-respondence"), *Passing* juxtaposes an envelope's exterior and the interior movements of its recipient's consciousness.

The materiality of letters persists as a vehicle of the struggle between Irene and Clare. Written, received, shredded, awaited: letters in *Passing* have a life of their own as material rather than expressive emissaries. The symbolic violence inflicted by Clare's letter (breaking through Irene's defensive barriers) is reciprocated by Irene's memory of having torn up a previous letter from her and scattering the fragments on the railroad tracks en route back to New York, foreshadowing Clare's violent death, and by the repetition of that gesture in the narrative present as she tears up Clare's inaugurating letter and throws the pieces into the wastebasket. Letters always originate from Clare, whose peripatetic existence makes them a necessary medium; Irene, who is threatened by Clare's rootlessness, refuses to respond, finding it preferable "to answer nothing, to explain nothing, to refuse nothing; to dispose of the matter simply by not writing at all" (*P*, 191).

More inclined to gaze at Clare than to open her heart to her, Irene (in good modernist fashion) keeps her interior life to herself. In this uneven distribution of expressive modes, letters fall on the side of a diasporic aesthetic that is both "furtive" and "flaunting," secretive and exhibitionist; the motions of the heart have moved inside (P, 143).

Underscoring this interiority, the decor of Irene's private room, like that of Clarissa's, is sketched very lightly. The furnishing is sparse: a narrow bed, book, and dressing table with a mirror for Clarissa; a writing table, chair, and mirror for Irene. The mirror's presence in both rooms calls attention to self-reflection. In Irene's case, the minimalist look, illuminated in the morning by a wash of October sunshine that imbues the scene with an auratic glow, contrasts with the overfurnished social spaces she shares with her husband, who "pilots" her from her private room to the dining room that stages, Pamela Caughie argues, "a send-up of the Black bourgeoisie."[55] The scripted gestures, the constraints of decorum, and the solidity of household objects and domestic workers during this breakfast scene, uncharacteristically rendered from an ironizing third-person perspective, suggest why Irene might want, as Richardson advised, to make "her closet her paradise."[56]

The distinctively modernist inflection of Larsen's version is the turn from Richardson's present-tense rendition of the flux of consciousness to a Woolfian cave of memory. It was through the process of crafting a new form for *Mrs. Dalloway* that Woolf made her "discovery": how to endow her characters with "humanity, humour, depth" by punctuating her narratives with self-contained scenes of memory.[57] As she fashioned a design "more remarkable" than any of her previous books, she developed what she called her "tunneling process" of telling the past by installments as needed.[58] The narrative breakthrough of *Mrs. Dalloway* is a method of spatializing temporality. The layering of memory is pervasive throughout the novel, but although Woolf refers in the plural to "caves" of memory, only one scene (and its subsequent reprise) has the spatial and temporal coordinates to warrant that metaphor fully. Unlike the ambulatory memories stirred by Clarissa's morning walk through Westminster, or Peter Walsh's more extended memory, upon awakening from a nap in Regent's Park, of his breakup with Clarissa thirty years earlier, only Clarissa's little attic room encloses what Woolf called in her memoir a "space of time" between four walls (Sketch, 79). Framed by Clarissa ascending and descending the staircase to her attic room, the scene that culminates in her memory of Sally Seton's kiss, "the most exquisite moment of her whole life," is as self-contained as the diamond that figures Sally's gift (MD, 35).

This is precisely the structure Larsen creates in *Passing*. For the entire first part of the novel, "Encounter," Irene remains seated at her writing table as she relives the memories catalyzed by Clare's letter. Before opening the envelope, Irene recalls scenes from their adolescence. Transitioning somewhat clunkily after Irene reads the letter, the second chapter announces: "This is what Irene Redfield remembered" (*P*, 146). "This"—the Chicago scenes triggered by her encounter with Clare on the top floor of the Drayton Hotel—unfolds over the next three chapters. Part 2, "Re-encounter," opens: "Such were Irene Redfield's memories as she sat there in her room" (*P*, 181). Having not moved for four chapters, Irene remains within a cave of memory (or perhaps, to align the metaphor more closely with the discourse of the novel, within a narrative envelope) that dilates the frame of Clarissa's attic-room recollection while retaining the architectural interior.[59] Although Irene's memories are more ambivalent and multifaceted than the scene of Sally's memorable kiss, both texts construct the constant backdrop of another time and place—Bourton in *Mrs. Dalloway*, Chicago in *Passing*—centered on enchantment by another woman.

As with the scene in Clarissa's attic room, Irene's memories are crystallized by the multisensory impression initially made simply by Clare's presence as she wafts through the rooftop restaurant of the Drayton Hotel, "a sweetly scented woman in a fluttering dress of green chiffon" whose flowered pattern turns the summer heat to spring (*P*, 150). Clare's husky voice, "peculiar caressing smile," and tinkling laugh add tactile and sonic details to the visual (and olfactory) image (*P*, 148). Despite the change in color scheme, Clarissa's impression of Sally at Bourton in a pink gauze dress that "*seemed*, anyhow, all light" and a beautiful voice that "made everything she said sound like a caress" similarly captures the almost magical appearance of a woman who seems to arrive at Bourton out of nowhere (*MD*, 35, emphasis in original). In both scenarios, the point of view rests entirely with the desiring rather than the desired woman. Although Irene suffers under Clare's steady gaze, which she suspects may have seen through her performance of whiteness, we never see Irene from Clare's perspective, or Clarissa from Sally's, or have access to the motives for the seductive woman's behavior. Clarissa can't take her eyes off Sally's "extraordinary beauty of the kind she most admired, dark, large-eyed, with that quality which, since she hadn't got it herself, she always envied—a sort of abandonment, as if she could say anything, do anything: a quality much commoner in foreigners than in Englishwomen" (*MD*, 33). Irene is similarly beguiled by Clare's provocative smile, unreserved manner, enigmatic history, and exotic black-eyed appearance. Characterologically as well as visually, the two pairs of women mirror one another. Clare, "stepping always on the edge of danger" (*P*, 143), exhibits the recklessness of Sally bicycling "round the parapet of the terrace" at Bourton (*MD*, 34), while Clare's dramatic ending seems to fulfill Clarissa's prophecy that Sally's "melodramatic love of being the centre of everything" would "end in some awful tragedy; her death; her martyrdom" (*MD*, 182). Most strikingly, both texts contain these romantic memories within a narrative enclosure that terminates with the arrival of a man—Peter Walsh, Brian Redfield—who proceeds to command the protagonist's attention.

Perhaps Larsen discovered this narrative technique independently of Woolf. More likely, it was an aspect of the assimilative reading through which she absorbed not only specific names and phrases, but also the formal strategies of the authors she admired.[60] Responding with a deep dive into Irene's subjectivity, rendered through a modernist mix of free indirect discourse and psychonarration, Larsen reenacts Woolf's narrative elaboration of the interior landscape given literary form by the epistolary novel. It is even tempting to read Clare's letter from an unspecified location as doubling as a metaphoric missive from Woolf. The cover design of the Modern Library edition of *Mrs. Dalloway* (fig. 1), published with Woolf's new "Introduction" in December 1928, as part of Random House's mission of disseminating affordable editions of major literary works, encourages such a reading. Featuring a large white envelope on which the title *Mrs. Dalloway* is written in oversize red cursive script (unfortunately not visible in the black-and-white reproduction), the cover presents Woolf's text as a letter to its readers. Although probably published too late to have influenced Larsen, who claimed that she had completed her manuscript the previous September (although it wasn't published until the following April), the cover invites us to imagine some atemporal conjunction that (like a dream image) condenses multiple exchanges exempted from linear chronology into an overdetermined image of literary transmission that travels from Woolf to Larsen and back again.

Clare's Envelope

What happens, then, to the surface of the envelope, whether inscribed in bold purple or red ink? The answer entails shifting to a different aesthetic that Woolf also intimates in a diary entry prompted by a sitting at *Vogue*, in which she notes her interest in investigating "the party consciousness, the frock consciousness," exemplified by the fashion world gathered in the studio, in which "people secrete an envelope, which connects them & protects them from others, like myself, who am outside the envelope, foreign bodies."[61] Here, the envelope is a bodily secretion, a protective shell that

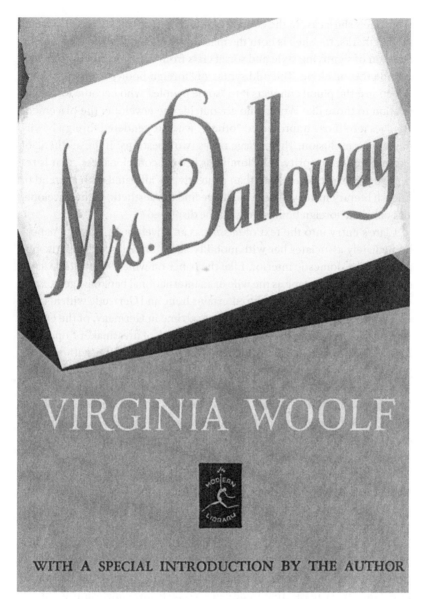

FIGURE 1. Book jacket for Modern Library's
edition of Virginia Woolf's *Mrs. Dalloway* (1928).

Woolf feels she lacks; in the context of the sitting for *Vogue* that occasioned these remarks, the shell is both the materiality of clothing and its symbolic function of signifying style and social class from which she feels excluded, outside the envelope. The odd syntax of "foreign bodies" toggles in both directions: the plural connects it to "some people," who become foreign in relation to those like Woolf who are outside the envelope; the placement attaches it to those unprotected "others" who are rendered foreign by virtue of their exclusion. The passage raises two questions: If the aesthetic of a transparent interiority, the "luminous halo of consciousness" that is receptive and expressive rather than protective, is affiliated with a strand of English literary history, where might we find the aesthetic of the envelope, and on what "foreign bodies" might it be displayed?[62]

Clare's entry into the text of *Passing* as an envelope of "foreign paper" immediately associates her with mobility and boundary crossing, the opposite of the domestic interior. Like the paper on which she writes, Claire circulates across Europe as the wife of an international banking agent. As in the "verbal feat" with which she entertains Irene and Gertrude with her stories "of wartime in France, of after-the-wartime in Germany, of the excitement at the time of the general strike in England, of dressmakers' openings in Paris, of the new gaiety of Budapest," Claire accumulates without integrating diverse European scenarios (*P*, 170). She strings them together in Harlem, James Weldon Johnson's "Negro metropolis," the theatrical site of his "cosmopolite self-concept" and the playful self-fashioning of a diasporic aesthetic that is syncretic rather than synthetic.[63] As Clare breezes in and out of Harlem in the narrative present, her cameo appearances captured by Irene's enraptured gaze introduce a visual counterpoint to Irene's inward-turning novelistic bent. Culturally both African American and European, Clare's performance in a series of stylish outfits locates a cosmopolitan Harlem Renaissance aesthetic in a female dandy's self-presentation.

The performance begins at the polished surface of Clare's skin. Whereas Irene is endowed with organic (and consequently vulnerable) "warm olive cheeks" that are susceptible to blushes that evidence the blood and emotions coursing beneath the surface (*P*, 145), Clare's "incredibly beautiful face" is an "ivory mask" that Irene can't "come to any conclusion about. . . . It was unfathomable, utterly beyond any experience or comprehension of hers" (*P*, 157, 176). Clare fosters this incomprehension through her "trick of sliding down ivory lids over astonishing black eyes" (*P*, 221). Her self-presentation, viewed through Irene's eyes, veers toward the inorganic. Even her laugh has "a hard metallic sound" (*P*, 159). Her skin is golden and her hair, rather than blonde or yellow, is "pale gold" (*P*, 161). Gold is both figuratively and literally the medium of Clare's alchemical transformation from

MRS. DALLOWAY IN HARLEM › 43

an impoverished Negro girl on the west side of Chicago to the glamorous wife of Jack Bellew whose return from South America "with untold gold" affords Clare a route through marriage to a gold-plated existence (*P*, 159). In her first impression of Clare in the Drayton Hotel, Irene watches "the silver spoon in the white hand slit the dull gold of the melon," revising the old saw "born with a silver spoon in one's mouth" while slipping the white hand between two precious ores in a way that seems to turn it to marble. Even "the ringing bells in her laugh had a hard metallic sound" (*P*, 159).

Irene also notes Clare's "dark, almost black, eyes and that wide mouth like a scarlet flower against the ivory of her skin" (*P*, 148). Aestheticized by a simile ("like a scarlet flower") that deploys a literary color (*The Scarlet Letter*, Scarlett O'Hara), the selective depiction of Clare's face in bold contrasting colors against the uniform backdrop of her ivory skin evokes the stylization of a Japanese mask: an impression reinforced by the Japanese print at which Irene finds herself staring immediately after Clare plunges to her death, as if Clare's spirit has migrated from her shattered body to a Japanese work of art.[64] Both the cultural associations and the color scheme Larsen chooses for Clare—gold, ivory, scarlet, black—evoke the classic dandy fashioned by Oscar Wilde (who invoked his own version of orientalism). When Dorian Gray, with his "finely curved scarlet lips" and "crisp gold hair," poses for a portrait by Basil Hallward, he sits "perfectly still" with "half-parted lips, and the bright look in the eyes."[65] When Irene tells Clare the story of her life, the golden Clare "sat motionless, her bright lips slightly parted, her whole face lit by the radiance of her happy eyes" (*P*, 155). More theatrical than Dorian's "picture," Clare's staging of the female dandy in Harlem brings Africa as well as Europe and Asia into the cultural mix.

A consistent feature of this mix is an emphasis on clean lines and polished surfaces. Typically, this takes the form of a metallic covering that repels light rather than absorbing it and that renders its wearer immune to the questions and gazes arrested at its polished surface. No frills, curls, ruffles, pastel colors, or exposed flesh: Clare's stylistic signature is constituted by sculptural lines, metallic coverings, and blocks of contrasting solid colors. Whether clad in "shining black taffeta," a stiff lustrous blend of silk and synthetic materials that originated in France and Italy, or a "shining red gown" for the evening or a "superlatively simple cinnamon-brown frock that brought out all her vivid beauty" for tea (*P*, 220, 223), Clare follows the dictates of simplicity and shine. The exception that proves the rule is her one moment of vulnerability when, after Irene fails to respond to her letter, Clare arrives at Irene's house and confesses her loneliness, while tears "ran down her cheeks and spilled into her lap, ruining the priceless velvet of her dress" (*P*, 196). To be vulnerable is to be dressed in a permeable covering (plush velvet rather than shiny taffeta) that both signifies and shows the cost of vulnerability.

The combination of clean lines and metallic shine that shapes Clare's sartorial performance shares key features with the international modernist aesthetic exemplified by the early twentieth-century architectural programs of Adolf Loos and Le Corbusier and theatricalized, as Anne Anlin Cheng contends in *Second Skin: Josephine Baker and the Modern Surface*, by Josephine Baker's performances in Paris.[66] Baker's exploration of what Cheng characterizes as the materiality of the modern surface began with her move to Paris from New York, where she had performed minstrel-style in Blackface, bandanna, and oversize shoes and lips in shows such as *Shuffle Along* (1921) and *The Chocolate Dandies* (1924), Broadway's version of the Black dandy as consumable candy. In Paris, she gradually refined and redefined her self-presentation from the famous *danse sauvage* in which she debuted at the Théâtre des Champs-Elysées in 1925 to the burnished performance that emerged in tandem with her growing allegiance to the aesthetic standards of her adoptive city. Upon returning to Paris in 1929 from a two-year tour through Europe and South America, she declared that in order to be an artist "worthy of Paris" she had renounced the Charleston and the famous banana skirt in which she had performed at the Folies Bergère. Embracing her hybrid identity as a Black French woman, she insisted: "Mais je suis française. Je suis une Française noire. Et j'aime Paris, j'adore Paris"; or, as she famously announced the following year in her signature song: "J'ai deux amours / Mon pays et Paris."[67]

Baker's expatriated reclamation of Blackness shares what Cheng calls the "dream of a second skin" not only with modernist European architecture, but also with the Harlem Renaissance aesthetic staged by Clare Kendry (*SS*, 13). Both women wear their "polished and flawless" skin as a protective costume and their shiny costumes as a second skin whose sheen renders them impervious to inquiry (*SS*, 116). Like Baker, Clare "gleam[s]" at the threshold where human skin morphs into modern surface" (*SS*, 12). The women share an "infinitely dressable surface" (*SS*, 81) and a "strangely fluid relation to the organic and the inorganic" (*SS*, 103). The luster of their "sartorial skin," at once organic and synthetic, renders their interiority inaccessible and their race illegible (*SS*, 162). Baker's performance of race as "neither pure illusion nor authentic embodiment, but a complicated and unceasing negotiation between the two" offers an excellent description of Clare's as well (*SS*, 163). This affinity can be brought into focus through a series of studio photographs of Baker taken in Paris in the late 1920s. One in particular, "Josephine Baker as Black Venus" taken in 1929

FIGURE 2. George Hoyningen-Huene, "Josephine Baker as Black
Venus" (1929). Copyright © Estate of George Hoyningen-Huene.
Photograph: George Hoyningen-Huene Estate Archives.

by the cosmopolitan fashion photographer George Hoyningen-Huene, coincides and resonates with Clare's presentation on the literary stage with the publication of *Passing* that same year (fig. 2). The photograph has become an iconic image, reproduced on the covers of two academic studies (among other sites).[68] Carefully arranged to distill its subject's defining features into a single concentrated image that contrasts with the performer's frenetic movements on the stage, the photograph features a vertical, statuesque, slender, naked Baker who commands our attention as a bronze figure sharply outlined against a shadowy background. Dramatically front-lit and frontally posed, she gazes directly at us, her oval face an ivory mask whose features are accentuated with lipstick and eyeliner. Brilliantly illuminated to bring out the gleaming bronze cast of her skin and the luminous vertical fall of the narrow panel of gold lamé cloth that shields the central portion of her body, the portrait draws metallic skin and golden fabric into a common medium.

Despite their obvious differences, the photographic portraits of Baker and the literary portraits of Clare share some defining features. "Photographed" in effect through Irene's gaze in seated or standing poses, Clare's stillness slows the pace of reading to a series of Bakerian tableaux. By contrast, when we see Clare dancing at the Negro Welfare League ball, it is through Hugh Wentworth's gaze, which seeks to fix her through a different mythologization of white female beauty: "But what I'm trying to find out is the name, status, and race of the blonde beauty out of the fairy-tale"; the narrative voice quickly intervenes to substitute "golden" for "blonde" (*P*, 204–5). The tableau that correlates most closely with the portrait of the Black Venus is produced by Irene's awed discovery of Clare and Brian in the Redfields' living room before the Negro Welfare Ball: "Clare, exquisite, golden, fragrant, flaunting, in a stately gown of shining black taffeta, whose long, full skirt lay in graceful folds about her slim golden feet: her glistening hair drawn smoothly back into a small twist at the nape of her neck; her eyes, sparkling like dark jewels" (*P*, 203). Stringing together adjectives that have characterized Clare elsewhere, the tableau renders Clare as a composite image of metallic shimmer and shine. Although Clare wears a formal full-length black gown and Baker only a vertical length of gold lamé cloth, Baker's way of "wearing her nakedness like a sheath" renders both portraits studies in black and gold (*SS*, 1). Clare's racialized Blackness is displaced onto her portable gown, while a protective golden covering is transposed to her skin that culminates in "slim golden feet" at one end and will extend in another to the accessory of a hat that resembles a "little golden bowl" (*P*, 220). Noting the "idealized goldenness" that offsets the potentially "abject darkness" of Josephine Baker's skin, Cheng calls attention in a chapter titled

"The Woman with the Golden Skin" to the centrality of gold highlights and accoutrements (jewelry, loincloth, fingernails, dress) in Baker's studio portraits (*SS*, 133). The photographic and literary scenarios correspond in other ways as well: the "graceful folds" of Clare's shining skirt are a more ample version of Baker's panel of gold cloth; Clare's smoothly drawn-back "glistening hair" may not be quite the "metallic helmet" of Baker's famously lacquered "Baker-Do," but both hairstyles favor sleekness and shine; Clare's sparkling, jewel-like eyes relocate to a different body part the jewels that adorn Baker's hands, neck, and ears (*SS*, 112). Baker may be more scantily dressed than Clare, but both are fully clad in the glossy envelope of a modern surface.

Since the two figures reach the public simultaneously, there is no question of influence here, but rather two manifestations of a shared aesthetic. As its caption indicates, "Black Venus" is a syncretic figure of Africa and Europe. The golden light that seems to pool at Baker's feet in the luminous material covering the pedestal on which she stands evokes the half shell from which Botticelli's Venus is born from the sea; the gold lamé cloth draped over Baker's private parts recalls the flowing golden hair that performs that service for Botticelli's goddess. What "Josephine Baker as Black Venus" eliminates are the curvy lines and flowery mythological surround of Botticelli's painting, producing a sparser form closer to a classical column than the reimagined classicism of Renaissance art, while blackening and illuminating the body of this twentieth-century Venus with a sheen historically associated with African aesthetics and Black skin.[69]

"Black Venus" was one of Baker's chosen nicknames (together with the variations "Bronze Venus" and "Black Pearl"), but its selection for this portrait was overdetermined by the name's previous and primary reference in French culture to Jeanne Duval, the Haitian-born cabaret performer and the mistress and occasional muse of the Symbolist poet Charles Baudelaire, who conferred that moniker on her. In the poems she inspired, Baudelaire endows his "maîtresse des maîtresses" with greater sensuality than Josephine Baker: she is variously the mother of memory, the child of midnight, and the "Faust of the Savanna"; the speaker drinks from the wells of her eyes, inhales her perfumed breath, and immerses himself in the fragrant "black ocean" of her hair that transports him to an exotic paradise far from quotidian Paris. Yet Baudelaire's evocation of his nineteenth-century Black Venus also anticipates her modernist iteration through the sonorous jewels she displays on her polished naked skin. By choosing the Baudelairean moniker as the caption for his photograph of Baker, whose own lavish jewels on naked skin seem to reference her predecessor, Hoyningen-Huene brings the Black Venus into the twentieth century and in so doing suggests how this modernized figure might help us envision—as the voluptuous Jeanne Duval could not—a feminine version of the dandy that Baudelaire theorized.[70]

Baker in Paris is a switch point through which we can elaborate the female dandy's properties along two axes: vertically across centuries and horizontally across cultures. Along with Clare, Baker reminds us that many of the dandy's presumptively masculine attributes (mobility, inscrutability, coolness, elegance) are no more intrinsically gendered than they are intrinsically raced. Differences in costume are immaterial. Both women conform to the model of the dandy Baudelaire offers:

> These beings have no other calling but to cultivate the idea of beauty in their persons, to satisfy their passions, to feel and to think. . . . Furthermore to his eyes, which are in love with *distinction* above all things, the perfection of his toilet will consist in absolute simplicity. . . . [Dandyism] is first and foremost the burning need to create for oneself a personal originality, bounded only by the limits of propriety. It is a kind of cult of the self which can nevertheless survive the pursuit of a happiness to be found in someone else. . . . It is the joy of astonishing others, and the proud satisfaction of never oneself being astonished. . . . The distinguishing characteristic of the dandy's beauty consists above all in an air of coolness which comes from the unshakeable determination not to be moved.[71]

Frock Consciousness

Larsen's intervention is to play the spectacle of the cosmopolitan female dandy against the inward turn of a Woolfian sensibility. In so doing, she reconfigures the relationships among race, surface, and interiority. Already destabilized by the fact that the character who passes as white performs a syncretic Black aesthetic while the character who affirms a Black identity is a vehicle of an English modernist aesthetic, the relationship is further unsettled by Larsen's exploration of the penalties incurred by interiority. Focalized through Irene, the narrative perspective (which is not the same as the novel's) consistently places Clare at an advantage by rendering her entirely through Irene's envious eyes. Despite her concerted attention to her own appearance (powdering her face, buying a new dress, pondering which outfit to wear, critically assessing the wardrobes of others, and rattling off the names of French couturiers—"Is it Worth or Lanvin? . . . Oh, a mere Babani"), Irene is unable to assemble the polished surface that signifies modernity; she lacks the sense of style that seems to come so effortlessly to Clare (*P*, 219).[72] Irene knows this, without knowing why. The unspoken assumption is that a zero-sum relation pertains between external shell and internal cogitation, as if the privileging of one entails the other's deficit.

As a result, Irene is touchable, penetrable, undefended: the sweat of bodies clings to her; letters and people intrude uninvited into her private space; an apparent stranger fixes her with a stare in a restaurant; proximate voices "rasp" on her, and she "intensely" dislikes the crunching sound of her husband eating toast (*P*, 148, 185). In this, Irene resembles her precursor Helga Crane in *Quicksand*, whose epidermal irritation registers the impingement of a racialized environment, although in the earlier novel Larsen puts more pressure on the aestheticizing alternative that Clare performs in *Passing*.[73] No wonder Irene needs a room of her own.

Like Woolf, Irene feels herself to be outside the protective envelope and consequently a "foreign body," which in her case means a conspicuously permeable and visible body whose exposure, like the flesh of a snail, is vaguely distasteful, even obscene. Parts of Irene's body remain awkwardly visible throughout her changes of outfit. After rendering her interior world in part 1, the narrative perspective pulls back to present her from the outside for the first time as Irene's husband Brian silently enters her private room while she draws "a fragile stocking over a pale beige-coloured foot" (*P*, 183). The transparent "fragile" stocking barely shields the nondescript beige of the foot that, unlike Clare's "slim golden feet" (a merger of shoes and skin), asserts its biological presence underneath. It is thus, perhaps, a compensatory logic that drives the swift turn of Irene's gaze from her image in the mirror to Brian, whose beautiful skin "of an exquisitely fine texture and deep copper colour" she singles out for praise (*P*, 184). Lacking that coppery covering (a color often ascribed to Josephine Baker), Irene's barely covered beige foot recalls the "appalling amount of leg, stout legs in sleazy stockings of a vivid rose-beige shade," exposed by Irene's unfortunate childhood friend Gertrude, another light-skinned, mixed-race woman whose only function in the novel appears to be to offer a foil for Irene (*P*, 167).

Looking "as if her husband might be a butcher" (as in fact he is), Gertrude is all body: her smooth "large white face," although unwrinkled, is "somehow prematurely ageing" (perhaps by virtue of its exposure to the air?), her "plump hands" are "not too competently manicured," her "black hair was clipt . . . by some unfortunate means," and, most egregiously, her "over-trimmed Georgette *crêpe* dress was too short" and consequently shows too much leg (*P*, 167). Incompetently styled, her body makes its presence felt. And, the narrative notes disapprovingly, Gertrude doesn't smoke: that is, she has disavowed not only a practical means of weight control, but also a signifier of compact, sleek modernity.

The novel seems to attribute the negative assessment of Gertrude to her provinciality: married to her high-school sweetheart, who has inherited his father's name and local butcher business, she is bound by the segregated Chicago neighborhood in which she grew up. Unlike Irene, who has moved to cosmopolitan Harlem, Gertrude never seems to have ventured beyond Chicago. Tethered to locality and body, she marks the opposite end of the spectrum from Clare and the pole into which Irene is at risk of falling.

Although Gertrude has married a white man, she doesn't exactly pass (since her husband and his family are aware of her race). Even though she could pass for white, or perhaps especially because she is phenotypically white, she is tied to her body: that is, she negotiates racial borders through her biological attributes rather than artistic transformation. In a surprising reversal, then, the unaestheticized body in *Passing* is (or appears to be) phenotypically white. Whereas Anne Anlin Cheng attributes what she calls "dumb flesh" to the unstylized Black body (where it serves as the motivating force for stylization), Larsen attributes it to the phenotypically white body that has not been called upon to stylize itself. "Dumb flesh" in *Passing* is at the mercy of biology: it perspires (as Black skin never seems to) like the red-faced man "mopping his neck and forehead with a big crumpled handkerchief" in the Drayton Hotel or like Gertrude, whose "perspiration stood out on her forehead" when she thinks about the risk of giving birth to dark babies; or it manifests as the "pasty-white face" of Clare's dead white father or the "unhealthy-looking dough-coloured face" of her husband (*P*, 148, 144, 168, 170). Like Gertrude's prematurely aging white face, there is something doughy and unbaked about white flesh; it lacks the protective covering of bronze or golden skin that we see on Clare, Brian, and Josephine Baker. (Perhaps Hugh Wentworth's wife, Bianca, is kept out of the picture to circumvent the question of intelligent white flesh.)

Precisely because she doesn't pass, Irene occupies a precarious midpoint between pasty white and gold (somewhere between olive and beige). Significantly, she sees this position as a failure in ways that align her more closely with Gertrude than with Clare. In the central scene of Clare's golden appearance in Irene's living room at the exact midpoint of the novel and turning point in the relationship between the two women, the second half of their contrasting dual portrait seems inadvertently to reiterate features of Gertrude. The evocation of "Clare, exquisite, golden, fragrant, flaunting, in a stately gown of shining black taffeta" is directly followed by Irene, who, "with her new rose-coloured chiffon frock ending at the knees, and her cropped curls, felt dowdy and commonplace" (*P*, 203). We could start by noting the verbal distinction between Clare's *gown* and Irene's *frock*, an old-fashioned word of Germanic origin (*hroc*) that traveled through Old French (*froc*) to Middle English. Uncommon in the U.S., it is repeatedly and exclusively associated with Irene, as the word *gown* is with Clare.[74] A *frock* usually refers to an informal dress that typically, and in Irene's case explicitly, ends at the knees. Unlike Clare's stately floor-length gown that reveals only a pair of golden feet, Irene's knee-length frock tacitly calls attention to her legs. In their exposure and color, which modulates between the beige of her feet and the rose of her frock, Irene's legs recall the "appalling amount" of Gertrude's "stout legs" in "rose-beige" stockings (*P*, 167). Irene's choice of a knee-length frock unconsciously repeats the style error of Gertrude's "too short" dress, as her choice of chiffon recalls Gertrude's Georgette *crêpe*: both soft, thin, pliable materials more revealing of the body underneath than is Clare's shiny black taffeta. Finally, Irene's "cropped curls" rhyme sonically with Gertrude's "clipt" hair and visually with her "over-trimmed" dress; ruffles, frills, or curls (whether on the body or the head) signal an outmoded or excessive femininity. In contrast to Clare's "unsheared" locks (*P*, 161), Irene's "set locks" (*P*, 183) are, like her knee-length dress, too short, implicitly leaving her neck (like her legs) exposed. Irene, like Gertrude, is trapped in a body she doesn't know how to artfully conceal. The attempts to be modern signaled by her cropped hair and dress fail, and she ends up feeling "dowdy and commonplace."

There's a logic (however cruel) to Gertrude's failures of taste, but how to account for those of Irene, who has traveled to Europe and lives in cosmopolitan Harlem at the height of the Renaissance? One clue might be derived from the framing of the dual portrait of Clare and Irene in a chapter that, for no obvious reason, is presented as a memory. Introduced by "The things which Irene Redfield remembered afterward about the Negro Welfare League dance" (*P*, 203), which parallels the sentence summarizing Irene's memories of Chicago, "Such were Irene Redfield's memories as she sat there in her room" (*P*, 181), the central chapter that recounts events that take place in the narrative present is set in the past and set off from the narrative flow. The Negro Welfare League dance, whose prelude is Clare's arrival in the Redfields' living room, is constructed as a cave of memory, underscored by the repetition of the phrase "She remembered" to introduce a sequence of the opening paragraphs (*P*, 203). It is as if Irene's inward turn, and the novelistic injunction with which it complies, correlate with or bear responsibility for her failure to fashion a protective envelope, as if her internal focus has left her exterior undefended.

Irene's sense of inferiority to Clare's stylish envelope aligns her with Woolf's self-deprecating impression of being "outside the envelope." Larsen wouldn't have known the diary passage, but she is likely to have read the narrative version of "frock consciousness" that Woolf published as the story "The New Dress" (1927). The self-critical perspective is unfolded in the story (one of several preparatory for *Mrs. Dalloway*) from the point of view of a character named Mabel, who arrives at Mrs. Dalloway's party in an old-fashioned yellow dress that had appeared charming and original in the dressmaker's workroom, but in the fashionable setting of the Dalloways' drawing room immediately seems "not right, not quite right. . . . No! It was not *right*."[75] Feeling "like some dowdy, decrepit, horribly dingy old fly," Mabel intensifies her sense of failure by contrasting herself to the elegance of another character, Rose Shaw, dressed "in lovely, clinging green with a ruffle of swansdown" (ND, 51, 55). Woolf's story anticipates, even sets the terms for, the juxtaposition of Irene and Clare: a possibility supported by the prominence of the adjective *dowdy* in the self-critiques of both Mabel and Irene and by the echo of Rose Shaw's dress in the "fluttering dress of green chiffon" in which Clare initially appears in Chicago (*P*, 148). Green chiffon is sufficiently alien to Clare's taste in Harlem to make us wonder what besides the difference of season and locale could account for this anomalous wardrobe item. Woolf's story provides an answer of sorts. Juxtaposing the stylishness of Rose and Clare and the self-denigration of Mabel and Irene suggests how "The New Dress" might have offered a template for feminine style competition in *Passing*. But since style extends beyond clothing, focalizing *Passing* from a perspective associated with Mabel would clinch Irene's identification with the narrative discoveries and sartorial anxieties of English modernism.

This is not as far-fetched as it may sound. Woolf published "The New Dress" in May 1927 in *Forum*, where she joined an impressive roster of her British compatriots (including Conrad, Hardy, Verne, and Wells) by appearing in one of the most respected American literary journals of the time.[76] Two years later, Woolf's essay "Women and Fiction," the digest of the lectures at Cambridge that evolved into *A Room of One's Own*, came out in *Forum* the month before *Passing* appeared in print (and almost two decades before "Women and Fiction" was published in England). *Forum* also had the distinction of soliciting more articles from African American intellectuals and spokespersons (most notably Booker T. Washington) than any other mainstream American periodical; consequently, it held special interest for African American readers. Three months after publishing "The New Dress," *Forum* published a debate featuring Alain Locke and Lothrop Stoddard on a question that would have captured Larsen's interest: "Should the Negro be encouraged to cultural equality?" That this is also the journal in which Larsen chose to publish her own short story "Sanctuary" in 1930—becoming the first African American woman writer to publish in the journal—suggests that she was aware of *Forum*'s reputation among Black readers and was likely to have been reading it for a while. Larsen's story manifests such an outsize debt to "Mrs. Adis" by Sheila Kaye-Smith, a popular British woman writer from Sussex, that it provoked the charges of plagiarism that ended Larsen's career. Perhaps this more blatant example might point retroactively to the subtler debt to the story a yet more celebrated London and Sussex-based precursor had published in the journal three years earlier.[77]

Finale: The Smashed Teacup

By transposing "Mrs. Adis" from the border of Sussex and Kent to the deep American South, "Sanctuary" offers a graphic example of African Americanization. *Passing* suggests a more nuanced transposition of the "frock consciousness" explored in "The New Dress" from London to Harlem, where the class division that accounts for the disparate sartorial success of Mabel and Rose evolves into the contending modernist aesthetics filtered through Irene and Clare. Both more subtle and more pointed than the wholesale transposition of working-class England to the American South, and more comprehensive than the fashion details aligned with "The New Dress," *Passing*'s "Finale" invites us to pull back and reconsider the novel's (modernist) form in relation to its (Harlem) setting and to evaluate the (ir)resolution of its alternative modernisms.

Revisiting the sequence of the novel's three sections—"Encounter," "Re-encounter," "Finale"—from a critical perspective, we could track the evolution from the coexistence of complementary aesthetics within Irene's interior psychological and architectural space (an "Encounter" closeted in memory), to the predominance of Clare's cosmopolitan aesthetic in the social spaces of the Redfield's home and the Negro Welfare League ball (a "Re-encounter" in the present), to the collision between the two aesthetics at parties at the homes of the Redfields and the Freelands, pressured and permeable social spaces that render both aesthetics precarious ("Finale"). The "Finale" is framed by two Harlem social gatherings separated by their hostesses' shopping expedition downtown, which opens an opportunity for the chance encounter with Jack Bellew that triggers his realization of his wife's race. *Passing*'s "Finale" is structured around a rupture in Harlem's boundaries that culminates in Bellew's dramatic appearance at the Freelands' party. This rude intrusion of difference both follows upon and amplifies Clare's earlier (and similarly uninvited) entry into the social world of the text as a foreign-looking envelope, an exoticism both enabled by and indissociable from the mobility of her white husband, who tracks her to and out the window of the Freelands' party. The "Finale" both brings to a dramatic close the disruption initiated by Claire's letter and inscribes a formal reminder of that breach in the narrative wedge between two parties. Or, if we envision the novel's form via the teacup that is the metonymic figure of Irene's earlier party, which launches the final section and anticipates its ending, the "Finale" both fulfills the formalist aesthetic suggested by the teacup and invites us to discern a crack in it through the fissured form of a conclusion that bookends the cave of memory with which the text begins.[78]

Clare's cosmopolitan flare ripples through Larsen's text and departs as abruptly as it enters; her death, mirrored by Irene's loss of consciousness, suggests the interdependence and irreconcilability of the twin protagonists' perspectives. There is no indication that a modernist aesthetic could reintegrate them. Instead, *Passing* achieves its denouement by recalling and revising the conclusion of *Mrs. Dalloway*. The "Finale" that begins by evoking the opening of *Mrs. Dalloway* ends by revoking its resolution. Both texts culminate in parties designed to bring the cast of characters together in a resonant conclusion; and both parties are punctuated by the unexpected intrusion of an unwelcome external reality. When Dr. Bradshaw enters Clarissa Dalloway's party "shockingly late" with the news of the suicide of the shell-shocked World War I veteran Septimus Warren Smith, Clarissa thinks, "Oh! . . . in the middle of my party, here's death" (*MD*, 183). Death, history, war, desperation: none of these has been invited to Clarissa's party, and yet she assimilates their intrusion quite readily by retiring to her little room (a reprise of the attic room in which she remembers Sally Seton) to reimagine Septimus's death in terms of her memories of Sally. Initially visceral— Clarissa imagines the rusty railing spikes penetrating Septimus's body—the rupture of corporeal and social boundaries is sutured over as Clarissa reinterprets Septimus's fatal plunge in a way that enables her finally to relinquish her attachment to her memory of Sally.

Mrs. Dalloway appropriates Septimus's death to Clarissa's cathartic restoration to the heteronormative social sphere. By equating Septimus's plunge with the heroic but self-destructive preservation of a pure but deviant erotic choice, Clarissa is newly able to embrace her married life: "It was due to Richard; she had never been so happy," she announces abruptly and unconvincingly (*MD*, 185). By bringing Sally to the party as a complacent middle-aged mother of five sons, Woolf underwrites Clarissa's questionable conclusion, which in turn underwrites Clarissa's radiant final appearance, "For there she was" (*MD*, 194). Clarissa's manifestation to Peter at the novel's end renders closure as the impression of a unified presence whose internal fissures have been magically repaired.

In contrast to the marshaling of secondary characters (both Septimus and Sally) toward the advent of a singular luminous presence at the end of *Mrs. Dalloway*, *Passing* ends in darkness for both protagonists. Larsen discretely but discernibly dismantles the negotiations that enable Clarissa's radiant return to her party. At an evening gathering of friends at the apartment of Felise and Dave Freeland, Clare ambiguously but spectacularly plunges to her death from a sixth-story window. The scene delves behind Dr. Bradshaw's report of Septimus's suicide to restage the earlier, more violent intrusion that actually precipitates Septimus's death: the forcible entry of Dr. Holmes, a cruder figure of medical authority, into the apartment Septimus shares with his wife, Rezia. Undeterred by Rezia's attempt to bar his entry, Dr. Holmes, "a powerfully built man," forces his way into the building, climbs the stairs, and bursts open the apartment door, symbolically propelling Septimus out the window. From within Septimus's consciousness, Woolf tracks the relation between the doctor's entry and his patient's death: "Holmes was coming upstairs. Holmes would burst open the door. Holmes would say, 'In a funk, eh?' Holmes would get him. But no; not Holmes; not Bradshaw. . . . There remained only the window, the large Bloomsbury-lodging house window, the tiresome, the troublesome, and rather melodramatic business of opening the window and throwing himself out" (*MD*, 149).

Clare's plunge from "one of the long casement-windows of which the Freelands were so proud" closely parallels Septimus's trajectory (*P*, 238). After Irene has opened the window to get some air, a forceful masculine authority, in this case John Bellew, rings the doorbell of the Freelands' building, climbs the six flights of stairs to their apartment, pushes past the host, and forces his way in to confront Clare with his newly acquired knowledge of her race. The result is the same. Bellew's roar "So you're a nigger, a damned dirty nigger!" provokes Clare's silent response, "a faint smile on her full, red lips, and in her shining eyes," and sudden fall from the sixth-story window (*P*, 238–39). As Judith Butler puts it, playing on Bellew's name, "Bellew bellows, and at that moment Clare vanishes from the window"; the bellows of a racist patriarchy propel Clare out of the scene.[79]

In both novelistic scenarios, a guardian of normativity propels a dissident figure beyond the boundaries of the social world. In *Passing*, however, this is the novel's climax rather than a subplot enabling the protagonist's regenerative return. Underscoring this, Larsen renders Irene's response to Clare's death in language that echoes Septimus's wife, Rezia, rather than Clarissa. After her husband's leap, Rezia listens to "a great deal of running up and down stairs" (*MD*, 150); left alone in the Freelands' apartment after the other guests race downstairs, Irene listens to "the sound of feet going down the steps" (*P*, 240). Both women lose consciousness at the end of their respective scenes. Rezia (assisted by sleeping medication) drifts off with an ominous impression of "the large outline of [Dr. Holmes's] body standing dark against the window" (*MD*, 151). Irene collapses and sinks to the ground. "She moaned and sank down, moaned again. Through the great heaviness that submerged and drowned her she was dimly conscious of strong arms lifting her up. Then everything was dark" (*P*, 242). Both stories end in darkness and the dubious assistance of a strong-armed masculinity. Whereas Septimus is sacrificed to spare Clarissa, who was originally intended to die at her party, as Woolf announced in the "Introduction" she wrote for the Modern Library edition of *Mrs. Dalloway* in 1928, Irene is granted no glimmer of the dawn that we know will soon break for Woolf's protagonist.[80] The controversial final paragraph deleted from the third printing of the novel, in which Irene recalls "the strange man saying: 'Death by misadventure, I'm inclined to believe. Let's go up and have another look at that window,'" redirects our attention to a space of interpretive possibility; but the exoneration provisionally offered to Irene carries no sense of her enlightenment, no impression (as for Clarissa) of a wind that has newly risen or a newfound ability (which Clarissa inherits from Septimus) to "feel the beauty . . . ; feel the fun" (*MD*, 186).[81]

Passing's final party teases out the tensions Woolf defuses between a formalist aesthetic and a heterogeneous social world. This has divergent implications for *Passing*'s twin protagonists. For Clare, Bellew's intrusion induces a spectacular exit from the text—as abrupt and cryptic as her entry—that maintains her signature theatricality. She goes out with a self-consuming flourish that resists interpretive mastery. "One moment Clare had been there, a vital glowing thing, like a flame of red and gold. The next she was gone" (*P*, 239). Does she jump, like Septimus? Or fall? Is she pushed by Irene? The inconclusiveness of Clare's disappearance fails to seal the historical boundaries of a mobile malleable cosmopolitan aesthetic that might flash through other contexts or assume other forms. The female dandy's mutability invites us to contemplate an afterlife.[82]

Although Clare's death affords a spectacular climax to *Passing*'s narrative, the novel's rhetoric devotes more energy to pressuring Irene's perspective, in part through conflicting figurations of Clare's death that blur decisive boundaries. Irene is subjected to a harsher judgment not only for her complicity in desiring (and possibly abetting) the resolution enabled by Bellew, her former adversary, or for her investment in maintaining the heteronormative family at all costs, but also for her implied adherence to an escapist aesthetic. Transposing an English modernist form to Harlem's more fractious and permeable social space subjects an aesthetic of bounded interiority to the racial disturbance from which it seems to offer refuge. As the locus of Anglophilia in *Passing*, Irene is also the site of a critique of England's service to the dream of an egalitarian society that could materialize a dera-cialized interiority. Whereas the first section of the novel winds backward into a Woolfian cave of memory, the final chapter opens onto America's tortured racial terrain: a newspaper report of a lynching that provokes an argument between Brian and Irene, who seeks to shield her children from the knowledge of racism by censoring all reference to it. The fantasy of color blindness has become a racial blindspot, the desire for a race-free refuge a susceptibility to racism. The closing chapter sets the progression to the ironically named Freelands' walk-up apartment against Irene's earlier as-cent, as if by a magic carpet, to the breezy freedom of the Drayton's rooftop restaurant. "Did you ever go up by nigger-power?" Brian asks Clare as they laboriously climb the six flights of stairs (*P*, 236), insisting on the deroga-tory term that Irene has banished from their domestic lexicon. There is no magic transport beyond race in the U.S., no refuge from the urban lynching enacted by Bellew.

Larsen, however, is not Irene; instead, the author exposes her charac-ter's self-deceptions and susceptibility to paranoia.[83] Rather than seeking like Irene to eject Clare (in fantasy or reality) from a bounded social world, Larsen inscribes her twin protagonists in a textual form indebted to Woolfian modernism at the same time that she gestures toward that form's precarious hold on the novel's social foundation. She draws from British modernism an aesthetic of enclosure while putting pressure on the homology it implies be-tween literary and social forms of enclosure. She insists both on the integrity of her narrative form and on the forces that exceed and disrupt it.

Formally, *Passing* is as tightly woven as *Mrs. Dalloway*: although it does not conform to the earlier novel's cycle of one day, it constructs an analogous narrative container that proceeds from Clare's appearance to her death, and from the "pathetic little red frock" Clare struggles to sew in Irene's childhood memory to the "shining red gown" in which she makes her spectacular exit (*P* 144, 233). Like Woolf, Larsen weaves elaborately patterned verbal surfaces through symbolically charged motifs: the shredded letters, flicked cigarette ashes, and smashed teacup that prefigure Clare's fall in *Passing* echo the rising and falling patterns of *Mrs. Dalloway*'s waves, leaves, and birds—except that *Passing*'s darker world affords only unrecuperated falls. Yet in its embrace of form, *Passing* sides with Woolf's claim in "The Art of Fiction" that "life" must be sacrificed to narrative pattern, quite literally in the case of Clare.

And yet not entirely, and that irresolution is a distinguishing feature of Larsen's mulatta modernism. Clare's mobile characterization enables her to serve not only as the locus of the cosmopolitan aesthetic manifested in the style of her final disappearance, but also as the site and sight of a residual margin, a form of "life" in extremis (i.e., death) that resists circumscription to aesthetic patterning. Irene's anxious imagination offers a glimpse of this material remainder and reminder through her fleeting apprehension of Clare's "glorious body mutilated" on the pavement below (*P*, 240). Echoing the "horribly mangled" body of Septimus on Mrs. Filmer's railings, the brief glimpse of Clare's mutilated body opens a crack in her protective envelope, forcing us to grapple with the loss—as well as the preservation—of her immunity: a loss that also rebounds on Irene (*MD*, 150).

The scene's implications are prefigured during the tea party at the Redfields' home. Prefaced by the walk through Harlem that occasions the nod to the opening of *Mrs. Dalloway*, Irene's tea party weaves together diverse allusions to English social and cultural forms. Clare's outfit in this scene is crowned by "a little golden bowl of a hat," an apparent gesture to Henry James's *Golden Bowl*, which Woolf cites in "The Art of Fiction" as exemplary of novelistic form, asking why "Life" should be presumed to be "absent in a pattern and present in a tea party" (*P*, 220). "Why is the pleasure that we get from the pattern in The Golden Bowl less valuable than the emotion which Trollope gives us when he describes a lady drinking tea in a parsonage?"[84] In this scene, Larsen brings the pattern to the tea party, while calling attention (as James does but Woolf does not) to the fracture in the pattern.

The intruder at this event is Clare herself rather than her racist husband. Brian has invited Clare to the party without informing his wife, who learns of the invitation, with its attendant implication that Brian and Clare have been conducting a secret affair, shortly before composing herself to go downstairs to perform her formulaic social ritual. A silent struggle unfolds between centrifugal passions and centripetal rituals that seek to contain wayward impulses within the signifiers of good English form. Key to this form is what Larsen calls the "ritual of tea" (*P*, 218) and Woolf the "tea table, the very hearth and centre of family life, . . . the centre of Victorian family life" (Sketch, 118).[85] Represented by the repetitive act of "pouring golden tea in thin old cups" (*P*, 219), the ritual is as old and as fragile as the cups through which it is funneled. *Golden* is the pivotal word that dissolves Clare's metallic skin into the symbolic beverage of English sociality. Irene, it seems, has gained the momentary victory of liquefying Clare's golden envelope and containing it within the porcelain skin of a thin old cup whose transmission from the English-affiliated Confederacy prompts the code-switching proposal "Be English if you want to and call it the underground."

Can these thin old cultural forms be transported effectively to Harlem? Assimilated to the visual icon of Englishness, Clare incites its demolition along with her own. The symbolic vehicle is unable to contain the pressure

produced by the three main characters' co-occupancy of a space infused with common knowledge. Weary of the pretense, Irene drops or throws a teacup onto the ground (the causality is as ambiguous as it is for Clare's plunge):

> Rage boiled up in her.
> There was a slight crash. On the floor at her feet lay the shattered cup.
> Dark stains dotted the bright rug. Spread. (*P*, 221)

The rage generated by Irene's suspicion of the affair flows into the tea that spills over as a figure of the blood that will spill from Clare's ivory body. Seeping and spreading beyond the contours of bodily and cultural forms, the stains become an overdetermined sign of excess, the punctuality of the single word "spread," like a dark stain on the rug, paradoxically calling attention to the word's meaning. Unlike the intactness that Irene can imagine in Clare's response to Jack Bellew's intrusion (which preserves both the neatness of the ending and the potential of a future return), Clare bleeds unmeasurably at Irene's hand.

The shattered cup and spreading stains recall the teacups cracked by the echoes of World War I and the "purplish stain upon the bland surface of the sea as if something had boiled and bled, invisibly, beneath" in "Time Passes," the narrative wedge that threatens to pry open the form of *To the Lighthouse* (*TTL*, 200–201). In Woolf's novel, however, that gap is recuperated by the formal balance of Lily Briscoe's concluding line "there, in the centre" (310), as the crack inscribed by Septimus's plunge is effaced by the plenitude of Clarissa's final appearance. Rather than the drive toward integration, *Passing* offers an unresolvable dualism that is reflected as well in the standoff between alternative endings of the text's different editions. The ideal of formal wholeness is both achieved as narrative pattern and rhetorically undermined by the figural residue that calls attention to the imperfect fit between Woolfian form and African American content and context.

The challenge of resolving racialized affiliations recurred throughout Larsen's career, starting with her application to the library school of the New York Public Library in 1922 (where she became the first African American student). In her insightful reading of this application, Barbara Hochman suggests that even this schematic form, especially the required list of "ten books you have read in the last two years," reveals "a cacophony that intensifies her [Larsen's] conflicted self-representation," torn between conciliation and resistance, between "radical and conservative views of genre, gender, nation, and race."[86] The choice of books, Hochman contends, reveals Larsen's "irreconcilable impulses—to conform and resist, to

conceal and reveal."[87] These unreconcilable impulses evolve from the un-spoken implications of the application to the verbal texture and structure of *Passing*, which refuses to choose sides or to integrate.

There is a tension at the core of Larsen's mulatta modernism, which insists on an irreducible duality whose terms may shift but whose structure persists. Larsen invests Clare's aesthetic with the vitality that galvanizes the narrative to whose pattern it is sacrificed; but that sacrifice both affirms and challenges the modernist form that exacts it. In the tense dance between the novel's modernisms, Irene's version sustains a partial victory, but the sacrifice of Clare is also pressed into overdetermined service to signal the constraints of English modernist form vis-à-vis a more dynamic cosmopolitan Black aesthetic and an alien and resistant social surround that both defers to and resists its circumscription. We are left with the impression of a tenacious form whose internal cracks and blurry edges compromise its hold.

The Smashed Mosaic

Woolf's Traces in Baldwin's Oeuvre

For what this really means is that all of the American categories of male and female, straight or not, black or white, were shattered, thank heaven, very early in my life.

James Baldwin, "Freaks and the American Ideal of Manhood"

Woolf's visibility in American letters in the 1920s, along with the bonds of gender and contemporaneity she shared with Larsen, make the established writer's imprint on the younger writer plausible even when it is unacknowledged. This is far from the situation with James Baldwin, divided from Woolf by gender, race, nationality, and history. The passage from Larsen to Baldwin also introduces new cultural terrain. Born five years before the publication of *Passing* in 1929, the year the stock market crash triggered the downward spiral of the Harlem Renaissance, Baldwin came of age in the 1930s and early 1940s in a bleaker Harlem, more impoverished, more violent, and more segregated than in the glory days of the Renaissance. Rather than the expressive possibilities afforded by Harlem's nightlife, Baldwin's essays on Harlem call attention to the increasing misery of a "captive population" living in "invincible and indescribable squalor" and "pervaded by a sense of congestion, rather like the insistent, maddening, claustrophobic pounding in the skull that comes from trying to breathe in a very small room with all the windows shut."[1]

Far from offering a room of one's own, Harlem yields only a cramped and crowded space from which, by age eighteen, Baldwin needed to escape. In contrast to Larsen's idealized interiority, challenged only by an alluring Black modernist exterior, the interior spaces of Baldwin's Harlem threaten to suffocate their inhabitants and the exterior spaces present both a danger and a moral obligation. Baldwin was deeply troubled by his first-hand knowledge of the racialized death-dealing streets, but he also needed to escape from the expectation that he confine his aesthetic vision to the priorities and boundaries of Harlem. Drawn to the Woolfian ideal of aesthetic integrity and autonomy figured by a room of one's own, he sought to reconcile it with a world beyond that room's entitlements. In the process, he cast light on Woolf's own efforts to negotiate the claims of a harmonious aesthetic interior with those of a disruptive social exterior.

Tracking the odd Baldwin-Woolf affinity has been made possible by the newly available James Baldwin Papers, acquired by the Schomburg Center for Research in Black Culture in 2017. In particular, the successive drafts of the novel that became *Giovanni's Room*, produced over a seven-year period from a stint at a writer's colony in upstate New York in 1948 through a formative period in Paris to the novel's publication in 1956, have opened a revealing window on Baldwin's compositional process. The traces of Woolf in the early drafts and their gradual (but incomplete) effacement disclose her silent imprint on the evolving novel. Rereading the published text in light of these drafts, we could say, as Woolf said of modern fiction generally, that "the accent falls a little differently; the emphasis is upon something hitherto ignored; at once a different outline of form becomes necessary."[2]

Paradoxically, the most revealing item in the archive, for the tracking of odd affinities, is one that has disappeared. Baldwin's personal journals, in which he recorded his reflections about his life and work, are neither referenced in the Schomburg Center's finding guide nor identified as missing. The existence of these journals has been amply documented by Baldwin's longtime friend, assistant, and biographer, David Leeming, to whom Baldwin granted unrestricted access to his papers.[3] In *James Baldwin: A Biography*, Leeming draws from the journals in considerable detail and in some cases recalls the circumstances under which he read them. One of Leeming's accounts, which is our only access to this vanished text, is tantalizing.

Leeming singles out for detailed paraphrase a "long, confessional journal entry, which was as carefully constructed as a draft for a short story."[4] Baldwin himself signals his literary aspirations for this journal entry by granting it a title: "The Last Days," a phrase he also uses in the penultimate draft of *Giovanni's Room*. Composed during a period of despair after the completion of *Giovanni's Room*, "The Last Days" encapsulates a dynamic that runs through the multiple drafts of the novel and across the years that separate it from its sequel, *Another Country* (1962), which was originally conceptualized as part of a single composite text. This textual thread is also the site of Baldwin's one explicit reference to Virginia Woolf.

Leeming's paraphrase of "The Last Days" uncovers Woolf's role as Baldwin's ghostly precursor, a role that comes sharply into focus at a pivotal moment in his career. What Leeming characterizes as Baldwin's "obsession" with suicide, manifest in his several attempts as well as recurring narrative accounts, was (as for Woolf) especially keen after finishing a difficult writing project.[5] In October 1956, depressed by the unraveling of a love affair as well as by the completion of *Giovanni's Room*, Baldwin wrote to Mary Painter in Paris from Corsica, where he was visiting his friend Mario Garzia in his house by the sea, to let her know that he feared he was at risk of losing his mind because of something terrifying that he knew he had to face.[6] A few days later, he wrote again to reassure her that he wouldn't throw himself into the sea. Baldwin did, however, come perilously close to walking into the sea, and he did so with a consciousness of following in Woolf's footsteps.

Paraphrasing "The Last Days," Leeming recounts how Baldwin escaped (glass of brandy in hand) from a social evening at Mario Garzia's home through an upstairs window that offered access to the roof, from which he swung down onto a stone wall that led to the sea. The paraphrase continues:

> He finished the brandy, threw the glass into the water, and thought of Virginia Woolf and her walking into the water to her death. He compared the death agony of drowning to the agony of his love affair. The death itself might be rather like the goal that seems unattainable in life. The sea seemed willing to embrace and accept him in a way that the 'world' and 'life' and 'love' had not. Holding his shoes in one hand, he advanced until the water reached his hips, and then he decided to wait. That night's encounter with the sea, he thought, could serve as an appointment for a later, more final meeting when there would be only the sea and Jimmy and no chance of rescue. The sea might digest him and then vomit him up some place where 'nobody knew my name.' Out of these suicidal thoughts, then, came the title of his next collection of essays. (Leeming, 131)

That Baldwin knew the details of Woolf's suicide and imagined them as a blueprint for his own tells us something about his investment in her writing and in narratives of suicide more generally. Given the disdain for suicide at that time within the African American community, which tended to view it as a decadent privilege and folly of whiteness, as taboo as homosexuality and for at least one vocal critic as indissociable from it, a white woman writer's well-publicized suicide might have elicited Baldwin's aversion more readily than his identification.[7] Beyond Woolf's personal choice of death by drowning, Baldwin's recurrent and ambivalent figure of a drive toward dissolution that both promises and threatens to annihilate identity, her fictional account of suicide in *Mrs. Dalloway* seems to have captured his attention.[8]

In "The Last Days," Baldwin navigates the draw of suicide through a strategy that recalls Clarissa Dalloway's. Even in Leeming's paraphrase, Baldwin's image of drowning as the path to an otherwise unattainable "embrace" draws close to Clarissa's response to Septimus's suicide: "Death was an attempt to communicate. . . . There was an embrace in death" (*MD*, 184). Although it is Woolf's biography that is the subject of the journal entry, Baldwin reads that biography through the lens of Woolf's fiction, especially the fictional suicide she invents for Septimus Warren Smith. As Baldwin begins to follow Woolf's footsteps into the water—that is, to turn from musing about to mimicking her drowning—he reaches a midpoint, the water up to his hips, at which he pauses and turns around. By turning back from drowning, while deferring and symbolically reaping a portion of its rewards (including the title of his next essay collection, *Nobody Knows My Name*), Baldwin reprises Clarissa Dalloway's psychic reenactment of and retreat from Septimus's uncompromising act: her passage from imagining the "blundering, bruising" rusty spikes and the "thud, thud, thud" in Septimus's brain to acknowledging that "she had once thrown a shilling into the Serpentine, never anything more. But he had flung it away" (*MD*, 184). Woolf now functions as Baldwin's Septimus, a sacrificial figure whose re-staged self-destruction gives form to and averts his own. Through this surrogacy, Baldwin seems to have found a way to face that very difficult "something" he explained to Mary Painter that he had to confront. The symbolic drowning and recovery that constitute, in David Leeming's words, "that fateful night in Corsica" were a turning point at which Baldwin resisted the embrace of death and "stepped out of the sea and turned back to *Another Country*" (Leeming, 132).

By recruiting Woolf to the function of Septimus, Baldwin not only salvages his own identity, as Clarissa salvages hers. His strategy also casts a retrospective light on the circuitry running through his drafts between the character he refers to as the "dead girl" (a locus of Woolfian echoes) and the diverse iterations of the character he refers to as the "dead boy" (a locus of Septimus's traces) in his essays and *Another Country*. The journal entry's disappearance seems to climax Woolf's gradual effacement from the drafts of *Giovanni's Room* at the same time that the evidence it offers of Baldwin's affinity with Woolf invites us to seek out more elusive traces elsewhere in his oeuvre. These affinities are more complex than those between Woolf and Larsen, for underlying the women's shared investment in narrative and social enclosures and foreclosures is the common ground of an urban feminine domesticity whose transracial manifestations are relatively straightforward. By contrast, the salient *differences* between Woolf's and Baldwin's gender as well as racial positions produce unlikely parallels between their struggles to define their respective positions in a dominant white masculine tradition.

These struggles, which Woolf and Baldwin articulate most fully in their nonfiction prose, illuminate a range of shared modernist sympathies traversed and troubled by advocacy for gender and racial equality. Anglo-American modernism's contributions to Baldwin's aesthetics are inevitably a vexed arena that has appropriately been sidelined by the priority of mapping his African American genealogies and pioneering roles as an eloquent spokesman for gay and civil rights and pathbreaking African American author. To honor Baldwin's resistance to pigeonholing, however, it is worthwhile to recover a minor but unrecognized contribution to his multifaceted oeuvre. A signal feature of the recent renaissance in Baldwin studies has challenged traditional identity categories by calling attention to his protean polymorphic identifications as a transnational, exilic, queer, and broadly defined trans writer.[9] Even these breakthroughs, however, have not considered the possibility of Baldwin's receptivity to the narrative craft of a white British woman: that is, to a writer who posed differences of gender as well as race, class, and nationality. This blindspot is especially striking in the context of Baldwin's move to Paris in 1948, a dislocation that galvanized both his literary production and his transnational, transgender and transracial identifications. During this period of literary self-discovery, he remarked: "I no longer felt I knew who I really was, whether I was really black or white, really male or female, really talented or a fraud, really strong or merely stubborn."[10]

To accommodate the wealth of new archival material, this inquiry is divided into three sections. The first elicits the surprising resonances between Baldwin's and Woolf's aesthetic values and argues that these resonances have been rendered inaudible by the reflexive attribution of Baldwin's early modernist inclinations to the influence of Henry James. Turning next to the specific practices Baldwin was developing in the drafts of *Giovanni's Room*, the second section adopts a more critical stance toward holistic aesthetic parallels that fracture when they hit the narrative ground. It is here that we can track the interwoven stories of the dead (white) girl and the dead (literally or figuratively Black) boy and uncover Woolf's tacit service in helping Baldwin navigate a path between the pressures exerted by his two dominant precursors: Henry James and Richard Wright.[11]

Baldwin's resistance to Woolf's narrative world comes most sharply into focus in the longest final section of this chapter, which plays Baldwin's *Giovanni's Room* (1956) against Woolf's *Jacob's Room* (1922) by unpacking the characteristics and contexts of the trope that links these texts. For Woolf, the room was a device for maintaining a continuous thread through a deliberately fractured text whose "main point is that it should be free."[12] Baldwin, by contrast, was seeking a form for a story that had never been granted one. The trope of the room helped him to create a narrative focus that both tightened his writing and offered a metaphor of psychosexual and economic constraint as well as racialized darkness (Giovanni as the dark-skinned Italian other to the blond American narrator, David).[13] Formally and thematically, Giovanni's claustrophobic room in a working-class district in Paris in the depressed aftermath of the Second World War is the opposite of Jacob's breezy serial rooms that mark his easy passage through the distinguished precincts of Cambridge and Bloomsbury in the emancipatory atmosphere before the First World War.

As the drafts of *Giovanni's Room* will show, however, Baldwin was drawn to Woolf's evocation of Jacob's solitary, absence-haunted childhood, which offered a potential point of departure for the queer trajectory he was trying to envision and for which he had few literary precedents.[14] Baldwin knew how to read the queer subtext of *Jacob's Room* and in so doing made it increasingly legible. By concluding with the violent death of their eponymous characters, moreover, *Jacob's Room* and *Giovanni's Room* are aligned within the framework of the antisocial thesis that holds that queerness challenges the "reproductive futurism" that structures social relations toward the future embodied in the child.[15] At their beginnings and endings, these texts constitute an example of what Carolyn Dinshaw describes as the "queer relations between incommensurate lives and phenomena," "new communities with past figures who elude resemblance to us but with whom we can be connected partially by virtue of shared marginality, queer positionality."[16] These relations play out on variegated turf, however. For on the extended middle ground between the beginnings and the endings of their novels, Woolf and Baldwin engage in very different narrative projects: in the first case, to evacuate character as a way to queer narrative conventions; in the second, to flesh out a homoerotic plot on uncharted and inhospitable literary and social ground.

Reading these two novels together, then, brings their contrasting projects into sharp relief. Their relationship is also triangulated, however, by the novel that followed *Jacob's Room*. To temper the claustrophobia of *Giovanni's Room*, Baldwin recruits the strategy of retrospective narration that Woolf develops while at work on *Mrs. Dalloway*. At the end of *Giovanni's Room*, he also redeploys the sacrificial strategy that Woolf deploys on Clarissa's behalf at the end of *Mrs. Dalloway* and that Baldwin summons on his own behalf in "The Last Days." This complexly mediated intertextuality requires careful unfolding, starting with essays in which both authors expressed their views about literature.

The Art of Fiction

The Paris to which Baldwin moved in 1948 was for him initially a place of silence (he spoke no French) in which he needed to find a novelistic "box" for the thoughts that swirled up in the absence of the usual distractions. In this "vacuum," Baldwin explains, "James became, in a sense, my master. It was something about point of view, something about discipline. . . . James was my key."[17] There is no shortage of evidence of Baldwin's explicit and implicit debt to James, whom he credits with the formal breakthrough that enabled him to craft his unwieldy Harlem-based, autobiographical first novel, *Go Tell It on the Mountain* (1953), around an organizing center of consciousness.[18] This narrative concentration, however, marked the beginning, not the culmination, of Baldwin's formal explorations. His second novel, *Giovanni's Room*, is linked thematically rather than formally to James's *The Ambassadors*, and is narrated retrospectively from a cave of memory: a Woolfian rather than a Jamesian narrative signature and a striking instance of a typically Jamesian story about a white American in Paris recounted in a typically Woolfian form.

Critics nevertheless can't affirm James's influence on Baldwin often enough, and they do so in strikingly repetitive terms that consolidate "Henry James" as the signifier of Baldwin's literariness.[19] This remains the case even for Colm Tóibín, the novelist who has become one of the most eloquent exponents of the figure he dubs "the Henry James of Harlem" and whose numerous essays on Baldwin display a keen ear for echoes from a range of Anglo-American writers from whom he claims Baldwin learned "a cast of mind" that "used qualification, the aside and the further sub-clauses" to render the complexity of thought.[20] But when it comes to questions of novelistic form and psychological interiority, there is only and always James. "Henry James would have been proud of him," Tóibín concludes after citing Baldwin's assertion of the writer's obligation to "the private life."[21]

Both the private life and syntactic qualification were, however, hallmarks of other Anglophone modernists whose work (like James's) was available to Baldwin in Parisian literary venues that catered to expatriate writers. Shakespeare and Company, the famous Anglophone bookstore resurrected in 1951, a few years after Baldwin's arrival in Paris, offered an important resource for literary émigrés, "a meeting place for Anglophone writers and readers, becoming a Left Bank literary institution."[22] It was especially hospitable to African American expats, most conspicuously Richard Wright, but also Baldwin, who gave a reading and book signing there of *Go Tell It on the Mountain* and *The Amen Corner* as he was completing work on *Giovanni's Room* in 1955.[23] Although frequented primarily by Americans in the early 1950s, the bookstore also made available the works of the earlier generation of Anglophone modernists on which it had staked its fame. Books published by the Hogarth Press, which distributed its publications internationally, were almost certainly on the shelves.

In addition to Woolf's novels, those books would have included collections of the essays in which she expressed her admiration for James's narrative form.[24] Borrowing the title of James's essay "The Art of Fiction" for her own critique of E. M. Forster's *Aspects of the Novel*, Woolf defended James's carefully wrought narrative patterns from E. M. Forster's complaint that they were "hostile to humanity" because they violated the ordinary experience of daily life.[25] That James's achievement of an impersonal, enduring novelistic aesthetic was a transformative moment in the history of the novel was a conviction Woolf and Baldwin shared: a silent mediation that suggests other unannounced affinities. For although Woolf lacked the bonds of gender and nationality (and implicitly of sexuality) that James shared with Baldwin, as well as the cultural authority that made James an attractive public "master," she shared Baldwin's extra-academic literary formation and investment in the "common reader" they both sought to address in the novels, essays, book reviews, and letters across which, to an exceptional degree, they both distributed their talents.

They were also, most significantly, both outsiders and insiders of the literary traditions through which they formed their distinctive points of view. If Woolf was a "step-daughter of England," Baldwin was a "kind of bastard of the West."[26] Baldwin's determination to find his "special place" in the scheme of the "white centuries" housed in New York's public libraries resonates with Woolf's quest to find the "essential oil of truth" about "Women and Fiction" under the "vast dome" of the British Museum "splendidly encircled" with the names of great men.[27] Both embraced with conviction and ambivalence the advocacy roles conferred by the conjunction of their historical moments, writerly eloquence, and gendered and racialized subject positions. Both insisted on the inimitable value of a point of view from within a subordinated group: Baldwin's critique of Faulkner's unnuanced representation of African Americans because "Faulkner could see Negroes only as they related to him, not as they related to each other" echoes Woolf's complaint that women have been represented almost exclusively "in their relation to men" rather than their relation to one another.[28]

As writers of imaginative literature, however, they both also feared the potential for a particular vantage point to calcify into a narrowly delimited perspective that would bar the full horizon of human experience. Baldwin claimed to have left America to prevent himself from "becoming *merely*

a Negro; or, even, merely a Negro writer."[29] Negotiating the dialectic between what he called a "specifically limited and limiting" inheritance and a
birthright that was "vast, connecting [him] to all that lives and to everyone,
forever," but could be accessed only by passing through that limiting inheritance was a defining feature of the project these writers shared.[30] Woolf's
seemingly contradictory position that "we think back through our mothers
if we are women" but that "it is fatal for a woman . . . to speak consciously
as a woman" resounds in Baldwin's suggestion that only those writers who
had accepted and thereby conquered their material could use it freely in
their writing.[31]

Beyond (and arguably as a consequence of) this balancing act, Woolf
and Baldwin drew from a common lexicon to articulate a shared goal of
conveying some transcendent, transpersonal, intangible, arguably metaphysical reality. In excess of Henry James's concern with subjectivity and
sociality, they shared the conviction that (in Woolf's words) "our relation
is to the world of reality and not only to the world of men and women,"
and that "whether we call it life or spirit, truth or reality," this is the "essential thing" in fiction.[32] Writing in opposition to American mass culture,
Baldwin asserts similarly that the creative writer's challenge is to convey
something intangible, since "the interior life is a real life, and the intangible
dreams of a people have a tangible effect on the world."[33] In strikingly
Woolfian language, Baldwin elaborates the point in another essay: "Every
artist is involved with one single effort, really, which is somehow to dig
down to where reality is . . . deeper than conscious knowledge or speech
can go."[34] Woolf describes her reaction to receiving a shock in similar terms
as the "revelation of some order; . . . a token of some real thing behind
appearances. . . . We—I mean all human beings—are connected with this"
(Sketch, 72). Baldwin concurs that "all lives are connected to other lives,"
and the writer's duty is "to suggest, through the order and discipline of art,
the much greater and hidden order of life."[35]

Both writers assume the voice of spiritual prophets in a materialist universe, although the materialism with which Woolf was concerned was that
of her Edwardian literary precursors, whereas Baldwin focused on the economic materialism of the mid-twentieth-century Americans who "depend
very heavily on this concrete, tangible, pragmatic point of view."[36] Both
seek to rouse their readers not only to aspire to spiritual heights but also to
plumb the darkness whose imagined terrors arrest our attention at the surface of things. Counterpointing the lofty philosophical register is a shared
psychological imperative to engage the unfathomable and potentially men-
acing emotional depths that Woolf describes as the "dark places of psychology" and Baldwin as "that darkness, which was the lot of my ancestors

and my own state."[37] Rather than private property, these dark places constitute for both a collective subterranean terrain. Both writers abided by principles of detachment and objectivity as bulwarks against what Baldwin called the "prison of my egocentricity" and Woolf "the damned egotistical self."[38] For Baldwin, the novelist should be "<u>disinterested</u>"; for Woolf, she must be impersonal.[39] Both asserted that the greatest writing emerged from what Baldwin called "the lives of the people" and Woolf "the common life which is the real life," and both found the exemplar of this truth in Shakespeare.[40] Together, they embraced the value of anonymity. Woolf proclaimed a "philosophy of anonymity" that forbade the quest for personal glory; Baldwin declared about an exhibit of African art: "All the artists are anonymous. Which, as Auden said once, is the real desire of the artist—to become anonymous."[41]

Woolf was hardly alone in asserting a modernist aesthetic of impersonal interiority. What is striking is that Baldwin was claiming this modernist inheritance against the grain of his time and place, and was reclaiming it in terms closely (albeit silently) aligned with the allegedly elite and provincial English whipping girl of the New York literary establishment. Although Baldwin was clearly familiar with the work of other Anglo-American modernists, such as Eliot, Joyce, and Faulkner, his resonance with Woolf is stronger, arguably because they shared a position as outsiders who felt compelled both to affirm a disallowed interiority and to assert the right to speak in universal terms. This dual mandate was especially urgent in a midcentury American literary culture that prioritized the social at the expense of the interior life that, according to Baldwin, infuses our more public lives.[42]

Baldwin found the emphasis on the social most prominent and problematic in the work of his Black contemporaries. His most provocative critique focused on the genre of the African American protest novel, which in his view sacrifices "this web of ambiguity, paradox, this hunger, danger, darkness. . . . It is this power of revelation which is the business of the novelist, this journey toward a more vast reality which must take precedence over all other claims."[43] The fiction of Richard Wright, especially *Native Son*, exemplified for Baldwin the reduction of African American subjectivity to a reflex of the dehumanizing conditions in which it was (de)formed. The portrait that results, in Baldwin's view, replicates the racist view of African Americans as less than human. Bigger Thomas's murderous rage, culminating in the brutal murder of a white woman, reinscribes his enclosure in a symbiotic bond with white America. Against this racial determinism, Baldwin insists that literature stake a claim to the full scope of African American humanity: the capacity for love, grief, tolerance, and fear as well as anger.

ANGER AND ANDROGYNY

Baldwin's concern about the psychological and literary damage inflicted by anger constitutes another affinity with Woolf, whose analogous position as a novelist from and advocate for a subordinated group created a similar perception of the threat that anger posed to the novel's formal integrity. If for Baldwin, hatred "never failed to destroy the man who hated" and to straitjacket the text he authored, for Woolf anger "disfigured and deformed" the poetry of Lady Winchilsea and Margaret of Newcastle and the novels of Charlotte Brontë in ways that seemed to ordain Brontë's premature demise, "young, cramped and thwarted."[44] Despite the differences between the African American protest novel and the Victorian novel of protofeminist protest, Brontë performs a function for Woolf analogous to Wright's function for Baldwin. Woolf cites the scene of feminist protest in *Jane Eyre* as evidence that "anger was tampering with the integrity of Charlotte Bronte the novelist. She left her story, to which her entire devotion was due, to attend to some personal grievance" (*AROO*, 76).

By dwelling on these symbolic figures, Woolf and Baldwin enact an anxious dialectic of identification and disidentification. To distance themselves from the anger that threatens to narrow their own perspectives to a single harsh glare, they berate the characters who voice their authors' racial and gender frustrations. Baldwin's anger at Wright (for which he eventually felt remorse) blinds him both to the anger his own provocation was bound to unleash and to the strengths that he eventually acknowledged in Wright's work.[45] Woolf's misreading of *Jane Eyre* as Charlotte Brontë's mouthpiece seems likewise to result from the anger that Woolf feels both with and (consequently) at Brontë and her protagonist.

Strikingly, Baldwin and Woolf embraced the same term—"androgyny"—as an antidote to anger. Woolf put "androgyny," borrowed from Coleridge's assertion that "a great mind is androgynous," into circulation in twentieth-century gender discourse as the name of an idealized mental state of gender equilibrium whose harmony eliminates anger and nurtures imagination (*AROO*, 102). Proffered in the final chapter of *A Room of One's Own*, and often viewed as a conciliatory gesture intended to mitigate the more assertively feminist claims that precede it, androgyny is presented as a spiritual counterpart to "the theory that the union of man and woman makes for the greatest satisfaction" (97). What that translates into for both genders, however, is an asymmetrical tempering of the masculine side of the brain, associated (for both genders) with anger, assertiveness, ego, and stridency. The seemingly heteronormative compromise is a cover for promoting the subtlety, suggestiveness, and indirection that Woolf associates with the

"feminine." What masculinity offers women is not a series of mental attributes, but a set of social possibilities: mobility, independence, and an expanded field of experience. Androgyny is an enabling fiction for Woolf, one
whose exclusions haunt her text.

It is, nevertheless, a compelling fiction and one to which Baldwin was
likewise drawn, most explicitly in his later years, with a similarly asymmetrical emphasis on the feminine as a vital component of a conception
of masculinity adequate to "the best sense of that kaleidoscopic word—a
man."[46] His turn to androgyny in "Freaks and the American Ideal of Manhood" (1985) is no doubt overdetermined by what he calls the androgynous
"craze" of the 1980s.[47] But unlike such self-conscious gender performers
of the 1980s as David Bowie or Michael Jackson, who might be considered
heirs to the Black dandy tradition traced by Monica L. Miller in *Slaves to
Fashion*, Baldwin's version of androgyny is not about gender presentation
or self-fashioning. Having been disparaged as a "sissy" from childhood and
a "faggot" or "pussy" after that, he had little interest in aspiring to "seem or
sound like a woman."[48] Instead, in a manner that reprises Woolf's spiritual
androgyny, he both possessed and proclaimed a strong psychological identification with the feminine as an essential step toward the "complexity of
manhood."[49] (Like Woolf, he was uninterested in the manly woman, as is
obvious from his characterization of Hella in *Giovanni's Room*.) In his uncensored moments, Baldwin spoke unselfconsciously about his own feminine identifications, as when he noted that he sometimes saw himself not as
he was, but, in a different universe, as alternatively masculine or feminine,
or that (like Woolf) he often experienced the writing process as a kind of
pregnancy.[50] He also bestowed (or tried to bestow) androgyny on some of
his fictional characters, as in his note for an early draft of *Giovanni's Room*
that his central character both wants and claims to be both a man and a
woman.[51]

Androgyny offers Baldwin an alternative to both "paralytically infantile" white and aggressively nationalist Black constructions of masculinity, which share the repudiation of difference whose most comprehensive
signifier is the feminine.[52] In language very similar to Woolf and her redeployment by second-wave feminism in the 1970s–1980s, Baldwin places
androgyny in the service of creating a less exclusionary conception of masculinity. Echoing Woolf's discourse on the "man-womanly" and "woman-
manly," Baldwin opens "Freaks and the American Ideal of Manhood" by
defining androgyny as the concept that "there is a man in every woman and
a woman in every man," so that all humans "have available to us the spiritual
resources of both sexes."[53] But unlike Woolf, when he revisits this definition
at the end of the essay, he incorporates racial along with sexual difference

in a comprehensive and perhaps overly idealistic assertion: "But we are all androgynous, not only because we are all born of a woman impregnated by the seed of a man but because each of us, helplessly and forever, contains the other—male in female, female in male, white in black and black in white. We are a part of each other."[54]

The Web of Histories

THE DEAD GIRL

How does this theoretical ideal play out in writerly practice, especially when race intersects with gender in the work in progress Baldwin described as his "web of histories"?[55] Disentangling this web and discovering Woolf's traces in it demand that we follow a circuitous route through a spectrum of recurring characters and scenes across many partial, variously titled, often undated, overlapping, and diverging drafts of the gradually emerging composite urtext that began with Baldwin's summer stay at a writer's colony in upstate New York in 1948 and extended through the literary apprenticeship in Paris that culminated in the publication of *Giovanni's Room* (1956) and *Another Country* (1962). Although many characters and scenes were eventually eliminated, that process of erasure informs what remains and allows us to reassemble the disparate fragments of the "smashed mosaic" of Baldwin's composition in ways that take the rejected as well as the recurring pieces into account.[56]

Baldwin evokes the metaphor of the smashed mosaic to characterize the enigmatic death of the figure he sometimes calls Eleanor and sometimes simply the "dead girl." Like the journal entry "The Last Days," the dead girl eventually disappears, but both the manner of her death and her function as a vehicle of Woolfian resonances capture key features of Baldwin's thinking as he worked toward the final version of *Giovanni's Room*. Making a brief but significant appearance in 1948 in "The Only Pretty Ring Time" (written variously in the drafts as Ring Time and Ringtime and occasionally as "All the Pretty Ring Time"), the earliest draft of what would evolve into *Giovanni's Room*, the dead girl evolves from a secondary figure who mediates two romantic triangles to the figure that enables Baldwin to mediate the models presented by his signal precursors: Henry James and Richard Wright.

From the first drafts of what would become *Giovanni's Room*, the plot centers on two relationships between two pairs of men. The first relationship, set in a provincial town in upstate New York, concerns an unspoken attraction between an adolescent protagonist variously named Peter, Mark, Johnny, and eventually Jon (the name I will use for him consistently) and a slightly older, more worldly friend named Julius (in some drafts Jewish, in others Italian). Over many revisions, this story would be condensed into David's recollection of his one erotic night as a teenager with Joey in *Giovanni's Room*. The second relationship, set several years later in New York City, involves an overt but tortured bond between Jon and Christopher, a bisexual former college English professor accused and then exonerated of the murder of a female student: a drama that would gradually evolve into David's adult relationship with Giovanni in Paris. The narrative apparatus that transports Jon from the first relationship to the second consists of two young American women who are college friends and alter egos, Nancy and Eleanor. Only one of these survives: Nancy, an attractive independent young woman who breaks up the relationship between Jon and Julius by drawing Julius to herself and who reappears in *Giovanni's Room* as the character Hella, the stereotypical American new woman who draws David away from Giovanni. Eleanor, her shadowy enigmatic counterpart, disappears. Her narrative function is to introduce Christopher, her falsely accused murderer, and to set him on a path that will intersect with Jon's. But her death is a strangely oblique and gratuitous way of accomplishing this outcome and one in which Baldwin invests far more rhetorical energy than Eleanor's ostensible function demands.

Whereas Nancy breaks up a homoerotic bond in conformance with conventional narrative expectations, Eleanor enables a new bond, but only by virtue of her death. Baldwin insists on this. In his first "Outline Edits" for "The Only Pretty Ring Time," written during the summer of 1948, he introduces Eleanor only as an attractive young woman student whose abrupt carbon monoxide death implicates a young college professor.[57] In the next iteration, undated but probably from 1950 to 1951, the young female student has been given a name, a nationality, a thumbnail romantic history, and most tellingly an appositive to which she is tightly bound: "Eleanor, the dead girl," who for a short time had been Christopher's mistress.[58] Her death is also given narrative prominence. Baldwin instructs himself early in his notes to open with Eleanor's death because her characterization is vital to the section. This characterization, however, proves elusive, which is, indeed, its point.

How to create a character whose singular function is to have died? One obvious place to go would be a murder trial, and Baldwin does reference one through a newspaper headline he cites in the 1948 "Outline Edits" as "Bond Alibi: Twisted Sex." The citation substitutes the name of his own character Christopher Bond for that of Wayne Lonergan, who was tried for murder in 1943 in a widely reported case headlined by the *Daily News* as "Lonergan Alibi/Twisted Sex." As the citation suggests, it was the alibi rather than the crime that captured Baldwin's attention. After changing almost every feature of the trial, transforming the wealthy heiress strangled and bludgeoned to death by her estranged husband into a college student who dies under mysterious circumstances, and the bisexual playboy husband (granted a 4F classification during the war on the grounds of his homosexuality) into a bespectacled English professor, he transforms Lonergan's alibi—that he had spent the night with a soldier—into the point of interest and enigma for "The Only Pretty Ring Tme." Christopher Bond's admission of "sexual ambivalence" to the enamored Eleanor becomes the precipitating cause of her death: presented in the "Outline Edits" as a suicide, which is suggested more ambiguously in an undated draft titled "Two."[59] But the historical case affords no help with the invented character of the dead girl or her death's precise relation to her lover's sexuality.

For this, Baldwin turns to literary sources. Eleanor is created at the interface—and, most critically, in excess—of Baldwin's two signal literary precursors, who occupy (literally) opposite sides of the pages on which her story is written. A Jamesian resonance is audible in the conflation of gender and nationality in Baldwin's description of both female characters as American girls on the brink of womanhood. Although Eleanor first appears to be a recognizable type, Baldwin quickly qualifies this assumption by denying that she is a caricature and insisting that her death, which at first appears baffling and "monstrous," comes to seem increasingly monstrous by virtue of its logic.[60] Initially, Baldwin tries to analyze the enigma of a character whose fate is both incomprehensible and logical by referencing Henry James's *The Princess Casamassima*. But Jamesian ambiguity fails to encompass the elusive Eleanor, as Baldwin suggests in a handwritten note in the margin and a follow-up to the allusion to James specifying that her death must partake of the "ambiguous force" and "unspecified chaos" that characterize this portion of his novel.[61] Ambiguous force and unspecified chaos go beyond James's psychological subtlety and the attribution of national character, for by exceeding (even as she shares) the sartorial and psychological registers of the American girl "seen in advertisements," Eleanor's contradictions escape circumscription within the parameters of a "country devoted to the death of the paradox."[62]

Baldwin criticizes the American aversion to paradox in "Everybody's Protest Novel," his 1949 essay on Richard Wright. He notes his plans for "The Only Pretty Ring Time" on the back of twenty-eight typescript pages of "Many Thousands Gone," his second essay on Wright (the last page of which is dated Paris, 1950). This recto/verso relation seems more than coincidental, since the essay also grapples with the enigma of violence in terms elicited but not satisfied by Wright's depiction of Bigger Thomas's murderous rage. While acknowledging the logic of Bigger's rape and murder of Mary Taylor, the daughter of his white benefactors, as the only outlet for the Black man's self-creation, Baldwin refuses Wright's equation of Blackness with an animus whose reach Baldwin sees as a more pervasively and profoundly human burden, "the heat and horror and pain of life itself where all men are betrayed by greed and guilt and bloodlust . . . [,] those forces which reduce the person to anonymity and which make themselves manifest daily all over the darkening world."[63]

By referring in this essay to the violence of the racial past as "the beast in our jungle of statistics," Baldwin transports Henry James from one side of the page to the other in the search for metaphors for the emotional intensity of repressed racial passions (given a queer twist by the allusion to James's novella) that the sociological analysis of race effaces.[64] But conversely, Baldwin also transposes his reading of Wright into his outline for "The Only Pretty Ring Time" by revisiting the murder of Mary through the violent death of Eleanor, who is both (like Mary) the white female object of aggression, albeit now only obliquely related to murder, and the site and sign of a more pervasively submerged and explosive violence.[65] Baldwin considered the possibility of racializing this violence in another early draft in which a Black chauffeur was charged with a rape attempt in a wealthy New York suburb, a relatively straightforward variant of Wright's (and America's) prototypical racial crime.[66] Quickly, however, Baldwin turned from racial hatred to the narrative arc of desire between (white) men and its potentially lethal implications for (white) women.

The stubborn ambiguity of Eleanor's death constitutes that death's singular ethical and aesthetic value. It is the challenge of embracing without explaining this enigma that nudges Baldwin into different writerly terrain, set in sharp opposition to the juridical scenarios of criminal investigation that structure the conclusion of *Native Son*. Baldwin's most striking points of contact with *Native Son* are his typed notes to parts of an essay on Richard Wright on verso, which include a series of pink index cards labeled "An Inquest," in which he specifies the types of evidence that could legally determine the causes and mode of death. His parenthetical reminder to himself in the notes that follow to open "The Only Pretty Ring Time" with Eleanor's death at the college provides its own kind of circumstantial evidence of his original intention to frontload the juridical scenario with which *Native Son* concludes.[67] This intention becomes increasingly explicit on the last two index cards, which specify that the inquest in "The Only Pretty Ring Time" should be followed by an autopsy and coroner's verdict.

How far Baldwin traveled from his original intention to map Wright's legal framework onto his fledgling novel through the verbal anatomy of a dead girl's body becomes apparent in his description of the aftermath of Eleanor's death. In an undated typescript simply labeled "Two," Eleanor's death moves from the opening scene to a midpoint that functions as a hinge between the two homoerotic stories: Jon and Julius, and Jon and Christopher. Beyond serving as a vehicle for bringing Christopher into the narrative, the death of Eleanor anchors a discursive shift from the register of narrative and character to the lyrical evocation of a heightened natural world that elevates individual death to cosmic proportions. The recounting of the death introduces an unfamiliar incantatory voice: "Now the summer . . . began in earnest; heat poured from the sky . . . Sound boomed dully on the air . . . at night there was a rustling, a whisper."[68] In this interlude between two narrative segments, nature signals some inarticulable unrest audible only as whispers and leaden booms. The extreme weather that carries this ominous message takes place in summer here, but it could also take place in winter, as in a comparable moment in an undated draft titled "One": "Now the skies . . . seemed heavy and hostile" and winter had never seemed "so long and cold" or summer weighed so relentlessly on "the sockets of the eye."[69] We could understand these polarized seasons, linked only by their extremity, through the historical context presented by these drafts: 1938, glossed in the text by a newspaper headline about the movement toward war in Europe. But there is a literary context as well.

If, as I have been suggesting, Woolf is the unnamed figure who enables Baldwin to write beyond the narrative range of both James and Wright, where might we find indications of her imprint? We could start by comparing the seasonal landscape Baldwin evokes as a premonition of the Second World War to the landscape Woolf evokes as a premonition of the First World War. Consider, for example, these passages from "Time Passes," the famously lyrical interlude between the two narrative segments of *To the Lighthouse*: "And now in the heat of summer the wind sent its spies about the house again. . . . There came later in the summer ominous sounds like the measured blows of hammers dulled on felt." Or "Night, however, succeeds to night. The winter holds a pack of them in store. . . . They lengthen; they darken."[70]

The omniscient perspective, the vatic voice, the rhetorical insistence on "now" as the marker of an unspecifiable immediacy, the evocation of sound as the conveyer of an impending and impersonal doom, and the imagery of seasons in extremis spin a web between these passages in Woolf's and Baldwin's texts. Both writers, moreover, focalize human bewilderment and loneliness through anonymous individuals: for Woolf, the sleeper who rises at night and walks on the sand in a futile search for answers to "those questions as to what, and why, and wherefore"; for Baldwin, the more quotidian citizens who rise at night, light and extinguish cigarettes, and go downstairs to raid the icebox before returning to sleep, "stunned, restless, exhausted under the heat."[71] Perhaps most significantly, both writers situate a singular human death at the heart of an existential quandary that coincides with, but is not circumscribed by, the advent of world war.

In *To the Lighthouse*, of course, the death is Mrs. Ramsay's; in "The Only Pretty Ring Time," it is Eleanor's. Different as these characters are, both pose the challenge of making sense of a death that provokes without answering those Woolfian questions "as to what, and why, and wherefore." As the charged premonitory landscape yields to the actual circumstances of Eleanor's death, however, the scenario is informed less by Mrs. Ramsay than by another of Woolf's characters. Baldwin's defense of the illegibility of a death whose ambiguous imbrication with homosexuality becomes the occasion for a broader defense of uncertainty brings echoes of *Mrs. Dalloway* into the frame. Following the precedent set by the Lonergan case, Baldwin starts by recounting Eleanor's death through a newspaper article headlined "Her Murderer Comes To Trial," which Jon reads on the Sunday morning after realizing that he has lost Julius to Nancy. By filtering Eleanor's death through this journalistic medium, Baldwin invests his story with the gloss of objectivity, which is both reinforced and undermined by the newspaper's photograph of "a dead girl, sprawled, face down, clutching the grass and the rocky ground."[72] The photograph, of course, like the fallen girl, is entirely Baldwin's invention, a device through which he revises his previous account of her death from carbon monoxide poisoning into an ambiguous fall from an upper-story window: a death associated with resistance by its literary genealogy. From this point on, the down-turned face of the dead girl, illegible from the start, becomes a lever for upending the logic of the inquest. In a voice that segues from pseudo-objective reportage to point-of-view narration to oracular pronouncement, the dead girl's silent body becomes a site of resistance to juridical and hermeneutic regimes and a locus of irrecoverable absence and impenetrable enigma.

The account begins neutrally enough by describing Eleanor's fourth-story college dormitory room whose disarray suggests drinking, smoking, and some scuffle. The description shifts abruptly midstream, however, to the agitated metaphors and rhythms of point-of-view narration reporting a "hunt" of investigators "sniffing, turning, noting," seeking out fingerprints, and sifting "through the stubborn substance of the dead girls [*sic*] life," demanding that "the earth and water, the silent air, give up the dead girls [*sic*] secrets."[73] Echoing the language of Baldwin's index cards, the mute testimony of the dormitory room points not only to a potential crime scene, but also to an aggressive attempt to interpret inconclusive evidence.

But who is speaking here? We seem to have segued from the voice of the journalist to that of its reader, Jon, whose anxious voice has already been heard between his Sunday morning awakening to a sense of a newly hostile world and his reading of the newspaper article about the murder trial: "Where am I, who, where, why?"[74] In addition to recalling the questions "as to what, and why, and wherefore" posed by Woolf's wakeful sleeper in "Time Passes," Baldwin draws a verbal parallel between the persecutory anxiety instilled in Jon by the knowledge that his homosexuality has become legible to Julius and Nancy and by the prosecution of Christopher, whose admission of sexual ambivalence informs (without causing) Eleanor's suicide. The two men's anxieties intersect in a shared stake in protecting the privacy of the dead girl who carries the secret of their closeted sexuality, which itself becomes a figure for the axiological privilege of the secret, or what Clarissa Dalloway calls "the privacy of the soul" (*MD*, 126–27).

If Jon's identification with Christopher, mapped onto the sanctity of a dead girl's secrets, offers an explanation for his anxiety, however, where does that voice itself come from? The short, staccato rhythms, the rapid pileup of participial phrases, and the persecutory fantasies suggest an inheritance from another hunted figure whose leap from an upper-story window may have facilitated Baldwin's transformation of the Lonergan murder into a fall that almost seems to be precipitated (psychologically rather than chronologically) by the intrusion of the hunters and sniffers. Both falls trace the forced arc of a guarded interior life that both echoes and exceeds the structure of the closet, and both deploy the metaphor of the hunt to characterize what precipitates or is precipitated by the fall. Feeling generally hounded by human beings who "hunt in packs," Septimus Warren Smith locates that pursuit in the medical, rather than juridical, institutions that seek to extract and diagnose his secret: "Holmes and Bradshaw were on him! The brute with the red nostrils was snuffing into every secret place! 'Must' it could say! Where were his papers? The things he had written? . . . Burn them! He cried" (*MD*, 89, 147). Jon's response to a newspaper photograph of Christopher (whose "horror-stricken eyes" recall the "look of apprehension" in Septimus's hazel eyes) elicits an image of the murder trial in which "every eye would watch" Christopher, "on trial for his life."[75] Septimus similarly feels "looked at and pointed at," for "he had committed an appalling crime and been condemned to death by human nature"(*MD*, 15, 96).

Beyond these characterological echoes, the Baldwin who cites the King James Bible as a signal stylistic influence seems in search of a more elevated idiom, for which a different Woolf novel seems to have offered assistance.[76]

In his depiction of Eleanor's death, Baldwin supplements the affective urgency of point-of-view narration by returning to the impersonal perspective and lyrical language of "Time Passes." The process begins with a turn from the dead body's refusal to offer up its secrets to the universal silence that mandates a shift in both locution and location: "No light broke on the waters. The sea, commanded to surrender its dead, threw up only . . . anonymous bones."[77] Suddenly, we are at sea. The unnamed girl face down on the grass has morphed into the anonymous bones of a silent world submerged beneath the sea. The dead girl assumes the burden of a universal loss through a metaphor that bears no relation to the narrative. In the historical context of an impending world war and the narrative context of a meditative interlude, the anonymous girl whose death on land becomes a figure of the underwater dead recalls Woolf's metaphorization of the dead Mrs. Ramsay as a "purplish stain upon the bland surface of the sea as if something had boiled and bled, invisibly, beneath" (*TTL*, 33–34). But it also evokes Woolf's own drowning, whose silent appeal Baldwin could resist only by repurposing it as Septimus's fall: that is, by reversing the narrative sequence of this draft.

After finally assigning a name to the dead girl (Eleanor) and attempting briefly to describe her in traditional social and narrative formulas, Baldwin abandons the attempt in order to revisit and revise the dead girl's body into its final figuration as a textual body, an invitation to a literary rather than a legal investigation, a critical inquiry instead of an inquest. "Where she had been was silence, space; a gap, a speechlessness forever. . . . The mosaic was smashed."[78] The metaphoric sea that swallows Eleanor, leaving only anonymous bones, anticipates and may register the imprint of the river that had swallowed Woolf in 1941. Both here and in "The Last Days," death by drowning portends the dissolution of identity for figures who are then subjected to a secondary erasure by the (voluntary or involuntary) disappearance of these passages from his oeuvre. Eleanor and Woolf, the dead girl and the dead writer, are Baldwin's forgotten places of silence. Eleanor is excised from the final version of *Giovanni's Room* in order to center and condense the stories of male homosexual desire. She is thus twice sacrificed: within the diegesis (through her death) and from the diegesis (through her excision). The Woolfian traces for which Eleanor's death serves as a nodal point vanish along with her. Eleanor's disappearance and the value accorded her silence prefigure, perhaps even predict, the disappearance and silence surrounding "The Last Days." Where Woolf had been in Baldwin's oeuvre, we might say as Baldwin does of Eleanor, there is only "silence, space; a gap," but fortunately not "a speechlessness forever," because she speaks obliquely through his drafts and essays.

THE DEAD BOY

Unlike the oblique presence of the dead girl, the figure of the dead boy traverses Baldwin's oeuvre, but these figures are less distinct than they might appear. Although the dead boy is strongly racialized and derives directly from Baldwin's experience, the narration of his death is informed by Septimus's sacrificial plunge, an offering that extends beyond Clarissa not only to Baldwin's own brush with suicide, as we have seen in "The Last Days," but also to a narrative dynamic that opens a path to *Giovanni's Room*.

Baldwin selects the story of the dead boy to illustrate his belief that every writer is "*really* telling the same story over and over and over again, trying different ways to tell it and trying to get more and more and more of it out."[79] Occurring near the end of an essay he originally titled "The Dead Boy" (retitled "Words of a Native Son"), this version of the story recounts his visit to a funeral parlor housing the coffin of a twenty-seven-year-old "boy" who had died in the Harlem neighborhood in which Baldwin had grown up. As he homes in on the challenge posed by recounting his recurring story, Baldwin echoes Woolf's tagline for the aesthetic hallmark of the text androgynously birthed in a room of one's own: "The story that one hopes to live long enough to tell, to get it out somehow *whole and entire*, has to do with the terrible, terrible damage we are doing to all our children."[80] Fleshing out the three-word sequence *whole and entire* that toggles between "Words of a Native Son" and *A Room of One's Own* (where it recurs four times in chapter 3 alone) is the implicit metaphor of giving birth by "getting out" a story from the writer's mind. The challenge is how to reconcile the birth of a well-formed text with the anguish provoked by the violent death of a child, which for Baldwin is a question not only about aesthetic distance but also about the personal risk of succumbing to despair.

As he walks from the funeral parlor along the block on which he had lived as a child, Baldwin unlocks an earlier and more disturbing memory:

> There was a railing on that block, an iron railing with spikes. It's green now, but when I was a child it was black. And at one point in my childhood—I must have been very, very young—I watched a drunken man falling down, being teased by children, falling next to that railing. I remember the way his blood looked against the black, and for some reason I've never forgotten that man.[81]

The scenario reprises an earlier version in which Baldwin elaborates on the scene's persistence in his memory:

> There's a figure I carry in my mind's eye to this day and I don't know why. He can't really be the first person I remember, but he seems to be, apart from my mother and father, and this is a man about as old perhaps as I am now who's coming up our street, very drunk, falling-down drunk . . . and he's stumbling past one of those high, iron railings with spikes on top, and he falls and he bumps his head against one of these railings and blood comes down his face, and there are kids behind him and they're tormenting him and laughing at him. . . . This figure is important because he's going to appear in my novel. He can't be kept out of it. He occupies too large a place in my imagination. . . . Who is he and what does he mean?[82]

Although Baldwin never wrote the hypothetical novel he envisioned in this essay, the "sight of that falling down, drunken, bleeding man" recurs in various guises across his oeuvre.[83] Despite his puzzlement about the scene's outsize place in his imagination, his rendition of what appears to be his first encounter with someone outside his family circle, a scene of violence staged at the fraught boundary between home and street, private and public, suggests why the moment might have endured. Sitting wide-eyed at an uncurtained window, the young Baldwin gazes at a fence intended to delimit and safeguard the interior against an outside world that nevertheless impinges, as if the iron-railed fence and the falling man press against his eyeballs with an almost physical pressure, leaving an indelible trace. The breached boundaries of the child observer mirror the spikes' penetration of the falling man's head, out of which blood spills onto the railings and down his face in a graphic index of a pierced interior.

This germinal scene of violence recalls the signal scene of boundary trespass in *Mrs. Dalloway*: the intrusion by Dr. Holmes that propels Septimus Warren Smith out of the window "down on to Mrs. Filmer's area railings" (*MD*, 226). As reimagined by Clarissa during the sudden interruption of her party, the violence of impalement becomes more graphic and immediate: "Up had flashed the ground; through him, blundering, bruising, went the rusty spikes" (*MD*, 134, 184). The recurring elements of these scenes—a man who is an object of public derision falls onto the spiky railings delimiting a property—suggest that Baldwin's account might even have been mediated by the memory of *Mrs. Dalloway* that also mediates his attempted suicide. For Baldwin, as for Clarissa, the intrusion of a violent scene demands some registration of the violence that, by stopping just short of its outcome, affords regeneration.

For Clarissa, as we know, Septimus is the medium of renewal. More indirectly, I suggest, he offers Baldwin a strategy for writing as well as for surviving. Baldwin's project of telling the dead boy's story over and over until it could come out whole and entire reached a crisis point with the suicide of his close friend Eugene Worth, who plunged to his death from the George Washington Bridge into the Hudson River in 1946. By taking his life at the age of twenty-four, Eugene enacted the most traumatic version of the dead boy: a promising young African American male, an "incandescent Negro boy," who rather than being a victim of violence ended his life by choice.[84] Although Baldwin recounts several versions of Eugene's story in his essays and interviews, highlighting different facets in different contexts, they all focus on the imaginative impasse produced by the gap dividing the "black man I loved with all my heart" from the "Hudson River corpse": a blank space where the suicidal subject should be.[85] Unable to enter the suicidal subjectivity of someone like himself, Baldwin explained that his imagination "simply kicks like a stalled motor, refuses to make contact, and will not get the vehicle to move."[86]

How to get the stalled vehicle to move? Unlike anonymous deaths, the suicide of an intimate friend exacts an imaginative leap into an abyss: a need to relive, rather than simply to redeploy, the suicidal act without reproducing it; to draw closer to Eugene's leap, and its Woolfian analogues, and further from Clarissa's facile management. This is a tricky balancing act. It would not suffice to cast away a token symbolic object, such as Clarissa's shilling or Baldwin's own wedding ring, which he tossed into the Hudson River in a gesture that he claims freed him to move to Paris and become a writer.[87] There had to be a more profound but not lethal reenactment, a form of mimesis that would enable him to relive without reproducing the choice of his dark double and thereby to reactivate his stalled imagination.

Moving from New York to Paris did not free Baldwin from the grip of Eugene's example, but it provided enough distance for him to begin working through the place of the dead boy's story in the novel that was becoming *Giovanni's Room*, as if writing out the suicide might free him from its hold. In the earliest draft of the text to assume the title, cast of characters, and compact structure of the published novel, the girl whose fatal fall launches "The Only Pretty Ring Time" (or its second half) has been absorbed into and displaced by the story of an unnamed friend modeled on Eugene. Both the compulsion and the struggle to incorporate Eugene's story into *Giovanni's Room*, to bridge the autobiographical story with a fictional form, New York with Paris, and Eugene with Giovanni, come to the foreground in this draft. Written for the first time in the first person, which may have facilitated the inclusion of personal memories, the text opens with the account of a good friend's suicidal wintertime leap from the heights of the George Washington Bridge into the "swollen and icy" Hudson River, from which he was recovered several days later "lacerated nearly beyond recognition."[88] This is an odd starting point for Giovanni's story, as Baldwin would acknowledge shortly. The narrator tries to build a bridge to the subject of his novel by anticipating Giovanni's execution through the image of the frozen water receiving his anonymous friend "with the brutality of an axe," an image that conflates drowning with falling onto land.[89]

The compulsion to repeat the story, and with it perhaps the act, of Eugene's suicide becomes increasingly intense as the narrative proceeds. After filling in some of the backstory about his relationship with his friend, the narrator describes how, after avoiding the George Washington Bridge for a year, he finds himself walking across it by accident. Looking down into the water, he begins to sweat and imagines his "boy—over and over and over again . . . going over the edge, and down—over the edge and down, into the water."[90] Repeating in language the compulsion he feels to repeat his friend's fatal leap "over and over and over again," language that reiterates the account he offers in "Words of a Native Son" of the novelist's compulsion to keep "telling the same story over and over and over again," Baldwin renders the circular force that threatens to propel his narrator over the edge. But as the narrator comes perilously close to reenacting his friend's plunge—that is, at a moment comparable to Baldwin's walk into the sea in Corsica—something comes to his rescue. The fictionalization that enables him to enter his friend's suicidal consciousness for the first time, and to enter it with such abandon that he wants to call for help, also shapes a pathway toward finding assistance. The crisis abates when the narrator puts words in his friend's mouth, giving him (imagined) direct speech that enables a less guilty, obsessional relation. But whose words are these, and where do they originate? The friend's parting words (underlined in the original)—"<u>Take this, too! Take it! I don't want it anymore!</u>"—echo the language and function of Septimus's final offering—"I'll give it you!"—as if Septimus's gift to Woolf and Clarissa now extends to Baldwin's narrator, set free by reexperiencing his friend's suicide as a sacrificial gift.[91] Upon hearing these words, and only upon hearing them, the narrator remembers the good times he had spent with his friend, and from that moment on he is freed of his compulsion and able to cry, connected to his friend through a cathartic flood of tears that enables him both to separate and to continue to write.

With this, the narrator can proceed toward recounting Giovanni's story, but only after continuing to wonder about the bridge he feels he needs to construct between his childhood friend and his fictional protagonist. Acknowledging the lack of real connection between past and present, he decides the association is a "trick of the bridge," for despite the manifest differences between the two bridges, the narrator thinks of Giovanni when he passes the Parisian bridge, because "*in the last days*," just before Giovanni was apprehended, he had been hiding near that bridge.[92] What fuels this dubious narrative "trick," fully acknowledged as such by the narrator, seems to be a desire to situate Giovanni's execution in a lineage of suicide: most immediately but not exclusively that of Eugene. This lineage is brought to bear on the story of Giovanni, who enters for the first time in this draft, as if Giovanni has to be assimilated to his precursors and carry their suicidal legacy forward, despite the obvious differences in context, for Baldwin to move forward with his text.

As with Eleanor's fall from a window into a metaphoric sea, the memory of Eugene's leap is ultimately excised from *Giovanni's Room*, but hints linger in the scenes in which David gazes down at the Seine from a bridge in Paris. Although the logic of the narrative makes it necessary that Giovanni be executed, Baldwin seems determined to blur the boundary between execution and drowning, to import one memory (of Eugene) into the memory of Giovanni, and the figuration of drowning into the narrative of execution. Reading back through the figurative language of these drafts, we can infer that Giovanni drowns under the bridge, joining Eugene, Eleanor, and Woolf there. Sometimes the lure of the sea is only figurative, as when David first encounters Giovanni leaning on the bar "as though his station were a promontory and we were the sea," or later in a more characteristic reversal recalls feeling that "Giovanni was dragging me with him to the bottom of the sea" (*GR*, 28, 114). Sometimes it is a feature of the material cityscape, as when Giovanni informs David about life under the bridges, or when David, walking along the quai by himself at night and recalling his own youthful fantasies of suicide, wonders about the people "who had looked down at the river and gone to sleep beneath it," and "how they had done it—it, the physical act" (*GR*, 103). But there is a pervasive sense, even though pared down from the earlier drafts, of the lure of the drowned.

Although he abandoned his original strategy for bridging Eugene and Giovanni, Baldwin did retain the scenario of Giovanni's hiding and eventual capture in a barge near a bridge on the Seine. But he cut three words from the final version: *the last days*. It is impossible to know whether he was reserving these words for potential future use or resuscitated them later as the title for the missing journal entry that suggests the autobiographical subtext of *Giovanni's Room*, flagged by David's disavowal of the "far-off boy" (himself) who had "thought of suicide when [he] was much younger" but no longer does (*GR*, 103). Either way, the transfer of the phrase from *Giovanni's Room* to the story of Baldwin's own Woolfian near drowning in Corsica constructs a verbal bridge from the exorcism of Eugene's suicide to the symbolic rite of passage through which Baldwin navigated the transition from the completion of *Giovanni's Room* to the composition of *Another*

Country, where the story of Eugene's suicide finds its final fictional and most explicitly racialized fictional form.

Only one year after starting to plan "The Only Pretty Ring Time," Baldwin jotted down his earliest notes for a novel he planned to call "The Long Farewell," which he intended to structure as the story of six people narrated retrospectively from the perspective of an elderly Black painter based on his close friend and mentor Beaufort Delauney.[93] Significantly later, sometime between a 25-page typescript dated February 1956 and an undated 200-page typescript closely resembling the final version of *Another Country*, Baldwin added a new figure to his cast of characters: Rufus Scott, the talented, desperate, angry, bisexual young African American jazz musician whose story spans the opening chapter of *Another Country* and whose spectacular jump from the George Washington Bridge at the chapter's end unleashes the novel's action. The invention of Rufus close in time to (and probably shortly after) the composition of "The Last Days" supports David Leeming's contention that the voice of the missing journal entry, which secures Baldwin's affiliation with Woolf, "would find fuller expression in the suicidal Rufus in *Another Country*."[94] As the final iteration of the series that begins with a stranger's fall against the fence of a childhood home and proceeds through Eugene's fatal plunge, Rufus performs the cathartic leap that completes the dead boy's story.

Once it became apparent that Eugene's story did not fit into the penultimate draft of *Giovanni's Room*, Baldwin developed the anonymous vehicle of Eugene's story in that draft into the fully developed character of Rufus, who differs in significant ways from Eugene. Whereas Eugene was biracial and light enough to pass, Rufus is the dark-skinned descendant of slaves. Whereas Eugene was educated, political, idealistic, and convinced of the ultimate efficacy of love, Rufus is down and out, apolitical, and consumed with bitterness and rage. Baldwin blackens Eugene racially and morally to make him a more apt representative of the dead Black boy, while preserving the sacrificial impulse that aligns him with Septimus. He also inscribes race more explicitly into the extended narrative, which tracks Rufus's progress via a subway ride from a primarily white downtown through Harlem, where the subway car is populated almost exclusively by African Americans, to the exit for the George Washington Bridge, which provokes an ironic comment about the "bridge built to honor the father of his country."[95] In his anger and desperation, Rufus more closely resembles Bigger Thomas than Eugene Worth. Yet Baldwin complicates this African American lineage by insisting on Rufus's sexual ambivalence and his suicide, which follows the tradition that proceeds through Eugene and Septimus.

Rufus and Septimus are parallel figures both thematically and structurally. Both were absent from their author's original conceptions. Woolf notes that "in the first version Septimus, who later is intended to be her [Clarissa's] double, had no existence; and that Mrs. Dalloway was originally to kill herself, or perhaps merely to die at the end of the party."[96] Baldwin explains that "now, in order to get what I wanted, I had to invent Rufus, Ida's brother, who had not been present at the original conception" of the novel.[97] Both figures are required to illuminate, by being sacrificed for, a central female character: Septimus to embody the darker side of Clarissa and to die in her stead; Rufus to explain the dark side of his sister Ida, since "Rufus was the only way that I could make the reader see what had happened to Ida and what was controlling her in all her relationships . . . , because of what happened to her brother, because her brother was dead."[98] Extending well beyond this narrative function, however, the sacrificial gesture is subsumed within a broader gesture of social protest. All three characters address their parting words to a generic social "you" that is at once the agent, target, and beneficiary of their self-destruction; and all mingle competing motivations that are legible as either sacrifice or threat. Rufus's final thoughts before jumping, delivered with a more accusatory and polished punch in internally rhymed iambic pentameter, *"You took the best. So why not take the rest?"* (*AC*, 77, emphasis in original), echo Septimus's "I'll give it you" as well as Eugene's "Take this, too!"

Beyond the mingled threat and sacrifice that bring Rufus's suicide into Septimus's orbit, this climactic scene suggests Woolf's imprint through a strand of imagery that has become a signature of Woolfian modernism. As Rufus looks down on the city from the George Washington Bridge, *Another Country* evokes and inverts the celebrated scene of skywriting in *Mrs. Dalloway*. The illegible words that fluttered from an airplane over London in "a thick ruffled bar of white smoke which curled and wreathed upon the sky in letters. But what letters?" (*MD*, 20) have become "the lights of the cars on the highway [that] seemed to be writing an endless message, writing with awful speed in a fine, unreadable script" (*AC*, 78). In this moment of contemplation just before he plunges, Rufus intuits an illegible message emanating from elsewhere, as enigmatic as the smashed mosaic of the dead girl's body. The "endless message" written in the lights of cars is another link in the associative chain through which Woolf signals in Baldwin's text "not indeed in actual words," as she writes of Septimus, who "could not read the language yet," but in "smoke words languishing and melting in the sky" (*MD*, 21–22).[99]

Woolf's faintly discernible words at the site of Rufus's leap offer an alternative to the lineage lamented by Eldridge Cleaver, for whom Rufus was "the weak, craven-hearted ghost of *Another Country*," an intolerable affront to the "black rebel" Bigger Thomas and a textual analogue to Baldwin's status as a pale shadow of "the fallen giant, Richard Wright, a rebel and a man!"[100] Pronouncing Rufus "a pathetic wretch who indulged in the white man's pastime of committing suicide, who let a white bisexual homosexual fuck him in the ass," Cleaver holds Baldwin's character up as evidence of the adulteration of Wright's legacy inflicted by the desire to bear a child by "the white man" (98). Blinded by homophobia and sexism, Cleaver could never have imagined that a white English woman might have offered Baldwin hints for writing about issues proscribed in the Black tradition, but by revealing just how prohibited they were, Wright points us toward their shadowy modes of transmission.

Shadow Genealogies

A white girl's enigmatic fall to her death enabled Baldwin to open a narrative space apart from the authority of James and Wright, but the lyrical voice he explored in that space ultimately wasn't his own. Although echoes of "Time Passes" fade from Baldwin's drafts with the excision of Eleanor, Septimus's version of her fall gave him a more functional tool for shaping the story he needed to keep telling until he could find a place for it in *Giovanni's Room* and *Another Country*. Eugene's suicide, reworked via Septimus's offering into Giovanni's sacrificial death, keeps Woolf's traces immanent in the text, as we will explore toward the end of this chapter. We will start, however, by tracing the lineage of the other central character: David, the first-person narrator, whose evolution requires that we revisit his precursor in the character of Jon in the undated draft titled simply "Two."

A key scene in "Two" begins with Jon's feverish awakening, after witnessing the budding romance between Julius and Nancy, to a sense of doom and terror on a hot Sunday morning. In that morning's newspaper he finds the photograph of a dead girl sprawled on the ground, along with the date that has been set for the trial of her alleged murderer, Christopher Bronson, a thirty-three-year-old English professor who stares out from his photograph with horrified eyes. Jon's panic at realizing his estrangement from the order in which Julius and Nancy are about to be engaged underlies his identification with Christopher, on trial in effect for a sexual ambivalence deemed tantamount to murder. At this crux in the prehistory of *Giovanni's Room*, "A shadow crossed the sun," falling on Christopher's photograph and sending a chill through Jon as if it were "an omen, a frosty wind; his doom alone."[101]

The shadow that crosses the printed page and signals doom to Jon emanates from a similarly foreboding scene in *Jacob's Room*, which opens with Jacob's mother on the beach in Cornwall writing to Captain Barfoot in Scarborough a "many-paged, tear-stained" letter, a repository of ink and tears that overflow in a "horrid blot" that spreads slowly across the scene in a collective lament for the coming of winter and the war in which Jacob, like so many young men of his generation, will die.[102] But another kind of nonfuturity is signaled at this juncture by Jacob's older brother Archer. Interrupting his mother's letter writing to complain about Jacob's refusal to play, Archer casts a shadow whose parenthetical depiction mimics both the shadow and the blot of ink on Mrs. Flanders's letter: "'Well, if Jacob doesn't want to play' (the shadow of Archer, her eldest son, fell across the notepaper and looked blue on the sand, and she felt chilly—it was the third of September already), 'if Jacob doesn't want to play'—what a horrid blot!" (*JR*, 4). As in Baldwin's draft, a shadow crosses the sun, falls on a written text, and produces a chill that is mingled with a sense of fatality. The shadow passes from Jacob (via Archer and Christopher) to Jon, who acknowledges himself as queer, and therefore as guilty, at the moment that Woolf's voice crosses Baldwin's text. If the dead girl's body is a figure of Woolf's absent presence in the composition of *Giovanni's Room*, the shadow that travels from *Jacob's Room* aligns the texts more closely in a genealogy identified in this crossing as queer.

Produced by Jacob's refusal to "play" by the rules of the game, the shadow that interrupts Betty Flanders's letter diverts it from its intended recipient, Captain Barfoot, with whom she carries on an always potential but never enacted courtship, and opens an alternative communicative circuit that transmits via shadows and absence. Perhaps like the letter in a bottle that Christopher Nealon imagines queer Anglophone writers in the first half of the twentieth century casting out for future readers to discern, the letter Woolf sends via Betty Flanders is received by Baldwin, the first reader of *Jacob's Room* to signal that he recognized its queer subtexts.[103] By reprising the shadow cast on Betty Flanders's letter, Baldwin situates his emerging novel in a "ghostly, impossible, interrupted" queer genealogy based on absence and implication, a shadow genealogy, unannounced, intermittent, oblique, occluded, indirect, and premised on death.[104]

Underwriting this shadowy genealogy is the scene that immediately follows: Archer's haunting attempt to conjure his brother's presence by a repeated one-line iteration of his name: "JA—COB! JA—COB!" (*JR*, 4). The rupture at the center of Jacob's name points to a gap at the center of his being, a fractured subjectivity that does not quite coalesce. Jacob's name cannot summon his presence, which remains elsewhere, unassimilated, somewhere in the gap between language and being, broken apart as the name breaks against the rocks.

"Ja—cob" slides out through the gap in his name into an early draft of the novel that would evolve into *Giovanni's Room*. Despite their different historical and material environments—the buildup to World War II in the U.S. rather than to World War I in England, and the recesses of an architectural interior rather than hideouts on a rocky beach—Jacob's habits of self-absenting recur in a game that Jon plays with his father. Taking off from an incident in which Jon gets tangled in the curtains and his father calls out for him, the game assumes an existential cast over time. The father's call becomes an echoing, drumlike sound, "Where's Jo-o-n?" at which Jon rushes out, announcing his presence.[105] Jon's hyphenated name clues us into Jacob's legacy, which becomes increasingly explicit as the game proceeds from hide-and-seek, whose goal is to be found, into an encounter with solitude, aloneness, existential isolation, and unfindability that reiterates Jacob's. Sometimes Jon plays both roles in the game by himself, calling out his name and hiding before answering the call, but the experience is not the same. As he matures into adolescence, which coincides with a breakdown of the social fabric during the Great Depression, Jon feels himself confronting for the first time "the vague, vexing riddle of himself." Intensifying the usual traumas of adolescence, he turns in anxiously on himself: "Now, Where's Jon? produced only an echo which thundered in a void . . . which isolated him forever."

Compare the void that echoes around the call for "J-o-n" with Archer's voice calling "Ja—cob! Ja—cob!" with an "extraordinary sadness. Pure from all body, pure from all passion, going out into the world, solitary, unanswered, breaking against rocks" (*JR*, 5). Ja—cob and J-o-n are two iterations of the same strange child, self-enclosed, absent, forever alone, no more at home to himself than to others, a name echoing in a void. Ja—cob and J-o-n share the loneliness of queer children marked in both cases by a "blackness" that renders their absence and negativity. When Jacob is finally located by the narrator rather than by his brother, he is gazing into a pool of water on top of a black rock roughly covered with seaweed and shells. Poised to jump down from the rock, he notices "an enormous man and woman . . . stretched motionless, with their heads on pocket-handkerchiefs, side by side. . . . The large red faces lying on the bandanna handkerchiefs stared up at Jacob. Jacob stared down at them"; and he races toward a "large black woman . . . sitting on the sand," whom he mistakes for his nanny, but who turns out to be another black rock: a refuge from the embodied heteronormative couple that represents the future from which he flees (*JR*, 6).

The black rock Jacob mistakes for his nanny—the strangely comforting alternative to embodied adulthood—is a figure of the queer child's perverse nurture, which by blocking one developmental path opens up another. Recurring in the "fragile, brooding blackness" and "long, black silences" that single Jon out from other children, the blackness Jon and Jacob share is aligned with the negativity of the death drive.[106] Acquiring a racial implication for Jon that associates him with the African American section of town, blackness represents the core of a "strangeness" that also distinguished Baldwin's own childhood.[107] Struggling to find a narrative logic for queer childhood that will lead to Jon's adult sexual orientation and anxious identification with Christopher, Baldwin turns to the vignette that Woolf intercalates between the lines of Mrs. Flanders's letter writing.

As Jon evolves into the adult first-person narrator David in a subsequent draft, the racial connotations gravitate to Giovanni (who inherits the story of the dead Black boy), and the status of David's queerness becomes increasingly explicit and problematic. Baldwin now defines his novel in progress as the study of the crisis precipitated for an "intensely ambivalent" American man in Europe by the recognition that he is attracted physically as well as emotionally to men.[108] Concurrently, the terrain on which this crisis is staged shifts from the symbolic architecture of Jon's family home to the densely material landscape of midcentury Paris that David has to navigate. As the queer deathliness that affiliates Jacob and Jon unfolds on disparate cultural ground, their trajectories highlight the contrasting perspectives of their authors. With his queer inclinations sanctioned by the Higher Sodomy, into which he is inducted at Cambridge, Jacob glides through his brief adulthood in London's pre–World War I environment buffered by the presumption of legitimacy, mobility, entitlement, and tradition in a world in which incomes and rooms seem to appear out of nowhere magically. Baldwin, by contrast, brings into focus the gritty precarity of queer outsiderhood in post–World War II Paris. Giovanni's room has none of Jacob's vacancy and mobility, but instead is encumbered with an accretion of personal and social detritus, a claustrophobic site of stasis and enclosure rather than a space of absence and possibility. Nevertheless, both authors plot their protagonists through parallel but contrasting stations on their trajectories. For both Jacob and David, a privileged adolescent room adjacent to his proper room constitutes a holding place of illicit desire, but these other rooms are rendered through different cultural filters: classical for Woolf, biblical for Baldwin. They also mark differently forsaken possibilities: shimmering in *Jacob's Room* as an untarnished, if unenacted, ideal; subjected in *Giovanni's Room* to the harsh judgment of a Judeo-Christian dispensation that consigns it to an inferior and anterior place in a developmental course that is doomed to revisit its repudiated promise. Both protagonists undergo a rite of passage: the university for Jacob, a gay Parisian bar for David; and both reach maturity in a major capitol: a well-preserved London in a bubble of prewar innocence and a war-damaged Paris that is both recovering from material deprivations and hosting a flamboyant style of effeminate gay masculinity antithetical to the manly love endorsed by the Anglo-Greek ethos that emanates from the British university.

Juxtaposing these trajectories brings into relief Woolf's insular British provenance vis-à-vis Baldwin's international perspective, which enables him to bring French and American homoerotic discourses into an agonistic encounter at the core of *Giovanni's Room*, as well as to incorporate elements of a British literary tradition. Yet despite the authors' multiple differences, we can map a shadowy genealogy that extends to *Mrs. Dalloway* as well as *Jacob's Room*. The wayward pathways of this lineage find a figure at the novels' conclusions, which bring Jacob and Giovanni to violent early deaths that leave the bereaved alone to decipher their meaning as a gust of wind unsettles the landscape, blowing fragments of the past toward an uncertain future.

FIRST ROOMS

Jacob's story takes off from a beach. Its trajectory is anticipated by his discovery of "an old sheep's skull without its jaw," which comforts him from the shock of suddenly encountering the "enormous" red-faced man and woman lying on the beach (*JR*, 7). Jacob's graphic encounter with these grotesque oversize parental surrogates plots his course away from embodiment, maturity, and reproductive futurity toward this "clean, white, windswept, sand-rubbed . . . unpolluted piece of bone" (*JR*, 7). Through this recoil from mortal flesh to immortal bone, from gross heterosexual coupledom to a sculptural purity reprised in the rose or ram's skull on the molding of his London room, the white marble columns of the Parthenon, and the classical sculpture to which he is repeatedly compared, queerness, death, and classical Greece enter the text together.

The nonprogressive nature of this trajectory is also figured at the beach. At the sandy bottom of a pool, Jacob suddenly sees and grabs a crab, as if wresting it from a womb, and transports it in a bucket he leaves outside the house. This opening chapter concludes with a description of the crab slowly circling the bottom of the bucket on its "weakly legs" and trying repeatedly and unsuccessfully to climb its steep side (*JR*, 11). More sharply focalized than the room Jacob shares with his brother, whose flushed outstretched body in the "hot; rather sticky steamy" sheets recalls the middle-aged couple on the beach, the bucket becomes a figure of Jacob's first room, and the cool, light, opal-shelled crab (who carries his room on his back) a figure of his alter ego or next of kin, his chosen rather than biological brother (*JR*, 10). Since Jacob's childhood room has been conscripted to the biological family, his own room, his individual room, which harbors his identity, must be outside, adjacent, another room, not within the familial architecture, but next door, away from the heat of flesh and blood.

Animals, according to Kathryn Bond Stockton, are often the queer child's chosen companions, and the animals that Jacob chooses are themselves decidedly queer: the sheep skull's jaw that he takes into his bed and the crustacean he brings home are at the far end of the spectrum of embodiment. The queerness of this kinship, reinforced by the famously lateral movement of the crab Jacob selects as his companion, sets in motion the developmental course of queer children who, as Stockton argues, grow sideways rather than "straight up" into roles for which they have little aptitude or desire.[109]

Jacob's room (always referenced in the singular despite the clear existence of a separate bedroom in his London flat) migrates laterally through the text without evolving functionally: light and mostly vacant, although increasingly encumbered after Cambridge, traveling as a single unit from Cornwall to Cambridge to London, accumulating and discarding bits and pieces of furniture, Jacob's room remains a site of forestalled potential, an insistent and insistently negated sense of possibility, as if the room were constituted by lack or awaiting some forbidden enlivening presence. Jacob's course through this anti-Bildungsroman is not only truncated and (like his name) interspersed with gaps, but also sideways through a world whose developmental sites and stages he inhabits without assimilating.[110]

CAMBRIDGE

The most formative site is Cambridge, where Jacob arrives in 1906 at a post-Wildean moment during which the university provided a rare sanctuary from an increasingly hostile public stance toward male love. Traditionally a kind of developmental shelter or parenthesis, at once central and peripheral to the formation of the English gentleman, Oxford and Cambridge afforded a particular kind of refuge for Jacob's generation. Building on the information transmitted by her brother Thoby and his Cambridge friends, especially Lytton Strachey and Maynard Keynes, who in 1903 took control of and reoriented the legendary Society of Apostles or Conversazione Society to which many of Bloomsbury's highest male achievers belonged, Woolf evokes the idealized world of what was known as the Higher Sodomy, which grounded its promotion of passionate male intellectual and affective bonds in a tradition of Greek love that shielded these attachments from association with the recently pathologized and criminalized homosexuality.[111] According to this ideal, the unconsummated but ever-alluring attraction between two intimate male friends was the highest form of love, a route to the apprehension of ideal beauty and wisdom, a source of spiritual exaltation both driven and threatened by physical desire: the balancing act crystallized by the figure of the charioteer in the *Phaedrus*, the dialogue Jacob reads in his London room. As Linda Dowling and Julie Anne Taddeo demonstrate regarding Oxford and Cambridge, respectively, Plato's dialogues were the vehicle of a homosexually coded inflection of the Greek ideal of civic manly education.[112]

Through its location in Nevile's Court at Trinity College, the crucible of Bloomsbury masculinity and the gathering site of the Conversazione Society, Jacob's room sits at the epicenter of Cambridge intellectual life, but a center whose intellectual and erotic passions were orthogonal to the values embraced by the university's more mainstream students. In her memoir "Old Bloomsbury," Woolf idealizes the Apostles as a "society of equals . . . questioning everything with complete freedom."[113] In *Jacob's Room* she renders the Society's "spiritual shape" as a pantomime glimpsed through a window that, barring sound, yields only the "gestures of arms, movements of bodies," that translate argument into art (*JR*, 44, 43). This spiritualized homosocial dance is both a rite of passage into and an interruption from the demands of heteronormative society whose routines are satirized brutally in the preceding depiction of Sunday lunch for undergraduates at the family home of a don. Unarticulated both culturally and within Woolf's text is how to negotiate the passage from one to the other: a task of assimilation at which Jacob manifestly fails. But that there could be another route is intimated in a depiction of the room that might have been, wants to be, but cannot be, its site.

That Jacob's Cambridge room, his first room of his own, is always already a site of lack, a mausoleum in advance of its final evacuation, is indicated not only by its inhabitant's absence when we enter it, but also by an abrupt shift to the past tense in its description, as if the room itself had receded into the past and become a historical artifact. The itemization of its contents—a round table and two chairs, numerous books, photographs, notecards, pipes, essays, slippers—renders at once the predictable accoutrements of an undergraduate room and a seemingly arbitrary assemblage of cultural artifacts that have lost the power to cohere. The dutiful catalogue seems to have fallen victim to the realist proclivities Woolf decries in "Mr. Bennett and Mrs. Brown." But whereas the protocols of realism seek to lend substance to a novelistic subjectivity, the description of Jacob's room serves an opposite purpose: to represent a shell without a center, a cultural rather than a personal formation.

SIMEON'S ROOM

That potential center, in *Jacob's Room*, is appropriately off-center in a room that is not Jacob's but (like the bucket outside his childhood room) adjacent to it. Its exact location remains ambiguous: prefaced by Jacob's proposal, "Let's go round to Simeon's room," it is also the newly vacated room on the next staircase through whose window the narrator has observed the "spiritual shape" of the students' conversation (*JR*, 41). As the site of high-minded conversations that evoke the Conversazione Society dissolves into the room in which Jacob visits Simeon, the text homes in on the potential of the intimate friendship at the heart of the creed of the Apostles. By reenvisioning the listless air in Jacob's empty room as a nurturing, encompassing, maternal presence that enfolds two loving friends in a sheltering embrace that suggests maternal generosity rather than masculine generativity, Woolf takes imaginative ownership of men's "spiritual procreancy."[114] In this room next door to, but importantly not, Jacob's—that is, a space not of continuous residence, but of temporal and spatial self-enclosure—Woolf crafts an early moment of being whose ephemerality is underscored by Simeon's disappearance from the text at its conclusion. With the infusion of affect that characterizes such moments, the material furnishings that are salient in Jacob's own room dissolve into a bath of intimacy.

Abandoning its characteristically ironic detachment, the narrative voice yields to the lyricism of this moment. Jacob's friendship with Simeon is oral, intimate, and lyrical rather than (as with Timmy) textual, cultural, and declamatory; importantly, their intimacy unfolds at the level of sound rather than symbolic meaning. Simeon's name (a Greek name from the Hebrew *shma*, "to listen," but affiliated as well with the Latin roots of *semen* as "seed") summons us to listen to what cannot be said. With the muffling of the outside world and the insulation of the world indoors by the noise of the wind, a new semiosis begins to emerge below the threshold of articulated language. What matters in this iteration of the Conversazione Society is what escapes verbalization, the murmurings that become audible when the meanings of words are blurred by the wind and "cancelled" by the tap of a pipe on the mantelpiece (*JR*, 45). Enfolded in an auditory envelope, undertones gain substance onomatopoetically through the repetition of words such as "murmuring" and "hum," which resonate in turn with the nasal intonations of "him," "mind," and "matter" that recur in the names of

Jacob's male friends: Timmy, Simeon, and Bonamy. The sound of humming is granted the status of a language as the "hum of talk" among the diners at Trinity College evolves into the observation that "perhaps Jacob only said 'hum.'" The palpable soundscape culminates in the achievement of "intimacy, a sort of spiritual suppleness, when mind prints on mind indelibly" (*JR*, 45).[115] Evoking and displacing the printing press, the figure of a tactile, unmediated, and reciprocal embrace between two equally agentic and corporealized minds transforms the Platonic figure of mental insemination into an egalitarian exchange.

As Jacob moves to stand and sway over Simeon's chair, the narrative voice confers an orgasmic bath of intimacy on characters denied its direct experience. Jacob's pleasure, we are told, "would brim and spill down the sides if Simeon spoke" (*JR*, 45). Simeon doesn't speak, as if speech would induce too climactic a consummation, but as if reprising the maternal wind's desire to endow masculine romance with procreative power, the third-person lyric voice intervenes to suffuse the scene with a gentler and more sustainable spermatic intimacy that dissolves the boundaries between body and mind, self and other, narrator and character, in a participially suspended moment that "rose softly and washed over everything, mollifying, kindling, and coating the mind with the lustre of pearl" (*JR*, 45). Brimming with what Woolf elsewhere describes as "a flood of the sacred fluid," Simeon's room grows "still, deep, like a pool," a generative space like the pool from which Jacob plucks the crab, a lustrous womb or pearly shell from whose inchoate murmurings the seed of a new life might emerge (*JR*, 45).[116]

But this scene of liquid generativity, where desire pools and swells, can take place only in a self-contained space of deviation from a room of one's own. The moment comes to an abrupt halt with the word "But" as Jacob moves, leaves, safeguards his identity by buttoning his jacket across his chest, and returns across the echoing courtyard to his own room, the refrain "back to his rooms" chiming with the "magisterial authority" of his footsteps on the stones (*JR*, 45). A different soundscape announces Jacob's return to the order of things. And yet Woolf has given the moment an enduring textual space that she imprints on the mind as Jacob's other room, the queer room he can visit but in which he can't remain.

JOEY'S ROOM

The first room that David recollects in *Giovanni's Room* is not his childhood room; in fact, the only childhood room he remembers is the living room, a site of familial tensions played out under the surveillant gaze of his dead mother's photograph. Like Jacob, David seeks a space of his own

outside the family home, but in contrast to Jacob's early recoil from social attachments, David's first remembered room is highly relational and
phobically rejected. Recalled under the sign of the guillotine with which
David's opening rumination concludes, Joey's room enters the narrative
as a deathly site of joy. Less an adjacent room like Simeon's that sustains
a lateral potential than an anterior room whose suppression will exert a
gravitational pull toward the dead center of Giovanni's room, Joey's room
is a sensuously detailed and stringently "bounded" scene of promise whose
mythos is Edenic rather than Platonic (*GR*, 8). After returning from an
idyllic summer outing to Coney Island, David and Joey, high-school bud-
dies, "gave each other joy" through a powerfully emotional "act of love"
during the night they spend together (*GR*, 8). David awakens the next
morning to a vision of Joey's body touched by the morning sun that seems
to caress it into being: "Joey's body was brown, was sweaty, the most beautiful creation I had ever seen till then" (*GR*, 8). Joey is the brown American
Adam, stroked by a recursive narrative gaze, a racialized flesh-and-blood
counterpart to *Jacob*'s white Greek statues, a beautiful "creation" molded
from the earth, the first man, naked, sleeping, prone, viewed through the
eyes of newborn desire. The scene quivers with emotion, a participial rip-
pling (beating, feeling, trembling, stirring) over a sensate body enlivened
by smell and touch.

We know what follows in the prototype of this creation scene: the formation of a helpmate whose fateful fall will give birth to the human race.
Baldwin seeks out alternative futures for his queer iteration of this scene.
Immediately following the reference to "the act of love" is a description of
Joey "curled like a baby on his side, toward me. He looked like a baby, his
mouth half open, his cheek flushed, his curly hair darkening the pillow and
half hiding his damp round forehead and his long eyelashes glinting slightly
in the summer sun" (*GR*, 8). After an implicit scene of anal procreation,
the birth of the beautiful queer brown baby signals the promise of a new
dawn, an alternative to the stillborn baby of Giovanni's thwarted attempt
at heterosexual reproduction, the Italian baby born with the cord wrapped
around its neck, strangled in the coils of its reproductive mechanism. The
beautiful baby of the future, however, is only half-formed, his mouth half-
open, his brow half-hidden, a potentiality waiting to be nurtured. We sense
David's readiness to be that nurturing lover, a maternal sensibility in a masculine form. But the outcome of queer procreation is nevertheless endangered. David feels that holding Joey is like holding "some rare, exhausted,
nearly doomed bird," exhausted before it can leave the safe nest of their
entwined bodies, nearly doomed because this nest may be its only safe place
(*GR*, 8). It may be impossible for this rare bird to spread its wings and fly:

it may be doomed to evolve into one of the *folles* who frequent Guillaume's bar in Saint-Germain-des-Prés. The wishful evocation of a masculinized Eden gestures toward a biblical counterpart of the spiritual procreancy of Simeon's room, but a queer Eden is unimaginable; before the banishment of Adam and Eve is a prior expulsion of the male couple from the cultural imaginary.

Into the nest of possibility crashes language: not the serpent's duplicitous language, but the prior, purer Adamic mode that (in the biblical narrative) gives names to the creatures of the universe. The book of Genesis sharply differentiates this generative naming from the beguilements of the serpent's tongue; Baldwin's queer revision, however, brings these linguistic modes into temporal proximity as both cause and consequence of the Fall. For the regulation of difference entails rules of exclusion and combination. David is expelled from Joey's room by an apparently innocent act of naming. As is customary after the birth of a child, the first words uttered proclaim the law of gender, italicized for emphasis in this case: "It was borne in on me. *But Joey is a boy*" (*GR*, 9). With the passive voice underscoring subjugation to a symbolic order that gives birth to the naming subject along with the one who is named, David understands that the gender binary that locates him and Joey on the same side of identity divides them along the axis of desire. As naming invades desire, the caressing gaze becomes anatomizing. Joey's brown skin and baby face dissolve into itemized, masculinized body parts: thighs, arms, fists. As abrupt as this transformation from infancy to manhood is the sudden reduction of Joey's holistic body into a single threatening orifice: "the black opening of a cavern in which I would be tortured till madness came, in which I would lose my manhood" (*GR*, 9). Although they are lying face-to-face, Joey figuratively turns his back.

The figure of the cavern (evoked three times in a single paragraph) anticipates the answer to Leo Bersani's titular question in "Is the Rectum a Grave?"[117] As David plunges imaginatively into this cavern, he finds "rumor, suggestion, . . . half-heard, half-forgotten, half-understood stories, full of dirty words," the waste products of the body transposed into toxic verbal offage (*GR*, 9). For the first time, he feels shame, along with the dictates of reproductive futurity. After imagining the disapproval of Joey's mother, he suddenly recalls his obligation to his own father, "who had no one in the world" but David through whom to generate a future (*GR*, 9). In its third iteration, the cavern becomes the casket of David's own future. The beautiful baby has become a corpse. The life cycle of queer futurity runs swiftly from infancy to manhood to death.

LONDON AND PARIS

The cultural differences encapsulated in the scenarios of Simeon's and Joey's rooms evolve with the central characters' progression into the adult worlds of London and Paris. Woolf and Baldwin both depict this step as a devolution into the historically real, but they view history through different lenses.

In *Jacob's Room* the process begins with Jacob "going down" from the rarefied atmosphere of Cambridge to the "real" world that Lytton Strachey disparaged (in terms that chime with the signal word in Simeon's room) as "the great limbo of unintimacy," in which the "prolonged innocence of boyhood" promoted by Cambridge confronted the imperatives of adulthood.[118] Jacob inhabits this world in a London room in a respectable Bloomsbury location in an eighteenth-century property where a rose or ram's skull carved in wood over the doorway is a clear reminder of the sheep's skull found on the beach. There are mitigating new elements, however, such as a bedroom visited exclusively by Florinda, in contrast to the sitting room where Jacob entertains his masculine visitors, preeminently Bonamy, the "good friend" who (although nominally present at Cambridge) enters the narrative at this point. Bonamy ushers in a turn from Greece to Rome, for whereas Jacob deems "the Roman civilization . . . a very inferior affair, no doubt. . . . Bonamy talked a lot of rot, all the same" (*JR*, 143). Bonamy's preference for "the definite, the concrete, and the rational" is manifested by his "mugging up Roman law in his rooms in Gower Street" (*JR*, 154). He is attracted to Latinate words such as "magnanimity, virtue," which Jacob uses to entice him to "play round him like an affectionate spaniel" so that "(as likely as not) they would end by rolling on the floor" (*JR*, 174). Under the aegis of Rome instead of Athens, Jacob and Bonamy gain entrée to an eroticized physical play (scorned by the Higher Sodomy) that sounds to Bonamy's housekeeper like "two bulls of Bashan" (*JR*, 107).

As homosexuality becomes an actual possibility rather than an incitement to sublimation, its representation becomes less inviting, but it remains within a frame of reference that forfeits transcendence but maintains order. Beyond Bonamy's personal taste for "books whose virtue is all drawn together in a page or two. . . . Sentences that don't budge though armies cross them," the London rendered in *Jacob's Room* showcases historical conservation through well-preserved neoclassical buildings that confer their distinction on the present (*JR*, 147–48). London's busy streets are full of motion, but it flows through orderly channels. Even the catastrophic world war in which Jacob dies offstage is depicted as a discrete event dictated by a flourish of old men's pens in a government office in Whitehall. Jacob's unrepresented death is rendered as a question of disposing of his belongings. The fall into history is into a kind of well-managed banality.

In *Giovanni's Room*, by contrast, history is the entropic condition of mortality. Baldwin's Paris evidences historical degradation, the erosion of the present by the weight of the past. As David characterizes Paris (in explicit contrast to New York, but arguably by extension to Woolf's London as well), "Paris is *old*, is many centuries. You feel, in Paris, all the time gone by" (*GR*, 49, emphasis in original). Rather than constellating in monuments, history is only ever a process of decomposition, manifested in an aging body. The history David witnesses in Paris is unanchored by cultural landmarks or events and unenlivened by perceptual intensity: we see no Gothic cathedrals or Renaissance hôtels de ville, no religious or civic buildings, no blocks of bourgeois apartment buildings, just seedy streets, markets, and cafés. Catalyzed by David's eviction from his hotel room in compliance with a code that demands that "whatever stinks" be cast outside, the route to Giovanni's room entails a slow traversal through the early morning streets and stalls of Les Halles that call attention to the microprocesses of consumption and digestion that break things down, rather than to enduring architectural structures, and that brings into the foreground the classed and racialized bodies excluded by the Anglo-Greek aspirations of the Higher Sodomy, whose ideal of "manly love did not encompass the dirty acts of 'buggers' who lurked in subway stations and dark alleys" (*GR*, 22).[119]

The embrace of permeable class and ethnic boundaries did not extend to gender, however. In contrast to *Jacob's Room*, in which the feminine is safely circumscribed within unthreatening if often foolish and ineffectual female characters, and perishable flesh in general is countered by marble statues, there is a pervasive threat of feminized bodily encroachment in *Giovanni's Room*. Narrativized most explicitly as Hella's disruption of David's relationship with Giovanni, this threat is registered more pervasively as the obtrusion of shapeless female flesh: either in the form of actual female bodies, such as Hella's "intimidating" breasts brushing David's arm or the "disquietingly fluid" yet hard body of Sue that he seduces as "a job of work" (*GR*, 158, 99), or that of an effeminate flabbiness in aging *vieilles folles* such as Guillaume. But more fundamentally than these particular forms, the feminine is figured as a ground of being, a biological foundation. Whereas the Higher Sodomy hinges on masculine sublimation, its declension to the lower registers insists on a feminized flesh, along with the lower senses of smell and touch. Subtending this world is David's nightmare of his mother's decomposing corpse.[120] Since we are "of woman born," a formulation invited by David's allusion to the apparition of the three witches from *Macbeth* during his hallucinatory encounter with a trans woman in a gay bar, the masculine body is a way station between an original and ultimate immersion in female flesh. There is no purity of bone in *Giovanni's Room*, no transcendence of the body, no flight to the aesthetic "comfort" of the skeletal. Whereas the classical frame that traveled from Athens to Cambridge and (in a Latinate version) to London offers the figure of the classical statue as the aesthetic telos of the skeleton or skull—that is, as a form of transcendence that makes death a paradoxical escape from mortality—the biblical frame that travels with Baldwin from Harlem to Paris feminizes a fall into mortality. Underlying Giovanni's personification of Paris as "an old whore" waking up is a pervasive presumption of feminine responsibility for the fallen condition of the present (*GR*, 45).

David and Giovanni navigate a fallen feminized universe that, like Sue's body, is disquietingly fluid. Rather than a patriarchal machine, as for Woolf in "A Sketch of the Past," society flows through the hands of women. The figure of Paris as a whore, Eve's descendant, conflates female sexuality and the cash economy. Instead of the pens of old men in Whitehall directing the course of history, middle-aged women "all over Paris . . . sit behind their counters like a mother bird in a nest and brood over the cash-register as though it were an egg" (*GR*, 50). The egg, of course, hatches more money. It is not the political domain that counts here (the inept police take a long time to capture Giovanni) but a market economy overseen by women. The consequent longing for a stabilizing paternal presence seems to underlie David's otherwise inexplicably auratic image of his ineffectual father "washed in the gold light which spilled down on him from the tall lamp which stood beside his easy chair" (*GR*, 11). But that singular point of light, the opposite of the decaying maternal corpse, does not provide a compass through a feminized, fungible material and social world in which men, vehicles, and money circulate.

SAINT-GERMAIN-DES-PRÉS

Giovanni's Room poses a fundamental question: how to salvage a notion of masculinity in a city perceived as a decaying female body, a queer male culture that prizes effeminacy, and social norms that assume one member of any couple will perform the role of the feminine. A critical site of this exploration is the bar in which David meets Giovanni. More narrative space is devoted to this single night, into which an entire developmental stage is compacted, than to the preceding twenty years of David's life. As the site of a cultural initiation, the queer Parisian bar and the underworld for which it serves as metonym, constitute a counterpart to Jacob's university, but rather than a rite of passage through the rarefied masculine world of

Cambridge, David is subjected to a process of degradation whose hallmark is the feminine.

The queer Parisian underworld that populates the bar consists of "knife-blade lean, tight-trousered boys," a few older "paunchy, bespectacled gentlemen" in search of "money or blood or love," and the gender-nonconforming effeminate *folles* "screaming like parrots the details of their latest love-affairs" (*GR*, 26–27). As an introduction or perhaps induction into *le milieu*, the first word of French in the chapter, the scene stages a particular intersection of history, culture, and sexuality that is as distinctively midcentury Parisian as the Conversazione Society in Cambridge was early twentieth-century English. The anonymous bar in *Giovanni's Room* exemplifies a particular social milieu: Saint-Germain-des-Prés in the early 1950s, "the only place in Paris where you can amuse yourself according to your tastes," and the hub for the performance of a flamboyant style of effeminate homosexuality.[121] Reinforced by the confluence of French writers, artists, and intellectuals in its cafés and theaters, the *milieu* became a well-known (if not always well-regarded) site of "out" queer visibility, especially noted for the "*folles* . . . who stood out by their effeminate mannerisms, their swishing walk, their elegant clothes, sometimes their facial make-up, and especially their mannered way of speaking, often punctuated with piercing shrieks, which distinguished them from other homosexuals."[122] The tolerance afforded gender and sexual deviance by the intermixture of high-minded artistic and philosophical debate makes the queer culture of Saint-Germain in the heyday of French existentialism an unexpected parallel to and inversion of the rites of passage afforded by the British university in the heyday of turn-of-the-century Hellenism.

The queer French bar and the English university are both male homosocial detours en route to adult masculinity: one passes through a rarefied masculinity that will need to adapt (or not) to the heteronormative world, the other through an exaggerated effeminacy that will need to be purged by a male couple exploring their gender roles. In the process, the bar inverts its university counterpart along a series of loosely related axes: Hellenic to Hebraic; masculine to effeminate; spirit to body; orality to anality; linguistic possibility to duplicity; adjacency to confusion. David describes his passage as an initiate through the bar scene in language that could apply to the university as well as to the holy orders he explicitly evokes: "It was as though they were the elders of some strange and austere holy order and were watching me in order to discover, by means of signs that I made but which only they could read, whether or not I had a true vocation" (*GR*, 27). The middle-aged businessmen buying drinks for young men in Guillaume's bar may engage in a more blatant form of exchange than the aging dons who serve up intellectual food to undergraduates in their chambers at Trinity College, but in both cases, a generational transaction undergirds an initiation rite that culminates in the proclamation of a sexual or professional vocation.

Accepting a sexual vocation in *Giovanni's Room* requires confronting its most distasteful features, a process of degradation rather than (as at Cambridge) of sublimation. Instead of facilitating assimilation into the elite, it is a process of relinquishing the markers of normativity. This is a necessary step in the project of breaking down David's straight white self-image, relaxing the boundaries of what Jacques derides as David's "pride and joy" in his "*immaculate* manhood" (*GR*, 30, emphasis in original). Only by acknowledging the desires on exaggerated display might it be possible for him to move beyond a bar scene that offers no middle ground between hungry youth and dirty old men, a scenario in which growth is simply a process of the young becoming old. Envisioning a different future entails both embracing and harnessing the disruptive force of queerness to another mode of life. The *milieu* sets the stage for the challenge of refashioning, rather than repudiating, a domestic realm colonized by heteronormativity. The desire for this future sounds in Jacques's wistful question to David after the imprisonment of Giovanni: "You two together . . . you weren't happy together?" (*GR*, 24). The auditory insistence—"you, two, to"—gives voice to the longing for and impediments to being two men together.

The path toward that goal begins by leading downward through a series of inversions of the Cambridge model. Instead of guidance by the "light of learning," the rite of passage in *Giovanni's Room* descends into an ill-lit underworld tunnel populated primarily by denizens of the demimonde, the "buggers" from whom the Higher Sodomists carefully distinguished themselves. The class inversion is echoed by a moral one: stripped of an elevating classical context, the terrain of the "lower" sodomists reverts to a biblical foundation in Sodom and Gomorrah. The desublimation of bodily desires elicits, even as it flaunts, the biblical ethos evoked by allusions to flames, heat, communion, and a (lost) Garden of Eden. The journey through the bar is more Dante's *Inferno* than Plato's *Symposium*.[123]

Although, as in the *Symposium*, there is ample drinking and talking, the scenario does not focus on orality. The pipe that Jacob Flanders takes in and out of his mouth, often in conjunction with a recoil from heterosexuality, disappears (along with the upper floors where the Conversazione members congregate) into tunnels that confound orality with anality. An anal imaginary that tunnels out a queer erotic refuge displaces the oral sublimation of homosexuality. In this new imaginary, spiritual suppleness descends into a tangle of animalized bodies and a preverbal hum crescendos into an animal

roar.[124] As David segues from being an onlooker to an object of the bar ha-
bitués' gaze, he feels himself joining the animals in a zoo. Standing behind
the bar, Giovanni has pride of place as the lion king, a singular figure of
masculinity perched on a promontory over a sea of undifferentiated bodies.
But his position of proud masculinity is precarious, as the text underscores
via David's evocation (provoked by a transvestite) of the nausea induced by
"the sight of monkeys eating their own excrement" (GR, 27). As masculinity
is contaminated with femininity, orality is contaminated with anality, and
humanity with animality. Confusion, in its full etymological sense, prevails:
distinctions between individuals, species, meanings, and genders dissolve
as proximate terms rub up against and infect one another. Adjacency, here
the site of an abjected other, slips from a visionary possibility to a boundary
threat.

The underlying source of this boundary confusion is the instability of
gender. Absent the "virilizing authority of the Greeks," the classical framework that masculinized queer manhood for Woolf, there is no bulwark
against the threat of the feminized homosexual culture of Saint-Germain-
des-Prés.[125] This threat is crystallized in the nightmare vision at the center of David's psychological journey: the trans woman who ups the ante of
the flamboyant self-displays of the *folles*. Emerging apocalyptically out of
the shadows, the "flaming princess" is the sole source of light in this queer
underworld, a figure that brings the theatricalizing flames of queer desire
together with the fires of hell (GR, 42). Straddling the boundary between
life and death, male and female, body and phantom, age and infancy, this
ambiguously gendered deathlike creature slowly approaches David with
an obscure and obscene intentionality. Seeming to quiver on the boundary
between the psychic and the social, "it" threatens annihilation, an undoing
of the categories that undergird world-making. "It looked like a mummy
or a zombie. . . . It carried a glass, it walked on its toes, the flat hips moved
with a dead, horrifying lasciviousness. It seems to make no sound. . . . It glit-
tered in the dim light" (GR, 39–40). As it comes close enough for David to
perceive the details of its flagrant makeup, hairless chest, and extravagant
outfit, the phantasm that seems as if it "might, at any moment, disappear
in flame" puts on display David's fears that he will be emasculated by his
awakening desire for Giovanni and consigned to a no-man's-land of boundary transgression. In spite of a bravura effort of syntactical deferral, David
realizes that "they had become visible, as visible as the wafers on the shirt of
the flaming princess, they stormed all over me, my awakening, my insistent
possibilities" (GR, 42). The religious resonance of the wafers on the shirt of
the flaming princess captures the ambiguity of feminizing possibilities that
are transformational and threatening in equal measure.

Critics agree about the impasse created by the conflation of homosexuality and effeminacy in the novel.[126] What they don't address as fully are the linguistic ramifications of the Judeo-Christian inflection of the "flaming princess." Among its other attributes, the princess that both entices and proscribes, that seems as if it "might, at any moment, disappear in flame," is a biblical temptress, a mixture of Satan and Eve, whose incitement to sexual knowledge ("You like him—the barman?") is also a religious admonition ("I fear that you shall burn in a very hot fire. . . . Oh, such fire!") (*GR*, 39–40). This trans Satan, like its biblical precursors, speaks with a forked tongue. The flaming that is a sign of queer flamboyance is also the hellfire of its enjoyment. Beyond the moral impasse, this double bind exposes the duplicity of postlapsarian language: not a generative plenitude but a paralyzing recoil through which adjacent meanings contaminate each other. This duplicity, which offers neither the suggestiveness of a pre-symbolic humming nor the stability of a patriarchal symbolic, is concentrated in a feminized figure of gender fluidity that undermines the sexual binary.

The rite of passage through the bar's "gloomy tunnel" leads to the knowledge of entrapment within an inhospitably ambiguous universe. There is no way back to an Edenic innocence. Indeed, as David reminds us, it is a "flaming sword" that bars the return to an Eden created through acts of binary division that culminate in sexual difference (*GR*, 25). At the other end of this passageway, and of the chapter that describes it, is an image of entrapment that doubles as its performance: Giovanni with the tunnel's dim light "trapped around his head" (*GR*, 63). The phrase refuses either to yield or to dispel the desired word *wrapped*, which we would expect (as well as desire) in the conjunction of light and head, from the rhyming but undermining *trapped* that evokes and excludes it. Whether as Satanic duplicity or Adamic transparency (which coexist in the text, as in the Garden of Eden), language in *Giovanni's Room* is always already rigged against the queer. Whether it serves heteronormative divisions or their collapse, the passage through the bar investigates what happens when a vision of Creation that culminates in sexual difference is called into question by the forked tongue of the serpent.

QUEER DOMESTICITY

The trajectory from trendy Saint-Germain-des-Prés to Giovanni's room in the working-class neighborhood of Nation, so "far out. It is almost not Paris," follows a transnational as well as an economic path to a site that is both the successor and challenger to the gay bar (*GR*, 46). After routing David and Giovanni through the prevailing French version of the homophilia that began to go public in the postwar years, Baldwin brings his male couple to the room in which they confront the possibility of a shared romantic life: a prospect advanced as a subject of debate by gay rights organizations in the U.S. in the early 1950s. The August 1953 issue of a periodical called *One*, for example, was titled with the question "Homosexual Marriage?" An essay by E. B. Saunders, "Reformers' Choice: Marriage License or Just License?," suggested that "to achieve acceptance, homosexuals should demand the right to marry in order to achieve social acceptance and dignity," but then questioned whether the forfeit of sexual freedom would justify the trade-off.[127] In contrast to *Jacob's Room*'s consistently queer Hellenism, *Giovanni's Room* brings contemporaneous French and American discourses of homosexuality into an agonistic encounter in which Giovanni's openness to the American model runs into the panic the biblically inflected French variety elicits in David.

The scene of a shared life opens part 2 of *Giovanni's Room* by revisiting the Edenic promise that had been tendered by Joey's room: "In the beginning our life together held a joy and amazement which was new-born every day" (*GR*, 75). This "high beginning," as David calls it, and the figure of new birth that also hearkens back to the memory of Joey, quickly yield to premonitions of death signaled by the skull that begins to be visible beneath Giovanni's brow (*GR*, 75). David's second attempt to recruit the opening of Genesis quickly runs into the problem of gender roles: "In the beginning . . . I invented in myself a kind of pleasure in playing the housewife after Giovanni had gone to work. . . . But I am not a housewife—men never can be housewives" (*GR*, 88).

Instead of the Garden of Eden, David finds a cavern, another repetition of his night with Joey, but invested now with a gritty adult-world gloss. To prepare David for the refuse overflowing his room, Giovanni characterizes the room as a dumping grounds for "all of the garbage of this city" (*GR*, 87). David proposes the more individualized figure of regurgitation; the text offers grounds for both, tacking closer to David's version of its contents and to Giovanni's account of its location. Situated "in the back, on the ground floor of the last building on the street" at the "end of Paris," Giovanni's room, accessed through "a short, dark corridor," is a figurative toilet (*GR*, 63, 131). Amid the accumulating clutter of dirty laundry, cardboard boxes, wallpaper scrolls, unused tools, sheet music, yellowing newspapers, empty bottles, and suitcases, its only visible piece of furniture is a perpetually unmade bed at the center. Bestialized by its proximity to the zoo, feminized by its former designation as a maid's room, darkened by the thick white cleaning polish that coats its exposed ground-floor windows, Giovanni's claustral, detritus-producing room is a site of anal generativity rather than rebirth.[128]

Lest we overlook this, the hinge between the novel's two parts is the bathroom that David cleans the night before leaving the great house in the South of France in which he recalls his life with Giovanni. This house's "tiny and square" bathroom with "one frosted window" reminds him of Giovanni's claustrophobic room, from which the two of them carry packages of bricks onto the street at night (*GR*, 71). It is hard, in this context, not to read the bricks as turds. In this cloacal space, in which useless production takes the place of reproduction, waste accumulates faster than it can be evacuated. The accumulation of waste despite Giovanni's and David's efforts at disposal suggests the symbolic burden of homosexuality's association with devalued body parts.

Only at this symbolic (rather than practical) level does the interminability of David's task of cleaning Giovanni's room make sense. The room is like some Augean stable, through which the detritus of civilization passes, that would require herculean strength to empty out. Compounding this challenge is the inchoateness of a desired goal. Bricks can be taken down and strips of wallpaper torn off: an especially urgent task for wallpaper displaying the hyperbolically heteronormative pattern of "a lady in a hoop skirt and a man in knee breeches [who] perpetually walked together, hemmed by roses" (*GR*, 86). And yet David tells us that one of the walls covered with this paper "was destined never to be uncovered," as if the perpetuity in which a man and woman walk (an aestheticized version of the red-faced couple from which Jacob flees on the beach) could only be disrupted temporarily (*GR*, 86).

The real challenge is not dismantling but remodeling: How does one design queer domesticity? What are its structural foundations? Its guidelines? How much of the heteronormative model can be made to serve? How to circumvent the role of housewife that David so resents? In search of a domestic alternative to the purgatory of the bar scene, *Giovanni's Room* stages the question of gay marriage that was beginning to emerge on the pages of *One*. But whereas the journal provided a forum for debate, Baldwin's characters are on their own. Giovanni's room is insular, cut off from the larger social fabric; aside from occasional calls from Jacques, no one visits; no mail arrives. There is no social framework or services or support; the queer couple is a self-contained unit on its own in a social environment presumed to be hostile (hence the cleaning polish shielding the windows from surveillance). There are no clues about how to integrate into, tear down, or reform the social fabric. Whereas the queer bar provides a social network for single individuals, the queer couple is on its own. The deficient social framework is echoed by an absent cultural tradition. Giovanni keeps removing bricks from the wall in order to install a bookcase for David: "It was hard work, it was insane work," in which Giovanni nevertheless perseveres as if only a structural act of rebuilding would be able to construct a conceptual world that would hold David in this room (*GR*, 114). But there are too many cultural bricks to remove and too few relevant books to install. Without the classical tradition that Cambridge channels into Jacob's room, there is no foundation for an alternative to the man and woman amid the roses on one side and the sewer of civilization on the other. There is only interminable remodeling, "plaster all over everything and bricks piled on the floor" (*GR*, 71).

On the ceiling of Giovanni's room hangs a "yellow light . . . like a diseased and undefinable sex in its center" (*GR*, 88). As if written with foreknowledge of AIDS, the description of "this blunted arrow, this smashed flower of light," associates the non-procreative penis with a blighted future (*GR*, 88). Focalized through David's phobic perspective, the rendition of queer sexuality gives voice to what Baldwin characterizes as "the most insistent and the most vehement charge faced by the homosexual: he is unnatural because he has turned from his life-giving function to a union which is sterile."[129] In an echo of *Jacob's Room*, the smashed light reprises one half of the ceiling decor of Jacob's London room: the rose or ram's skull carved in wood over the doorways. In Giovanni's room, the rose has been appropriated by heterosexuality; what remains for homosexuality is a more explicitly queer version of the ram's skull that is the overdetermined sign of death in *Jacob's Room*.

Both texts are haunted by death, but *Giovanni's Room* also raises the question of the future that is held in suspension in Simeon's room. It will not be a return to the Garden of Eden, but another not-yet-visible possibility glimmers at a moment of desperation. In their final encounter, when David returns to Giovanni's room to say goodbye, Giovanni recounts the story of his earlier life with his girlfriend in their native Italian village. This is a story of failed nativity. The baby boy they conceive by the walls of their village was supposed to have grown into "a wonderful, strong man" who would embody Giovanni's future; instead, he is born dead, "all grey and twisted" (*GR*, 139). Buried in the churchyard where his father and his father's fathers are buried, the dead baby is the end of the heterosexual line that has been twisted metaphorically around his neck. This climactic end to reproductive futurity has launched Giovanni on his path to Paris as the queer new beginning of a story that unfolds according to Lee Edelman's dictum of "no future." But although the baby's death conforms to Edelman's model by dividing Giovanni's life neatly between hetero and homo phases, the sexual liberation is not into the homoerotic *jouissance* that Edelman theorizes, whose narrative locus would be the bar in which Giovanni works but does not frequent as a patron. Rather, the release from heteronormativity enables an attempt to invent a queer version of domesticity: a release into the question of "homosexual marriage" posed by the American journal *One*.

This unexplored terrain draws a theoretical crossroads in the text. Shortly after hearing the story of the dead baby, David leaves Giovanni's room for the last time, but only after confronting Giovanni with the underlying source of his resistance to imagining a shared future. "What kind of life can we have in this room—this filthy little room. What kind of life can two men have together, anyways?" (*GR*, 142). David can envision this domestic life only in heteronormative terms as a gendered division of labor that would reduce him to being Giovanni's "little *girl*," tantamount in David's view to murder (*GR*, 142, emphasis in original). Disregarding Giovanni's protests—"I am not trying to make you a little girl. If I wanted a little girl, I would be *with* a little girl"—David finally voices the bottom line that is also the novel's bottom line or fundamental question, which reprises his anguished realization with Joey: "'But I'm a man,' I cried, 'a man!' What do you think can *happen* between us?'" (*GR*, 142, emphasis in original). Rather than answering, Giovanni reconfigures the question as a space of possibility: insisting that David already knows "what can happen between us," he walks to the window that has been protectively coated with white cleaning polish and opens it. Although we don't see what is outside, we know there is fresh air because Giovanni's hair is blowing in the wind when he turns around.

This brief aperture opens a utopian moment in the novel: we can't yet see what is possible between men, but the novel insists that *something* is possible. It is a gesture that anticipates what José Esteban Muñoz, disputing Edelman's *No Future*, calls "a doing for and toward the future."[130] For the brief moment until David demands that Giovanni "Close the window"— and with it the possibility of a different life together—there is an opening toward something else, still unnameable, not quite visible, but affirmed as what Muñoz describes as "the warm illumination of a horizon imbued with potentiality."[131] The potential depends on some larger context, some exterior world whose outlines remain inchoate but whose glow of possibility, apprehended on the skin rather than discerned with the eyes, offers an alternative to the degradation of the smashed electric light or the ram's skull. Although David and Giovanni cannot invent this future on their own, Baldwin inserts it into the text as a window of possibility that, by evoking what cannot be conceived, advances what is imaginable. As the moment passes and the window is closed, the wind becomes a metaphoric force blowing David away from Giovanni's room. The weather changes; fall arrives; Giovanni murders Guillaume, is caught, imprisoned, tried, and guillotined; David and Hella leave Paris for the South of France, where Hella, after discovering the truth about David's sexuality, leaves to return to the U.S.

What, then, becomes of Muñoz's critical utopianism and the herme-
neutics of hope? Characterizing his critical practice as "a backward glance
that enacts a future vision," Muñoz contends that the seed of the future is
often planted in the past. But whereas Muñoz finds that seed in the "wow"
and "gee" of Andy Warhol and Frank O'Hara, the cultural productions of
the pre-Stonewall decades of the fifties and sixties in New York, which he
characterizes as a form of "astonished contemplation," Baldwin looks back
to the cultural production of the 1920s.[132] There he found, beyond the horizon of *Jacob's Room*, the novelistic future it anticipates: Woolf's next novel,
her own novelistic breakthrough, through which she discovered what she
called her "queer" design: a word with a different yet not entirely unrelated
meaning of a skewed relation to narrative convention.[133] Rather than a solution to the social problem of queer domesticity, *Mrs. Dalloway* suggests a
formal strategy for envisioning a future not chained to the past. In addition
to the Clarissa/Septimus dynamic, the nonlinear design of *Mrs. Dalloway*
models a way to subsume a death-bound plot within a form that could enable a release from it. Between the action and narration of *Giovanni's Room*,
between the closing of the window in Giovanni's room and the closing of
the text of *Giovanni's Room*, is the retrospective gaze from a house in the
South of France that concludes with the rising of dawn. This intervention,
this turn to the literary past as a "field of possibility . . . in the service of a
new futurity," asks us to turn our critical gaze from the queer Parisian room
of the action of *Giovanni's Room* to the "great house" in the South of France
that is the site of its narration.[134]

THE GREAT HOUSE

It took some work for Baldwin to situate the rural site of David's retrospective narration in relation to the site of the narrative action, since David doesn't arrive at the house in the South of France until after Hella's
return from Spain precipitates his exit from Giovanni's room. The "Publisher's Mss." opens, for the first time, in the "great house" as the seat of
David's consciousness; and subsequent drafts document the transposition
of textual chunks in ways that sharpen the distinction between the multichambered country house that accommodates what Baldwin elsewhere
describes as the "antechambers of consciousness" and the linear drive of
the narrative action that tracks Giovanni's "short road ending in a common
knife" (*GR*, 153).[135]

Architecturally underdetermined but culturally overdetermined, the
"great house" in the South of France—actually a two-bedroom rental property under the watchful eyes of an Italian caretaker across the street—points

to a distinctively British legacy. The phrase, for starters, has no equivalent in French; the closest counterpart would probably be "villa," but despite the fact that Baldwin wrote a significant portion of *Giovanni's Room* in the Villa Lou Fougau near Grasse in the South of France, this is not the word he chose to describe the novel's site of narration. Nor, conversely, did he use the phrase "great house" to characterize the eighteenth-century stone house in Saint-Paul-de-Vence that became his home and writing refuge for the last seventeen years of his life; known among locals as "Chez Baldwin" or "Chez Jimmy," that intimate yet capacious space was simply "the spread" in Baldwin's own parlance.[136] Within *Giovanni's Room*, the house is loosely planted on French soil in an unnamed village that lacks the vivid particulars of the Swiss village Baldwin describes in detail in "A Stranger in the Village." Primarily a container that seems almost devoid of household belongings despite the fact that we see it through the eyes of the inventory-taking caretaker, the "great house" offers evidence of partial habitation only in the tangled sheets and rumpled clothes of the guest room in which David sleeps after Hella's departure. If an obvious formal question to which *Giovanni's Room* seeks a response is how the "great house" of fiction could more fully accommodate the queer bedroom, a more subtle literary historical question is how the provenance of the architectural trope inflects the text's cultural geography.

As Virginia Woolf explains in her essay "American Fiction," "The English tradition is formed upon a little country; its centre is an old house with many rooms."[137] By contrast to this singularity, which remains remarkably consistent across historical and architectural variations, America's social and geographic diversity has generated a spectrum of symbolic houses that run from lonely cabins to Gothic mansions.[138] For Baldwin, however, the "American House"—the phrase he uses instead of "great house" everywhere except for *Giovanni's Room*—is also singular: an inescapably racialized "house of bondage" (the title of an essay he wrote for the *Nation* in 1980) he paid a high price to inhabit: "If I am part of the American House, and I am, it is because my ancestors paid—*striving to make it my home*—so unimaginable a price."[139] In *Giovanni's Room*, the phrase "great house" is both anomalous and insistent, a conscious or unconscious signal of a different cultural landscape in which the "great" or "country" house has an enduring symbolic legacy quite different from the house in which Baldwin imagines himself sitting in part 1 of *Nobody Knows My Name*.[140]

Henry James's trope of the "house of fiction" is grounded in the English tradition. Woolf made abundant use of the English house tradition as well, most conspicuously in *Orlando*, to which we will return in a later chapter. Relevant here is the notion and nomenclature of the great house as a narrative holding space, a figure that emerged gradually for, and as a bridge between, Woolf and Baldwin. Reviewing the narrative breakthrough she achieved in *Mrs. Dalloway*, Woolf described her dissatisfaction with the conventional literary "house": "The novel was the obvious lodging, but the novel it seemed was built on the wrong plan. Thus rebuked the idea started as the oyster starts or the snail to secrete a house for itself."[141] That new house was constructed via the narrative "design" of her famous "tunneling process." In the course of composing *Giovanni's Room*, Baldwin discovered his own tunneling process, through which he converted the narrow room of queer male sexuality and the anal tunnels of queer male sociality into a commodious space of reflection. Aided, perhaps, by the 1953 publication of Woolf's *A Writer's Diary*, which contains her reflections on designing *Mrs. Dalloway*, Baldwin began to reconfigure his own narrative design.

In a note penciled into the typescript titled "The Only Pretty Ring Time" (February 13, 1954), Baldwin wrote that the action takes place "on the surface" in a single day: "morning to very early morn."[142] The formula maps precisely onto the time frame of *Mrs. Dalloway*. Gradually adapted to the nighttime tonalities better suited than Clarissa's day in June to David's somber confession, this breakthrough played the condensed temporality of David's narration against the longer duration of Giovanni's story. Running from David's evening "reflection in the darkening gleam of the window pane" to his fading reflection the next morning in the same windowpane, the narration opens into a Woolfian cave of memory (*GR*, 3).

The fundamental breakthrough, the decision to enfold the story of Giovanni within David's retrospective narration, coincides with the decision to locate the narration in a great house in the South of France. Through a restructuring that makes David's consciousness the vehicle that subsumes the room of the story to the house of its narration, the American author constructs a British-inflected (Jamesian, Woolfian) novelistic structure as the container of a queer Parisian story. This way of enacting the theoretical proposition that "homosexuality is a closed and withdrawn place that is transformed into a redeeming space" resolves the narrative impasse produced by incompatible queer national and personal psychologies by assimilating them to a whole and entire narrative form designed to conclude with the break of a new day.[143]

This conclusion is achieved through the most emotionally exacting and transformative version of the Clarissa/Septimus dynamic. David's imaginative experience of Giovanni's death follows the Woolfian model closely. Both David and Clarissa receive word of a violent death from a secondary source (Jacques's letter, Dr. Bradshaw's report), after which they retreat to a solitary site of reflection where they undergo a cathartic reenactment that yields some acceptance of their lives and deepens their capacity to greet the future. For both, the imagined death is visceral and violent and focuses on the impact of hitting the ground. David imagines Giovanni's fall in the present tense: "Then the door opens and he stands alone, the whole world falling away from him. . . . Then the earth tilts, he is thrown forward on his face in darkness, and his journey begins" (*GR*, 168). Unlike Clarissa's effortless reception of Septimus's offering, however, David experiences Giovanni's execution as a baptism in sweat, an embrace of bodily corruption that enables him to accept what stinks as a medium of revelation. No easy redemption, this is a grave embodiment, "scoured with the salt" of David's life and burdened with mortality and sexuality (*GR*, 169).

Replacing the Old Testament's judgmental language, the redemptive stance of the New Testament, represented by the figure of the Virgin, brings a spiritualized feminine presence to bear on this final scene. For the first time in this text, femininity assumes a positive because disembodied form. As he imagines the preparations for Giovanni's execution, David hears an instruction that hovers in some indeterminate space between an internal voice and that of Giovanni's priest, telling him to "*Take off your clothes . . . , it's getting late*" (*GR*, 167, emphasis in original). After imagining Giovanni being dragged down the stairs into "the heart of the prison," David pictures him in the office of the priest, where "he kneels. A candle burns, the Virgin watches him" (*GR*, 167). Framed between two iterations of Giovanni's prayer, "*Mary, blessed mother of God*," David summons the courage to look at his own naked body trapped in his bedroom mirror: "dull and white and dry" and, like Giovanni's, "under sentence of death." Under the icon of the Virgin Mary, the bodies of David and Giovanni draw close (*GR*, 168, emphasis in original).

The feminine figure of grace in the "heart" of Giovanni's prison, a figure whose invocation frames the inscription of David's body at the site of Giovanni's passion, seems to bless the union of the two men, or at least to enable David to experience their mutual embodiment at the moment of Giovanni's death. Although David will survive, Giovanni's physical impression lingers in the "dreadful weight of hope" David feels as he walks out of the house the next morning, burdened not only with the knowledge of mortality, but also with the memory of another man's body (*GR*, 169).

The feminine can be a form of grace: a spiritual or aesthetic form. Although echoes of Woolf's texts were attenuated during the composition of *Giovanni's Room* as the dead girl morphed into the dead boy, perhaps like Mary her immaterial presence lingers in the novel's form. "I suspect," Baldwin wrote in a late essay, "though I certainly can't prove it, that every life moves full circle—toward revelation: You begin to see, and even rejoice to see, what you always saw."[144] Anticipated by David's apprehension that the mystery residing in his body "hurries toward revelation," the move toward revelation is both a religious and an aesthetic mandate (*GR*, 168). By bringing David's narrative full circle, allowing him to see what had always been there, Baldwin confers a version of Woolfian plenitude on his text: the circular form of *Mrs. Dalloway*; the "globed, compacted things" extolled by Lily Briscoe; the "silver globe" of life that Woolf wanted to take in her hands and feel it "quietly, round, smooth, heavy. & so hold it, day after day."[145]

Is Woolf then hidden behind or an implicit secular backdrop to the figure of the Virgin Mary, an immanent textual presence legible only in the novel's form? As Baldwin declares about the circular form of life, I suspect but certainly can't prove it. Nor can we determine David's future. As he closes the door on his night of reckoning and heads down the road toward the bus stop, he embarks on an uncertain trajectory as the sky is "awakening," and the horizon "is beginning to flame" (*GR*, 169). By summoning the vexed verb of queerness in this text (*flame*), Baldwin leaves David's future radically unknown but gives us reason to hope that in this context it signals Muñoz's "warm illumination of a horizon imbued with potentiality."

LAST ROOMS

Our final view of Jacob's room reveals that he has died in the war. It also lets us know that Bonamy has replaced Jacob's brother, the more plausible companion to help Jacob's bereaved mother sort through her son's belongings, by repeating Archer's childhood cry for his always already absent brother. The repetition with a difference—Jacob has died and his closest mourner is not his next of kin but the "dark horse" of a friend with a "peculiar disposition"—brings the novel to a full but empty circle (*JR*, 163). As Bonamy crosses to the window before uttering his cry for Jacob, his gesture anticipates the window of possibility that Giovanni opens in his room during his last desperate encounter with David. The wind is blowing in both scenarios: it lifts Giovanni's hair and the leaves on the street outside Jacob's room. After Bonamy's call for Jacob is disseminated into the world by a "harsh and unhappy voice [that] cried something unintelligible" in the street outside, "suddenly all the leaves seemed to raise themselves. 'Jacob! Jacob!' cried Bonamy, standing by the window. The leaves sank down again" (*JR*, 186–87). To know that cry's final destination, we would have to be able to read the leaves, whose message may be as unintelligible as the anonymous voice, but that the future is at stake and that it will run through odd rather than obvious affinities is suggested by Jacob's mother as she turns to Bonamy in the text's closing lines:

> Bonamy turned away from the window.
> "What am I to do with these, Mr. Bonamy?"
> She held out a pair of Jacob's old shoes. (*JR*, 187)

If it would be too much to say that Baldwin's David inherits Jacob's shoes—a trope better suited to more conventional genealogies—the wind that blows intermittently but at critical junctures through these texts affiliates them more loosely and idiosyncratically. In its final appearance at the end of *Giovanni's Room*, the wind flaunts its capriciousness. Walking toward the morning bus that will carry him away from the great house in the South of France toward some unknown destiny, David shreds the letter in which Jacques has informed him of Giovanni's execution and watches the wind carry the pieces of paper away. As he turns, however, the wind blows some of those fragments back on him: the past, literary and personal, cannot be so readily dispatched.

Echoing the scene in *Passing* in which Irene shreds a letter from Clare, which doubles as a missive from *Mrs. Dalloway*, the conclusion of *Giovanni's Room* resumes a larger trajectory: the fugitive paths of the metaphoric letters that interleave Woolf with African American modernism. With this culminating instance, our framework pivots to the darker terrain of late twentieth-century Europe. Odd Woolfian affinities continue to leave their subtle yet revealing traces, but the modes and lines of transmission change. Letters, with their individual signatures and addressees, their presumption of language's communicative power, and their enclosure in envelopes that indicate a legible interiority, yield to more diffuse, fluid, and collective modes of transmission. European philosophical discourses— phenomenology, psychoanalysis, and cultural materialism (to name only the most salient)—also come into play in new ways. In conversation with these discourses, Woolf's signature tropes assume new forms. The figure of the multichambered house of fiction acquires an increasingly urgent but precarious appeal as a stay against the turbulence of European history. And as the weight of the past signaled by the wind's final turn in *Giovanni's Room* assumes greater complexity and force, the cave of memory that had offered a refuge from the tyranny of time threatens to engulf, haunt, or paralyze— while still offering to enliven—the present.

∴

Part Two

WOOLF'S REFUGE IN LATE EUROPEAN MODERNISM

∵

[CHAPTER THREE]

Light Rooms

Virginia Woolf, Roland Barthes, and the
Mediums of Maternal Mourning

I like going from one lighted room to another, such is my brain to me; lighted rooms.

Virginia Woolf, *The Diary of Virginia Woolf*

It is a mistake to associate Photography, by reason of its technical origins, with the notion of a dark passage (*camera obscura*). It is *camera lucida* that we should say.

Roland Barthes, *Camera Lucida*

Although it may seem counterintuitive to associate Woolf with Larsen and Baldwin, their shared language, engagement with modernist aesthetics, and formal exploration of narrative closure secured by a violent, untimely but ultimately recuperable death formed common ground that extended across national, racial, and class differences. This foundation, and the narrative forms developed to accommodate it, dissolve when we turn to our pair of late European authors, who are engaged less with negotiating a narrative and social space for the dissident individual than with navigating the dark passages of visual technology and historical decline.

The insistence of a past that can be depressingly present or mournfully absent (or some combination of both) makes the backward-turning but formally inventive *To the Lighthouse* the salient (but not ony) Woolfian reference point. Some paradoxes attend this affinity. Looking backward through the optic of the nuclear family (as *To the Lighthouse, Camera Lucida*, and *Austerlitz* all do) rather than forward (like *Giovanni's Room*) toward a queer futurity would seem to be an intrinsically conservative gesture at odds with formal innovation. Thematically, however, the intensely matricentric focus of all three texts puts pressure on the nuclear family and its psychoanalytic underpinnings, calling into question the necessity of the paternal function, depathologizing the mother/son dyad and the modes of mourning incited by its loss, and counterpointing the biological mother with a figurative surrogate who opens a space for a shadow genealogy. Formally, the challenge of reckoning with an ambivalent, maternally coded past disrupts the boundaries of medium and genre.

Since for Barthes and Sebald, the warm illumination that Carlos Muñoz discerned from the future emerges (if at all) only from a past that also threatens its transmission, the search for alternative modes of expression extends to nonverbal mediums. The visual arts function in *Camera Lucida* and *Austerlitz*, as in *To the Lighthouse*, as literal and figurative vehicles of affects that travel beneath the surfaces of words. Rendering the absent presence of the past, however, is also a narrative project that prompted nonfiction writers such Barthes and Sebald to attempt to remake themselves as novelists and thereby to open a potential link to Woolf.

As the only writer in this study to write (in German) in England, Sebald was most attuned to a Woolfian genealogy. His final (and arguably only) novel is thus the overdetermined endpoint of this inquiry, which begins with Barthes's late turn to the novel. Although Barthes depicts this overtly as a turn to Proust, it opens up covertly shared terrain with Woolf as well. In *À la recherche du temps perdu*, *Camera Lucida*, and *To the Lighthouse*, the transformative event that launches the writing of the novel is the death of the mother. After examining the sites at which Barthes signals his awareness of Woolf's work, this chapter turns to a comparative reading of the two pairs of texts in which they both struggle to come to terms with the death of their mothers: "A Sketch of the Past" and *To the Lighthouse* for Woolf; *Mourning Diary* and *Camera Lucida* for Barthes. Challenging psychoanalytic and literary orthodoxies, this hybrid quartet questions the presumption of elegy's linguistic medium and the hierarchical ranking of mourning and melancholia. Collectively, although in different ways, these texts bring into the open a photographic discourse of light that illuminates an obscured third psychoanalytic term associated with both maternal presence and maternal death: mania. By concluding with the recovery of mania as a mode of mourning instead of a pathology, this chapter disrupts—perhaps we could say *queers*—the binary of healthy and unhealthy mourning that has shaped our paradigm of grief.

Proust's Mediation

On October 19, 1978, one year after his mother's death, Roland Barthes delivered a lecture on Proust in which he announced a new direction for his own writerly practice. Writing himself into Proust's masterwork by choosing its opening line as his title, "Longtemps, je me suis couché de bonne heure . . . ," Barthes reconstitutes himself as a novelist, remaking his authorial identity as he saw Proust remaking *his* in the aftermath of his own mother's death in 1905.[1] It is a radical turn exacted by a radical loss that compels both writers to renounce "the way of the Essay (of Criticism)," on which Proust had embarked in *Contre Sainte-Beuve*, a path that "argue(s) theory," "traumatizes or desiccates affect," and "has difficulty acknowledging *pathos* as a force of our reading," for "the way of the Novel," "that uncertain, quite uncanonical Form" whose "power is the truth of affects, not of ideas" (L, 278–79, 289). This new form summons Barthes as a way to break with the "uniformly intellectual nature" of his previous writings, a rupture necessitated for him, as for Proust, by a "unique and somehow irreducible bereavement" that makes the linear trajectory of "literary science" unacceptable: "What! Until my death, to be writing articles, giving courses, lectures, on 'subjects' which alone will vary, and so little! . . . I see my future, until death, as a series. . . . Can this be all?" (L, 289, 286, 287). Taking his lead from Proust, whose quest for "a form which will accommodate suffering (he has just experienced it in an absolute form through his mother's death) and transcend it" leads to his creation of "*a third form*," Barthes declares his allegiance to "the *intimate* which seeks utterance in me, seeks to make its cry heard, confronting generality, confronting science" (L, 279, 280, 284).

This forking of paths constitutes, for Barthes, the midpoint of a life. Positioning himself firmly in a literary (rather than critical) lineage, he begins the second half of his essay with the opening line of Dante's *Commedia*, "*Nel mezzo del camin di nostra vita . . .*" (L, 284). This "middle of our lives," Barthes explains, is a "semantic point" rather than "an arithmetical point"; it is the moment, whenever it occurs, when there is "the summons of a new meaning, the desire for a mutation: to change lives, to break off and to begin, to submit . . . to an initiation, as Dante made his way into the *selva oscura*, led by a great initiator, Virgil" (L, 284). Virgil, Dante, Proust, Barthes: the lineage accords maternal death the gravitas of the breaking point that launches an epic quest through the dark space of the self out of which a new life might emerge. For a writer, that new life could only be "a new practice of writing," a practice on which Barthes embarked most boldly in his notes toward the text he called his *Vita Nova*, the novel on which he worked in the last years of his life and which he considered "a radical gesture: (discontinuous—necessity of discontinuing what previously continued on its own momentum)."[2]

Since for Barthes, as for Proust, "the 'middle of life's journey' was certainly his mother's death" (L, 286), the absence of literary mothers in his genealogy is striking, especially the absence of Proust's most ardent British fan and heir. More explicitly than Proust, Virginia Woolf placed the death of the mother in the narrative lacuna that constitutes the midpoint of *To the Lighthouse*, the novel that "expressed some very long felt and deeply felt emotion" about her mother (Sketch, 81). Not an arithmetical middle of her own life any more than of Barthes's—at ages thirteen and almost sixty-three when their mothers died, they were nearer to opposite poles of the life spectrum—maternal death is the "semantic point" that hollows out the dark corridor of "Time Passes" that divides and connects the two narrative portions of Woolf's autobiographical novel. The lure of Woolf that beckons just below the surface of Barthes's late texts was masked as well as mediated by their shared admiration of Proust.[3]

Immersed in reading Proust for most of her career, Woolf pronounced him "far the greatest modern novelist."[4] Her admiration was not without anxiety. "Oh if I could write like that!" she cried upon her first reading. "And at the moment such is the astonishing vibration and saturation and intensification that he procures—theres [*sic*] something sexual in it—that I feel I *can* write like that, and seize my pen and then I *can't* write like that. Scarcely anyone so stimulates the nerves of language in me: it becomes an obsession."[5] Only after publishing *To the Lighthouse*, and perhaps because of that novel's thematic and stylistic resonance with Proust, did Woolf gain the confidence to read him with equanimity. As she began to envision *The Waves* in terms that echo her earliest appreciation of Proust's style—"What I want now to do is to saturate every atom"—she came to view him as a model for eliminating "this appalling narrative business of the realist: getting on from lunch to dinner": "I should like to take the globe [of life] in my hands & feel it quietly, round, smooth, heavy. & so hold it day after day. I will read Proust I think. I will go backwards & forwards."[6] This backward and forward, this englobing of time, this affective saturation and dilation of the moment, suggested a way for Woolf to move beyond the linear plot of the novel. Whereas Proust modeled a path toward the novel for Barthes the critic, he modeled a path for Woolf the novelist to move toward the affective intensity of lyric. In language that seems to reach out unconsciously to Woolf, Barthes associates this intensity with "the recognition of *pathos*"—especially the *pathos* of grief—that is located in "moments of truth" that have "nothing to do with 'realism'" and that have been "absent from every theory of the novel" (L, 287).[7] From their different starting points, Woolf and Barthes follow Proust's guidance to a genre that escapes or exceeds conventional designations: for Woolf the closest name for this genre is "elegy."[8]

Proust, Woolf, and Barthes are the signal maternal elegists of the twentieth century, but Proust's more visible association with the other two along the established lines of literary history (with Woolf) and national tradition (with Barthes) has obscured a more oblique affiliation between Woolf and

Barthes that cuts across the boundaries of periodization and nation, gender and genre. Although there is little evidence of direct transmission between Barthes and Woolf, Barthes does gesture occasionally and evasively to her, nowhere more provocatively than in his quasi citation in the margin of his notes for his lecture series "Preparation of the Novel" at the Collège de France from 1978 to 1980. In a seminar on "the internal story of the man who wants to write" (December 19, 1979), Barthes explains: "This man—my not especially heroic hero—will obviously be a composite man, a pseudonymic man, for he'll have several proper names: he'll be called, in turn, Flaubert, Kafka, Rousseau, Mallarmé, Tolstoy, Proust—and . . . he'll also be called: *me* →"[9] Displaced from her (chrono)logical place in this sequence (following Proust), Woolf's name appears instead in a marginal reference to "Woolf, Seuil, 65" (171). Tracking this reference leads to *L'art du roman* (1963), the French translation of several of Woolf's essays on the novel, and specifically to "Mr. Bennett and Mrs. Brown" (1924), where Woolf meditates on some of the recent manifestations of her imaginary character, Mrs. Brown: "Ulysses, Queen Victoria, Mr. Prufrock—to give Mrs. Brown some of the names she has made famous lately."[10] Barthes transposes what Woolf predicts will be "one of the great ages of English literature" into a lineage of mostly French, mostly nineteenth-century, and entirely male authors.[11] The elusive Mrs. Brown—whose challenge to the modern novelist is "catch me if you can"—has morphed into the European canon. Should we read this as a straightforward appropriation of Woolf or as a sly intertextual wink that transports her from the status of descendant to that of source? Barthes's hallmark playfulness inclines me toward the latter. "Catch me if you can" teases the author of "The Death of the Author," as he teases us in his 1975 pseudo autobiography, *Roland Barthes by Roland Barthes*, whose opening instruction is "It must all be considered as if spoken by a character in a novel": an instruction reminiscent of Woolf's proposal in *A Room of One's Own* that "'I' is only a convenient term for somebody who has no real being."[12] If "books continue one another," as Woolf proposes in *A Room of One's Own* (79), we must tease out the continuity in this case by pursuing hints, echoes, resonances, silences, and ellipses, starting with Woolf's cameo appearance in Barthes's maternal elegy.

Victoria's Secret (What a Novel!)

Of the twenty-four photographs in the body of *Camera Lucida* (the frontispiece is explicitly set apart), one stands out in several ways: George Washington Wilson's 1863 portrait of Queen Victoria at Balmoral mounted astride her horse Fyvie, whose bridle is held by the queen's faithful servant John Brown. The queen and her horse are shown in profile against a blank white background: this is the outline of majesty beyond its empirical grounding.[13] This is the only photograph of a monarch or national leader, the only one of or by a British subject, the only one with a history of usage as a carte de visite, and—most importantly—the only one not captioned with a passage from *Camera Lucida*. The portrait of Queen Victoria, unlike all the other photographs (including many by American photographers), is captioned in English—the only words of English in the French text—in words attributed not to Roland Barthes but to Virginia Woolf: "'*Queen Victoria, entirely unaesthetic* . . .' (Virginia Woolf)" (fig. 3).[14] Here, England slips into *Camera Lucida* through the antithetical personae of Virginia Woolf and Queen Victoria. Adopting Barthes's own terms, we might call this a textual *punctum*, that contingent, wayward, inassimilable detail that suddenly "rises from the scene, shoots out of it, like an arrow that pierces me. . . . That accident which pricks me (but also bruises me, is poignant to me)" and "overwhelms the entirety of my reading" (*CL*, 26–27, 49). Or, adopting Woolf's language, we could call it a piece of "foreign matter" that is conspicuously "unconsumed" (*AROO*, 58), even that "(Virginia Woolf)" is the name of foreign matter in the text by Roland Barthes, the parenthetical space of a potential but exorbitant genealogy (*CL*, 56).

Barthes encountered the photograph (along with several others he reproduced in *Camera Lucida*) in the November 1977 "Spécial Photo" issue of the *Nouvel observateur*, where it is one of the photographs chosen to illustrate the French translation of excerpts from Walter Benjamin's 1931 essay "A Short History of Photography."[15] He almost certainly discovered Woolf's comment (from her diary entry December 27, 1930) in Monique Nathan's *Virginia Woolf par elle-même*, a compendium of excerpts from Woolf's work, biographical information, and photographs that appeared in 1956 as part of the Éditions de Seuil's series "Écrivains de Toujours": the same series in which the self-consciously parodic *Roland Barthes par Roland Barthes* appeared nineteen years later. Perhaps Woolf also enters *Camera Lucida* as a guilty reflex or symptom of her conspicuous absence from an essay Barthes had just completed on the diary as an ambiguously literary form, in which he discusses the literary journals of Kafka, Gide, and Mallarmé.[16] Woolf finds a voice instead in the liminal space of the caption (as she had in the margins of his lecture notes) that negotiates between photograph and text. Captions, Barthes tells us in "The Rhetoric of the Image" (1961), either anchor the meaning of an image or propel it into other associative circuits; here, conspicuously at odds with the text's linguistic fabric, the

FIGURE 3. Roland Barthes, "'*Queen Victoria, entirely unaesthetic . . .*'
(Virginia Woolf)." "Queen Victoria on 'Fyvie' with John Brown, Balmoral"
(1863). © His Majesty King Charles III 2022. Photograph: Courtesy of the
Royal Collection Trust. Photograph by George Washington Wilson.

caption locates the portrait of Queen Victoria only as a site of contestation between disruption and continuity.

As a caption, Woolf's verdict on the queen, whose letters she had been reading, offers a comment on the blanketing force of the conventions that Victoria, and her portrait, emblematize. The queen, Woolf concludes, "knew her own mind. But the mind radically commonplace, only its inherited force, & cumulative sense of power, making it remarkable."[17] This inherited force of the commonplace, this body of cultural consensus, derived from a common education and social formation, sanctions the dulling mode of photographic reading that Barthes associates with what he calls the *studium*. Within this photograph, Barthes locates the *studium* in Queen Victoria's skirt, "suitably draping the entire animal (this is the historical interest, the *studium*)" (*CL*, 57). Victoria's skirt, that is, not only constitutes a site of historical interest (in clothing styles, codes of decorum, gender roles, etc.), but also illustrates how these generic categories function to cover an entire field (as emphasized in the English translation), draping particulars, especially those that might provoke particular curiosity or excitement (*CL*, 91). It is this homogenizing cover, Barthes suggests through Woolf, that is "entirely unaesthetic," or entirely contrary to the aesthetic of *Camera Lucida* and its narrator, whose stance is that of a "primitive" before and beyond the cultural codes through which (due in large measure to Barthes's influence) photography is customarily "read" (*CL*, 51).[18] In fact, despite its seemingly adventitious entrée to Barthes's text—"Here is Queen Victoria," the narrator casually announces as if the queen had just trotted into his study to pay a social call—this photograph arguably instantiates what he describes somewhat ambiguously as "the Victorian nature (what else can one call it?) of the photograph"—or, less redundantly, of photography itself ("la photographie" could be either) as a medium that not only developed in tandem with Victoria's reign (her ascension to the throne coinciding almost exactly with the first announcement of the daguerreotype process), but that also continues to bear her imprint through the authority of the cultural codes that govern its interpretation (*CL*, 57).

Against this Victorian inheritance, Barthes recruits Woolf to, indeed constitutes her as, a performance of the unruly *punctum*, a modernist protest against the blanketing force of Victorian conventions. Within the photograph, Barthes locates the *punctum* in the "quilted groom [who] holds the horse's bridle." The groom's function is "to supervise the horse's behavior: what if the horse suddenly began to rear? What would happen to the queen's skirt, *i.e.*, to *her majesty*?" (*CL*, 57, emphasis in original). Within this carefully staged and static photograph, Barthes detects both a visual allusion to the founding gesture of civilization, the assertion of human hegemony over the animal kingdom, and the possibility of its disruption, associated with the text's broader project of freeing the photographic medium from its domestication by a "society [that] is concerned to tame the Photograph, to temper the madness" (*CL*, 117). If the groom's hands relaxed their grip on the bridle of culture—and we might note how frequently hands attract Barthes's attention in *Camera Lucida* as the body part that either serves or breaks with service to social demands to engage in pleasures (touching, piercing, weaving, writing) at the intersection of the erotic and aesthetic— what kind of topsy-turvy saturnalian horseplay might ensue (Barthes's equestrian expression in the French text is *caracoler*)?[19] We can easily envision Woolf joining imaginatively in these insurrectionary capers, given her propensity to unseat figures of authority from their saddles, especially in the context represented by Queen Victoria as Empress of India: Percival tumbling from his horse in India in *The Waves*, or the narrator's maiden aunt from hers, to the narrator's economic gain, in *A Room of One's Own*. But although a shared destabilizing bent aligns these writers under the aegis of the *punctum*, figured as a horse cavorting with the norms of gender and genre, status and sexuality, a less obvious and playful alliance comes into view through a related set of terms that are also introduced at this juncture in the text.

Barthes's commentary on "Queen Victoria, 1863" intervenes between his discussion of two pairs of contrasting terms: still photography and cinema, and erotic and pornographic images. Spanning these contrasts—and elaborated on the page facing this photograph—is his concept of the "blind field" (*champs aveugle*) that in cinema "constantly doubles our partial vision" of the characters through the lives we project beyond the frame, but that is usually absent from still photography, whose subjects "do not *emerge*, do not *leave*: they are anesthetized and fastened down, like butterflies" (*CL*, 57, emphasis in original). When a *punctum* is galvanized through the chain of associations triggered by a visual detail, however, "a blind field is created (is divined)" that transports the viewer to a space outside the photographic frame (*CL*, 57). The blind field is a narrative off-frame, a novelistic elaboration of the still image, a hypothetical space in which Barthes can indulge his novelistic desires: indeed, he indulges them in precisely these terms regarding Ernest, a schoolboy photographed by André Kertész in 1931: "It is possible that Ernest is still alive today: but where? how? What a novel!" (*CL*, 83).[20]

Barthes's novelistic desire, awakened by the death of his mother, awaits the reader's intervention in the blind field between Woolf's words and Wilson's image. As with Proust, Barthes uses citation to open a novelistic space, but whereas in "Longtemps, je me suis couché de bonne heure . . . ,"

Barthes writes himself seamlessly into Proust's narrative world by claiming the novel's celebrated opening line as his title, in *Camera Lucida* his citation of Woolf's unfamiliar words in an untranslated tongue points the reader toward a space he invites us to fill in ("but where? how? what a novel!" we might respond). For although Barthes ends his citations of both Proust and Woolf with ellipses, as he does in most of the captions in *Camera Lucida*, the passage from Woolf is the only one whose ending we don't already know. The text proposes one way to uncover the field cloaked by Victoria's skirt in the photograph that follows, Robert Mapplethorpe's "Young Man with Arm Extended," the only image of a naked torso—and a beautiful, youthful masculine torso—different in every way from the cloaked figure of Queen Victoria. This uncloaking offers a climactic eruption of the erotic that is augured by the prancing of the unbridled horse. But this photograph is placed just before the crucial juncture in *Camera Lucida*: the turning point at which the narrator, like Proust, breaks from his former path and makes his "recantation": "I would have to descend deeper into myself," veering from "desire" to the intertwining of "love and death" (*CL*, 60) ("l'amour et la mort" in *La chambre claire*, 115).

There is another "novel" to be written about Virginia Woolf and Roland Barthes that uncovers another body also cloaked by the queen's dark robes. This is the body of death rather than of love—not exactly the dead body, but the social body of assumptions, emotions, and conventions that comprise the field of mourning that dominates the second half of *Camera Lucida*. The encounter between Barthes and Woolf at the site of Queen Victoria heralds this descent into mourning. Queen Victoria is the icon of interminable, unrelenting mourning. Photographed by Wilson two years after Prince Albert's death, on the second anniversary of their last joint "Great Expedition" into the Highlands, the queen looks soberly at the camera, wearing the somber clothing she continued to wear throughout the forty years between Prince Albert's death and her own. Remembered "for her seemingly never-ending old age: her years of mourning, her black dress, her dour expression, her iconic stature," she blankets the affective field, as she does the horse, with a self-imposed set of formulaic practices.[21] Cloaked here are the particulars not of the erotic body (whether of the generic "animal" or of Mapplethorpe's young man), but the individual lineaments of grief: that intensely personal and socially monitored experience of loss.

What lies underneath the queen's cloak is a question posed by Woolf, who was subjected to the Victorian regulation of mourning after her mother's death in 1895. In "A Sketch of the Past," she recalls the "shrouded, cautious, dulled life" of covered windows and "muffled voices," of "unbroken black" clothing and of notepaper "so black bordered that only a little space for writing remained" (94). In the place of "merry, various family life . . . a dark cloud settled over us; we seemed to sit all together cooped up, sad, solemn, unreal, under a haze of heavy emotion. It seemed impossible to break through. It was not merely dull; it was unreal. A finger seemed laid on one's lips" (Sketch, 93). Three-quarters of a century later, Barthes confronted a different set of protocols, as Victorian social codes gave way to a psychoanalytic regime that imposed the "work of mourning" as a form of affective labor. "Don't say *Mourning*. It's too psychoanalytic. I'm not *mourning*. I'm suffering," Barthes protested a month after his mother's death.[22] The finger had been lifted from one's lips, but the language was still scripted.

Victoria and Freud: variously aligned under the sign of *eros*, conjoined here under the cloak of *thanatos*. Peeling back that cloak, as Woolf and Barthes both do, to illuminate more tenuous affective fluctuations requires us to read across their work, divining the "novel" toward which *Camera Lucida* gestures. If the critical project that elicits this story appears novelistic, however, the mode in which Barthes and Woolf both work is elegiac. Both elaborate this mode across two different kinds of texts; the richness of their individual projects, and the resonance between them, derive from this internal dialogue. In each case, the acclaimed centerpiece was written in a rush, a sudden outpouring after a delay (several decades longer on Woolf's part) that was supplemented by more personal reflections. Woolf's retrospective account is legendary:

> It is perfectly true that she [her mother] obsessed me, in spite of the fact that she died when I was thirteen, until I was forty-four. Then one day walking round Tavistock Square I made up, as I sometimes make up my books, *To the Lighthouse*; in a great, apparently involuntary, rush. One thing burst into another. . . . Blowing bubbles out of a pipe gives the feeling of the rapid crowd of ideas and scenes which blew out of my mind, so that my lips seemed syllabling of their own accord as I walked. I wrote the book very quickly; and when it was written, I ceased to be obsessed by mother. I no longer hear her voice; I do not see her.
>
> I suppose that I did for myself what psycho-analysts do for their patients. (Sketch, 81)

When the finger is lifted from the lips in this instance, the mind blows bubbles through a pipe (a submerged allusion to elegy, perhaps), a seemingly effortless effusion that eventuates in a meticulously crafted text. The release is sufficiently profound for Woolf to suspend her usual skepticism about psychoanalysis. Although Barthes takes a very different stand toward what had become a psychoanalytic orthodoxy, especially the course of mourning it prescribed, he likewise wrote *Camera Lucida* very quickly, in apparent confirmation of his guarded intuition that the writing might be therapeutic: "[No doubt I will be unwell, until I write something *having to do with her* (*Photo*, or something else).]"[23] Both of these rapidly composed but carefully shaped texts are complemented and complicated by more private modes of writing (memoir, diary) that were published only posthumously: Woolf's "Sketch of the Past" (composed April 18, 1939–November 1940, published 1976); and Barthes's *Mourning Diary* (*Journal de deuil*) (composed October 26, 1977–September 15, 1979, published 2009). The insights offered by these more unguarded texts—Woolf's written after, Barthes's before, the more deliberately crafted public texts, but both published only decades later—both illuminate the well-known version and enter into a dialogue with it that stretches the boundaries of genre.

Despite their biographical and cultural differences (Woolf, who lost her mother as a teenager and who, as one of eight children, could barely recall a moment alone with her; Barthes as the adored child of the single mother with whom he lived until her death at eighty-four), Woolf and Barthes both ground their sense of loss in an idealized, rural childhood home: Bayonne for Barthes, St. Ives for Woolf. Each mourns the loss of a childhood world, an affective landscape, bathed in the retrospective glow of memory and saturated with the auratic presence of the mother. This geographic and affective concentration endows biographical givens with a mythological structure and lyric intensity that justifies applying the term "elegy" to prose works that mourn the passing of what Woolf calls a "space of time" and Barthes "the Land of Childhood."[24]

What creates the elegiac affect, however, also troubles a genre devised to resolve the loss of an individuated "object." Enmeshing the memory of the mother in an environment as a diffuse presence—an atmosphere or ambience or radiance that saturates a world but is not localized within it, at once "there, at the very center" and "one of those invisible presences," both central and invisible, indeed invisible because central, everywhere and nowhere at once—confronts less the practice than the theory of elegy that has evolved in recent decades in conversation with broader cultural narratives of loss (Sketch, 83).

Mourning, Melancholy, Medium

This theory reads the elegiac process through the oedipal narrative and takes the genre's linguistic medium as a theoretical necessity rather than a historical contingency. The elegist's "reluctant resubmission to the constraints of language," according to Peter M. Sacks, the primary exponent of this line of argument, is the defining gesture of the genre, the only way for it to perform, rather than simply to describe, the act of substitution on which both the genre and the "work of mourning" depend.[25] "At the core of each procedure is the renunciatory experience of loss and the acceptance, not just of a substitute, but of the very means and practice of substitution" (*English Elegy*, 8). Consequently, not only are the linguistic signs that substitute for presence the constitutive medium of elegy; the acceptance of substitution and the aesthetic consolation it affords constitute the singular model of mourning.

It is the model, Sacks proposes, that is underwritten by the master psychoanalytic narrative: the renunciation of the mother as the cost of entry to the symbolic register. The process unfolds through various iterations: the fort/da game through which the child gains the symbolic tools to master maternal absence; the paternal prohibition that enforces substitution; and ultimately the achievement of verbal prowess through which the poet gains figurative mastery over death (and his poetic/paternal precursor). Several assumptions need unpacking here: most obviously, that the subject and object of elegy are constitutively masculine; but also more particularly that maternal loss can only be a training ground for elegy, and if a mother were to evolve into an elegiac subject, she could be legible only as an oedipalized "object" (coherent, individuated, delimited) for whose loss language might offer compensation. That an earlier, more diffuse and proximate multisensory presence (auditory, tactile, olfactory) might persist along with (rather than being displaced by or subsumed within) the bereaved individual—and that the loss of this encompassing environment might elicit specific inflections of mourning—does not enter the theoretical picture. But what, we might ask, could substitute for light or air? What if, at some level, there is no "fort" in the fort/da game, if the embodied individual comes and goes, lives and dies, but the environment that holds her as an enveloping presence persists or is regenerated as a felt sensation after she is gone? Proust's observation that "people do not die for us immediately, but remain bathed in a sort of aura of life which bears no relation to true immortality but through which they continue to occupy our thoughts in the same way as when they were alive" suggests an economy of presence and absence that does not fit into the calculus of affective loss as aesthetic gain.[26]

Recent debate has approached the issue differently. Taking its lead from the alternative to mourning proposed in Freud's classic 1917 essay, "Mourning and Melancholia," which Barthes was reading as he worked on *Camera Lucida*, theorists now routinely embrace Freud's devalued secondary term as an ethical, political, and aesthetic imperative. Attempting to rescue melancholia from the pathology Freud ascribes to it, they have refused the logic of substitution that constitutes both the normative "work of mourning" and the consolation of elegy. The festering melancholic wound has become the sign of the irreplaceability of the lost object, the unrecuperability of social and cultural deprivations, and the ethical integrity of the grieving subject who refuses the commodifying model of exchange implied in Freud's account of mourning as a "withdrawal" and "reinvestment" of the ego.[27] For some of these theorists, who draw inspiration from the Frankfurt School to pivot from the individualism of psychoanalytic discourse to the pervasive and pervasively obscured social underpinnings of grief, modernity itself is characterized by "difficult-to-mourn losses" whose elusiveness is compounded by the lack of rituals for the collective processing of grief. In Jonathan Flatley's compelling formulation, melancholia is an "allegory for the experience of modernity . . . , the place where modernity touches down on our lives in the most intimate of ways."[28] For Flatley and for cultural critics such as Lauren Berlant and Ann Cvetkovich, who have organized work on "public feelings" and "feel tanks," a "non-depressive" and politically informed understanding of melancholia can be leveraged into an impetus for social change; for others, melancholic social formations, such as race, inflict a mode of grief that political grievance can't assuage.[29] In either case, however, and in spite of the inversion, the binary division between mourning and melancholia remains intact. The late twentieth-century turn to mourning reprises and revises a modernist discourse of lost objects; a more expansive social theorization of melancholia engages a more pervasive and less punctual experience of loss. The perverse result is that an approach that seeks to take the temperature of intangible social moods focuses almost exclusively on negative affects, while theoretical projects that seek to give new voice to mourning continue to unfold via a discourse of lost objects that narrowly delimits the experiential boundaries of loss.

The genre of elegy presents a different but equally frustrating version of the mourning/melancholia binary. A poetic tradition of mourning that originated with shepherds' pipes performing a lament for the death of a friend who was also, typically, an aesthetic precursor affords little space for mourning a mother.[30] Even as the genre evolved over the centuries, mothers rarely became its central subjects. On the few occasions they did, the revisions they elicited were closely intertwined with the conventions of lyric form: new tropes of enmeshment and structural patterns of continuity and return rather than transcendence.[31]

Conversely, mothers have been at the center of the "melancholic" variant of the recalcitrant, anticonsolatory twentieth-century elegy. The cataclysmic events of the twentieth century, inaugurated by a world war that exploded the pastoral foundations of the genre, generated what Sandra M. Gilbert (following Wallace Stevens) calls "monsters of elegy" that struggle to adapt an inherited poetic form to the clinical realities of modern death, stripped of consolatory fictions of transcendence.[32] As Gilbert points out, maternal elegies surface at the historical moment when the shock of death's materiality finds expression in the confessional mode of post–World War II American poetry; indeed, the maternal body becomes a privileged site of uncovering death's monstrosity. The exposure of this body in a deliberate affront to elegiac conventions of encomium serves as an affective locus for the ugly feelings that characterize the melancholic elegy: anger, disgust, contempt, revulsion, exultation, denunciation. Whereas the normative elegy is restitutive and idealizing, the melancholic counterpart is violent, unresolved, and fueled by ambivalence rather than love.

As poetic versions of elegy reinscribed the mourning/melancholia dichotomy, the complex and contradictory affects triggered by maternal loss found a more accommodating home in prose. The expansive, hybrid adaptations that Woolf and Barthes composed out of a blend of fiction, memoir, image, and essay reinvigorated a traditional form and inflected it with the broader concerns these authors engaged as cultural critics. Their involvement with nonverbal mediums allowed them to challenge assumptions about medium and mourning, including the assumption of elegy's linguistic medium and the inevitability of the mourning/melancholia binary.

This engagement with visual culture was inflected by their historical moments and milieus: the post-Impressionist aesthetic that Woolf's Bloomsbury circle made available to England during the second decade of the twentieth century and the theory of photography that flourished in France in the late 1970s. Each medium supports a specific variant of maternal elegy. The most available comparison is between Woolf's evocation of painting to exemplify a traditional process of mourning as working through and Barthes's recruitment of photography to stake a claim for melancholia, a claim that arguably launched or at least heralded the melancholic turn of recent theory. The distinction is immediately legible in the contrast between the three-part structure of *To the Lighthouse*, which follows the classic elegiac sequence of presence, absence, and aesthetic consolation, and the resolutely nondialectical two-part structure of *Camera Lucida*, which emphatically refuses consolation. For reasons that are overdetermined— the time lag between the death of the mother and the composition of the text (thirty years for Woolf, less than two for Barthes), as well as the consequences of the visual medium each invokes to articulate grief—their signal elegiac texts seem to restage the mourning/melancholia split.

That is not the whole picture, however. Because Barthes (as we will see) draws a critical distinction between the melancholic nature of the photographic print and the euphoric connectivity of the photographic process, he also enables us to discern retrospectively a protophotographic discourse of light that is already nascent in Woolf. This discourse points to an alternative to both mourning and melancholia. It points, indeed, to the third term that this binary occludes, a term specifically implicated with maternal death, a term that turns our focus from the logic of symbolization on which psychoanalysis and elegy are both premised to modes of proximity and presence that other mediums might register. Rather than reading elegy through the lens of psychoanalysis, we can reread psychoanalysis through the lens of elegy.

Running across these discourses is an association of mother, mania, and light. Teasing out these associations allows us to materialize a conventional elegiac figure and to recover a neglected psychoanalytic category. Rather than a trope of spiritual consolation achieved at the end of a journey through the night, the "new day" of "Lycidas," the "Intimations Ode," or "In Memoriam," photographic light, as evoked by Woolf and Barthes, is a constant ingredient of processing loss, an agent of mediation rather than a figure of illumination. Through its association with the third term in the triad of mourning, melancholia, and mania, light grants maternal mourning a specific medium and mode. No panacea, this medium and mode raise as many questions as they answer. While offering an alternative to the language of (and language as) object loss, they impose their own burden of idealization, their own discordance with the materiality of the maternal body that has been a prime site of cultural anxiety about the deterioration of the flesh. Woolf and Barthes struggle with these contradictions within a common set of terms.

Woolf's *To the Lighthouse*, Barthes's *Camera Lucida* (the French title *La chambre claire* means literally "light room"), the "lighted rooms" that figure Woolf's brain in the diary entry that is an epigraph to this chapter: How have we not noticed this commonality? Perhaps the similarities have been blinding, for as Barthes (citing a Chinese proverb) reminds us, the darkest place is always under the lamp.[33]

To the Light House

Uncertain about how to begin the story of her life, Woolf plunges into her memoir, "A Sketch of the Past," with two "first" memories that point in opposite directions: the first away from St. Ives toward London, evening, and Julia Stephen's eventual death; the second, which emerges as a reflex or displacement of the first, toward St. Ives and dawn as they converge in a self-replenishing Land of Childhood.

> I begin: the first memory.
>
> This was of red and purple flowers on a black ground—my mother's dress; and she was sitting either in a train or in an omnibus, and I was on her lap. I therefore saw the flowers she was wearing very close; and can still see purple and red and blue, I think, against the black; they must have been anemones, I suppose. Perhaps we were going to St Ives; more probably, for from the light it must have been evening, we were coming back to London. But it is more convenient artistically to suppose that we were going to St Ives, for that will lead to my other memory, which also seems to be my first memory, and in fact it is the most important of all my memories. (Sketch, 64)

We can understand why Woolf might have wanted to defer the first of her two "first" memories. The ominous black ground, instantiating the "background of knowledge" about death that her mother had acquired from her first husband's early death, establishes death as the common ground of the young Virginia's connection with her mother (Sketch, 82). There from the first, we might say in Woolf's own language, along with an intimation of pain in the contact zone. The vivid, even violent colors of the anemones—purple, red, blue—pinned against her mother's black dress suggest that abrasion may inhere in bodily intimacy. The implication surfaces when the memory recurs later in the memoir after the first mention of Julia's death: "My first memory is of her lap; the scratch of some beads on her dress comes back to me as I pressed my cheek against it" (Sketch, 81). At this scratchy interface the colors of blood and bruising bloom, like the "purplish stain upon the bland surface of the sea as if something had boiled and bled, invisibly, beneath" that figures the conglomerate unspoken pain of World War I and Mrs. Ramsay's death in "Time Passes" (*TTL*, 133–34). But here, the "something" that boils and bleeds to the surface comes from both sides of the contact zone, indeed seems to come as a consequence of contact that is bound up with mortality from the first. The juxtaposition of brightly colored, perishable flowers, whose fleeting blossoms suggest the soft vulnerability of flesh, and the black ground on which these flowers bloom encapsulates the life of the flesh pinned to the certainty of death.

Against this vulnerable mortality, Woolf offers her other "first" and "most important" memory, about which she claims that "if life has a base that it stands upon, if it is a bowl that one fills and fills and fills—then my bowl without a doubt stands upon this memory" (Sketch, 64).[34]

It is of lying half asleep, half awake, in bed in the nursery at St Ives. It is of hearing the waves breaking, one, two, one, two, and sending a splash of water over the beach; and then of breaking, one, two, one two, behind a yellow blind. It is of hearing the blind draw its little acorn across the floor as the wind blew the blind out. It is of lying and hearing this splash and seeing this light, and feeling, it is almost impossible that I should be here; of feeling the purest ecstasy I can conceive . . . ; the feeling, as I describe it sometimes to myself, of lying in a grape and seeing through a film of semi-transparent yellow. (Sketch, 64–65)

As numerous readers have noted, the narrator moves imaginatively inward here from the mother's lap to her womb, underneath the heart whose rhythmic pulsing blends with the breaking waves. Enclosed within a translucent yellow film, the narrator floats in a liminal state of golden light and rhythmic sound. As the infant's emerging consciousness is shielded from the world by the womb's semitransparent yellow veil—this is the originary site of the "luminous halo of consciousness that surrounds one from childhood through death"—the veil's smooth skin is protected from hardening or puckering by the suspension of time.[35] Lying, hearing, breaking, sending, feeling: participial verb forms prevail. This intermingling of mind and matter seems exempt from—but cannot ultimately forestall—change.

From these two memories Woolf spins out two elegiac trajectories, each of which aligns key scenes in "A Sketch of the Past" and *To the Lighthouse* along a specific axis and with reference to a specific visual medium. The first, which pivots on a moment of puncture, acknowledges, even embraces, the trauma of early loss and struggles to redeem it through the consolations of painting suggested by the vivid colors of the memory of Julia's lap. The painterly implications are reprised shortly after Julia's death in the blaze of color the thirteen-year-old Virginia perceives after escaping briefly with her siblings from the shrouded house of mourning at Hyde Park Gate to meet their brother Thoby at Paddington Station.

It was sunset, and the great glass dome at the end of the station was blazing with light. It was glowing yellow and red and the iron girders made a platform across it. I walked along the platform gazing with rapture at this magnificent blaze of colour, and the train slowly steamed into the station. It impressed and exalted me. It was so vast and so fiery red. The contrast of that blaze of magnificent light with the shrouded and curtained rooms at Hyde Park Gate was so intense. Also, it was partly that my mother's death unveiled and intensified: made me suddenly develop perceptions, as if a burning glass had been laid over what was shaded and dormant. (Sketch, 93)

With the rending of the maternal veil, things become hyperclear, viewed from within a lens of burning glass. The bruises implicit in the memory of Julia Stephen's lap gain force as the train that carries Thoby to his mother's funeral steams under Paddington's great glass dome. The glass dome functions as an ocular membrane that transmits impressions of the outside world. The steaming train that carries Thoby to his mother's funeral pierces that membrane, as if death penetrates the young Virginia's field of vision with an almost sexual "rapture." "It was so vast and so fiery red," she declares, as the piercing of the ocular membrane seems to issue forth in blood—or paint.

For the scene of Paddington Station is highly painterly. The intensity of the blazing colors (no subcutaneous bleeding here) is held within an iron-girded structure that transposes Lily Briscoe's post-Impressionist aesthetic—"colour burning on a framework of steel, the light of a butterfly's wing lying upon the arches of a cathedral"—to the privileged urban site of Impressionist painting (*TTL*, 48).[36] Instead of tears, the eye unveiled by maternal death bleeds paint. This should come as no small surprise, given Woolf's detailed rendition of mourning as painting in part 3 of *To the Lighthouse*. As Lily Briscoe struggles to complete her painting ten years after Mrs. Ramsay has died, she encounters an unformed, ambiguously situated "mass . . . pressing on her eyeballs. Then, as if some juice necessary for the lubrication of her faculties were spontaneously squirted, she began precariously dipping among the blues and umbers" as "her mind kept throwing up from its depths, scenes, and names, and sayings, and memories and ideas, like a fountain spurting over that glaring, hideously difficult white space, while she modeled it with greens and blues" (*TTL*, 159). Becoming integral to Lily's practice (as opposed to her theory) only after Mrs. Ramsay's death—for Lily's accounts of her painting in part 1 are almost entirely formal—pigment is the expressive medium of mourning that transposes the fluxes of grief and memory onto a canvas where they can be modulated and given form (a modulation we observe in the contrast between the fiery red of Paddington Station and the blues, umbers, and greens that pay tribute to Cezanne).

Through Lily's painting, Woolf shifts mourning from the "entirely unaesthetic" Victorian social conventions to the fine-tuned aesthetic register catalyzed by the puncture of the maternal veil. What originates with modernist shock, however—"I surmise that the shock receiving capacity is what makes me a writer"—unfolds in accordance with the narrative arc of mourning (Sketch, 72). In contrast to Freud, who associates the breaching of the mind's protective shield with traumatic experience that, like the mechanical record produced by a camera, bypasses conscious recognition to register only in the unconscious, where it remains inaccessible to mourning, Woolf routes traumatic rupture through an analogy to painting that makes it amenable to conscious resolution.[37] The analogy offers a medium well suited to resolving maternal loss: it yields a vocabulary of color, in contrast to mourning's unbroken black, and of rhythmic stroking on the white skin of a canvas on which Mrs. Ramsay might be conjured back in a new form. Recourse to the tangible medium of paint appears to mitigate the substitutions on which linguistic signs are based, while submitting painting to the project of substitution that subtends the work of mourning. In the elegy that constitutes its literary form, mourning reaches closure when loss achieves symbolic form. "I have had my vision" are the novel's closing words (*TTL*, 209).

Counterpointing the trajectory from Julia's lap to Paddington Station to Lily Briscoe's painting is a pair of mirroring scenes that resists mourning's narrative arc toward closure in an effort to preserve the mother's presence as a timeless continuity. The point of departure is the second of Woolf's early memories, set in the nursery of St. Ives and routed through the biographical daughter rather than her fictional surrogate (Sketch, 64). Rather than traversing the burst of painterly color at the station, this version of a maternal elegy turns to the light-writing suggested by the lighthouse of Woolf's fictional elegy. Unfolding between two "lighted rooms" (or two versions of one room), recalling her state of mind while concluding *Mrs. Dalloway* ("such is my brain to me; lighted rooms"), the memory of the yellow grape finds an anticipatory echo in a similarly encapsulated scene in *To the Lighthouse* (section xi). In her only scene alone, wedged between the departure of her son and the appearance of her husband, Mrs. Ramsay sits (like her infant daughter/author) by the window of a now-darkening room in a fictional version of Talland House. Emptied of personality, as the room appears vacant of furniture, she becomes a pure receptacle of the light from the lighthouse. In this singular and solitary scene, Woolf places the fictional character of her mother, as she later positions herself, entranced with light pouring through a window. As she offers her first memory as a dawning of consciousness, she presents her final image of her fictional mother (for although Mrs. Ramsay remains active within the fictional world until the end of part 1, she is never again viewed from a narrative perspective trained exclusively on her) on the evening before her death. In this valedictory scene, the yellow light of morning has turned silver, as if the lighthouse beam blends with the rays of the evening star. Through these mirroring scenes, mother and daughter gaze at one another across an ocean of time. As the section "Time Passes" both connects and divides two mirroring moments in the life of the Ramsay family, time both passes and does not pass between the two scenes at the windows of Talland House. The suspended temporality of the nursery scene expands here to reach backward and forward to the fictional scene of the lighthouse that precedes it in the chronology of writing and succeeds it in the biographical chronology.

In the lighthouse scene, Woolf occupies the narrative perspective of the lighthouse beam, sweeping through the darkened chamber of Mrs. Ramsay's mind, lifting up her "wedge-shaped core of darkness" for our contemplation (*TTL*, 62). She has plucked her fictional mother from the distractions that she describes in "A Sketch of the Past" as the "panoply of life" that left her mother "not time, nor strength, to concentrate . . . upon me, or upon anyone—unless it were Adrian. Him she cherished separately" (83). Having dispatched James (modeled on Adrian) to bed just before this scene, Woolf brings Mrs. Ramsay to be present, to be silent, to sit for a portrait of her interior life by her daughter-writer. The privacy of this inner chamber, "something invisible to others," becomes visible only through the lighthouse beam that Woolf sends her way. Acknowledging this beam as "her own eyes meeting her own eyes, searching as she alone could search into her mind and her heart," Mrs. Ramsay opens herself to be written in light (*TTL*, 63). The access denied to Lily Briscoe, who in strikingly similar language imagines "how in the chambers of the mind and heart" of Mrs. Ramsay were secrets that would "never be offered openly," is granted to the daughter-writer through the agency of light (*TTL*, 51).

Setting up a tension between the daughter who paints in color and the one who writes in light, Woolf recasts the traditional rivalry between the sister arts of literature and painting (personified by herself and her sister-painter Vanessa Bell) as a submerged contestation between photography and painting as mediums for processing maternal death.[38] Evoking photography as the tactile registration of light that enters through the single aperture of the camera obscura of Mrs. Ramsay's mind, Woolf directs toward her fictional mother a mode of susceptibility to impressions that she repeatedly claims for herself in the language of photography. In a strangely doubled allusion to photography that sums up her childhood at St. Ives, she explains: "Figuratively I could snapshot what I mean by some image; I am a porous vessel afloat on sensation; a sensitive plate exposed to invisible rays" (Sketch, 133). Taking a snapshot of the photographic plate—that is, looking from the outside at the inside of the camera—reproduces the narrative optic of the lighthouse scene, which photo-graphs the sensitive plate of Mrs. Ramsay's mind through an opening into her obscure interior space.[39]

The photographic metaphor allows Woolf to shift attention away from personalities without renouncing interiority. In experimental texts such as *The Waves* that seek to imagine "the world seen without the self," she extracts the sensitive plate from the mind entirely and turns it to producing an impersonal record of the object world.[40] A different transaction takes place within and between Woolf's autobiographical texts, which recruit the impersonal technology of the sensitive plate to an interpersonal exchange among objects and subjects and subjective objects like the lighthouse beam that "expressed one . . . became one . . . knew one," entities whose imprint we register without the abrasive touch of individuals (*TTL*, 63). Photography is a medium and a figure of mediation that can align memories, scenes, and bodies in relations that are neither so close as to leave bruises nor so far as to leave no traces.

Photographic metaphors in Woolf's autobiographical texts are less about vision than about touch, less about the impersonal perspective of the sun that presides over *The Waves* than about the transmission of impressions via "strokes" of light from a salvific, man-made object endowed with the eyes and fingers of a lover. In a key passage in the lighthouse scene, the third stroke of the beam caresses Mrs. Ramsay's eyes "as if it were stroking with its silver fingers some sealed vessel whose bursting would flood her with delight" (*TTL*, 165). The "silver fingers" echo early photography's defining metaphor, the "pencil of nature" that William Henry Fox Talbot, the British originator of photography, adopted as the title of his pathbreaking treatise (1844–46) about his newly created "sun pictures" that are "impressed by the agency of Light alone, without any aid whatever from the artist's pencil."[41] The treatise details his development of the calotype process that refined his earlier discovery (contemporary and competitive with Daguerre's) that silver chloride would render the surface in a camera obscura sensitive to light; he now revealed a more efficient process of chemical development that used silver nitrate to make a negative from which multiple positives could be printed. The intersection of light's "pencils" with the salts of silver that allow them to register an enduring impression creates a context in which, beyond the nod to evening light, Woolf's "silver fingers" can be seen to concatenate in a single figure the two mutually essential ingredients of "light writing."

As a member of a family of amateur and professional photographers, Woolf was well acquainted with early photographic technologies, especially those practiced and transmitted by her great-aunt, the photographer Julia Margaret Cameron. This aesthetic lineage must have been on her mind as she was composing *To the Lighthouse*, for in 1926, the Hogarth Press published a collection of Cameron's photographs (including two of Woolf's mother) with introductory essays by both Woolf and Roger Fry. Following in the tradition of her mother, who wrote the entry on Julia Margaret Cameron in Leslie Stephen's *Dictionary of National Biography*, Woolf's contribution is primarily (and at times humorously) biographical, but the essay by Roger Fry, to whom she was planning to dedicate *To the Lighthouse* and whose biography she would write concurrently with "A Sketch of the Past," uses Cameron's work as an occasion to elevate early photography from a mechanical to a fine art compatible with the values of post-Impressionism. In Fry's account, early photographic technologies (in contrast to those of both representational painting and snapshot photography) share with post-Impressionism a concern with the formal values that are fully realized in the work of Cameron, whom he proclaims "far and away the most distinguished" of the "artists [to] have ever used the medium," singling out her formal abstraction, volume, and compositional unity and "the incidence, intensity, and quality of light" as her distinctive legacy.[42]

Cameron thematizes this engagement with light in a self-reflexive photograph whose title resonates with Woolf's "silver fingers." In "Cupid's Pencil of Light" (fig. 4), she depicts a naked androgynous child personifying Cupid, who points with two luminous fingers—pencils of light—at a glowing metallic plate under streaks of light in the sky. In Carol Armstrong's compelling reading, both the process and product of photography "are imaged as light itself, both as disembodied force and as embodied shape: amorphous light above, which images the making of the photograph itself; blinding light within, on the plate upon which Cupid draws, light embodied in the form of the child . . . Photography under the sway of the Mother, rather than the law of the Father. For the light above Cupid is Mother Light, the Light of Cupid's Mother Venus," who, we might recall, is also the evening star through whose fingers photography's light would run silver.[43]

The reading of photography as a function of maternal light provides a thematic as well as theoretical link to Mrs. Ramsay's lighthouse scene. Like Cameron's "maternalization of photography," which conflates heterosexuality (Cupid) with mother-child eroticism, Woolf figures the intense eroticism of the lighthouse scene as "a bride [rising] to meet her lover," but gestures intertextually toward an eroticized rapport between mother and daughter (*TTL*, 64). The intimate scene with the lighthouse rewrites as a caress Woolf's last actual encounter with her mother, laid out in death in her bedroom, her cheek, when kissed, like "iron cold, and granulated," and assuages the figuration of maternal death as the puncture of the daughter's eyes (Sketch, 92). By sending "silver fingers" to stroke her fictional mother's eyes, a stroking whose orgasmic climax will burst a "sealed vessel" not into blood-as-paint, the rupture-as-rapture she will experience as daughter, but

FIGURE 4. Julia Margaret Cameron, "Cupid's Pencil of Light" (1872). Photograph: © Royal Photographic Society Collection / Victoria and Albert Museum, London.

into the mother's "delight . . . , exquisite happiness," Woolf solaces, in advance and in reverse, the wound her mother's death inflicts on her own eyes (*TTL*, 65). Culminating in an "ecstasy" that races in "waves of pure lemon" across the beach and the floor of Mrs. Ramsay's mind, the mother's ecstatic moment both anticipates and echoes the daughter's "purest ecstasy" as she listens to the waves inside the yellow film of the maternal body (*TTL*, 65; Sketch, 65).

This reverberation across time suggests that, against the narrative of mourning worked out through Lily's painting, a nonlinear, nonsequential mode of connection is transmitted through light. Arguably a mode of light-writing with a lineage from Julia Margaret Cameron, this tactile connection resists sequence and closure. Perhaps that is why this protophotographic discourse is not articulated in a form comparable to Lily's painting. Allowing the photographic metaphor to develop into fully actualized form could undermine its function as an alternative to the narrative arc of mourning that finds closure in a painting. For it is striking that although Woolf, like the other members of her family, regularly photographed friends and relatives and collected these images in her own family album, she neither reproduces these photographs nor makes significant reference to them in "A Sketch of the Past," unlike her deliberate and provocative use of the medium for satiric or comic purposes in *Three Guineas* and *Orlando*. Despite her repeated effort to recall the physical appearance of her mother, an often-photographed subject in Woolf's visual world, there are only two rather distant references to photographs of Julia. The risk appears to be that memory would congeal around the visual image. Woolf seems to have shared Proust's attitude toward the freezing of memory in snapshot exhibitions or family albums; however worthy in themselves, they are incompatible with the project of literary memory.[44]

How the photographic process might be salvaged from this calcification of memory is suggested by the most extended and nuanced allusion to it in "A Sketch of the Past." In a famous passage in which she meditates about the interplay between the past and the present, Woolf describes the present as the "sliding surface of a deep river" that must run smoothly for the past to become visible beneath. This creates one of her "greatest satisfactions. . . . For the present when backed by the past is a thousand times deeper than the present when it presses so close that you can feel nothing else, when the film on the camera reaches only to the eye" (Sketch, 98). In contrast to older photographic technologies that incorporated a depth dimension through the duration of the exposure that, as Woolf and Fry both point out, create a "slightly generalized" effect that avoids "the too acute, too positive quality from which modern photography generally suffers," the film of the snapshot is glued to the eye of the present.[45] Photography obscures memory rather than abetting it, for memory resides in the back of the mind, not on the surface of the eye.

In the same passage, however, Woolf proposes a somewhat different relation between photography and memory as she seeks to recover a less agitated vision of the current moment (July 19, 1939) "by getting the past to shadow this broken surface" of the present (Sketch, 98). Memory as shadow: perhaps rather than either clinging to the immediacy of the present or memorializing a vision of the past, photography might negotiate their interplay through a formal composition of light and shadow. This is in fact the language that Lily Briscoe invokes to explain her nonrepresentational painting of Mrs. Ramsay to Mr. Bankes as a tribute expressed "by a shadow here and a light there." The formula is repeated twice: "A light here required a shadow there," for it was a question "of lights and shadows" (*TTL*, 52–53). This insistence on light and shadow derives from the lexicon of photography, for which these terms, enshrined in popular memory by such phrases as "words of light" and "fixing a shadow," may constitute the definitive pair. Certainly, they were the defining pair with which to describe Julia Margaret Cameron's chiaroscuro effects. But this photographic discourse is entirely displaced by the painterly language of pigment once Lily returns to her canvas after Mrs. Ramsay dies. As Woolf is determined to have mourning transpire through the medium of paint, she is determined to withhold a memorial function from photography.[46] To allow even the highest form of photography to be fully developed within her texts—that is, to be developed as a figure of a fully developed art form—would be to undermine the contrast between the closure of mourning and the continuity bestowed by light.

The present tense "It is enough!" in which Mrs. Ramsay's scene with the lighthouse culminates, in contrast to Lily Briscoe's past perfect tense "I have had my vision," speaks to the sufficiency of light as a medium of presence (*TTL*, 65, 209). The protophotographic discourse that hovers in the resonance between the scene with the lighthouse and the scene in the grape suggests a medium that is in and about suspension, an elegiac process rather than a print. In more medium-specific terms, we might say that Woolf is more drawn to the indexical process of photography, the inscription of light on a sensitive surface, than to the iconic features of the photographic image. To explore how this indexicality might register a nondefinitive experience of death, a lingering impression of presence slowly textured with loss, we have to turn to Roland Barthes.

The Light Room

1977: Barthes's mother is dying in their summer home in Urt in the South West of France, near his village of origin. They spend the summer together there as usual, with Barthes participating in his mother's care. In July, he writes "The Light of the South West," published in *L'Humanité* the following September. Half a century after the publication of *To the Lighthouse*, Barthes tries to put into words the sensory world of childhood, the only world that matters, since "in the end, there is no Land other than the Land of Childhood."[47] Like St. Ives, despite the geographic differences, Barthes's childhood land is constituted by a quality of light that emanates from a maternal source, a holding environment for the disoriented son who knows he will "drift painfully, without existence" after his mother's death. Anticipating the disappearance of the "gratifying Mother [who] shows me the Mirror, the image, and says to me: 'That's you'"—Barthes has been reading Winnicott—he reimagines the mother as a luminous space that will embrace them both after she is gone.[48]

What Barthes calls "that South-West sunlight, which has accompanied my life," is both an atmosphere he carries with him as a permanent and portable microclimate and a specifically regional ambience.[49] "The great light of the South West appears, noble and subtle at the same time; it is never grey, never gloomy (even when the sun isn't shining); it is light-space, defined less by the altered colours of things (as in the other Midi) than by the eminently *inhabitable* quality it gives to the earth. I can think of no other way to say it: it is a luminous light" (SW, 7, emphasis in original). This redundantly luminous light-space is less a visual phenomenon—it is a vehicle of neither color nor form—than one that, in the absence of the mother or the sun (if these can be differentiated, given Barthes's depiction of his mother as "a radiant, irreducible core"), makes it possible to survive on earth (*CL*, 75). The South-West light that Barthes had previously appreciated as a "view without contours, without object, *without figuration*, the view of a transparency, the view of a non-view"—that is, as an aesthetically self-sufficient, noninstrumental medium—thickens, with his mother's approaching death, into a tangible vehicle of presence, an atmosphere to inhabit with open pores and eyes half closed.[50]

Barthes's anticipation that his mother might linger in the light of his childhood evolved into the suggestive title *La chambre claire* and one of its most memorable chapters, which opens by rejecting the received account of photography's shared lineage with painting via the inventions of Albertian perspective and the camera obscura. Against painting's presumed status as photography's "absolute, paternal Reference" (*CL*, 30), Barthes proposes (in terms that anticipate and perhaps inspired Armstrong's reading of Julia Margaret Cameron) an alternative and alternatively gendered genealogy that derives not from strategies and technologies of representation, but from the physical and chemical properties of light. Photography's sensory modality here is touch rather than vision, its founding science chemistry, not optics. In Barthes's most extreme formulation, the photographic mechanism (heir to the camera obscura) disappears in the transmission of light rays between two bodies. Photography became possible only on the day when a scientific circumstance (the discovery that silver halogens were sensitive to light) made it possible to recover and print directly the luminous rays emitted by a variously lighted object. The photograph is literally an emanation of the referent. From a real body, which was there, proceed radiations which ultimately touch me, who am here; the duration of the transmission is insignificant; the photograph of the missing being, as Sontag says, will touch me like the delayed rays of a star. A sort of umbilical cord links the body of the photographed thing to my gaze: light, though impalpable, is here a carnal medium, a skin I share with anyone who has been photographed. (*CL*, 80–81)

Although the passage begins by emphasizing the inscription of an image, that image rapidly recedes, first into a relay between the object and the viewer and then into light itself. Light rays become an independent "carnal medium" that, more than a means of transmission, constitutes a sensuous environment of its own, a full-body immersion in an enveloping skin that encompasses two beings in the primal unit suggested by the umbilical reference. Like Woolf, Barthes is more interested in the moment and mode of inscription than in the production of an image that would reorient the sensorium from skin to eyes and shift the object of perception from "the photographed body [that] touches me with its own rays"—an experience more akin to sunbathing than to spectatorship—to "the surface which in turn my gaze will touch" (*CL*, 81).

The magical thinking that enables Barthes to sustain a primal connection to his mother leads him to invent a Latin alternative to the Greek etymology that locates photography (as a form of writing, photo-graphy) in the register of culture: "'imago lucis opera expressa'; which is to say: image revealed, 'extracted,' 'mounted,' 'expressed' (like the juice of a lemon) by the action of light" (*CL*, 81). Barthes's photographic process is as natural as sunshine, a ripening that extracts the hidden essence of an object to make it manifest elsewhere; or, in a less explicit variant of the metaphor, the camera is like a nursing infant that expresses (in both senses) the vital juices of its beloved object without the intervention of the Name of the Father. In yet a further permutation, the natural shades into the supernatural, and the expressed fluids morph into the chemical—and then alchemical—substances that make it possible to give birth to (as opposed to writing) the image: "The loved body is immortalized by the mediation of a precious metal, silver (monument and luxury); to which we might add the notion that this metal, like all the metals of Alchemy, is alive" (*CL*, 81). The camera as nursing child monumentalizes the mother through the photographic plate's living skin of silver.

This sensitive skin, flecked with "sprouting silver grains," melds with that of the viewer, on which, as for Woolf, the image is fantasmatically imprinted (*CL*, 93). Alchemy takes a Christian turn as Barthes asserts that photography is closer to resurrection than to remembrance, giving life to the absent, the disembodied, and the dead like the cloth of Saint Veronica on which "the image of Christ" is "impregnated" (*CL*, 82). Softening to cloth, the photographic plate dissolves into skin so that the son can be impregnated (surely not an accidental verb choice) with the image of the mother, whom he resurrects on the surface of his body, inverting the Virgin Mary's insemination by the Holy Spirit. If, as various critics have proposed, the mother in *Camera Lucida* is, like a camera, an "incunabulum of images," or conversely and more darkly, that the camera is "a mechanical mother that mimes, distorts and disrupts the maternal function" with "as great a capacity to kill as it does to procreate" its subjects—that is, that a process routed through a dark interior reproductive apparatus results in the birth of an alienated image—the relocation of that image to the skin of the son circumvents photography's deadening effects by transforming the child into the generative mother.[51]

What then becomes of the photographic print that, bypassed in this magical transfer, emerges from the passage through the chambers of the camera and dark room as an independent, material object? Barthes's suggestive title seeks to sidestep this outcome by extending the promise of the light-space of the South West. The text supports this vision with an etymological and technological derivation from a luminous alternative to the camera obscura: the Latin version of a light room, the camera lucida (the title of the English text), which Barthes describes as an "apparatus, anterior to Photography, which permitted drawing an object through a prism, one eye on the model, the other on the paper" (*CL*, 106). Caught between the downside of preserving photography's link to painting (here, drawing) that he otherwise disputes and the benefit of granting photography a lineage of light, Barthes chooses the latter, but his wishful conjuring of the maternal still has to contend with the materiality of the photographic print that is both a locus of and barrier to the transmission of light.

Photography is thus a deeply contradictory medium for Barthes: light is both its vehicle and rival, its source and circumvention. With the intervention of the camera whose "click" divides life from death by "separating the initial pose from the final print" (*CL*, 92)—Barthes collapses mechanical and chemical processes here—the living alchemical process is cut off and the "treasury of rays" in front of which the viewer "burns" can be accessed only as a referent that inflicts a lacerating wound (*CL*, 82). Once an image is developed, the intractable temporality of the photograph takes hold, declaring of its referent: "That-has-been" [*ça-a-été*] and, therefore, is not present here and now. The indisputability of the referent's former existence—the unique and therefore defining feature of photography, whose referent, in contrast to the "*optionally* real thing" that painting sets before us, is "the *necessarily* real thing which has been placed before the lens"—enforces recognition of that referent's nonexistence in the present (*CL*, 76, emphasis in original). The referent the photograph drags into view, the referent to which the photograph is inextricably "glued," the referent that "adheres" to the photographic surface, can thus be apprehended only as a corpse, a thing whose life could only have been in the past (*CL*, 6). With no way to recover the referent's living presence, the "superimposition . . . of reality and of the past" that is "the very essence, the *noeme* of photography" elicits anguish rather than nostalgic remembrance "(nothing Proustian in a photograph)" (*CL*, 76, 82). This intractable temporality becomes the ultimate *punctum* of photography: "Time, the lacerating emphasis of the *noeme* ('*that-has-been*')" (*CL*, 96). With the camera's intervention, the viewer's skin morphs from Saint Veronica's napkin to the site of Saint Sebastian's stigmata. As for Woolf, wounds and light are the ingredients for processing maternal loss, but they operate for Barthes within discrete and irreconcilable spheres.

Camera Lucida, then, both fulfills the protophotographic discourse of *To the Lighthouse*, making it legible retroactively, and provides a different account of the medium's engagement with maternal death. It is tempting to read the half century dividing these texts as an extended version of "Time Passes" from which Barthes's light room emerges as a fully theorized photographic space. Barthes's elegy for his mother looks back at Woolf's as the two narrative portions of *To the Lighthouse* face one another across a corridor of time. But "after a night's passage and a day's sail," there is complication as well as clarification, for the trajectory from Woolf to Barthes, a metaphoric passage through a dark room—Barthes describes the camera obscura as a "dark passage"—does not lead simply to the light, as in the consolatory journey of traditional elegy, nor to the aesthetic compensation staged by Lily's painting, but to the developed photographic print that imposes a confrontation with unrecuperable loss (*TTL*, 3; *CL*, 106). Rather than bleeding into paint, time's lacerations issue in a contradictory medium that resists the work of mourning.

Mourning also changes with the course of history. What had been sufficiently unorthodox in the 1930s to allow Woolf to bracket her resistance to psychoanalysis long enough to propose an analogy between writing and therapy had emerged by the 1970s as a reigning paradigm, as constraining in its way as the Victorian protocols it superseded. While reading George Painter's biography of Proust half a year after proclaiming, "Don't say *Mourning*. It's too psychoanalytic," Barthes reiterates his protest through an affirmation of the common language that literature shares with daily life:

Mourning/Suffering
   (Death of the Mother)
   Proust speaks of *suffering*, not *mourning* (a new, psychoanalytic word,
   one that distorts). (*MDY* [July 5, 1978], 156)

Barthes's proposed pair of contrasting terms (suffering/mourning) revises
the dyad Freud put into play with the title of his influential essay "Mourning
and Melancholia" ("Trauer und Melancholie," 1917, translated into French
in 1936 as "Deuil et mélancolie"), a binary that, over the course of the following century, came to exert a stranglehold on the discourse of mourning. Barthes's intervention was the first to contest their asymmetry, which
invested mourning with the positive value of a healthy process of working
through versus a malingering, recalcitrant, and consequently pathologized
melancholia. By substituting the everyday word "suffering" (*chagrin*) for
the emotion that resists Freud's normative model of mourning, Barthes
purges it of its opprobrium, and gives it the theoretical and ethical space
that is its due, inverting Freud's dyad in a gesture that, in the decades following *Camera Lucida*, but without acknowledging its pioneering role, has
become almost as engrained as the original pair.

By invoking photography as (in different words) a melancholic medium,
one that provokes and sustains inconsolable suffering, Barthes offers an alternative not only, implicitly, to the model of Lily's painting, but also to
a contemporaneous theorist's attempt to recruit photography to Freudian
mourning as a "form of mental hygiene." Robert Castel's "Images et phantasmes," which appeared in the fourth special issue on photography published by *Le nouvel observateur* in December 1978 (and which Barthes, a
regular subscriber and frequent interviewee, would have read as he was
preparing *Camera Lucida*), quotes extensively from "Mourning and Melancholia." Castel proposes that photography supplements Freud's account
by "allowing the dead to 'live on in the memory,'" thereby helping "the
mourner to rationalize death, and to go on living. Some of the pain of loss
is exorcised through the photograph, which is often piously preserved and
contemplated, along with other souvenirs, in the respectful ceremonial of a
private religion. The horror of decomposition is allayed by a frozen, faded
smile."[52] That Barthes was already grappling with "Mourning and Melancholia" is clear from repeated references in *A Lover's Discourse* (1977), but
Castel's attribution of therapeutic value to the pious preservation of a "frozen, faded smile" would have galvanized and focused his critique on the
relationship of photography to mourning.

Barthes is piqued, most profoundly, by the smugness of Freud's endorsement of mourning as a liberating form of "work" that enables the subject to

divest from the lost object and reinvest in substitutes. If Victorian mourning is overly protracted and insufficiently narrativized, Freudian mourning, in Barthes's account, is overly contracted and excessively scripted to culminate in closure. Against Freud's assertion that the "normal" result of mourning is the "withdrawal of the libido from the object and transference of it to a new one," Barthes insists that "true mourning is not susceptible to any narrative dialectic," not only because the diversity of personal narratives cannot be abstracted to the formula that Freud both normativizes and naturalizes as an organic process of "ripening," but also and more fundamentally because the notion of the dialectic—that some reconciliation between presence and absence can be negotiated through a substitute (erotic or aesthetic) that makes it possible to come to terms with loss—disregards and disrespects the irreplaceability of the lost object.[53]

In the uncensored *Mourning Diary*, more explicitly and extensively concerned with suffering than *Camera Lucida*, Barthes rejects the foundation on which Freud's account of mourning rests. Declaring that, unlike mourning, "pure *suffering* [*chagrin*]" is "without substitutes, without symbolization," Barthes refuses the renunciations and substitutions that, especially in the Lacanian version that flourished on his home turf, form the gateway to the symbolic register and the training ground for "working through" all subsequent losses (*MDY* [June 11, 1978], 144). It is the structure of the oedipal narrative that Barthes ultimately challenges. *Mourning Diary* opens with this provocation the day after his mother's death:

First wedding night.
But first night of mourning? (*MDY* [October 26, 1977], 3)

The internal dialogue with cultural norms, the juxtaposition of love and death that gently pushes back against sanctioned rites of passage, becomes more audacious with the accusatory voice that opens the next entry:

— You haven't known a Woman's body!
— I have known the body of my mother in illness, then dying. (*MDY* [October 27, 1977], 4)

Invoking the language of sexual knowledge, Barthes positions his own knowledge of the maternal body—the scene of oedipalization—as an undesired consequence of *thanatos* rather than *eros*. "Before, she had made herself transparent so that I could write," he explains two days later (*MDY* [October 29, 1977], 16). Illness and death spell the end of this enabling transparency. The trigger for oedipalization is not some organic maturation of the son's bodily zones and libidinal drives; in Barthes's world there is no preordained or natural end of the preoedipal holding environment, which could extend indefinitely, as Barthes's elongated legs in a childhood photograph of himself in his mother's arms suggest.[54] Barthes's bleak version of Oedipus derives instead from the mother's fall into the body toward the end of her life. There is no climactic end to this phase either, no paternal interdiction, no need—and no desire—to substitute for or to symbolize the maternal body. Rather than an early lesson in symbolization, the undesired gain, followed by an even more undesired loss, of access to the mother's body finds an analogue in the photographic click that makes the body accessible only as a corpse. Written from the vantage point of maternal death, the narrative task is not to find a substitute in body or in language but to craft a form to convey an unspeakable burden:

> Suffering, like a stone . . .
> (around my neck,
> Deep inside me). (*MDY* [March 24, 1978], 106)

Read in the context of the *Mourning Diary*, *Camera Lucida*, often viewed as a hasty emotional outpouring, comes to seem almost as carefully composed as *To the Lighthouse*, although in a strikingly contrasting way. Instead of a narrative dialectic whose tripartite structure—presence, absence, reconciliation—is foundational to mourning in a form *To the Lighthouse* demonstrates vividly, *Camera Lucida* insists on nondialecticized binaries. The text's two-part structure, presented as an ode and palinode, affirmation and recantation, refuses any third term that might lead to resolution. Whereas the thematic binaries within the text—*studium/punctum*, mourning/suffering—recall Barthes's other signal pairs (denotation/connotation, text/work, pleasure/jouissance, author/scriptor), they are elevated here to a structural principle of suffering. Refusing the label "melancholia," Barthes nevertheless appropriates Freud's central metaphor of "a painful wound" that is incurable, and hence intractable, immobile, because it cannot be spoken (MM, 179). Barthes's turn to photography to make his case against mourning is as overdetermined as Woolf's turn to painting, for photography in his account "is without culture: when it is painful, nothing in it can transform grief into mourning. And if dialectic is that thought which masters the corruptible and converts the negation of death into the power to work, then the photograph is undialectical" (*CL*, 90). "With the Photograph, we enter flat Death. . . . The horror is this: nothing to say about the death of one whom I love most. . . . I have no other resource than this irony: to speak of the 'nothing to say'" (*CL*, 93).

If this were in fact all there is to say, the difference between suffering's attachment to the "flat, platitudinous," surface of the melancholic medium that "teaches me nothing" and mourning's alignment with the rhythmic strokes of pigment on canvas that (although nonverbal) enable the catharsis that can lay the mother to rest would outweigh Woolf's and Barthes's shared investment in light as a medium of maternal presence (*CL*, 106). But there *is* more to say because Barthes is unwilling to relinquish the possibility that the silence of the photograph might also preserve the moment prior to the fall into the body. If the nonverbal (the nonsymbolic, the intractable) could be reconfigured as the preverbal (the utopian, the preoedipal, the imaginary), the unspeakable as the unspoken, a different alternative to mourning might be conceivable. The other side of this possibility of silence is the relation Barthes shared with his mother who "never made a single 'observation'" and to whom he "never 'spoke' . . . , never 'discoursed,'" a relation in which "nothing to say" is an expressive alternative to language ("the very space of love") rather than its failure or impossibility (*CL*, 69–72). Barthes torques the intransigent Freudian mourning/melancholia dichotomy toward a broader spectrum of possibilities by routing it through two terms of the Lacanian triad. (The Symbolic is never in question in this version of a-cultural photography.) Barthes references Lacan only once, in relation to the Real: the "matte and somehow stupid" contingency of the photograph is "what Lacan calls the *Tuché*, the Occasion, the Encounter, the Real, in its indefatigable expression" (*CL*, 4). But Barthes also makes Lacan a pervasive presence through the recurrent invocation of the Imaginary as the psychic register of childhood.[55] Deciphering the relation of the Imaginary, which Richard Howard translates as the "image-repertoire," to the flat surface of the photographic medium is a challenge both to Barthes and to the reader, however. Bringing the Real under the aegis of the Imaginary (or at least in a dialogue with it) entails negotiating two divergent but intersecting projects: realigning with childhood a medium associated with mortality, death, the maternal corpse through a photograph that reimagines the mother as a child, and from that position reengaging with the material surface of the photographic print in more particularized terms than the adherence of the Referent whose scandalous assertion has preoccupied critics. This struggle, which constitutes an underlying, if unannounced, project of the palinode, entails filtering psychoanalysis through phenomenology.

Barthes's strategy for repositioning the mother-as-child (*mère-enfant*) pivots on the "discovery" of a single photograph that propels the "palinode" to spiral deeper into the self as it contracts the critical focus to a material image that is both visually absent (not reproduced) and descriptively present. The description of the photograph evokes an image whose physicality (unlike that of its subject) bears witness to the passage of time. That this is a strategy rather than the fortuitous "discovery" announced halfway through the text is revealed by the *Mourning Diary*, where Barthes reports his encounter with the photograph on June 13, 1978, ten months before beginning *Camera Lucida*. Beyond its richly articulated affective claims, this photograph does critical work by forcing into crisis the tension between image and embodiment.

Part 2 of *Camera Lucida* returns to the beginning through a clarification and particularization of time and place. The focus narrows from the indefinite temporal setting of part 1, "One day, quite some time ago," to "Now, one November evening shortly after my mother's death" (this is the first mention of his mother's death) as Barthes turns his attention from the public photos he encounters in books and journals to the family photographs he holds up "one by one, under the lamp" as he sits "alone in the apartment where she had died" (*CL*, 3, 67). The dark room of Barthes's inquiry—staged on an evening in November, although we know from the *Mourning Diary* that he found the photograph on a morning in June—comes into focus only with the mention of his mother's death, as if her death and his reinhabitation of its site occur at the interior of a coffin or a camera obscura, from which he seeks to resurrect her as he holds her images to the sole source of illumination (*MDY* [June 13, 1978], 143). Out of this dark space, through a kind of fairy-tale transformation, signaled by the language of a "sudden awakening," Barthes "discovers" the photograph that displaces the site of death with the place of birth: the house at Chennevières-sur-Marne in which his mother was born. Adjacent to the house is a "glassed-in conservatory, what was called a Winter Garden in those days," in which his mother as a five-year-old child stands with her brother (*CL*, 67).

Winter gardens are sites of conservation designed to keep in bloom flowers that would ordinarily die in the winter. In this instance, the photograph duplicates that function by preserving the image of the mother-as-child, distilling her essence under the aspect of eternity, fresh forever like Snow White in her glass coffin. Through the intervention of two layers of glass, the conservatory dome and the camera lens, the mother is recovered as "that essential child": both herself and Barthes's self-as-child, not just the "little girl" into which she declined as she aged, but the internal "feminine child" that "never ages" (*CL*, 72). This self lives on as an intact homunculus inside the adult: "For it is not the irreversible I discover in my childhood," as Barthes explains in his mock autobiography, "it is the irreducible: everything which is still in me, by fits and starts."[56] What Barthes recaptures as he "studied the little girl and at last rediscovered" his mother derives not from the child's resemblance to the mother that he knew but from her "expression" of innocence, which survives as the essential being of his mother (*CL*, 69). This "expression" links Barthes's mother to the Latin definition of photography (*imago lucis opera expressa*) he invents to dispense with the camera. The Winter Garden photograph elicits an "expression" from the mother that is "more than what the technical being of photography can reasonably offer" (*CL*, 70).

The conservatory as a light room, the eponymous *chambre claire*, the camera lucida, displaces the dark room (camera obscura) in which Barthes sits, peeling away the accretions of time and flesh that constitute the photograph as maternal corpse through a technological return to origins that doubles the biographical movement backward in time. The Winter Garden photograph is able to exceed what photography can offer by its identification with a setting that precedes the technology of photography. The conservatory was one of early photography's sites: Barthes notes that the first photographic portraits had to be produced "under a glass roof in bright sunlight" (*CL*, 13), which was in fact the setting of Julia Margaret Cameron's portraits, as she acknowledges in the title of her autobiography, *Annals of My Glass House*. But the light-filled, glass-enclosed room also works as an enlargement of the camera lucida. This essential childhood—revealed by stripping away the layers of time and life from the photograph as maternal corpse to uncover the irreducible essence of childhood as "the Sovereign Good" that is also "an essence of the Photograph"—is preserved by virtue of a prism of glass through which one could draw an image that need not be fixed or stabilized (*CL*, 71, 73).

Yet, unlike the free-floating images of the camera lucida, the Winter Garden photograph has a material form to which Barthes calls attention before describing the image: "The photograph was very old. The corners were blunted from having been pasted into an album, the sepia print had faded, and the picture just managed to show two children standing together at the end of a little wooden bridge in a glassed-in conservatory" (*CL*, 67). The five-year-old subject of the photograph may be magically enclosed in glass, but her image is mediated, even imprisoned, by an ancient body through which we can barely discern her face. Suddenly, and uniquely, here, in an overdetermined catachresis, the photographic surface Barthes elsewhere describes as a "weightless, transparent envelope" has become opaque (*CL*, 5): not only because this 1898 photograph is in fact old, but also because it functions symptomatically as a repository of or stand-in for the very old maternal body that Barthes seeks to hold at bay. Unlike the conservatory, or the image refracted through the prism of the camera lucida, the photograph, Barthes continues in a frustrated meditation sparked by *this* photograph, shares "the fate of paper (perishable) . . . it is still mortal: like a living organism, it is born on the level of the sprouting silver grains, it flourishes a moment, then ages. . . . Attacked by light, by humidity, it fades, weakens, vanishes: there is nothing left to do but throw it away" (*CL*, 93). Light that is the photograph's source has become its enemy. Sharing their human subjects' mortality, photographs on paper devolve along with them into disposable flesh: a condition of photographs in books that Carol Armstrong graphically describes as "this chemical process of aging, this liver spotting, this disintegration and disappearance of the print."[57] Unlike glass conservatories, photographs on paper that "yellows, fades, and will someday be thrown out" thwart our best efforts to make them serve as monuments (*CL*, 94).

Since Barthes is flipping through books and journals as he composes his thoughts about photography, virtually all the photographs he encounters are "given right there on the page," as he puts it, rather than exhibited behind glass or even printed on specially treated paper (*CL*, 43). Consequently, they all are subject to the vulnerability that printed matter shares with human skin. But it is only when the essential self is bound to an aging body that paper becomes visible in *Camera Lucida*. In an early instance, Barthes registers his dismay when an unusual photograph of himself that seemed to register "the distress of a recent bereavement"—some interiority—is transformed into a "horrible disinternalized countenance" when it appears on the cover of a pamphlet (*CL*, 15). But the dissonance between some internal affective self and the paper on which the image is printed emerges primarily as a rebound from Barthes's effort to extract his mother's childhood face from the medium in which it appears. The more fervently Barthes seeks to "outline the loved face by thought, to make it into the unique field of an intense observation," the more he tries to "clean the surface of the image to accede to *what is behind*," "to enter into the paper's depth, to reach its other side," the more the paper intrudes: "If I enlarge I see nothing but the grain of the paper: I undo the image for the sake of its substance" (*CL*, 99–100, emphasis in original). Whereas his discovery of the Winter Garden photograph prompts an exultation over the "distinctness" of his mother's face (*CL*, 69), a later return reveals her face as "vague, faded," "lost in the depths of the Winter Garden," as if the face has succumbed to its embodiment within the medium (*CL*, 99). The ecstatic present-tense first encounter with the Winter Garden photograph—"There she is! She's really there!" (*C'est ça!*)—language that recalls Woolf's signature phrase for beholding the presence of the other, cedes to the resigned acceptance of the medium that allows us to see it; *ça a été*, becomes "There she was." Barthes's hypothesis early in *Camera Lucida* that taste in photography is as idiosyncratic as "would be . . . a science of desirable or detestable bodies," an aside that has been interestingly read in terms of race, seems instead to register the distinction between the bodies of childhood and old age, especially when these are conjoined catachrestically, rather than consecutively, in a medium in which a very old body is the holding environment of the very young (*CL*, 18).[58] The intractability of the medium prevails over the irreducibility of the childhood imaginary.

To purge the image from the medium in which it is embedded, Barthes enlists phenomenology to mandate reducing photography to its "very essence, the *noeme* of Photography," which he at one point defines as "'That-has-been,' or again: the Intractable," to which the materiality of paper recalls us, but which he also, contradictorily, associates with the exemplary photograph, "the essence of the Photograph," "the only photograph which assuredly existed for me," which captures the irreducibility of the childhood self (*CL*, 76–77, 73). In antiphonal relation with the Intractability of the melancholic photographic Real stands the Irreducibility of a photographic Imaginary crystallized by the Winter Garden photograph through which Barthes submits to "the Image, to the Image-Repertoire" (*CL*, 75). To leverage the tension between the Intractable and the Irreducible in the interest of the latter, Barthes also recruits phenomenology more covertly, beyond the more "casual" and "cynical" uses he acknowledges (*CL*, 15), to enlist a perceptual register that is alternative to (rather than the essence of) photography, to pry the mental image from its material support and to constitute an unconstrained and unconstraining field of mental images. Dedicating *Camera Lucida* to Sartre's *L'imaginaire*, Barthes invokes phenomenology to temper psychoanalysis, redirecting Lacan's Imaginary (associated developmentally with childhood) toward a Sartrean imagination whose defining attribute is the separation of mental images from material support. He gestures toward this by stating that "the image, says phenomenology, is the object-as-nothing" (*CL*, 115), which segues into his familiar claim that the photograph that absents the object also bears witness to its anterior presence. Yet despite funneling phenomenology back onto the terrain of the referent, Barthes also indirectly invites us to consider the negation of the photographic object: not just the absenting of the object by the photographic image, but the purging of the image from the photographic object. It is this severance of the mental image from the object of perception on which Sartre insists. To posit an image, Sartre asserts, is "to hold the real at a distance, to free oneself from it," but the cost of this freedom is the sensory impoverishment of the mental (as opposed to perceptual) image.[59] Sartre's recurrent figure for this difference is skin: we can see the "grain of the skin," the enlarged pores, the "intimate texture" of the object of perception, whereas the object of imagination is skinless and vague.[60] Barthes's distress over the "grain of the paper" of the Winter Garden photograph suggests his attraction to Sartre's dematerialized images, a desire to dislodge the perceptual image presented by the photograph from its material prop and transfer it to the mind's eye. Or as Barthes says later, "The Photograph separates attention from perception, and yields up only the former, even if it is impossible without the latter" (*CL*, 111). Barthes's dedication and reference to Sartre's *L'imaginaire* betray his wish to untether the perceptual image from the aging skin of the photographic body and transfer it to a safely immaterial imaginative home: a preservative light room.

The closest Barthes can get is to give the Winter Garden photograph a younger, cleaner skin and restore it to a new "glassed-in" home. He explains his decision not to reproduce this photograph within *Camera Lucida* as a way to safeguard its uniqueness. No one else would experience its wounding force, he explains; and we can imagine his reluctance to submit the treasured image to mechanical reproduction by the printing press. Barthes doesn't simply keep the photograph out of circulation, however. Contrary to his claim that he "cannot reproduce the Winter Garden Photograph" (*CL*, 73), he sends it out for reproduction, as he mentions in his *Mourning Diary* on December 29, 1978 (a few months before starting *Camera Lucida*), but only for himself and in a way that enhances rather than endangers its aura. Although he doesn't explain his reasons for sending the photograph out for reproduction, it is presumably to restore it, to clean the surface in order to minimize the dissonance between the youthful face and the skin of yellow paper. Cleaned, restored, the photograph is then framed behind glass, transforming the mortal image into a lasting monument. And although he also notes that he can't bear to keep the photograph in front of him on his worktable because "it's too much—intolerable—too painful" (*MDY* [December 29, 1978], 220), three weeks later he does just that, and subsequently hangs it on the wall between two other photographs, one of the house at Urt, the other of camels (fig. 5). It has become a central, rather than a singular, image, one among several, positioned, as Laura Wexler argues, "at the edge of sight," where Barthes has neither to look at it directly nor to lose sight of it entirely.[61]

This process of distancing has been completed before Barthes begins to write *Camera Lucida*. Sheathed in glass, the photograph on the wall, returned to a conservatory, presides from the beginning over the composition of a text that does not acknowledge it is there. The photograph-as-monument of the mother-child, frozen in time, is arguably a condition of Barthes's ability to write *Camera Lucida*, to resubmit himself to suffering under the aegis of this monument as the guarantor of something that endures.

FIGURE 5. François Lagarde, "Roland Barthes at His Desk in Paris" (April 25, 1979). Photograph: Courtesy of Agence Opale.

Monuments are distant, chilly to the touch. Even the warm air enclosed in a conservatory, or the radiant expression of a five-year-old child, cannot be felt on the skin from the far side of the glass. If the Winter Garden photograph unframed has been too often touched, and touches Barthes too strongly, the framed version on the wall may not touch him closely enough, may veer too far toward the iconic, the eternal, the frozen Imaginary. Barthes is not ready to relinquish the light of the South West even after its source has disappeared. In the final sections of *Camera Lucida*, he renegotiates a relationship to light by introducing a new term, "air." Mediating between the photographic subject and its viewer, "the *air* (the expression, the look)" is "that exorbitant thing which induces from body to soul—*animula*, little individual soul" (*CL*, 107–8). A near synonym for "expression" minus the etymological link to the Latin formula for photography, the "air" of Barthes's mother is educed by but not resident in the Winter Garden photograph. As the "intractable supplement of identity" (*CL*, 109), it transfers the name of the photographic "that-has-been" to an imaginary realm that is "consubstantial" with the mother's face but independent of her aging body, a less corporeal locus that is also a cooler version of the carnal medium. The turn to "air" marks some attenuation, some distance from the source of rays, some turn away from the glow intensified by the imminence of maternal death toward the transparency of the early mother.

This turn is inflected by a new term that, in tandem with Barthes's signature metaphor, generates an apprehension of death that is different from—even antithetical to—the melancholic corpse:

> Thus the air is the luminous shadow (*l'ombre lumineuse*) which accompanies the body, and if the photograph fails to show this air . . . there remains no more than a sterile body. It is by this tenuous umbilical cord that the photographer gives life; if he cannot, either by lack of talent or bad luck, supply the transparent soul its bright shadow (*l'ombre claire*), the subject dies forever. (*CL*, 110)

The umbilical cord that linked "the body of the photographed thing" to the viewer has grown tenuous, a thing of air; it etherealizes a sterile body and materializes a transparent soul. Barthes's name for this attenuated medium is "luminous shadow." The photograph renders the transparent soul as the bright shadow of an absent body, the afterlife of a being that lingers in a photograph of air.

Rather than emanating light, the body of the dead casts a luminous shadow, a vacancy bearing traces of a presence. As the preservative magic of the *chambre claire* fades into an *ombre claire*, the scant auditory difference between *chambre* and *ombre*—not the sharp click of the shutter that divides the living body from the dead—suggests that life shades into death almost imperceptibly, the difference of a syllable, or a shadow tingeing the air.

This liminal zone entangles and grants equal weight to photography's defining terms: light and shadow. Both recalling and diverging from Lily Briscoe's painterly discourse of formal balance and distinction ("A light here required a shadow there"), Barthes envisions light and shadow as interpenetrating terms that can modulate an enduring impression of presence with an evolving acknowledgment of absence (*TTL*, 53). His figure of the light-filled shadow is not casually chosen: in "Loving Schumann," it recurs in his description of Schumann's lied as "continually taking refuge in the luminous shadow of the Mother."[62] Barthes ultimately exchanges the inhabitable light of the South West for neither the artificial air of the conservatory nor the lacerating wound of the photographic print, but rather for an air in which he could continue to breathe, an air that hovers in an indeterminate space between the living and the dead, the photograph and the viewer, but that remains an attenuated link between child and mother, felt on the skin rather than seen with the eyes. This is neither mourning (moving on) nor melancholia, but something else, some third term.

The search for a third term directs us to a discourse that triangulates the exchange between Woolf and Barthes. Psychoanalysis has informed their juxtaposition, but it can also be transformed by the light they bring to its own submerged third terms.

Bright Radiance

"The shadow of the object fell on the ego" (*Der Schatten des Objekts fiel so auf das Ich*)—perhaps the most celebrated phrase in "Mourning and Melancholia"—has been cited so frequently that it has developed a life of its own (MM, 249).[63] In a single dramatic moment that mimics the fall of a body as it passes from life to death, this body-object extends into the shadow that it casts. Beyond figuring the negative affective penumbra of the melancholic object, the shadow functions as a medium of concretization through which a lost object—or more accurately, a libidinal attachment to that lost object—enters the ego as an alien presence. Likening Freud's unusually visual scene to the representational mode of a "photo-graph, a writing with light," Jonathan Flatley points out that it describes less a melancholic identification with the lost object than "a kind of shadow play in which a certain portion of the ego has been marked in the *shape* of the lost object as darker than the rest."[64]

But in order to mark the ego, the shadow must traverse the bodily surface that is a troubled site for Freud. Although he eventually accords it a significant function in *The Ego and the Id* (1923) by asserting that "the ego is first and foremost a bodily ego" that is "ultimately derived from bodily sensations, chiefly from those springing from the surface of the body," Freud does not resolve how these bodily sensations might intervene in the phenomenology of mourning.[65] When he revisits the issue in an addendum to *Inhibitions, Symptoms and the Anxiety* titled "Anxiety, Pain, and Mourning" (1926), he struggles to reconcile the general understanding of physical pain as a stimulus that breaks through the body's protective shield (whose psychic counterpart would be anxiety) with the psychic pain of (nonmelancholic) mourning for an object in the outside world. The argument involves a series of displacements from the "peripheral stimulation" that gives rise to physical pain to the "psychical representatives" of the object that allow "the peripheral causation of physical pain" to be "left out of account."[66] Left out of the account more unequivocally is how the bodily periphery that registers pain might also register sensations of pleasure. At the opposite pole of the affective spectrum from pain, and the opposite side of the object from its shadow, there must be a source of light. As necessary to as it is excluded from Freud's framing of the shadow, that light and its imprint on the mourner's bodily surface and its psychological correlate—what we might call the unconscious of the shadow-figure—flicker briefly before waning in the language of psychoanalysis.

Teasing them out entails revisiting the displaced term from the title of the text Freud acknowledges as the "most important" of the precursors of "Mourning and Melancholia": Karl Abraham's 1911 paper, "Notes on the Psycho-Analytical Investigation and Treatment of Manic-Depressive Insanity and Allied Conditions" (MM, 242). Freud's interest in Abraham's paper, as evidenced in his own title, is the distinction Abraham draws between ordinary grief and "neurotic depression" (which Abraham intermittently calls melancholia). Abraham's title, by contrast, highlights a different pair: manic depression. Dropped out of Freud's own title, the terms *mania* or *manic* emerge only toward the end of his essay as a reaction formation and theoretical afterthought.[67] For both Freud and Abraham, mania is the flip side of melancholia, a libidinal rebound from melancholia's severity. Acknowledging Abraham's lead in linking these antithetical states, Freud does not address mania's association with renewal in Abraham's account of a reversion to "infantile freedom" that demonstrates "how deeply mania is rooted in the infantile."[68] Rooted in the infantile means rooted in the mother, a terrain that Abraham continues to explore and bequeath to Melanie Klein, along with the emphasis on libidinal development that constitutes his major contribution in "A Short Study of the Development of the Libido, Viewed in the Light of Mental Disorders" (1924), published the year he became Klein's supervisor. Within this framework, Abraham depicts mania as a regression to the oral drives, cannibalistic fantasies, and states of exaltation that characterize the early merger with the mother. Although he claims to find this libidinal stage's anthropological corollary in primitive rites of mourning as festivals of consumption and intoxication, he insulates the psychology of mania from that of mourning, both temporally (mania can only follow melancholia) and psychodynamically (mania is incorporative, mourning renunciatory). Whereas mourning trades in substitutions, mania and melancholia both refuse them, melancholia by identifying with the lost (paternal) object, mania by denying that the (maternal) object has been lost.[69]

Abraham was also the first to elicit what the shadow-figure obscures, and to do so in a way that flares out from his later paper, "A Short Study of the Development of the Libido, Viewed in the Light of Mental Disorders." In an untheorized burst of figuration, Abraham inverts Freud's figure in the course of a case study that resonates with Barthes's account of his relation to his mother. After describing the lost "paradise" of a bisexual patient's early years, Abraham focuses on this patient's response to his mother's death:

He was with her during her last illness and she died in his arms. The very great effect which this experience had on him was caused by the fact that in a deeper stratum of his mind it represented the complete reversal of that unforgotten situation in which he, as an infant, had lain at his mother's breast and in her arms.

No sooner was his mother dead than he hurried back to the neighbouring town where he lived. His state of feeling, however, was by no means that of a sorrowing son; he felt, on the contrary, elated and blissful. He described to me how he was filled with the feeling that now he carried his mother safely in himself, his own for ever. . . .

It is astonishing to find that this process of introjection should have resulted in such a feeling of happiness, in direct contradiction to its effect on the melancholic upon whose mind it weighs so heavily. But our surprise is lessened when we recollect Freud's explanation of the mechanism of melancholia. *We have only to reverse his statement that 'the shadow of the lost love-object falls upon the ego' and say that in this case it was not the shadow but the bright radiance of his loved mother which was shed upon her son.*[70]

Abraham presents this as a case of nonmelancholic introjection, but doesn't clarify whether *nonmelancholic* in this instance signifies its manic opposite or what he refers to as "the normal person" or (as I propose) some intermediate position. Nor does he account for his turn from the discourse of orality (the infant at the breast) to the rhetoric of light—and not only of light, but of "bright radiance" (*strahlende Glanz*), the adjectival intensifier that is absent for Freud's shadow suggesting what is also at stake in Abraham's silent emendation of Freud's "object" (*Objekt*) as "love-object" (*Liebesobjekt*) or of Freud's active verb (*fallen*) to a more ambiguously shared experience (*mitgeteilt*). Most strikingly, Abraham doesn't speculate about the import of his yoked reversals from shadow to light and from father to mother. Although he references the early paradise of merger with the mother, he doesn't ask whether a father's death could generate this luminous aftermath or whether (manic) radiance is as intimately linked to the death of the mother as the (melancholic) shadow is to the death of the father. The flash of light that suddenly erupts in Abraham's text—and erupts in the English translation, published by the Hogarth Press, the year before it published *To the Lighthouse*—seems to emerge from some unconscious source or memory that we might call (following Woolf) the "foreign matter" of psychoanalysis, although here that matter is light (*AROO*, 56).

Just how foreign is suggested by the response Melanie Klein developed across two essays: "A Contribution to the Psychogenesis of

Manic-Depressive States" (1935) and "Mourning and Its Relation to Manic-Depressive States" (1940). Having supplanted her mentor's assumption of an early preambivalent stage by her concept of an original paranoid-schizoid position characterized by the mechanisms of projection and introjection that split the mother into a "good" (gratifying) breast protected from the aggressive fantasies now channeled toward its "bad" (withholding) counterpart, Klein portrays mania—now exclusively a "manic defense" against the acknowledgment of damage psychically inflicted or received—as inseparable from a sense of triumph in possessing the "good" breast. "What in my view is quite specific for mania is the *utilization of the sense of omnipotence* for the purpose of *controlling and mastering* objects."[71] This critique of manic omnipotence precludes the recognition of any positive potential, as we see in Klein's redaction and reduction of Abraham's case study in her second essay. Relegating his key phrase to a footnote—as if it is too provocative to ignore but cannot be assimilated into the discursive body of psychoanalysis—Klein recasts Abraham's "bright radiance" as "passing states of elation" (that is, as circumscribed temporally as well as textually) that "are manic in character" and "due to the feeling of possessing the perfect loved object (idealized) inside."[72] Bracketing the figure of light, she reinstates the language of objects and interiors that displaces affects and surfaces. Most significantly, she summons her own experience, disguised as a case history, to reverse Abraham's scenario of mourning, substituting (her own) maternal mourning for a son for the luminous experience of maternal death.[73] Implicit in this generational reversal is a perspectival shift from a son's loss of a radiant external light source to a mother's loss of the life she has carried inside: an interior now doubly vacated by birth and by death. It is this painfully empty interior that urgently needs replenishing: a vacuum Klein had previously theorized in her reading of the "empty space" within the painter Ruth Kjär.[74] This need, manifested in the solace "Mrs. A" (Klein's stand-in) receives from looking at attractive houses in the country and wishing for her own, reduces the affective locus of skin to an invisible, insensate outer boundary of an internal object world. Abraham's inversion is thereby reinverted; the radiant potential of mania is circumscribed; and the work of mourning is revalorized as a hard-won struggle against manic defenses and paranoid fantasies.

The more conceptual and emotional effort devoted to replenishing an internal object world, the more remote and irrelevant the bodily surface becomes. Despite the busy psychic traffic between internal and external worlds propelled by the dynamics of projection and introjection, these transactions seem not to traverse a mediating sensory zone. Rather than granting Klein's premise that the site of reparation can only be "a complex

object-world, which is felt by the individual, in deep layers of the unconscious, to be concretely inside himself"—the adverb "concretely" suggesting how the tools and techniques of play therapy have materialized
the grammatical "objects" of psychoanalysis, investing them with weight
(both ethical and theoretical)—we could follow the lead of Woolf and
Barthes and ask why the work of reparation could not be undertaken along
a boundary.[75]

The luminous, tactile boundary zone Barthes and Woolf envision as their
earliest environment is just as endangered by maternal death as the internal object world. It is also just as needy and deserving of repair: whether
preemptively, in anticipation of maternal death, or retroactively, or both.
Empty space can be experienced outside the body as well as at its interior.
Unsurrounded by the translucent yellow film later in her life, Woolf felt:
"Very lonely. . . . Very useless. No atmosphere round me. . . . I have no pro-
tection. And this anxiety & nothingness surround me with a vacuum."[76] An
atmospheric void can be lethal: imagining that his mother will never return,
Barthes feels "a sort of black wing (of the definitive)" descend on and stran-
gle him (*MDY* [August 3, 1978], 180). The luminous stroking Woolf imagines
with her mother, like Barthes's evocation of the carnal medium, attempts
to repair a catastrophic loss that can be experienced as rupture, vacuum, or
darkness. Read through a photographic lens that amplifies and validates the
tactility of light, their writing complicates the distinction between manic defense and reparative mourning on which psychoanalytic theory insists.

Skin Envelopes

Recent scientific developments in the diagnosis and treatment of manic
depression (with depression as the modern melancholia) have sought to
detach the condition from the negative judgments with which it has been
burdened by psychoanalysis. Anchored in a bedrock of neurochemistry,
manic-depressive (now more commonly bipolar) illness has been legiti-
mized as a medical condition. Alleviating the moral stigma has enabled
new autobiographical accounts to emerge that have greatly enriched our
understanding at the same time that they have reinforced the dominant
paradigm of alternating (albeit sometimes coexisting) antithetical states:
emotional highs and lows, racing thoughts and mental stagnation.[77] Woolf
has been a prime example of this shift in critical attention. According to
Thomas C. Caramagno, who supports his case with scientific studies as well
as passages from the diaries of both Virginia and Leonard Woolf, "Virginia
Woolf's symptoms fulfill the manic-depressive paradigm."[78] Shifting to the

rhetoric of light that Woolf shares with Barthes, however, opens up a paradigm beyond the clinical register.

"I've had some very curious visions in this room too, lying in bed, mad, & seeing the sunlight quivering like gold water, on the wall. I've heard the voices of the dead here. And felt, through it all, exquisitely happy," Woolf wrote in her diary on January 9, 1924.[79] Woolf's language of ecstasy here—which in tandem with hearing the voices of the dead would presumably be diagnosed as manic—anticipates the imagery of ecstatic merger with the lighthouse beam that she imagines for her mother and her own earliest memory of the "purest ecstasy" in the luminous envelope of the St. Ives nursery. Ecstasy, light, and the dissolution of the boundaries between life and death, mother and daughter: whether this is manic denial or psychological merger, whether it defers, refuses, or enables mourning, is difficult to determine.

It is this relationship between mania and mourning (rather than melancholia/depression) that has been overshadowed by the focus on biochemistry. While illuminating mania's exhilarating (as well as debilitating) features, including its kinship with and spur to creativity, these studies have not explored the relationship to mourning left hanging by psychoanalysis. Nor have they explored the possibility that mania might bear a relation to the maternal that could make it a precondition, rather than a denial, of mourning, a psychic shelter that enables mourning to take place, a solution to the paradox of how to proceed when the environment that is prerequisite to mourning is the one that must be mourned.[80]

Instead of moving toward biochemistry, Woolf's ecstatic light and Barthes's carnal medium engage a different set of overlapping turns to the sensory modalities and sites variously addressed by affect theory, surface reading, new materialisms, and discourses of mourning (and psychic life more generally) that prioritize the intersubjective and intersensorial environments of emerging and grieving subjectivity. Anticipating psychoanalytic theories of an original tactile psychosensory envelope or "skin" (an exemplary case is Didier Anzieu's *moi-peau*) on which "systems of intersensory correspondences come to be inscribed," they suggest how these theories can be articulated with the indexical features of photography and the phenomenology of mourning for a lost maternal world.[81] Their maternal elegies open a window onto a general shift in contemporary approaches to mourning from a discourse of psychic objects and interiors to one of tactile deprivations and urgencies, and from the "private mise-en-scène of the psyche" to its material and social surround.[82] Constellating these shifts under the sign of "mania" offers a way to bridge the language of classical psychoanalysis with an emergent discourse of affects and sensations that deflects the critique of mania as a fantasy of omnipotence masking a failure to symbolize.

Attending to the fluctuating intensities of light makes it possible to bring mania into the orbit of mourning rather than stigmatizing it as a flight from loss. Disrupting the two canonical dyads—mourning and melancholia (the healthy/pathological pair) and mania and melancholia (the paired pathologies)—with mourning and mania as an interpenetrating alternative pair (a form of manic mourning rather than a manic-depressive malady)— demands that we negotiate between the suffering of "object" loss and the affective registers of the boundary zone. This requires an approach aligned with Barthes's concept of the "neutral" as "a back-and-forth, an amoral os- cillation" that "would defeat, annul, or contradict the implacable binarism of the paradigm by means of a third term."[83] Barthes's attraction to photog- raphy late in his life coincided with the urgency of rendering loss beyond the binaries of the psychoanalytic paradigm. The third terms he sought skirted the language system for "something of the opacity of film."[84] Following his path helps us remobilize a couple of eclipsed third terms—Woolf by Barthes and Proust, mania by mourning and melancholia—whose intersections and ramifications expand the possibilities of reading and grieving.

CHAPTER FOUR

Invisible Subjects

Woolf's Flickering in Sebald's *Austerlitz*

> Memory, even if you repress it, will come back at you and it will shape your
> life. Without memories there wouldn't be any writing; the specific weight an
> image or a phrase needs to get across to the reader can only come from things
> remembered—not from yesterday but from a long time ago.

W. G. Sebald, interview by Maya Jaggi, 2001

Woolf seems to remain in eclipse in the dark world of W. G. Sebald, but her
narrative forms and images linger among the memories that inform his final
text. Since Sebald embraces an aesthetic of nuance and modulation rather
than fixed definitions or oppositions, however, she is not a static or mono-
lithic presence, nor does she yield a Barthesian third term, for there is no
possibility of a dialectical synthesis in Sebald's fluid literary world. Instead,
Woolf's oeuvre offers a mobile textual repository whose diverse features
perform different roles at different points in *Austerlitz*'s textual web. Across
a sequence of four sections, this chapter explores how Sebald introduces
Woolfian allusions into covert conversations with his more explicitly referenced European precursors. After situating Sebald's hybrid photo-text
in a complex relationship to Barthes's photographic and literary legacy,
the chapter proceeds to examine Woolf's contribution to a carefully constructed cultural geography that plays a British landscape and literary architecture, for which *Orlando* affords a hyperbolic instance, against Walter
Benjamin's melancholic vision of history. It turns next to Woolf's role in the
contrast between a set of Austerlitz's recovered childhood memories that
resonate with *To the Lighthouse* and a childhood photograph that recalls
a famously contrived childhood portrait of Kafka. The final (and longest)
section sharpens the focus to a trope that Woolf and Sebald share for negotiating the claims of literature and history. The most relevant Woolfian text
in this section is the story-essay "The Death of the Moth": a contemporaneous and deceptively minor irritant to *Orlando*'s comic grandiosity. Here,
rather than leavening a darker universe, Woolf's figure of the death-bound
moth counterbalances the spiritual transcendence implied by the trope

associated with another of Sebald's European precursors: Nabokov, whose passion for lepidoptery offers a fitting figure of an aesthetic virtuosity and cosmopolitan mobility that Sebald came to deem too lightly tethered to place and history.

Rather than a linear progression, this series of encounters is intended to spotlight Woolf's subtle role in sustaining the conceptual fluidity of Sebald's novelistic universe. The moth's fluttering wings signal this mobility at the same time that its oscillations are encumbered by mortality. Although Sebald evokes the potential of manic flight in a lyrical scene of airborne transit across England's dazzling night sky in an airplane piloted by the best friend of Austerlitz's youth, this aspiration toward transcendence yields a dual resolution: the friend's paradoxical release from the burden of history by death and Austerlitz's assumption of that burden by his figurative fall onto the Holocaust-ridden European ground on which he will meet the narrator (the friend's adult replacement) who will write his story. The brilliant night sky yields no permeating radiance—not even a luminous shadow—as a buffer against the wounds of an embodied history that the protagonist (rather than his expendable surrogate) must endure. The photographs that Sebald incorporates into his photo-texts are (unlike Barthes's) not vehicles of luminous connection. Any reparative possibilities in *Austerlitz* derive from literary rather than graphic mediums, but to fully grasp Woolf's function as a literary mother and the site of an unrecognized novelistic genealogy, we need to start with Sebald's linkage of the visual with the biological mother.

Uncanny Returns: W. G. Sebald Revisits the Light Room

When we first encounter Austerlitz, the eponymous protagonist of W. G. Sebald's phototextual masterwork (2001), he is making notes and sketches in the "subterranean twilight" of the *Salle des pas perdus* of Antwerp's Centraal Station.[1] In this liminal moment between the last rays of the setting sun, which illuminate the gold and silver frames of huge mirrors facing the windows, and the onset of darkness, Austerlitz takes out his old Ensign camera and photographs the mirrors "which were now quite dark"(*Aus*, 7). Reporting the scene offhandedly, the narrator notes that he has been unable to find these photographs among the many hundreds that Austerlitz entrusted to him thirty years later. And so the stage is set for the unfolding and refolding of the narrative that springs from the absent photographs of an empty mirror.

A great many of the novel's driving concerns are compacted in this opening encounter. The narration of this scene is (as elsewhere) so matter-of-fact

that we don't initially notice how strange it is. Why is Austerlitz photograph-
ing empty mirrors? Rather than an answer, Austerlitz offers his own speculation about the number of workers who died from inhaling the mercury
and cyanide fumes emitted during the manufacture of the mirrors. Voiced
without explanation in French (a language tainted in this text by French
collaboration with the Nazis) and set off by italics, the question seems dis-
connected from its surrounding context. Only later, when we hear from
Vera Rysanová, Austerlitz's childhood caregiver, about the fumigation of
his mother's evacuated apartment by a German pest-control officer, "a particularly sinister figure with an unpleasant look in his eye" (*ein mir besonders
unheimlicher Mensch mit einem bösen Auge*) that Vera still sees in her dreams
"surrounded by clouds of poisonous white smoke," do we recognize the
association between the lethal gases of the Holocaust—evoked a few pages
later through the "poison-green" field and "clouds of smoke" emitted by
the petrochemicals plant near the former internment camp Terezín—and
the poisonous fumes concealed by the mirrors' "dimly shimmering surfaces" (*Aus*, 255, 263).[2] With this, we grasp as well what underlies Austerlitz's fascination with the vacant mirrors and the source of their vacancy: the
incineration of all traces of his mother into poisonous fumes has agitated
and evacuated the foundational metaphor that D. W. Winnicott named the
"mirror-role of the mother."[3]

We could hardly be further from the sun-kissed elegies of Barthes and
Woolf. And with good reason. Although written only a couple of decades
after *Camera Lucida*, the work of this German-born author looks back at the
spectral aftermath of the Holocaust, whose unacknowledged residue clogs
the atmosphere.[4] There is no carnal medium here; no habitable light of the
South West or caressing lighthouse beams; no day's sail after a long night;
no lighthouse at the end of the tunnel.

As the dark night's passage that in *To the Lighthouse* conflates maternal
death with the First World War evolves into the cataclysm of the Holocaust
into which Austerlitz's mother vanishes, the encounter with confounding
loss calls visual access to knowledge into question. The eighty-eight black-
and-white photographs reproduced within the text offer little grounding
for this attenuated narrative world, relayed through a web of syntacti-
cally embedded, disembodied voices. The grainy quality of the images—
intentionally degraded in some of Sebald's work by passage through a Xerox
machine—registers the particulate afterlife of disintegrated bodies instead
of the maternal caress of the sun.[5] Rather than anchors, these uncaptioned
photographs are "emanations of the dead" that offer windows into a broader
critique of the visual register.[6]

This critique puts on display a perversely hypertrophied visuality

precipitated by immersion in a dark impenetrable world. Initiating us into
the darkened universe of the Antwerp Zoo's Nocturama, where the text begins, the opening graphics present a vertical row of lithographs by Jan Pieter
Tripp, Sebald's friend and collaborator. Each of the four narrow rectangu-
lar frames displays a close-up of a pair of staring eyes: the two pairs above
the two lines of text depict what the narrator describes as "denizens of the
Nocturama" (variously interpreted as owls, bats, and raccoons) (*Aus*, 3).[7]
The two pairs below depict the eyes of Tripp and Wittgenstein, two of Sebald's alter egos and representative examples of the figures referred to in the
framing text's exposition of the "strikingly large eyes, and the fixed inquiring gaze found in certain painters and philosophers who seek to penetrate
the darkness which surrounds us purely by means of looking and thinking"
(*Aus*, 3).[8] The conjunction of painters and philosophers—with the implied
identification between looking and thinking—extends the critique of vision's privileged status to the ocularcentrism of Western philosophy more
broadly.

This initial figuration of a "fixed inquiring gaze," an adult iteration of
young Austerlitz's "piercing, inquiring gaze," finds a formal counterpart
later, on the opening page of the serial photographs of the fortified city of
Terezín, which Austerlitz visits in his quest to uncover his mother's story
(*Aus*, 260). Here, the front and rear facades of a house, perhaps one of the
houses in which his mother had been interned before being deported east,
are divided by two lines of text recording Austerlitz's impression that the
closed "gates and doorways" of Terezín are "obstructing access to a darkness
never yet penetrated" (*Aus*, 268). The first page of the sequence of Terezín
photographs and the first illustrated page of the text—and *only* these two
pages—are configured as two vertical visual blocks divided by two lines of
closely related text. Beyond revealing the historical locus of the metaphor
of the Nocturama, the mirroring relation between these pages lays bare the
underlying conditions of our existence: isolated, disembodied eyes open
wide in a futile effort to penetrate an impregnable barrier to a darkness that
intensifies the visual effort it also dooms to failure.[9]

These conditions require us to remap the ground that Sebald shares with
Barthes. Critical consensus has located their shared terrain in an engagement with photography, narrativized in both cases through a search for
traces of a vanished mother and a strategy of magnifying, or in Austerlitz's
case slowing down, the visual traces they discover. Sebald calls these in-
vestments into question, however, by having Vera dismiss the image that
Austerlitz believes to be his mother in the Red Cross propaganda film of
Terezín and by having Austerlitz dismiss the photograph that Vera offers
of his mother instead. Barthes's version of the photographic register is not

consequential in *Austerlitz*. The text is invested neither in the photographic print's melancholic inability to reanimate a past that now confounds representation nor in the manic potential of a luminous medium whose animating source has faded. Instead, Sebald distributes melancholy more broadly across the historical field of *Austerlitz*, which he aligns with the backward-turning gaze of Walter Benjamin's angel of history, who perceives "one single catastrophe which keeps piling wreckage upon wreckage" that the angel longs but is unable to "make whole."[10] Melancholy, as Sebald reminds us in *The Rings of Saturn*, is both an attitude toward and attribute of "our history" as "a long account of calamities."[11]

Dissociated from melancholy, the visual register in *Austerlitz* is relocated under the aegis of the uncanny. The *unheimlich* German pest-control officer ("sinister" is a weak translation of the German term famously translated from Freud's essay as "uncanny"), whose dispersal of all traces of Austerlitz's mother renders the maternal home similarly *unheimlich* (here literally "un-homey") and does so not only with his chemical gases but also with his evil gaze (*bösen Auge*), suggests how the visual functions as the sensory channel of the uncanny. Within the psychoanalytic tradition in which Sebald was well versed, the *unheimlich* derives from the repressed association of the home with the maternal body: "It often happens that neurotic men declare that they feel there is something uncanny about the female genital organs. This *unheimlich* place, however, is the entrance to the former *heim* [home] of all human beings, to the place where each one of us lived once upon a time and in the beginning. . . . The *unheimlich* is what was once *heimisch*, familiar; the prefix '*un*' ['un-'] is the token of repression."[12] Freud is explicit about the centrality of vision to the experience of the uncanny. He devotes a central section of his essay to a reading of E. T. A. Hoffmann's *The Sandman*, the basis for the first act of Offenbach's opera *Tales of Hoffmann*, in which Austerlitz's mother performs the star role of the mechanical doll Olympia at the Estates Theater in Prague. Hailing the "quite unparalleled atmosphere of uncanniness evoked by the story," Freud directs our attention to the figure of the Sandman who tears out children's eyes.[13] Correlating the fear of going blind with the fear of castration, he attributes "the uncanny effect of the Sand-Man to the anxiety belonging to the castration complex of childhood."[14] In his subsequent essay "Medusa's Head," Freud underscores the centrality of vision—and specifically the sight of the female genitals—to the fear of castration that undergirds the uncanny.

Sebald preserves Freud's focus on the gaze, but as with the evil-eyed German pest-control officer, he complicates the specular exchange and regrounds it in a specific geographic and historical location. The uncanny features of *Austerlitz*'s European landscapes (and only of those

landscapes)—the "silence, solitude, and darkness" that Freud specifies as
attributes of the uncanny, the ghostly doubles, the inexplicable but ineluc-
table coincidences, and the impression of returning to places one has been
before—derive from a condition of estrangement from a maternal home.[15]
The meanderings of the text's deracinated, disoriented, and doubling narrator and protagonist, split halves of a single exilic subject who run into
each other repeatedly and unaccountably on the Continent, are the bewil-
dered products of the historical upheavals that hyperbolize and thrust onto
a world stage the foundational condition of estrangement from a maternal
home. Passing through the various homes offered by and as the text of *Austerlitz*, the mutually traversing trajectories of the protagonist and narrator
reveal that the *heimlich* is always haunted by its opposite.

Following the lead of the Frankfurt School theorists whose displacement from their native land gave historical ballast to the psychic power of
an estranged yet familiar place of origin, Sebald transposes the Freudian
uncanny from a constitutive and biologically determined consequence of
human derivation from a maternal origin to the compromises entailed by
a specific historical moment. For Adorno, a lifelong influence and (according to Sebald's biographer) a "substitute father" during Sebald's formative
years, the conception of home in the post–World War II world had been
contaminated by the domestic sphere's tacit acquiescence to, or at least
failure to contest, the Third Reich's political and economic designs.[16] As a
result, according to Adorno, "the house is past. . . . It is part of morality not
to be at home in one's home."[17]

Austerlitz's mother, who haunts the empty center of *Austerlitz*'s textual
and psychic maze, is a case in point. She is poised at a painful crux of complicity as both the Nazis' representative victim (the only character in the
text we know they murdered, since the fate of Austerlitz's father remains
uncertain) and their oblivious enabler. One inference we could draw from
Sebald's careful narrative timing is that Austerlitz's mother, who names her
son Jacquot after Jacques Offenbach, remains in Prague, putting her family
at risk, in order to safeguard her debut in the role of Olympia, which "she
had dreamed of since the beginning of her career," in mid-October, 1938:
the precise moment that the Munich Agreement ceded the Sudetenland
to Hitler, who planned his invasion of Czechoslovakia for that month (later
deferred until mid-March) (*Aus*, 226).[18] Since the text offers no account of
why she refuses to flee with Austerlitz's father, which would have kept their
family intact, she implicitly bears some responsibility for the "sense of rejection and annihilation" that Austerlitz experiences as a young child "suddenly cast out of his familiar surroundings" when he arrives in Britain via
Kindertransport in 1939 (*Aus*, 322). Austerlitz's mother is an explicit figure

of origin (the apartment she shares with Austerlitz's father is listed under her own last name, which she confers on her son) who is implicated (however unwillingly) in the catastrophe she fails to offer shelter from.

When Sebald sends his adult protagonist back to his place of origin, the text insists that there can be no unmediated recovery of the mother after Auschwitz. The figure of the good mother inscribed in the very name of Austerlitz's mother—Agáta (from the Greek ἀγαθός [agathos] for "good")—has become entangled not only with the specific agent of the German pest-control officer, but also with the mythic figure of the uncanny: Medusa. Sebald's claim that "the horror of the Holocaust is like Medusa's head: you carry it with you in a sack, but if you looked at it, you'd be petrified," captures both his own dilemma as a writer and (as we will see) his protagonist's dilemma as a son.[19]

This dilemma drives a wedge between Sebald and Barthes in ways that are crystallized by Sebald's comments on a passage from *Camera Lucida*. In section 16 of that text, Barthes offers a meditation on Charles C. Clifford's 1854–56 photograph "The Alhambra (Granada)," which he captions with a phrase from the text (which in turn echoes Baudelaire): "I want to live there . . ." (CL, 39). The photograph (fig. 6) depicts an old stucco structure built over a round archway above which sits an arched double window: a facade readily legible as the face of a welcoming interior that distills the comforts of the maternal body from their potentially disturbing biological roots. Arriving at the end of the section at the body toward which the photograph gestures, Barthes admits the threat of the Freudian uncanny, but only under the sign of a de-negation that protects his vision of the ideal home: "Now Freud says of the maternal body that 'there is no other place of which one can say with so much certainty that one has already been there.' Such then would be the essence of the landscape (chosen by desire): *heimlich*, awakening in me the Mother (and never the disturbing Mother)" (CL, 40). Written in the German that reminds us of the negative prefix of which it has been shorn, the adjective *heimlich*, attached here to a maternal origin that is consciously embraced rather than compulsively revisited, siphons the disturbing mother away from her idealized form.

Unheimlich, Sebald wrote in the margin of this passage in his copy of *Camera Lucida*, administering a stern corrective to Barthes's wishful thinking.[20] Yet *Austerlitz* suggests that Sebald was drawn to (although he would also depict the limitations of) a certain kind of utopian *literary* architecture that, like Barthes's ideal home in a different medium, could offer a defense against the uncanny. Sebald and Barthes cross paths beyond the photographic field in a turn to the novel form: a turn they both depict as an entrée to an elevated literary tradition informed by the elegiac instead of the

FIGURE 6. Roland Barthes, "I want to live there . . ." [The Alhambra, Granada. The Wine Tower] (1862). Photograph: © The Metropolitan Museum of Art, New York. Source: Art Resource, New York. Photograph by Charles Clifford.

uncanny. This other genealogy, which stretches back to Dante and forward to Proust, also opens a pathway to Woolf.

Let us start by noting how Sebald's account of his turn from criticism to literature self-consciously echoes Barthes's deliberate echo of Proust (and via Proust of Dante) in his own account of his turn "toward the middle point" of his life from academic to literary writing (from the "way of the essay" to "the way of the Novel").[21] We may recall that, after drawing his essay's title from the famous opening line of Proust's *Recherche* ("Longtemps je me suis couché de bonne heure"), Barthes launches the essay's second half with the yet more famous opening line of Dante's *Commedia*: "Nel mezzo del camin di nostra vita" ("At the middle of the path of our life"). Here is Sebald, gesturing to Dante and Barthes (and via them to Proust) in his own account in an interview with Joseph Cuomo on March 13, 2001, shortly after the completion of *Austerlitz*:

> But what I felt towards the middle point of my life was that I was being hemmed in increasingly by the demands of my job at the university, by the demands of various other things that one has in one's life, and that I needed some way out. . . . This preoccupation with making something out of nothing, which is, after all, what writing is about, took me at that point. And what I liked about it was that if you just changed, as it were, the nature of your writing from academic monographs to something indefinable, then you had complete liberty.[22]

Yet more pointedly, Sebald routes his turn to "writing" through the same photograph in *Camera Lucida* that elicits Barthes's announcement of the novelistic potential of still photography: that is, a turn not only from the essay to the novel, but also from the visual to the literary. In his caption to André Kertész's photograph "Ernest," we recall, Barthes exclaims: "It is possible that Ernest is still alive today: but where? how? What a novel!" (*CL*, 83). Responding to Barthes's provocation, Sebald elaborates:

> But the fact remains: each image interrogates us, speaks to us, calls to us. In *La chambre claire*, the wonderful text by Barthes, there's a photograph of a little boy who had stepped out from behind his school desk [and] into the walkway. He is wearing this little apron worn by French schoolboys. I can't remember exactly how Barthes comments on the image, but he asks the question about what might later have happened to this boy named Ernest. One can imagine that it's perhaps the year 1903 or so: and that fourteen years later this now about twenty year old man sacrificed his life on the Somme or in Passchendaele, or at another horrible place. One can imagine the life-trajectories that emanate from these photographs in a much, much clearer way than from out of a painting.[23]

That Sebald, who does not have the photograph in front of him, misremembers its date as 1903, a date seemingly determined (as it would be in a novel) by the foregone conclusion that the boy would die on the battlefields of the First World War, tells us something about Sebald's own novelistic imagination, but despite the differences in the motive forces that drive the "novels" that Barthes and Sebald envision, these aspiring novelists share a conviction about the invitation to narrative extended by photography—especially, it seems, by photographs of young boys.

But the photograph (fig. 7) captioned "Ernest" (an unusually personal choice for a photographer who usually preferred more generic captions) actually depicts two child subjects. Behind Ernest, who seems to have been summoned from the activity represented by the open book on the desk to pose formally in the foreground in what seems an imitation of an adult pose, sits an unnamed little girl. She is in less sharp focus and wears light-colored clothing that, unlike the contrast between Ernest's brightly illuminated face and hands and his dark schoolboy smock, blends in with her skin. Rather than posing like Ernest somewhat fatuously for the camera, with an expression that takes for granted her status as the appropriate object of the camera's gaze, this unnamed girl observes the photo session that both excludes and includes her with an expression that is hard to read: attentive, thoughtful, skeptical, knowing. Like Ernest, her arms are crooked at the elbow, but unlike him she is writing. As the anonymous writer who observes but is unobserved by the photographer or his commentators—an especially surprising oversight in view of Sebald's insistence (indebted to Barthes) that narrative can be sparked by "something that is entirely in the margins of the image"—she is the counterpart inside the photograph to the aspiring novelists outside.[24] What story might she be writing? *Quel roman* indeed!

The anonymous girl's palpable but unacknowledged presence in the background introduces a depth dimension—psychological, temporal, and formal—to the project of novelization: a reminder of spaces and stories that shadow the narrative surface traced by Sebald's migratory characters. Seated rather than standing, the girl is a figure of contemplation rather than peregrination. We might speculate that the novel she would write would complement and complicate the straightforward narrative arc projected (however tragically) for Ernest. Rather than eliciting identification, she introduces difference: the second viewpoint of the second sex that, rather than narrative elaboration, invites the reconsideration of premises and places.[25] The narrative surface is opened through her presence to the recessive layering of the Woolfian novel: the work of memory without which, as Sebald claimed in the epigraph to this chapter, there "wouldn't be any writing," or at least any writing in the mode of *Austerlitz*.

The gendering of the background in this instance both is and is not coincidental: an artifact of this particular scene, it is nevertheless congruent with the countless cultural and social scenarios that prompt Kertész, Barthes, and Sebald to single out Ernest as their photographic subject. The woman in the background is a recurrent figure in *Austerlitz*, nowhere more poignantly than in the image of his mother that Austerlitz believes he can

FIGURE 7. Roland Barthes, "It is possible that Ernest is still alive today:
but where? how? What a novel!" André Kertész, "Ernest" (1931). © Estate
of André Kertész. Photograph: Courtesy Stephen Bulger Gallery.

glimpse between the longer shots of the Red Cross propaganda film of
Terezín. Hovering similarly between visibility and invisibility, the feminine
presence in the background of "Ernest," to recall Sebald's own words, "in-
terrogates us, speaks to us, calls to us," but in ways that require an effort to
discern.

One route might follow Sebald's attraction to Wittgenstein's concept
of a "family resemblance." The phrase occurs in a charged scene in which

Austerlitz sits alone in his London home arranging "in an order depending on their family resemblances" the black-and-white photographs that, as he later explains to the narrator, "one day would be all that was left of his life" (*Aus*, 168, 408). In contrast to Barthes's focus on particular responses to particular details in specific images, Sebald calls attention to the potentially revealing family resemblances that might affiliate numerous photographs without, however, telling us how these resemblances are to be determined. The phrase's colloquial meaning, suggested by the row of similar coats hanging along the schoolroom's back wall in "Ernest," is manifestly suited to the childhood subject of that image. There is, however, a more rigorous meaning of the term that more closely approximates Wittgenstein's privileged example: the rule-governed games whose commonality encompasses all potential iterations, comprising a relation based on structural, rather than substantive, similarities.[26]

We have already seen a prime example of the structural nature of family resemblances in the formal parallel between the vertical pair of staring eyes, including those of Wittgenstein, and the vertically aligned photographs of the closed doors of Terezín. What if we took this as a model for situating Kertész's pivotal photograph in a "family" constituted by formal relations rather than similitudes? It might encourage us to look beyond the similarities among boyhood photographs to a photograph whose family resemblance to "Ernest" derives from a structural parallel. In it, a ten-year-old Virginia Stephen peers out from the background of a photograph of her parents reading in the sitting room of their summer home, Talland House, in St. Ives (fig. 8).[27] Like Kertész, the photographer seems unaware of the pensive young girl's presence, but Virginia (like the writing girl in "Ernest") seems acutely aware of the photographer. Holding her chin in her hand (the classic gesture of the thinker), the young Virginia seems to be imagining the scene as she would recreate it thirty-three years later in *To the Lighthouse*, whose first part concludes with the depiction of Mr. and Mrs. Ramsay reading side by side at night in the sitting room of Talland House. But rather than depicting the physical appearance of the scene or its inhabitants, the adult writer dissolves the external scene into the interior worlds of her fictional parents. Displacing her sister behind the camera lens, Woolf substitutes a modernist novelistic practice for the photographic surface.

Whether or not Sebald was aware of this photograph (and it is likely that he was, since it was reproduced in a critical study of Woolf included in his personal library), it would have been part of "the archive that gathers behind the lid of an eye": the site at which cultural and personal imaginaries intersect.[28] At this site, and in the novel so richly informed by it, Woolf is an overdetermined source and figure of novelistic depth that complicates

FIGURE 8. Virginia Stephen (behind Leslie and Julia Stephen reading) (1893). Leslie Stephen's Photograph Album, Box 1, plate 38h. Photograph: Smith College Special Collections, Northampton, Massachusetts.

the narrative surface with the layering of memory. One reason she has not been seen within or behind Sebald's work is that (like the writing girl in the background of "Ernest") she has been obscured by the presumed centrality of a masculine alternative. As for Barthes, whose turn to the novel Sebald reenacts, this eclipse is routinely effected by Marcel Proust, who has been taken for granted as the sole modernist source of the elegiac affect, hypotactic syntax, and temporal stratification that differentiate *Austerlitz* from Sebald's earlier work. Hence when Eric Homberger notes in his obituary for Sebald that "reviewers grasped for the right comparison. Was it a gloomy Proustian? Or was it Jamesian?" one obvious answer to the reviewers' dilemma—that Woolf might occupy the space between Proust and James—appears to have been unthinkable.[29]

As Austerlitz slows down the film of Terezín to coax the woman he takes to be his mother out from "the black shadows" (350), we need to tease Woolf out of the textual shadows of *Austerlitz* by slowing down our reading in order to catch the traces obscured by Sebald's more explicit "monuments" to the writers often referred to as his "band of brothers." Drawn from Sebald's reference in his long poem *After Nature* to the works of art in which it seemed that "men had revered each other like brothers, and / often made monuments in each other's / image where their paths had crossed," the trope of the fraternal band—an elastic category whose core members include (with variations) Benjamin, Kafka, Nabokov, Hoffmannstal, Bernhard, Calvino, Canetti, and Borges—has guided the map of Sebald's literary genealogies.[30] Although diverse, these writers share an allegiance to an aesthetic of the improbable, the uncanny, the perverse, the ironic, the irreverent, and a certain darkly comedic tone and insouciance about the classification of genres. When Proust makes an appearance in this cast of characters, as he does only after the publication of *Austerlitz*, it is solely in relation to this final text, whose elegiac tone and more direct engagement with the Holocaust invite a broader set of Sebaldian affiliations, ranging from Proust to Primo Levi.[31] Never is Woolf (or any woman writer) included in this expanded cast of characters.

The section that follows uncovers Woolf's role as the anchor of an alternative genealogy underwritten by the figure of the missing mother. In contrast to the migratory modernist figures of exile routinely cited as Sebald's literary kin, Woolf is a nonexilic figure of origin, the one who stayed at home and consequently becomes an implicit source of figures of home exempt from Europe's catastrophic history. Recasting Woolf from her pejorative designation as (in Hugh Kenner's memorable phrase) a provincial "English novelist of manners, writing village gossip from a village called Bloomsbury for her English readers," hence unworthy of the stature granted "International Modernism," Sebald reclaims her as a counterfigure of literary genealogy, a British alternative not only to the band of brothers (the affiliations with Benjamin, Kafka, and Nabokov in particular), but also to the problematic of maternal origins, firmly rooted on the Continent, that undergirds their aimless wandering.[32]

The Architecture of Elegy

In "An Attempt at Restitution," a speech he delivered three weeks before his death, Sebald explained: "There are many forms of writing; only in literature, however, can there be an attempt at restitution over and above the mere recital of facts, and over and above scholarship."[33] The statement re-prises his previous account of his turn from scholarship to writing, now called "literature" and weighted with the mission of restitution for human cruelty and suffering. Offering both accounts shortly after the completion of *Austerlitz*, Sebald suggests that this text marked a turn in his writing that reaches back to Dante (and through him to Proust and Barthes) in a form that counterbalances the uncanny plots and peregrinations of his central characters through a desolate European landscape.

Austerlitz is Sebald's first and only novel, a crossroads in his career that points beyond the previous generic experiments that, as John Zilcosky puts it, "wandered along the borders between travel diary, memoir, collage, and short story."[34] Sebald is explicit about the distinctive generic features of each of his works, characterizing *Vertigo*, for example, as a mixture of crime fiction and (the narrator's) autobiography, and *The Emigrants* as "a form of prose fiction" that "exists more frequently on the European conti-nent than in the Anglo-Saxon world."[35] Although Sebald foregrounds the European genealogy of his "form of prose fiction," in which "there isn't an authorial narrator" and "dialogue plays hardly any part in it at all," it is also worth noting, conversely, the implicit association of the novel form with the "Anglo-Saxon world": a geographic region whose worlding, in parallel to the "European continent," evokes an analogous totality of the novel as genre. It is the formal complexity and integrity of the novel, whose multiple perspectives and temporalities are distinct from the first-person commentary of *The Rings of Saturn* and the four discrete narratives of *The Emigrants*, that enable the uniquely restitutive capacity Sebald attributes to literature.[36]

The interconnections among the Anglo-Saxon world, the formal archi-tecture of the novel, and the project of restitution have been obscured by Sebald's critique of the traditional novel genre, his objection to "standard novels . . . whose purpose is just to move the action along."[37] The critique, however, aligns *Austerlitz* with the tradition of fractured chronology, lay-ered narration, and self-conscious fictionality of the modernist novel; his dislike of realist novels in which an omniscient narrator "pushes around the flats on the stage of the novel" echoes Woolf's own complaints about "this appalling narrative business of the realist" that is "false, unreal, merely con-ventional."[38] Sebald attributes his break with the traditional novel—a break that he asserts is fully manifest only in *Austerlitz*—primarily to the writings of Thomas Bernhard, who developed a "periscopic" narrative technique of recounting only what is heard via others, but this debt to a German pre-cursor does not account for *Austerlitz*'s signature multilayered temporality: the highly crafted spatialization of time that formalizes the protagonist's perception that "time did not exist at all, only various spaces interlocking according to the rules of a higher form of stereometry" (*Aus*, 261).[39]

The interlocking spaces that organize *Austerlitz*'s narrative design align it with the formal hallmarks of the modernist novel, especially its articulation within the "Anglo-Saxon world" that constitutes the setting of the first third of the novel and the scene of its narration for a more extended portion. Not only does this mean (as we will see) that the literary allusions for which Sebald is renowned reach out in this section primarily to British authors (Woolf, Eliot, Auden, Conrad, Browne, and the contemporary poet Stephen Watt, among others); it also means that the distinctively British troping of the twentieth-century novel as (in Henry James's celebrated phrase) a "house of fiction" meshes with the domestic architecture of rural Britain to offer an affective and aesthetic alternative to the architectural exemplars of capitalism that prevail in the European capitals and constitute Austerlitz's scholarly obsession. The British framework, grounded in Woolf's figure of the multichambered house as a stay against the linear passage of time, is a critical component of the dialogue between modernist literary architecture and the historical pressures that engulf Austerlitz's biological mother. Rather than seeking solace (as Barthes did) in photography, it is the three-dimensionality of architecture, its metaphoric capacity to house diverse "pockets of time," whose elusive promise haunted an author who sought "redemption" in "release . . . from the passage of time."[40]

Beyond any particular loss (a parent, a house, a nation), *Austerlitz* evokes—in order to mourn—Woolfian modernism's faith in art's potential to transform an impoverished temporal landscape into a more commodious habitation. The centrality of form to this literary project reverberates in Sebald's characterization of *Austerlitz* as "in the *form* of an elegy, really, a long prose elegy."[41] The form of Sebald's elegy reconfigures the temporal sequence of loss and restoration as the accommodation of diverse moments of time. In *Austerlitz*, these temporal pockets are constituted as what Woolf called "space(s) of time," even as these subjective recollections are ultimately enmeshed with the traumas of European history.[42] Recovered and narrated in fits and starts, memory fuels and gives depth to narrative sequence. Designed to complicate the linear passage of time, Sebald's "house of fiction" hues more closely to Woolf than to James, whose figurative house centers on the "millions of windows" through which the outside world can be observed; as Jamesian observation yields to Sebaldian memory, windows open into rooms.[43] It is not coincidental that Sebald's temporal pockets recall Woolf's spatialized memories, for both writers grant memory specific architectural and narrative locations: Clarissa Dalloway's attic room, for example, or the clearly delineated spaces (restaurants, waiting rooms, sitting rooms, bars, observatories, taxis) in which Austerlitz relays his memories to the narrator, memories often recounted to Austerlitz himself in similarly dramatized scenes of storytelling. As Austerlitz's house in London is set up, by the transmission of his keys to the narrator, to be the future site of the text's composition, individual narrative segments are housed within specific times and spaces of narration.

An intricate but integrated narrative architecture results from the enfolding of stories within stories and the interplay between diverse sites and subjects of narration. Unlike the impasses, aporias, and flattenings of postmodern literary and material architecture, *Austerlitz*'s complexly crafted narrative design enlists its formal dispersals in the project of negotiating compromises between the acknowledgment and the refusal of time's passage.[44] The temporal and affective depth that results is quintessentially modernist, as is the wager that aesthetic form can salve the wounds of history. *Austerlitz*'s British-inflected formal architecture tempers the horrors of European history, enabling the reader to contemplate, rather than to be paralyzed by, "the full measure of the horrific . . . , because if you existed solely with your imagination in *le monde concentrationnaire*, then you would somehow not be able to sense it."[45]

Austerlitz is the only of Sebald's texts to straddle and contrast the Anglo-Saxon world and the European continent, each of which contributes a distinctive strand to the novel's cultural geography. In contrast to *The Rings of Saturn*, set in a Britain that is complicit in and scarred by history, *Austerlitz* draws on the mythology of a pastoral island nation to depict a cultural landscape that seems immune to, and therefore can be tapped as a resource for reshaping, the traumas of European history.[46] The text underscores Britain's apparent immunity by enclosing between asterisks the entire extended section (and only this section) covering the period from Austerlitz's arrival in London in 1939 to his encounter with the narrator in Antwerp in 1967. This self-contained narrative pocket, as insulated as the Britain it depicts from entanglement with Europe, tracks Austerlitz's path across a series of residences whose insistent and proliferating signifiers for "house" (translated into English as "manse," "grange," "lodge," and "grove") suggest a drive toward some elusive aesthetic, as well as domestic, domicile. Even when they are anti-homes, as in the young protagonist's emotionally and physically frigid first residence in Bala, Wales, there is nothing *unheimlich* about them or the relationships they sponsor. Instead, the domestic architecture of rural Britain underwrites the trope of the house of fiction as an affective and aesthetic refuge from the uncanny plots and civic fortifications that prevail in Europe's capitals.

Woolf is Sebald's vehicle for probing the fictional strategies that encourage our belief that time is open to cultivation through narrative in-tervention.[47] Many of Austerlitz's musings about time's passage echo tropes and scenes from Woolf. Standing under the "mighty clock" at the Antwerp station in 1967, Austerlitz delivers a disquisition on the "new omnipotence" of time that echoes the centralizing presence of Big Ben in *Mrs. Dalloway*, while the narrator's observation that the clock's six-foot hand is "slicing off the next one-sixtieth of an hour from the future" recalls Clarissa's impres-sion, upon hearing Big Ben's chimes, that "year by year her share was sliced" (*Aus*, 9; *MD*, 30). Conversely, by narrating Austerlitz's childhood arrival at London's Liverpool Station in 1939 through his delayed recollection half a century later, when he finds himself inexplicably drawn back to the station during his nocturnal wanderings in London in the early 1990s, Sebald con-figures this originary scene as a Woolfian cave, or multiple caves, of mem-ory "behind and within which many things much further back in the past seemed to lie, all interlocking like the labyrinthine vaults . . . which seemed to go on and on for ever" (*Aus*, 192). Sebald gently hints at the Woolfian connection by situating Austerlitz's recovered memory in a disused "Ladies Waiting Room" that he imagines to contain "all the hours of [his] past life": the unusual choice of "hours" (rather than the traditional psalmist "days") echoing Woolf's original title for the novel in which she discovered her "tunneling process."

Austerlitz engages most intensively with the text that most exuberantly, even parodically, puts on display Woolfian modernism's temporal ambi-tions. Commonly viewed either as comic relief from the work of mourn-ing undertaken by *To the Lighthouse* or as a playful exercise in gender and genre bending, *Orlando: A Biography* (1928) also clinches Woolf's engage-ment with the links among architecture, elegy, and temporality. Written as a literary compensation for Vita Sackville-West, who was legally barred by gender from inheriting Knole House, her family's ancestral home, *Orlando* performs a fanciful act of aesthetic restitution, an elegy on steroids, a hy-perbolic iteration of literature's ability to restore in language what has been forfeited to law. And not only to human law, but also to the ultimate law, mortality: subjection to time's passage. In addition to extending Orlando's life over several centuries, Woolf seizes the opportunity presented by Knole House's architectural oddities and stature as one of England's five largest country homes to remodel time itself, which for Sebald was "that most ab-stract of humanity's homes."[48] Knole House had already given that abstrac-tion material form in its 365 rooms, seven courts, and fifty-two staircases, lodged firmly in an architectural exemplar of England.[49] "No other country but England" could have produced Knole House, Vita Sackville-West de-clared, since it is "above all, an English house" with "the tone of England"

and a distinctly English mandate of exemplifying an ideal commonwealth capable of harmonizing the natural and the social.[50] In what is arguably the most English of her texts, the one devoted most explicitly and exclusively to English literary history, Woolf renders Orlando's recovery of her home as restitution for the losses wrought by history.

Sebald demonstrates his intimate knowledge of *Orlando* by echoing numerous passages that conjure the arrest of time. One cluster references the celebratory scene of skating on the frozen Thames during the Great Frost in *Orlando*'s Elizabethan youth. Austerlitz evokes the scene in passing in his final conversation with the narrator at the tellingly named Glacière metro station in Paris, where he informs the narrator that "there were great swamps here where people skated in winter, just as they did outside Bishopsgate in London" immediately before handing him the "key to his house in Alderney Street" (*Aus*, 408). The key to the house in which *Austerlitz* will be composed offers a key to a text that informs its composition. The intertextual echoes begin with a contrast between Orlando's exuberant Elizabethan youth and Austerlitz's privative childhood in Bala, Wales, where his sense of living "in some kind of captivity" comes fully into focus during his returns from boarding school in 1947, "the coldest winter in human memory" (*Aus*, 87), an echo of Orlando's description of the Great Frost as "the most severe that has ever visited these islands" (*O*, 25). When Austerlitz returns at half-term to find his foster mother dying from a mysterious illness that compels her to suffuse herself and her environment with a layer of fine white talcum powder, we hear an echo of *Orlando*'s description of a young country-woman during the Great Frost in Norwich who "was seen by the onlookers to turn visibly to powder and be blown in a puff of dust over the roofs" (*O*, 25). But the sense of the miraculous is absent from *Austerlitz*, and the scene is less magical than simply odd, verging on pathological.

During his second visit over the Christmas holidays, both of Austerlitz's foster parents seem to be dying from the "chill in their hearts" that internalizes the iciness of a winter in which

> even Lake Bala . . . was covered by a thick sheet of ice. I thought of the roach and eels in its depths, and the birds which the visitors had told me were falling from the branches of the trees, frozen stiff. (*Aus*, 89)

Many of these images derive from Woolf's description of the festival on the frozen Thames during the Great Frost in *Orlando*:

> Birds froze in mid-air and fell like stones to the ground. . . . [But] London enjoyed a carnival of the utmost brilliancy. . . . Here and there burnt vast

bonfires of cedar and oak wood. . . . But however fiercely they burnt, the heat was not enough to melt the ice which, though of singular transparency, was yet of the hardness of steel. So clear indeed was it that there could be seen, congealed at a depth of several feet, here a porpoise, there a flounder. Shoals of eels lay motionless in a trance, but whether their state was one of death or merely of suspended animation which the warmth would revive puzzled the philosophers. (*O*, 25–26)

But whereas the freezing of water and time in *Orlando* opens a space of aesthetic spectacle whose layers anticipate the fantastic architecture of the great house, the more subdued evocation in *Austerlitz* seems more deathly than enchanted.

The tension between a wishful time-suspending vision and an oppressive temporality culminates in a fleeting evocation of Orlando's house during Austerlitz's visit to the Royal Observatory at Greenwich, the world's prime meridian and the standard of world time, in the winter of 1995–96. Sebald underscores the scientific basis for standardized time at Greenwich, the epicenter and guarantor of global time, by guiding us through the display of "ingenious observational instruments and measuring devices, quadrants and sextants, chronometers and regulators" to the octagonal observation room whose 360-degree panorama is made visible through "unusually tall windows" (*Aus*, 140–41). Standing here at the apex, and in defiance, of the global site of temporal regulation, Austerlitz issues his "disquisition of some length on time." His language—virtually a modernist manifesto against the tyranny of clock time as the "most artificial of our inventions"—is manifestly Woolfian (*Aus*, 141). Austerlitz's insistence that a clock strikes him "as something ridiculous, a thoroughly mendacious object," echoes *Orlando*'s assertion of the "extraordinary discrepancy between time on the clock and time in the mind" (*Aus*, 144; *O*, 72). What links Austerlitz's critique most specifically to Woolf's, however, is his vision of the spatial coexistence of different moments of time. Taking off from a challenge to a Newtonian conception of time's uniform flow and density, Austerlitz's disquisition turns from the figure of time-as-river to the figure of a multichambered house. In a careful choice of words that reworks Orlando's insistence on "the sixty or seventy different times which beat simultaneously in every normal human system," Austerlitz translates time into space, anteriority into posteriority, in his wish that "time will not pass away, has not passed away," that he could "turn back and go *behind* it" (rather than *before* it) and there "find everything as it once was, or more precisely . . . find that all moments of time have co-existed simultaneously" (*O*, 233; *Aus*, 144, emphasis added).[51] In contrast to Proust, for example, Austerlitz's goal is not a release of personal memory that defeats time's linear thrust, but the conversion of time into an estate as capacious as Orlando's great house and as global in its reach as the prime meridian. There are numerous parallels between the two locations. With a panoramic vista of "half of England with a slice of Wales and Scotland thrown in," Orlando's great house rivals the 360-degree panorama afforded by the Royal Observatory (*O*, 71). Geographically local and aspirationally global, both the Royal Observatory and Orlando's great house stake their competing claims to universality in and as a manifestation of England.

As the image of the woman Austerlitz takes to be his mother flickers between the longer shots of the Red Cross film, a subliminal image of Orlando's estate glimmers between the lines of Austerlitz's disquisition on time. It is not just any version of Orlando's house, however, but the derealized version that is restored in the final pages of Woolf's novel. As the moon rises at midnight over the weald,

> its light raised a phantom castle upon earth. There stood the great house with all its windows robed in silver. Of wall or substance there was none. All was phantom. All was still. All was lit as for the coming of a dead Queen. . . . A Queen once more stepped from her chariot.
> "The house is at your service, Ma'am," she [Orlando] cried, curtseying deeply. "Nothing has been changed. The dead Lord, my father, shall lead you in." (*O*, 328)

The past has been restored, history transcended, and the visionary house presented to a resurrected queen reverts to its original owners in an elegiac form.

Austerlitz's vision cannot be sustained, however. In a final deflationary turn, his lofty disquisition on time submits to the pressure of history. Set in the narrative present of 1995–96, and interrupting Austerlitz's account of his formative years in Britain, the Greenwich scene both resists and registers the knowledge of history the adult Austerlitz has painfully acquired on the Continent, as if his very protest against clock time has been a defense against acknowledging the relentlessness of human history. That knowledge gains implicit recognition as, after a dash that underscores the break, the narrator's voice takes over from Austerlitz's with an uncharacteristically precise notation of clock time—"It was around three-thirty in the afternoon and dusk was gathering" (*Aus*, 144)—as the two men descend from the panoramic vista of the Royal Observatory to a darkening temporal world ruled not only by the mechanics of clock time but also and more painfully by the melancholic declines and uncanny repetitions of history.

We will return to this juncture and *Orlando*'s underside in a concluding section that will track a more nuanced interaction between aesthetic contemplation and historical immersion. For an intermediate position that sidesteps these extremes to explore the modest building blocks of narrative composition, we turn from the totalizing figure of literary architecture to the intimate architecture of interpersonal relations. As Austerlitz reverses his journey to Britain to revisit his childhood in Prague, we can follow his course backward from his professional identity as an architectural historian to a dual site of origin that houses adjacent versions of his childhood experience: a classically psychoanalytic version oriented toward his biological mother and a British object relational version oriented toward a second maternal figure who occupies the place of Kertész's writing girl.

Vera and the Writing Girl

At the affective center of *Austerlitz*, the protagonist journeys from London to Prague. Sebald renders this story obliquely: not just as the narrator's relay of Austerlitz's narrative as they sit together in Austerlitz's London home in the late winter of 1997, but also as Vera's recounting of her memories to Austerlitz during his visit to her Prague apartment. The technique of periscopic narration gains special prominence in this portion of the text. "Vera told me, said Austerlitz" (*Aus*, 244, 248), "Vera remarked, said Austerlitz (242)," "Vera continued, said Austerlitz" (246), "Vera described them to me, said Austerlitz" (250), punctuate the narrator's report, as if this string of oral transmission, and the proximity on which it depends, extend signal features of the childhood era into the narrative present. The text sets up a resonance between the domestic spaces harboring the storytelling duos in Prague and London: the first prepares the groundwork for the second, which offers a material and cultural surround attuned to the value of intimate talk.

After encountering each other by accident and design in a range of public spaces (railroad stations, cafés, parks, museums), the conversation in London is the first time Austerlitz invites the narrator to his private home on Alderney Street: a scene that is carefully scripted to proceed from a front room furnished only with a large table on which Austerlitz plays a solitary game of arranging his black-and-white photographs "in an order depending on their family resemblances" and a long ottoman on which, exhausted from the mental effort of striving to reconstruct his past, he reclines and feels "time roll back" (*Aus*, 168). The conventional psychoanalytic scenario implied by Austerlitz's position on the ottoman is given a different cultural twist by his tacit invitation to the narrator not only to fill the vacant space

of the analyst, but also to join him in an intersubjective space of imaginative play. With the narrator prepped for his dual role as auditor and participant in a two-person game, they proceed from the front room to the
sitting room, where they assume a more egalitarian position on two chairs
placed on either side of the hearth, the symbolic heart of the house. In this
sustained and attentive listening environment, Austerlitz reaches back to
the childhood memories restored by his earliest caregiver and reserved for
a scenario, elaborated by the British object relations theorist D. W. Winnicott, in which therapy and narrative intersect as forms of collaborative
play.[52] We have noted Sebald's evocation in absentia of Winnicott's concept
of the mirror function that Austerlitz's mother fails to fulfill. More generally, Austerlitz's childhood in Britain echoes a number of Winnicott's case
studies of inadequate mothering, especially a study of a woman who had
been traumatized as a child by her evacuation to England during World War
II.[53] Surprisingly unremarked, however, is that *Austerlitz* also renders an
affirmative version of Winnicott's key figure of nurturance. The negative
and positive versions are represented by the two central figures that shape
Austerlitz's early life: not his parents, since Austerlitz's father, guided by political convictions that take him to France and Germany, is primarily a vivid
figure of departure, waving goodbye at the doorway to the plane in which
he makes his escape to Paris the day before Hitler's troops enter Prague, but
a pair of maternal figures. In one apartment Austerlitz lives with his biological mother, Agáta (represented primarily on stage as an object of the gaze);
in the apartment next door he visits Vera Rysanová, his mother's closest
friend ("almost a sister") who has functioned as a surrogate mother and co-
parent who assumes the daily tasks of his emotional and material nurture:
taking him for walks, preparing his dinner, reading him stories, putting him
to bed, and fostering his imaginative development (*Aus*, 216).[54]

Adjacent to the mirror function left blank by Austerlitz's biological
mother, Vera fulfills the Winnicottian function of the "good enough" (not
necessarily biological) mother, the "enough" marking her as less idealized
than the unmodified "good" mother written into Agáta's name, but more
adapted to her charge's evolving creative needs.[55] Situated to one side of
the visual frame in which the longed-for face in the empty mirror can invert
into the head of Medusa, Vera operates in an unobtrusive verbal register.

Because our lexicon lacks a name adequate to her role, Vera has been
sidelined as a nanny or nursemaid and relegated to the margins of critical analysis.[56] Austerlitz, however, seems to have internalized the knowledge of her psychic presence, for although he journeys to Prague in search
of information about his biological mother and revisits the building in
which they had lived together, he never inquires about or tries to see their

former apartment. Instead, he simply climbs to the top of the staircase at 12 Sporkova Street and rings the bell of the right-hand flat. The probable existence of a flat to the left—the flat in which he had lived with his mother—is faintly registered and sealed from our eyes. Once evacuated by the German pest-control officer, the maternal home persists as an invisible and imaginatively vacant space that can be accessed only circuitously. In contrast to this empty space, the reencounter with Vera takes place primarily in her richly furnished apartment in which "everything was just as it had been almost sixty years ago" because "she could not bear to alter anything" (*Aus*, 215).

Vera's role is also endowed with a narrative refurbishing that affirms the special potency of the periphery. She is aligned with Sebald's indirect approach to the Holocaust/Medusa, in which the periphery enables an oblique perspective toward a story with the power to paralyze. She is also aligned with the narrator's peripheral vision, produced by a blind spot at the center of his right eye that redirects his gaze to the edges, where he can see "as clearly as ever" (*Aus*, 47). The periphery, moreover, is a gathering place for a range of off-center writerly presences. Vera has an antecedent in Kertész's "writing girl," who sits behind and to the side of the focalized subject, the position that Virginia Stephen also occupies in her childhood photograph with her parents. Vera and Virginia, whose peripheral contributions to *Austerlitz* are both underacknowledged, are affiliated by more than their first initials (a consonance that should not be entirely discounted in a text in which the letter *A* is the perseverating initial of Austerlitz, Auschwitz, Agáta, Alderney, Andromeda, and Ashkenazi, and a context in which the letter *V* similarly perseveres in the intimate world of Virginia, Vanessa, Vita, and Violet).[57] These decentered sources of narrative share a Winnicottian conception of childhood imagination as an enduring creative resource.

In addition to anchoring a peripheral lineage, however, Vera is Sebald's vehicle for transmitting the story of Austerlitz's biological mother. Centered in Prague, this story, grounded in a signal memory and photograph that Vera passes on to Austerlitz, explores the problematic of the historically compromised maternal origin from the perspective of her son. In so doing, it draws from the discourse of the uncanny elaborated by Kafka (a native son of Prague) and Benjamin, his self-declared double: a duo at the core of Sebald's band of brothers, affiliated at this juncture through a boyhood photograph of Kafka that shares a family resemblance to both Austerlitz and to Kertész's Ernest. Operating through visual similitude rather than (as for Vera, Woolf and Kertész's writing girl) positional analogy, this resemblance illuminates a shared specular dynamic. Vera is thus the site of a culturally freighted diptych of modernist childhood. On one side, rendered legible by Kafka and Benjamin, a set of visual scenarios distills the literary and cultural conventions for representing a traumatic European legacy grounded for Austerlitz in Agáta; on the other, rendered legible by Woolf and Winnicott, a storytelling chain initiated by Vera draws its affective resonance from a British literary mother and its theoretical support from a British clinician turned theorist of cultural experience.

CHILDHOOD PHOTOS

Agáta's sole material legacy to her son are two small photographs that Vera discovers "by chance" in a volume of Balzac's Comédie humaine that Agáta had borrowed from and returned to her. The first photograph, which shows a provincial theater stage with two tiny figures in the lower left-hand corner against a dramatic scenic backdrop, offers a generic image of theatricality rendered entirely through Vera's associations. The second, more intimate portrait presents the young Jacquot Austerlitz, dressed in a snow-white costume made by his mother for a masked ball at the house of an admirer in 1939 (fig. 9).[58] Jacquot is to accompany his mother dressed as the page boy of the Rose Queen in Strauss's Rosenkavalier. Looking directly at the camera, with his left arm bent at the elbow, the page boy assumes a posture very similar to Ernest's, but in contrast to Ernest, he fails to elicit a response from his adult viewer. Rendered "speechless and uncomprehending" by this photograph of a younger self he refers to simply as a "boy," the usually fluent Austerlitz remains untouched by a photograph he also dares not touch, as if he has internalized a prohibition on touching or as if the only form of touch he can imagine is a wounding one, as implied by his speculation that the child's bent arm might be broken (Aus, 260, 259).

Why does Austerlitz's only tangible inheritance from his mother evoke alienation instead of connection? It is not simply the elaborate costume that estranges him, but something in the setting of the image and the page boy's "piercing, inquiring gaze" (Aus, 260). Although Agáta is not included in the photograph, we feel her presence in the role she has fashioned for her young page boy. If, as Marianne Hirsch has argued, "every picture of a child is also, however, indirectly, a picture of the mother" . . . and "mothers are always exposed by and through their children," this picture exposes a mother who has groomed her child to play an ancillary role in her own performance.[59] The discomforts of the photo session are suggested by its time and place: this child is not en route to a masked ball, but has been summoned at what Austerlitz describes as the "grey light of dawn" to pose in fancy dress in an empty field (260). There is little evidence of Hirsch's "familial look" in the unsmiling face and stiff frontal posture Jacquot turns toward a camera that, regardless of who operates the shutter, is aligned with a maternal gaze more

FIGURE 9. "Jacquot as the Rose Queen's Page." From *Austerlitz* by W. G. Sebald.
Copyright © 2001 by W. G. Sebald, used by permission of The Wylie Agency LLC.

coolly appraising than affiliative. As the recipient not only of the photo-graph, but also of a photographic gaze that freezes, rather than affirms, its subject, Austerlitz cannot adopt the affiliative stance he believes that the photograph asks of him or grant his younger self the recognition of which he has been deprived. Even when, in an echo of Barthes's Winter Garden photograph, he uses a magnifying glass to scrutinize the image, he finds nei-ther himself nor his mother as a child but rather an unmothered child who "had come to demand his dues": but from whom and why? (260).

Although Austerlitz assumes that he is the guilty party, another answer is suggested by a larger family of boyhood photographs that share anxiety about the maternal gaze. In the same 1997 interview with Christian Scholz in which he positions himself in a novelistic genealogy with Barthes and Kertész by elaborating on Barthes's response to "Ernest," Sebald also ex-tends a visual alignment with the two key members of his band of brothers by describing a childhood photograph of Kafka that had riveted Benjamin as well (fig. 10). Sebald's keen interest in the photograph of Kafka as a five-year-old child—the same age as his own protagonist—is not surprising in view of his lifelong identification with Kafka as an exilic ghostly precursor who, like himself, was obsessed with uncanny narrative coincidences and photographic doubling. Indeed, he had described the same photograph in almost identical terms in an essay he had written on Kafka twenty-five years earlier.[60] Both iterations call attention to what Sebald describes in the later interview as the "absolutely desolate expression" of the young boy in a photographic studio in Prague looking "into the camera or halfway past the camera, with these giant, dark eyes, his gaze somewhat dejected."[61] In the more expansive version of the essay, Sebald develops the sense of coer-cion suggested by "the infinitely somber gaze of the five year old boy who, dressed in a sailor suit and with a shiny black walking stick and a straw hat in his hand, was dragged into the gloomy exoticism of a photographer's studio in Prague."[62] Anticipating the photograph of Jacquot in fancy dress, this ac-count also draws from another member of the band of brothers.

Like Sebald, Walter Benjamin had engaged with this same photograph twice. His more direct encounter is in "A Short History of Photography" (1931), where his description of the "immeasurable sadness" of the pho-tograph of the five-year-old Kafka whose "boundlessly sad eyes" stare out above a tightly fitting outfit against a backdrop of upholstered palm trees in a studio that resembles a cross between "execution and representation, torture chamber and throne room," seems to have inspired the "infinitely somber gaze" of Sebald's young Kafka.[63] But the more uncanny doubling that reverberates as well through the key childhood scenes in *Austerlitz* is Benjamin's ekphrastic evocation of Kafka's photograph the following year

FIGURE 10. Franz Kafka as a young boy (studio portrait, undated).
Photograph: Courtesy of Leo Baeck Institute, Inc.

in *Berlin Childhood around 1900*. In a section titled "The Mummerehlen," Benjamin contrasts his childhood love of self-disguise in language to his hatred of the imposed disguises of the photography studio. Segueing from the "tortured smile" on his own face in a childhood photo to a redescription of Kafka's childhood photo, he now presents the photograph *as if it were his own*. "I am standing there bareheaded," he writes, and proceeds to fictionalize the perspective of the child looking out from his niche in the photography studio toward an imaginary space: "Over to the side, near the curtained doorway, my mother stands motionless in her tight bodice. As though attending to a tailor's dummy, she scrutinizes my velvet suit, which for its part is laden with braid and other trimming and looks like something out of a fashion magazine."[64]

Benjamin's ventriloquization of Kafka's childhood image is more powerful in German: *die Mutter starr*, "the mother stares" (rather than the pallid and personal "my mother stands"), a generic figure that concatenates his own mother and Kafka's into an extension of the camera whose petrifying gaze travels across the studio to the upholstered palm trees that (in the language of the "Short History") "stand frozen in the background."[65] This is the generic Medusan figure whose permutations will resurface (along with her somberly gazing son) in one of Austerlitz's signal efforts to recall his childhood. And despite its outdoor setting, Jacquot's photograph also reflects the conjunction of the studio and the maternal gaze, as if *die Mutter* in her manifestation as the Rose Queen were standing to one side of the photographic frame and scrutinizing the elaborate costume she had made for him to wear. Sebald even mimics Benjamin's appropriation of someone else's childhood photo by borrowing from a colleague the photograph "of" Jacquot (whose reproduction on the book's front cover, where it mirrors the author's photo on the back cover, fosters the illusion that it depicts Sebald as well).

Sebald also arguably borrows the retributive strategy that Eduardo Cadava discerns in Benjamin's masquerade as Kafka. By deploying the power of the word against that of the image, in Cadava's astute account, Benjamin avenges Kafka by projecting a Medusan gaze back at the gorgonizing mother; mother and son transform each other into mannequins—or, if we add Sebald to this lineage, into versions of Olympia, the mechanical doll.[66] But in the struggle between verbal and visual powers in *Austerlitz*, the visual seems to triumph in Sebald's rendition of Agáta as Medusa. In the first and defining memory Vera offers Austerlitz of his mother, she recounts his childhood visit to Agáta's dress rehearsal on the evening before her debut as Olympia in the *Contes d'Hoffmann* at the Estates Theater in Prague in October 1938. Agáta enters Austerlitz's memory through her performance as a mechanical doll in a theater that takes the name of an estate rather than the home that is always offstage. Unsurprisingly, perhaps, the result is an auditory petrification: Austerlitz, usually a garrulous child, falls into a "reverent silence," seemingly because he fears that his mother has become "a complete stranger" to him (*Aus*, 227–28).

Prompted by Vera's narrative, the adult Austerlitz returns to the Estates Theater the following morning. The scene is meticulously staged: "Before me the proscenium arch of the stage on which Agáta had once stood was like a blind eye" (*Aus*, 227). The ocular metaphor translates the "heavy folds" of the "drawn curtain" into a closed maternal eyelid whose failure to see threatens, like the gaping hole at the center of the stage, to paralyze the child viewer. Young Kafka's imprisoning velvet suit reappears here as a "sort of velvet-lined casket" into which Jacquot feels shrunk to "to the stature of a little Tom Thumb" by the blind eye of his mother's empty stage (227). Austerlitz is freed from this miniature burial/castration only when someone walks behind the drawn curtain, sending ripples that stir the folds of memory.

The scene bears comparison to Mrs. Ramsay's reappearance at the window in part 3 of *To the Lighthouse* as Lily Briscoe struggles to complete her painting and her mourning: "Suddenly the window at which she was looking was whitened by some light stuff behind it. At last then somebody had come into the drawing-room. . . . Mrs. Ramsay—it was part of her perfect goodness—sat there quite simply, in the chair" (*TTL*, 202). Having built up to an equivalent sighting of a lost mother, however, Sebald takes a turn toward the perverse by echoing Hugo von Hofmannsthal instead of Woolf as Austerlitz imagines glimpsing a "sky-blue shoe embroidered with silver sequins" between the stage and the hem of the curtain (*Aus*, 228).[67] Since the curtain on *Austerlitz*'s stage is figured as both an eyelid and a dress, it covers both an eyeball and a leg; the fetishistic sky-blue shoe that sparkles in the blind eye of the curtain's slightly raised lid occupies the space where the pupil should be (the space that emits the blue-green light that draws Barthes toward his mother's inner being). Rather than the missing phallus, the eye is the organ for which the blue shoe substitutes, and does so problematically, for the glitter through which it achieves its function as a fetish impedes its function as an instrument of seeing. By deflecting the threat posed by one version of maternal insufficiency, Olympia's shoe participates in a scene of monocular and unreciprocated seeing that is mandated by Agáta's function as Medusa and insures that she will fail at mirroring.

Jolted by Vera's confirmation that the sequined blue shoe had actually been part of Agáta's costume as Olympia, Austerlitz recalls lying awake on the couch at the foot of Vera's bed "filled by a grief previously unknown to" him as he waits for his mother to come home from the dress rehearsal at the theater: home to him and home from her transformation into a mechanical doll (*Aus*, 229). The scene puts an uncanny spin on a classic modernist scene of childhood memory: the long wait for the mother's nighttime kiss, a scene inscribed into literary history by Proust but evoked by Woolf and Benjamin as well.[68] In *Austerlitz*'s version, longing is tinged with fear and mixed with ashes, as if Sebald were rewriting this touchstone of childhood memory in order to show how anxiety reimagines it. Long past Jacquot's usual bedtime, his eyes remain "wide open in the dark": the classic posture of exposure to the Sandman. When Agáta finally appears after an agonized period of waiting (*waiting* is repeated three times), Austerlitz sees her at his bedside in an "ashen-grey [*aschgraues*] silk bodice laced up in front" that recalls the tight bodice of Kafka/Benjamin's motionless mother. The adjective for "gray" (*grau*), moreover, is closely associated with the noun and verb forms for "horror" (*Grauen*), the word Freud uses to describe the head of the Medusa: *das abgeschnittene Grauen erweckende Haupt der Medusa* ("the horror-inspiring/-arousing decapitated head of the Medusa").[69]

Like Benjamin, Sebald deploys the power of language to transform the mother into a Medusa, although this does not redound to his protagonist's advantage. In contrast to Benjamin, however, Sebald also provides an alternative to the claustrophobic psychoanalytic scenarios through the very first memory that Vera recounts, which similarly culminates in Jacquot's little couch at the foot of Vera's bed but takes off from a different relation to a different mother.

STORYTELLING DUOS

We might wonder how Austerlitz, struck silent by the theatrical performance of his mother, the only member of this pair who seems encouraged to play, develops his impressive narrative skills and drive. For guidance we must turn to the mother next door and to a context in which play shifts from theatrical performance to improvisatory collaboration, and from the specular to the auditory. Rather than commissioning or cherishing a photograph of Jacquot, Vera encourages the "conversational gifts" that he demonstrates from age three (*Aus*, 218). Nurturing these through her boundless willingness to listen, she also prepares him to enlist an auditor like herself, someone "to whom he could relate his own story" and who will become in turn the narrator of *his* stories (as she is of his mother's) (60). Their encounters in the narrative present are characterized by reciprocal storytelling—"I don't remember in what order Vera and I told each other our stories" (216)—that magically restores Austerlitz's long-forgotten knowledge of Czech, the

198 ‹ CHAPTER FOUR

intimate mother-tongue in which they had conversed indoors about "more domestic and childish matters," in contrast to the French they spoke in public places "by agreement with Agáta" (219). As a result, "like a deaf man whose hearing has been miraculously restored," all Austerlitz wants to do in Vera's company is to close his eyes and "listen for ever to her polysyllabic flood of words" (219).

Austerlitz's immersion in this verbal bath flows into Vera's narration of a primal scene of storytelling. At once entirely ordinary and possessed of a magical quality, the scene, ritually enacted every evening during the warm season, takes place on the boundary between interior and exterior worlds. Perched on Vera's window seat after they return from their afternoon walk, Jacquot looks out at the enclosed space of an interior courtyard, blossoming with lilacs and bordered on the far side by a low building in which the "hunchbacked tailor Moravec" has his workshop. The simplified setting and archetypal triad of characters—child, guardian, and hunchback in a "walled garden," reminiscent of the "father & mother & child in the garden" that germinated into *To the Lighthouse*—brush the scene with the aura of a fairy tale that is "always the same, yet always slightly different" (*Aus*, 221, 220).[70] In the safety of this protected world, a quintessentially transitional or third space between walking and supper, inside and outside, self and other, Jacquot explores the relationship between the external world and his own subjective states.[71] Anchored indoors by Vera, performing the everyday routines of cutting bread and boiling tea, and outdoors by the hunchbacked tailor mending and sewing with the needle, thread, and scissors that are the "tools of his trade," Jacquot hones the tools of his own emergent trade by translating the tailor's actions into the "running commentary" he recounts to Vera (220). Stitching together with words what the tailor stitches with needle and thread, Jacquot weaves his own imaginative cloth. His special interest in narrating the tailor's preparations for supper while Vera is preparing his own evening meal demonstrates how the given world serves the shaping of a psychic interior. That the liminal space of the window seat that fosters imaginative play is for Sebald, as for Winnicott, a locus of cultural experience, that there is continuity between rudimentary narration and the transposition of observation into a more complex text, is suggested by Moravec's careful placement of his supper on a double sheet of newspaper "blackened with print," on which his curd cheese, radish, smoked herring, and boiled potatoes seep into the print medium that weaves readers into the fabric of an imaginary community while Jacquot translates supper into story (220).

Complementing the spatial imaginary that aligns the scene with the discourse of object relations in general and Winnicott in particular, this paradigmatic childhood scene, repeated at the same time every day, enlists the temporal strategies of the modernist novel. Suspended in time as well as space, the self-contained, affectively saturated childhood scene constitutes a modernist moment of being, set off from temporal flux, "ringed round" by memory, as Lily Briscoe might put it, cherished, preserved intact in a form that can be reinhabited, perhaps most fully, retrospectively (*TTL*, 174). For Woolf in particular, the moment is most fully actualized in memory, not the capricious version figured in *Orlando* as a seamstress who (despite her resemblance to *Austerlitz*'s tailor) "runs her needle in and out, up and down, hither and thither" (*O*, 78), connecting all sorts of incongruous materials, but the elegiac version exemplified by the memory scenes that Lily Briscoe and James Ramsay summon (in their different ways) in part 3 of *To the Lighthouse*. In the generational reversal of *Austerlitz*, Vera is the custodian and catalyst of Austerlitz's childhood memories, which enables her to recount to him the stories that he had told her as a child sixty years ago. By retelling them increasingly in Jacquot's own voice, segueing from the hypotactic syntax of the adult's retrospective narration to the parataxis of the child's present-tense narration—"He's putting the sleeve dummy in the wardrobe, he's going out into the kitchen, now he's bringing in his beer, now he's sharpening his knife, he's cutting a slice of sausage . . ."—she embeds a verbal trace of Jacquot's childhood voice, the seed from which the future text will grow, within the larger scene of its recreation (*Aus*, 220). Compensating (as would a therapist) for the insufficiencies of an impoverished early environment of play, Vera launches the narrative relay that will culminate in the text recounted to us by a narrator who reinstantiates her attentive listening environment.

Woolf's imprint on the scene resounds more fully as past and present draw more closely together when Vera rises in the course of her narration to open "both the inner and outer windows," allowing Austerlitz to revisit this privileged moment firsthand at the same time of day and year (evening in spring) as in his childhood (*Aus*, 221). Enhanced by the sound of church bells, the fragrance of lilacs in bloom, and the sight of the waxing moon (a Woolfian signature of plenitude), memories that had been "deeply buried and locked away" now come "luminously back" to Austerlitz's mind as he reoccupies his childhood position at the window. The echo of Woolf's "luminous halo, a semi-transparent envelope surrounding us from the beginning of consciousness to the end" gathers force as Vera unlocks another pathway to the past by opening the door to her bedroom, in which Jacquot had slept as a child on the couch at the foot of her four-poster bed, the furnishings unchanged (as in a fairy tale) over the intervening sixty years.[72] Austerlitz's recollection of Vera's "uncommonly beautiful eyes misting over in the twilight" as she bent down to kiss him goodnight, a marked contrast to the

blind eye and blue-sequined shoe presented on Agáta's stage, segues into
his feeling of safety in the care of this "solicitous guardian and the pale glow
of the circle of light where she sat reading" (222). The enchanted circle that
emanates from the figure of the reading mother sustains the child in a safe
space that recalls Woolf's memory of "lying in a grape and seeing through a
film of semi-transparent yellow": now a literary rather than a natural light,
and a solicitous guardian rather than a mother (Sketch, 65). The literary
resonances amplify as Austerlitz's adult consciousness dissolves into the
memory of his childhood consciousness dissolving into the "poppies and
leafy tendrils etched into the opaque glass of the door before [he] caught
the slight rustle of the page turning" (*Aus*, 223). The unraveling boundaries
between past and present, waking and sleeping, hearing and seeing, evoke
scenes from part 3 of *To the Lighthouse* in which consciousness interleaves
with the shapes of plants and the sounds of pages turning: Cam Ramsay
drifting off as she looks backward from the boat sailing to the lighthouse at
the receding leaf-shaped island of her childhood while her father turns the
yellowing pages of his book; James Ramsay remembering from that boat
the garden world of childhood over which at night "a very thin yellow veil
would be drawn, like a vine leaf" through which he could perceive the figure of his mother stopping and "hear, coming close, going away, some dress
rustling" (*TTL*, 185).

From the vantage point of the late twentieth century, Vera and Austerlitz cast this tender backward gaze at the last possible modernist childhood
idyll extended through Jacquot's early years in the late 1930s and cradled
between the turning pages of Vera's book. Vera consolidates its pastness by
redirecting her narrative as they proceed from the intimacy of her bedroom
to the living room to the walks they used to take through the Lesser Quar-
ter to the observation platform on Petrin Hill from which they had looked
down together at the towers and bridges of the city. Spatial distance registers temporal distance for Vera as she recalls her own childhood memories,
frozen as if seen in a diorama or "through a glass mountain" with the "un-
naturally enlarged pupils" of her eyes (*Aus*, 24). Is this vitrification the inevitable fate of Austerlitz's memories as well, or can the imaginative life Vera
has fostered in the luminous halo of his prewar childhood years be brought
to bear on the trauma that ensued and was already closing in on Jacquot and
his mother? Vera's commemorative mission requires her to fix her gaze on
the past to preserve it from the historical turbulence into which Agáta and
Austerlitz are thrown, but is there a way to transmute and transmit what
was fostered within that prewar past that does justice to the legacies of both
of Jacquot's mothers?

Austerlitz begins to suggest an answer in his final addendum to his instructions to the narrator before they separate at the Glacière metro station in Paris, where Austerlitz hands the narrator the keys to his home on Alderney Street. Recently, Austerlitz comments, he discovered an eighteenth-century Ashkenazi cemetery when a gate suddenly and magically stood open for the first time in the brick wall adjoining his house on Alderney Street. Despite its casual mention, this secret burial "plot," manifest only after Austerlitz's return from Prague, is a crucial supplement to the habitable space of his house. The enclosed memorial space in which the dead have rested peacefully for two hundred years offers some symbolic closure not only for the "plot" of genocide but also for the narrator's relationship with Austerlitz, whose parting admonition is to be sure to ring the bell in the cemetery's gateway.

With this injunction, Austerlitz bestows on the narrator an adult iteration of the interior courtyard that had fueled his storytelling from Vera's window seat. Like its childhood predecessor, the cemetery adjacent to the living space of the home is rendered in bright spring light and harbors lilacs (mingled here with lime trees as befits a memorial space). Marking the end of a life story (of Austerlitz, of the Jewish dead) rather than the beginning, and the end of a lived relationship with the narrator as the beginning of a literary one (as the narrator prepares to fulfill his charge of rendering Austerlitz's stories into a text), the cemetery in London nevertheless shares the Prague courtyard's fairy-tale ambience, now presided over by an "almost dwarf-like woman of perhaps seventy years old" and her aging Belgian sheepdog (*Aus*, 409). An avatar of Vera that replaces the hunchbacked tailor in Prague, this latest iteration of the writing girl extends her legacy into the present. By verbally transmitting this sanctuary along with the key to his house, Austerlitz bequeaths to the narrator the primary creative space of storytelling that is a necessary supplement to the work of composition he enjoins the narrator to undertake indoors.

But the legacy has become "a fairy tale which, like life itself, had grown older with the passing of time": one that has aged, along with Austerlitz and Vera, who had seemed almost unchanged, despite her fragility, in Prague. Does the "almost dwarf-like woman" ten years her senior mark her decline, or that of her version of modernism more generally (*Aus*, 409)? If we can infer from the replicating images of Kertész, Kafka, Benjamin, and Sebald that one iteration of modernist childhood—let's call it the European one as a shorthand—may survive into the present of Sebald's text (and beyond) through a process of doubling that they also thematize, the survival mechanisms of Woolfian modernism are less clear. How can they engage with the violence of history from which the fairy-tale courtyard and cemetery seem sheltered even if they submit to the passage of time? Is Virginia Woolf—or her writing—a fairy tale grown old?

If we glimpse Woolf, along with Vera, in the aging guardian of the Ashkenazi cemetery, we might be tempted to dismiss her work as a beautiful anachronism. That is not, however, her only guise in *Austerlitz* or the only yield of the Ashkenazi cemetery, for in a characteristically understated aside, Austerlitz also informs the narrator that he now suspects that the cemetery breeds the "moths that used to fly into his house" (*Aus*, 408). This trope, casually referenced near the novel's end, constitutes a complex thread through which Sebald weaves Woolf into a more dynamic relationship to history in general and to World War II in particular. Particularly apt figures of the transit between death and life, body and spirit, outside and inside, moths also figure the travel between the literary bodies of Sebald and Woolf in ways that modulate the binary oppositions within and between their oeuvres.

The Moth Aesthetic

For both Sebald and Woolf, it is the multidimensionality and mutability of moths—their tendency to swarm in loops and swirls rather than to fly in straight lines, their metamorphosis through diverse incarnations in a life cycle that nevertheless culminates inevitably in death—that enable them to serve as multifaceted figures of mediation. Conventionally, the moth's evolution from earthbound caterpillar to winged insect fosters a narrative of transcendence. For Sebald, by contrast, the moth's biological position in a life cycle that proceeds from egg to caterpillar (larva) to cocoon (pupa or chrysalis) to insect, a trajectory whose economic appropriations he charts (with the help of Sir Thomas Browne) in *The Rings of Saturn*, renders it a mediating figure of the conflict and collaboration between embodiment and transcendence, matter and spirit, melancholic history and aesthetic transformation. Rather than aligning Woolf with one pole in Sebald's negotiation between literary form and material reality, this shared trope nuances the interactions between aesthetic transformation and historical necessity. Through the figure of the moth, Woolf and Sebald engage in a complex dance that Sebald names, by echoing the title of Woolf's essay through the voice of Great-Uncle Alphonso, "the life and death of moths" (*Aus*, 132).

Austerlitz affords a welcoming twenty-first-century home to the moths that had an earlier genesis in Woolf's own work and life, beginning with the Stephen family's passion for entomology, manifested in a family Entomology Society of which the young Virginia was both chairman and treasurer, and a family publication by the same name. As a number of critics have observed, this passion recurred in different forms across Woolf's oeuvre, most intensively in *Jacob's Room*, where, as Catherine Lanone points out, the character of Jacob himself, in a textual mimicry of the butterflies he loves to chase, flickers between presence and absence throughout the text.[73] Lanone argues insightfully that the flickering of moth wings often signals a code switch, but rather than the switches between presence and absence that engaged Woolf in *Jacob's Room*, it is the oscillation between transcendence and mortality that claimed her attention at the end of the 1920s, a juncture that produced both the culminating modernist text of *The Waves* and the growing recognition of the burden of history.

This juncture begins with a letter to Virginia from Vanessa Bell in Cassis on May 3, 1927. In it Vanessa describes sitting "with moths flying madly in circles round me & the lamp. You cannot imagine what its like. One night some creature tapped so loudly on the pane that Duncan said 'Who is that?' 'Only a bat,' said Roger, 'or a bird,' but it wasn't man or bird, but a huge moth—half a foot, literally, across."[74] Virginia responded: "Your story of the Moth so fascinates me that I am going to write a story about it. I could think of nothing else but you & the moths for hours after reading your letter. Isn't it odd?—perhaps you stimulate the literary sense in me as you say I do your painting sense."[75] Vanessa stimulated her sister's "literary sense" in two quite different ways. The moths flying madly in circles remained a potent figure of instinctual life rhythms, as a diary entry of November 28, 1928, attests: "The Moths still haunts me, coming as they always do, unbidden, between tea & dinner, while L[eonard] plays the gramophone."[76] Hovering between the literal and the literary, as the curious slippage between her plural subject ("Moths") and the singular verb ("haunts") in the diary entry indicates, the imaginary moths that arrive unbidden with the sound of music on Leonard's gramophone between tea and dinner—those anchors of the realist novel ("getting on from lunch to dinner")—open a space for the airborne rhythms to which the formal patterns of *The Waves* aspire.[77] Originally titled *The Moths* until Woolf realized that moths don't fly by day, *The Waves* manifested the fascination with life's rhythms that the moths had catalyzed.[78] A subsequent diary entry confirms the enduring importance of the moths as a figure of nature's rhythms: "I am trying to convey: life itself going on. The current of the moths flying strongly this way. A lamp & a flower pot in the centre. . . . I shall have the two different currents—the moths flying along; the flower upright in the centre; a perpetual crumbling & renewing of the plant."[79]

If Vanessa's description of the current of moths in the plural inspires the abstract choral poem that evolved into *The Waves*, however, Vanessa's

"story" of the singular oversize moth that (as she proceeds to recount) she
captures and chloroforms inspires a different kind of "story-essay" that
Woolf titled "The Death of the Moth."[80] Precipitated out from the impersonal life rhythms flowing outside the window, the particular moth
of Woolf's story is entrapped (like Vanessa's moth) within a house that
doubles as a figure of the body. The narrator of this story watches with admiration and resignation as the moth flutters helplessly against the "square
of the window-pane" that divides it from the waves of vitality outdoors.[81]
Unable to restore the moth to its upright position by stretching out her
pencil, the narrator accepts that this "tiny bead of pure life" enclosed in
a hay-colored body and a human habitat cannot be "righted" by writing
(DM, 4). Neither the moth nor the writer can alter its allocated life span.
Like the windowpane whose transparency belies the reality of the material boundaries it imposes, the body of the moth cannot be sublimated
in an aerial form. Rather than offering aesthetic transformation, the "decently and uncomplainingly composed" body of the moth seems, like a
stoical soldier, to acknowledge that "death is stronger than I am" (DM, 6).
To write without righting is to propose the recognition, not transfiguration, of mortality.

The duality of the moth as a figure of both transcendence (from the caterpillar) and mortality appeals similarly to Sebald, who explains his position in terms that closely echo Woolf's. When Sarah Kafatou comments
in a 1998 interview with Sebald, for example, that an "elusive figure for the
spirit of art is the Nabokov-like butterfly collector" or "the butterfly itself,
or the moth," he sidesteps the reference to Nabokov in order to pay homage
to moths:

> I've always been interested in invertebrates, in insects, and very much
> in moths. They are infinitely more numerous than butterflies, more vari-
> ous, and often more beautiful. They exemplify the so-called biodiversity
> which is now being lost. A thing that appeals to me particularly in the
> moth is its secretiveness. Butterflies flit about in daylight, moths hide in
> darkness. You only see them when, for instance, they get into a house.
> Then they sit absolutely still in a fold of curtain or on a whitewashed
> wall, for days on end, until all life has gone out of them and they fall to
> the floor. Suppose that you had lost your way back out to the garden,
> to anything living and green! What the moth does in that case is simply
> to hold quite still until it just keels over. Perhaps that is what we should
> do, instead of bustling about going to see the doctor and causing trouble
> to everyone around us. The idea of transformation, metamorphosis, in
> terms of turning from a pupa into a beautiful winged thing, doesn't par-

ticularly appeal to me. It strikes me as rather trite. To me the really wonderful thing about these insects is the way they perish.[82]

Acknowledging that moths can represent both metamorphosis and mortality, Sebald follows Woolf's lead—contra Nabokov—reiterating even her setting of entrapment in a human habitat and her narrative arc by concluding
with the word "perish." Without repudiating Nabokov, whose artistry he
continued to admire, Sebald mimics the subtle ways of moths to indicate a
shift in his allegiance from the butterfly-collecting Russian émigré seeking
to net an elusive spirit of art to the moth-observing British novelist who
acknowledges the material boundaries that delimit both life and art.

The echoes of Woolf's story implicit in Sebald's interview with Sarah
Kafatou become explicit in a subsequent interview with Michael Silverblatt
that took place shortly after the publication of *Austerlitz*. Here, the focus on
mortality expands into a broader engagement with history in Sebald's only
explicit acknowledgment of reading Woolf:

> You know, there is in Virginia Woolf this—probably known better to you
> than to me—wonderful example of her description of a moth coming
> to its end on a windowpane somewhere in Sussex. This is a passage of
> some two pages only, I think, and it's written somewhere, chronologi-
> cally speaking, between the battlefields of the Somme and the concen-
> tration camps erected by my compatriots. There's no reference made to
> the battlefields of the Somme in this passage, but one knows, as a reader
> of Virginia Woolf, that she was greatly perturbed by the First World War,
> by its aftermath, by the damage it did to people's souls, the souls of those
> who got away, and naturally of those who perished. So I think that a sub-
> ject which at first glance seems quite removed from the undeclared con-
> cern of a book can encapsulate that concern.[83]

Sebald's critical purchase on Woolf's essay reveals him to be an astute and
wide-ranging reader of her oeuvre, for although "The Death of the Moth" is
not one of her better-known texts (testifying to the scope of his reading), its
selection by Leonard Woolf as the title essay for the first posthumous collection of her essays published in 1942, during the darkest phase of World
War II, corroborates Sebald's intuition that the text speaks presciently
about *both* wars and the implication of the second in the first.

Vanessa Bell's design for the jacket of the Hogarth Press edition (fig. 11),
which positions the elm tree under which Woolf's ashes are buried and the
banks of the river in which she drowned between the large black-lettered
title of the volume at the top and the black-lettered name of its author at the

THE DEATH of THE MOTH

VIRGINIA WOOLF

FIGURE 11. Book jacket by Vanessa Bell for *The Death of the Moth* (1942). ©
2022 Artists Rights Society, New York / DACS, London. Photograph: The
Henry W. and Albert A. Berg Collection of English and American Literature,
The New York Public Library, Astor, Lenox and Tilden Foundations.

bottom, further aligns the death of the moth with Woolf's own demise and situates them both in the context of war.[84]

Sebald's reading reflects his grasp both of the historical referent whose insistence in Woolf's work puts pressure on her embrace of imaginative transformation, *and* of the stylistic indirection through which she both registers and distances the burden of history ("There's no reference made"). The moth is a meta-figure of history *and* of its figuration; its capacity to straddle divergent realms, a capacity derived from its dual incarnation as a caterpillar and flying insect, enables Sebald to gesture both toward the unspeakable *and* toward its aesthetic antithesis.

An appreciation of the moth's duplicity emerges most fully in the portion of *Austerlitz* set at Andromeda Lodge, the rural Welsh family home of Austerlitz's childhood friend Gerald, whose untraditional family offers a refuge from the hardships of boarding school. Spanning Austerlitz's extended adolescence from his arrival at Stower Grange at age twelve in 1947 through the Lodge's sale in 1957, this surrogate home provides a cocoon for an emerging self, a misty dream-home whose inevitable but always deferred foreclosure only intensifies its charm. Perched in a blue-ceilinged room that seems open to the sky and the sounds and scents of the Irish Sea below, in a house surrounded by an orangerie enlivened with flocks of white cuckatoos, Austerlitz inhabits a moment suspended in time and space, bathed in birdsong and ocean spray, cocooned in a liminal zone in which "all forms and colours were dissolved in a pearl-grey haze" without contrasts, "only flowing transitions" whose evanescence paradoxically confers "something like a sense of eternity" (*Aus*, 135). Suspended in this scenario's mix are diverse attractions, kinship and friendship relations, and interspecies bonds that traverse multiple generations and positions woven together by ties of affinity rather than biology.

Austerlitz's mentor during this era is Gerald's Great-Uncle Alphonso, a naturalist and watercolorist whose signal gesture is the replacement of his eyeglass lenses with gray silk tissue that mutes colors and blurs divisions. As an advocate for subtle gradations and interstitial spaces, he becomes a spokesman for the moth aesthetic that he contrasts to the "passion for collecting" displayed in the cabinets of natural curiosities that fill Andromeda Lodge with the boxes of meticulously taxonomized specimens that have turned it into a "kind of natural-history museum" (*Aus*, 119). By contrast, Great-Uncle Alphonso takes the two young men outside at night to "spend a few hours looking into the mysterious world of moths." Austerlitz recalls their "amazement at the endless variety of these invertebrates, which are usually hidden from our sight" (127–28).

Through Great-Uncle Alphonso's induction into the world of moths,

Sebald separates himself from Nabokov, the member of the band of brothers who had flitted in word and image throughout his earlier work *The Emigrants* (1992) as the spectral "butterfly man" with a white gauze net that
Sarah Kafatou references in her 1998 interview with Sebald.[85] Whereas in
"Dream Textures: A Brief Note on Nabokov," written contemporaneously
with *The Emigrants*, Sebald had celebrated the ghostly features of Nabokov's
prose as a consequence of the disembodied perspective generated by exile,
from which he argued Nabokov's fascination with butterflies emerged, by
Austerlitz his perspective has changed.[86] One indication of the change is the
evolution of Great-Uncle Alphonso from the character of Great-Uncle Ambros Adelwarth in *The Emigrants*, who is associated with Nabokov through
their common residency in Ithaca. There, Nabokov chases butterflies—the
lifetime passion that he only half facetiously claimed to prefer to writing
novels—and teaches literature, while Great-Uncle Adelwarth, increasingly
driven by his self-imposed rules, interns himself in a sanatorium, which affords a final glimpse of him strapped down in a position that anticipates
the pinned-down specimens in Andromeda Lodge's collector boxes.[87]
In *Austerlitz*, Sebald gestures toward Nabokov obliquely by calling attention to the product rather than the process of the quest for butterflies, the
specimens pinned to the collector's board rather than the "beautiful winged
things" that had aroused Nabokov's childhood desire upon awakening to the
butterfly-engendering "rectangle of framed sunlight" in the family estate in
Vyra (a dramatic contrast to the "square of the window-pane" against which
Woolf's trapped moth struggles).[88] He clinches this critique by including
a photograph of a glass-cased specimen box displaying rows of butterflies
pinned to a white backboard. Although like all the images in *Austerlitz*, it is
unattributed, it has been identified as a photograph by Arwed Messmer that
is widely (albeit wrongly) believed to represent Nabokov's butterfly collection in St. Petersburg (fig. 12).[89] As taxonomic specimens become Nabokov's signature in *Austerlitz*, the tormented Great-Uncle Ambros Adelwarth
morphs into the contented watercolorist Great-Uncle Alphonso, whose philosophy of moths, based on contemplation rather than capture, appreciation
rather than classification, nighttime observation rather than daytime expe-
ditions, becomes a countervoice to a member of Sebald's band of brothers.
     Moreover, Sebald draws Great-Uncle Alphonso from Nabokov's orbit
explicitly into Woolf's. As Alphonso's critique of collecting segues into his
initiation of Austerlitz and Gerald into the world of moths that emerges
only at night, Sebald recalls a scene that Woolf first sketches in her essay
"Reading" and revisits in *Jacob's Room*. During a nighttime moth-hunting
expedition, a lamp is placed under a tree "and the insects came scrambling
from all quarters . . . so sitting on the ground we felt we were surrounded by

FIGURE 12. Arwed Messmer, "In the Zoological Museum in St. Petersburg" (1996). Photograph: Courtesy of Arwed Messmer.

life, innumerable creatures were stirring among the trees; some creeping through the grass, others roaming through the air. . . . Perhaps it was alarming to have these evidences of unseen lives."[90] In both of Woolf's texts, this is a moment of derealization that initiates a profound shift in perspective, a breach in the fabric of reality that "makes us stand still, in amazement."[91] Echoing this moment in *Austerlitz*, Great-Uncle Alphonso leads the two young men outside on a moonless night to a promontory above Andromeda Lodge and places an incandescent lamp in a hollow to which clouds of moths immediately fly "as if from nowhere, describing thousands of different arcs and spirals and loops, until like snowflakes they formed a silent storm around the light," a "wonderful display" at which the three men gaze spellbound until dawn (*Aus*, 128). For Austerlitz, as for Woolf, this constitutes a moment of revelation. Sebald transforms an inconspicuous moment in Woolf's oeuvre into an optic into a hidden universe that continues to expand throughout the night. After a detailed evocation of the infinite variety of moths, "perhaps some ten thousand of them by Alphonso's estimate," the three men marvel at the trails of light they seem to leave behind "in all kinds of curlicues and streamers and spirals" that are "merely phantom traces created by the sluggish reaction of the human eye" (131). It is this "sudden incursion of unreality into the real world," Great-Uncle Alphonso explains, that kindles "our deepest feeling" (131–32).

For both Sebald and Woolf, this moment of illumination in the darkness, this incursion of unreality into the real, is an opening into both beauty and death. In both *Jacob's Room* and "Reading," the moment is followed by, even seems to precipitate, a "terrifying volley of pistol-shots" in whose silent aftermath it appears that "a tree has fallen, a sort of death in the forest" (*JR*, 31). The allusion to the First World War that Sebald discerns in "The Death of the Moth" becomes more explicit here; in "Reading," it is reinforced by a narrative shift from the swirling moths whose description in Vanessa's letter fired Woolf's imagination to the capture of the individual moth that epitomizes the death-bound subject. The sudden turn from wonder to capture, from life to death, characterizes Sebald's narrative as well. After a brief aside about Darwin's description of a flock of migrating butterflies, an aside seemingly designed to rebound in the privileging of moths, Austerlitz reprises Great-Uncle Alphonso's discourse on what Austerlitz now calls "the life *and death* of moths" (*Aus*, 132, emphasis added). As death makes its quiet entry as a supplement to life, Sebald imports the title of Woolf's story into what Austerlitz describes as this "especially memorable" lesson of Great-Uncle Alphonso's (132). Through his transmission of this lesson, Austerlitz becomes the spokesman for the encomium to moths that Sebald offers in his interview with Sarah Kafatou and Woolf offers in "The Death of the Moth."

Austerlitz's narration closely follows Sebald's, which in turn hews closely to Woolf's. Austerlitz explains about moths:

> Of all creatures, I still feel the greatest awe for them. In the warmer months of the year one or other of these nocturnal insects quite often strays indoors from the small garden behind my house. When I get up early in the morning, I find them clinging to the wall, motionless. I believe . . . they know they have lost their way, since if you do not put them out again carefully they will stay where they are, never moving, until the last breath is out of their bodies. . . . Sometimes, seeing one of these moths that have met their end in my house, I wonder what kind of fear and pain they feel while they are lost. (*Aus*, 132)

The focal point of all three is the moth that strays indoors and meets its death with dignity, "clinging to the wall, motionless" in Austerlitz's exposition, "hold[ing] quite still until it just keels over" in Sebald's, and lying "most decently and uncomplainingly composed" in Woolf's.[92] Counterbalancing the emancipatory trajectory from body to spirit, caterpillar to moth—the sentimental subject of Nabokov's story "Christmas"—they trace

FIGURE 13. Photograph of a moth. From *Austerlitz* by W. G. Sebald. Copyright
© 2001 by W. G. Sebald, used by permission of The Wylie Agency LLC.

the moth's final passage across the threshold between nature and culture, life and death.

By transporting the moth from the vitality of its natural habitat into a domestic interior, Austerlitz, Sebald, and Woolf segregate the green world from the built world, reinscribe divisions in a landscape in which there had been "no contrasts," and import death into the solidifying architecture of the permeable dream-home. Through a series of coordinated and seamless transitions that soften this passage into a hardening world, life bleeds into death, Great-Uncle Alphonso's voice segues into Woolf's, and the plural moths (tens of thousands) that had swarmed around the lamp outdoors contract to the singular moth stilled (as in Woolf's essay) against a flat backdrop in the photograph that illustrates this turn in the narrative (fig. 13).[93]

SIR THOMAS BROWNE

Shortly after this photograph, Austerlitz breaks off his recollections of Andromeda Lodge and the scene returns to the narrative present in the winter of 1995–96 in the bar of the Great Eastern Hotel. The following morning (in a scene we have already discussed), Austerlitz and the narrator ascend to the Royal Observatory at Greenwich, where Austerlitz delivers his impassioned declaration of the multiple times experienced concurrently in the mind. As they descend from this elevated vantage point and the modernist declaration it supports, the moth recurs in a new iteration. As daylight dims and the narrator's voice takes over from Austerlitz's, the narrator notes the "drone of the great planes flying low . . . towards Heathrow. Like strange monsters going home to their dens to sleep in the evening, they hovered above us in the darkening air, rigid wings extended from their bodies" (*Aus*, 144–45). The description seems calculated to remind us of the fluttering wings of the insects and birds that populate this text as figures of mobility and flexibility. But despite the airplanes' animation through the trope of returning to their dens to sleep, their rigid wings evince their conscription to industrial modernity. Guided by instruments rather than instincts to their airport "home," these mechanical monsters bear witness to the name assigned to the first generation of British recreational aircraft: Moths.

In their declension from animate to mechanical creatures, the airplanes that accompany Austerlitz and the narrator on their descent from Greenwich also guide us downward from the utopian aspirations evoked at its pinnacle to their architectural and affective underside and the precursor who authorizes them. Rather than the restoration of the phantom house that shimmers between the lines of Austerlitz's modernist declaration, the downward trajectory of the moths directs us to Orlando's crypt, to which he descends in the chapter that follows the dissolution of the Little Ice Age and the glittering Elizabethan festival it had sustained. After the thawing of the Great Frost draws the boat carrying his beloved Russian princess, Sasha, out to sea, Orlando plunges into a melancholy that propels him downward into the seventeenth-century ambience of the "ghastly sepulcher" of the great house (*O*, 53). There, amid the scattered skulls and bones of his ancestors, he recalls that "there was a writer called Thomas Browne, a Doctor of Norwich, whose writing upon such subjects took his fancy amazingly" (*O*, 54).

The seventeenth-century writer and physician Sir Thomas Browne, who replaces Shakespeare as an idol as Orlando matures from an exuberant adolescent in the courts of Queen Elizabeth and King James to a melancholy young adult, is also a literary ancestor who connects Woolf and Sebald. Both writers were drawn to Browne's dark and fertile imagination and labyrinthine prose style, and both considered him a gateway to English writing. Moreover, it seems likely that Sebald discovered Browne through Woolf. Consider, for example, the echo between Orlando's recollection of Browne and Sebald's assertion that he began his "enquiries about Thomas Browne, who had practiced as a doctor in Norwich in the seventeenth century and had left a number of writings that defy all comparison"; or between Woolf's salute to "the sublime genius of Sir Thomas Browne" and Sebald's tribute to the "sublime heights" from which Browne sought to view the world; or between Woolf's account of Browne's "swooping and soaring at the highest altitudes" before "stoop[ing] suddenly with loving particularity upon the details of his own body" and Sebald's account of Browne "rising higher and higher through the circles of his spiraling prose" to offer a view of "the tiniest of details with the utmost clarity."[94] Most importantly, Woolf and Sebald shared Browne's concern with mortality and transcendence, historical circumscription and aesthetic transfiguration, body and soul, which were figured for all three by the dual embodiment of caterpillar and moth.[95]

Revisiting *Orlando* through a Sebaldian lens uncovers the seventeenth-century writer's critical role in the emergence of Orlando as a writer. Upon returning to his room from the ancestral crypt, Orlando opens Sir Thomas Browne's works and proceeds for an hour "to investigate the delicate articulation of one of the doctor's longest and most marvelously contorted cogitations," which leads Orlando to review his own experiments in writing (*O*, 54). As the figure Woolf describes in "The Elizabethan Lumber Room" as the "first of the autobiographers," the writer who focused attention on the "lonely life within" in contrast to the brilliance of the Elizabethan theater, Browne plays a pivotal role in Orlando's evolution.[96] Despite Orlando's glimpses of the "rather fat, rather shabby man" with a pen in his hand that we eventually recognize as Shakespeare, it is not Shakespeare but Sir Thomas Browne who gives birth to Orlando the writer (*O*, 59). Whereas Orlando the lover comes of age in the carnivalesque courts of Queen Elizabeth and King James, Orlando the writer needs to pass through an experience of loss and the emergence of memory articulated by Browne in the seventeenth century. The sequence concludes with Orlando's return to the book of Sir Thomas Browne, still open on his table. Meditating on "what remained" of human endeavor—"A skull; a finger"—Orlando hears rising from the open pages of Sir Thomas Browne "an incantation rising from all parts of the room, from the night wind and the moonlight"—for "this man and his words were immortal" (*O*, 60).

THE FALL OF ICARUS

If Sebald shifts our perception of Orlando's literary formation, he also uses *Orlando* to reimagine Woolf's literary affinities. In Orlando's passage from his ancestral crypt to his room, he paces through the long picture galleries of the great house, "looking for something among the pictures, which was interrupted at length by a veritable spasm of sobbing, at the sight of a Dutch snow scene by an unknown artist" (*O*, 54).[97] It is at this juncture, strategically positioned between Orlando's initial mention of "Thomas Browne, a Doctor of Norwich" and the reading that redirects his sense of his literary vocation, that Sebald intervenes on behalf of his own protagonist by evoking the same painting during Austerlitz's conversation with the narrator when they meet on the promenade of the river Schelde in Antwerp on the bright summer morning following their first encounter at the Antwerp station in 1967. Here, shortly after he has absorbed Great-Uncle Alphonso's lesson about the life and death of moths, Austerlitz describes his recollection of a late sixteenth-century Flemish painting (fig. 14). In one of the rare sunny moments in the text, spotlighted as a privileged moment, Sebald intervenes intertextually by translating the "Dutch snow scene by an unknown artist" which elicits Orlando's grief in "the great house in the country" into Austerlitz's ekphrastic depiction of "a picture painted by Lucas van Valckenborch towards the end of the sixteenth century during what is now called the Little Ice Age" (*Aus*, 15).

By specifying the Little Ice Age in his description of the painting rather than mentioning its title (*View of Antwerp with the Frozen Schelde*, 1593), Sebald nods to Woolf's evocation of the painting as the cause of Orlando's spasm of grief over his lost romance with Sasha on the frozen Thames during the Little Ice Age. But *Austerlitz* translates Orlando's personal grief into an allegory of human falling and failing. Through an extended present-tense ekphrasis, he evokes the painting so vividly that it displaces the sparkling summer scene immediately before them: "A shower of snow is falling from

FIGURE 14. Lucas van Valckenborch, *View of Antwerp with the Frozen Schelde* (1593). Photograph: Städel Museum, Frankfurt am Main.

the lowering sky above the tower of the cathedral of Our Lady, and out on the river now before us some four hundred years later, said Austerlitz, the people of Antwerp are amusing themselves on the ice" (*Aus*, 15). He then calls attention to a particular detail of this busy scene, using uncharacteristically vivid primary colors to render "very conspicuous" in his verbal redescription what is barely visible in the painting (and even less visible in the black-and-white reproduction): "In the foreground, close to the right-hand edge of the picture, a lady has just fallen. She wears a canary-yellow dress, and the cavalier bending over her in concern is clad in red breeches" (15–16). Focalizing the "lady [who] has just fallen" prepares for the pivotal final sentence, which segues from the present tense to the subjunctive in order to transpose the painted moment into the present one:

> Looking at the river now, thinking of that painting and its tiny figures, said Austerlitz, I feel as if the moment depicted by Lucas van Valckenborch had never come to an end, as if the canary-yellow lady had only just fallen over or swooned, as if the black velvet hood had only this moment dropped away from her head, *as if the little accident, which no doubt goes unnoticed by most viewers, were always happening over and over again, and nothing and no one could ever remedy it.* (16, emphasis added)

On the one hand, this expanded moment, imaginatively held in the mind's eye for four hundred years, is able to collapse time's passage into the recurrence of a single action. On the other hand, the moment is indirectly situated in history, enacted in this instance via reference to one of Woolf's compatriots who critiqued the evasion of politics and history in the preceding generation's iteration of literary modernism. For the language chosen to render this obscure sixteenth-century Flemish painting, whose selection appears to be driven by its resemblance to Orlando's "Dutch snow scene," seems intended to evoke its celebrated counterpart: Pieter Bruegel's *Landscape with the Fall of Icarus* (ca. 1558), a springtime scene that is compositionally very similar (a river opening to the sea on the right, a populated shoreline on the left) and whose key detail, a "fall" situated in the identical location, is just as visually inconspicuous and thematically central as Sebald's redescription of van Valckenborch's painting (fig. 15). The discrepancy between the mythic calamity Bruegel identifies in his title and the tiny space he accords it on the canvas has provoked the meditations of more than one poet. Sebald's rendition of the *View of Antwerp with the Frozen Schelde* signals the imprint of one of them. For there is no other reason for Austerlitz to dwell on the "little accident" of a fall, which "no doubt goes unnoticed," unless he wants to summon the

FIGURE 15. Pieter Bruegel the Elder, *Landscape with the Fall of Icarus* (ca. 1558). Photograph: Royal Museums of Fine Arts of Belgium.

interpretive lens of W. H. Auden's "Musée des Beaux Arts" (1938), whose present-tense ekphrasis of one Flemish Master's painting is likely to have offered a model for Sebald's own.

Composed during a visit with Christopher Isherwood to Brussels in December 1938, Auden's meditation on the marginality of human suffering in the work of the Old Masters condenses several paintings, as the plural in the opening lines indicates: "About suffering they were never wrong, / The old Masters." Art historians have argued persuasively that two other Bruegel paintings in the Museum of Fine Arts in Brussels (*The Census at Bethlehem* and *The Massacre of the Innocents*) contributed to the wintry landscape Auden depicts in his first stanza.[98] But the formal and iconographic similarities to van Valckenborch's *View of Antwerp with the Frozen Schelde* are so much more striking that, whether or not Auden also had that painting in mind, Sebald's rendering demands that we read the works by these two Old Masters together. For only these two paintings enable an understanding of human suffering, consigned (in Auden's words) to "a corner, some untidy spot," as emotionally marginal and conceptually central.

Sebald's investment in Auden's poem and Bruegel's *Landscape with the Fall of Icarus* is manifest elsewhere: he evokes the painting in *After Nature* and hung a reproduction of it on his office door at the University of East Anglia.[99] His decision to evoke rather than to specify these texts in *Austerlitz* reflects the modernist strategy of indirection he identifies in Woolf (mistress of the "undeclared concern"). The flickering of Bruegel's painting between the lines that describe van Volckenborch's anticipates the phantom house apprehensible in the interstices of Austerlitz's disquisition on time. But unlike the phantom house, the "Musée des Beaux Arts" carries its own historical weight, which engages the other pole of Woolf's aesthetic.

The poem's second stanza turns explicitly to the myth of Icarus, who (in Ovid's exposition) fell into the ocean when he defied the admonition of his artificer father, Daedalus, by flying too close to the sun with the waxen wings Daedalus had fashioned for them both to escape their confinement in a Cretan labyrinth. Although Auden's image of Icarus's fall—"a boy falling out of the sky"—will map complexly onto *Austerlitz* (as we will see), the poem itself, like the figures it depicts, averts its gaze from this disaster, but only to call attention to the act of turning away that is rendered succinctly in the poem's concluding lines: "and the expensive delicate ship that must have seen / Something amazing, a boy falling out of the sky, / Had somewhere to get to and sailed calmly on." Whether understood as a figure for the work of art or for the ship of state (or both), the "expensive delicate ship" that turns away from what it "must have seen" inevitably registers Britain's equivocal position in the aftermath of its acquiescence to the Munich Agreement, which ceded the Sudetenland to Hitler. This is the context in which Auden's reference to the "torturer's horse [that] / Scratches its innocent behind on a tree"—a scene that exists in neither painting—makes sense. The poem poses a choice, which Sebald also poses, between bearing witness to and turning away from a disaster that is historical as well as mythological, intentional as well as accidental. For human observers, unlike animals, are confronted with an ethical (arguably existential) question about engaging or ignoring what they "must have seen."

Written in December 1938, "Musée des Beaux Arts" was published the following spring, spanning the period during which Agáta was performing as Olympia on the stage of the Estates Theater in Prague and turning a blind eye toward history as well as toward her son. The poem's publication also coincides with Jacquot's arrival via Kindertransport in a Britain that shielded him from the knowledge of post-Napoleonic European history and afforded a prolonged period of innocence until the death of Gerald in 1967 thrusts him forcibly from the cocoon in a staging of the death of the moth and the fall of Icarus.

Bringing "Musée des Beaux Arts" into the textual mix enables Sebald to offer a final reflection on Austerlitz's fall into European history and Woolf's position in literary history. In a passage of sweeping lyricism that concludes the era of his British formation, Austerlitz recalls a nighttime flight with Gerald, whose passion for flying has led him to join the Air Cadet Corps, to study astrophysics at Cambridge, and to buy a Cessna plane with the proceeds from the sale of Andromeda Lodge after the deaths of Great-Uncle Alphonso and Uncle Evelyn in 1957. The Cessna is the distillation of Andromeda Lodge, and the night flight through the star-speckled sky the fulfillment of the celestial allusion embedded in the house's name. In the most intensely lyrical scene in the text, a liminal moment of unspecified (but arguably queer) possibility as the two young men seated side by side in the cockpit soar through the heavens and generative galaxies, Austerlitz bids farewell to an England newly visible beneath them and to an Andromeda Lodge transfigured into a celestial abode. Released from gravity and swirling through the constellations, the two men seem headed toward a transcendent home divested of the burdens of embodiment.

This is our last view of Gerald. After a brief reference to their subsequent walks in Geneva, Austerlitz reports in a flat voice: "I suppose it was inevitable that he would fail to come home from one of those flights. . . . It was a bad day when I heard that he had crashed in the Savoy Alps" (*Aus*, 165). Because that crash is only reported, not described, however, it appears that Gerald has indeed gone home by vanishing into the star-speckled sky, that he has achieved the escape from history Austerlitz himself has desired and that his insular adoptive nation has afforded. By fulfilling Austerlitz's desire to "have vanished without trace in the peace that always reigned" at Andromeda Lodge (111), however, Gerald also drains the visionary potential from their world, leaving Austerlitz on his own to succumb to the burden of history. Gerald's crash precipitates Austerlitz's own decline. The second half of the sentence reporting Gerald's death enacts that psychic plunge: "and perhaps that was the beginning of my own decline, a withdrawal into myself which became increasingly morbid and intractable with the passage of time" (165). Rather than yielding a new mode of mourning, manic flight precipitates a fall into melancholy.

In a pivotal moment that could be titled "the life and death of moths," the two young men split apart the moth's dual incarnations: shedding the mortal body of the caterpillar, Gerald is released into the "thousands of different arcs and spirals and loops" performed by Great-Uncle Alphonso's nighttime moths, while Austerlitz enacts the stoical death of the single moth that Sebald and Woolf both extol and associate with the inevitability of war. Enacting Great-Uncle Alphonso's description of the arc of life, "which, once the meridian is reached, leads without fail down into the dark" (*Aus*, 128), Austerlitz's fall also bears the symbolic weight of the lady's fall in Lucas van Valckenborch's painting and the fall of Icarus into which it is transposed by Sebald's evocation of Bruegel's painting and the Auden poem that has framed our reading of it.

Gerald's quest for the "liberation" enabled by the "lifting capacity of the air" is a quintessentially Icarian aspiration performed via airplane rather than wax wings (*Aus*, 161). Without any representation of Gerald's crash, Auden's "boy falling out of the sky" stands in as a description of the depressive aftermath of their shared euphoric flight. (It is worth noting that the term *Icarian* has been adopted as a name for manic depression.) By mentally reenacting the fall of Icarus rather than (like Auden's compatriots) averting his gaze from the falling boy, Austerlitz assumes the burden of confronting a melancholy cultural as well as personal past. In the context of mid-twentieth-century European history, there is no possibility of the manic mourning Barthes and Woolf could envision in the framework of a personal loss. Underscoring the ethical and political stakes of depression, Sebald splits it decisively from mania. The flight Austerlitz shares with Gerald is both a psychological prelude and an ethical counterexample to the burden he assumes. Austerlitz's "decline" into a melancholic state readies him to meet the narrator, Gerald's European replacement, to whom he redescribes the painting in Orlando's gallery in a way that clinches the chain of historical witnessing that extends from Austerlitz (and his informants) through the narrator to us.

By evoking Auden's poem via Austerlitz's revision of the painting that provokes Orlando's sobs at the center of his own melancholic decline, Sebald also refashions Woolf's reputation as a high modernist who averted her gaze from the mounting political pressures of the 1930s. In the crypt in which Orlando discovers a literary ancestor Woolf and Sebald share, Sebald also insinuates Woolf's contemporary, the titular head of the generation reputed to have superseded and repudiated hers.[100] Echoing *Orlando*'s turn from the artistic and erotic exuberance of the sixteenth century to their melancholy sequel in the seventeenth century is a turn from the artistic achievements of the high modernist decade to the next generation's ideological critique. Sebald's evocation of Auden's poem at a turning point in Orlando's vocation redraws the British literary map by refashioning the conventional account of the adversarial relationship between the socially engaged "Auden generation" of the 1930s and the previous generation they disparaged as an effete and ahistorical literary elite (an expensive delicate ship). This is not an opposition that Sebald's more capacious understanding of Woolf could endorse. By proposing an intersection between Orlando's picture gallery and Auden's visual museum, Sebald enlists Auden in the service of his own nuanced perception of Woolf as a modernist capable of torquing the poetics of indirection toward the registration of history: a capacity displayed as deftly in "The Death of the Moth" as in "Musée des Beaux Arts."

In Sebald's reading, "The Death of a Moth" is located conceptually as well as chronologically between the two world wars, encapsulating what Paul K. Saint-Amour describes as the "tense future" of the interwar years, the proleptic recognition that the fragile peace negotiated at the end of World War I was doomed to eventuate in another war.[101] The life and death of the moth gesture beyond the life span of an individual to delimit the arc of the interwar period during which a modernist poetics of suspension was increasingly haunted by the apprehension of the ending inscribed in its post–World War I origins. By bringing Auden's Icarus into proximity with Woolf's moth, Sebald amplifies Woolf's struggle as an interwar writer to negotiate the aesthetic priorities of two decades and the two phases of the moth's life cycle.

ALDERNEY STREET

The death of Woolf's moth makes its strongest appearance in *Austerlitz* in a setting that underscores the essay's anticipation of the Second World War: Austerlitz's relay of what he has learned about his childhood in Prague during the narrator's overnight visit to his London home. Austerlitz's narrative is divided into two installments separated by the narrator's description of the bedroom in which he processes the stories he has heard from Austerlitz. Folded between the two installments, the reflections in the bedroom constitute a textual analogue to the interior childhood space that Vera slips between the pages of her book and to the walled cemetery that Austerlitz encloses in his parting words to the narrator. In the privacy of a consciousness separated only by a thin wall from Austerlitz (we might recall the "crepuscular walls" of Mr. and Mrs. Ramsay's intimacy from *To the Lighthouse* or the adjacent apartments of Agáta and Vera), the narrator transposes the protagonist's memories into a different register that reprises and reinflects the death of the moth (*TTL*, 123).

The room is furnished only with a camp bed that resembles a stretcher and a wine crate that serves as a nightstand on which Austerlitz has placed (in seeming anticipation of the overnight stay) a carafe of water, a lamp, and "an old-fashioned radio in a dark-brown Bakelite case" (*Aus*, 232). Only after the narrator thinks about Austerlitz, whom he "could now hear moving about the room next door," does he look up and see "seven variously shaped Bakelite jars on the mantelpiece," no more than a few inches high, each containing "the mortal remains of one of the moths which—as Austerlitz had told [him]—had met its end here in this house" (232). Any question of whether the death of these moths alludes to "The Death of the Moth" should be settled by the specification (otherwise gratuitous) of the seven Bakelite jars, a nod to the seven attempts the moth in Woolf's essay makes to resume its flight before accepting its death. In constructing an altar to the moths, Austerlitz has also fashioned an homage to Woolf that fulfills the historical foresight Sebald attributes to her. For whereas Austerlitz in 1966 shared Woolf's assumption that the moths that meet their end in a house must have strayed in from a garden, the narrator's report in the winter of 1997 betrays the knowledge he and Austerlitz now share of Agáta's death in the Holocaust. Referring to the jars explicitly as tombs, each appropriate to the size of the moth body it contains, the narrator renders the bedroom an echo of the Ashkenazi cemetery whose discovery has led Austerlitz to derive the moths from the Jewish dead.

After tipping into his hand an individual moth whose delicate anatomy recalls the "frail and diminutive body" of Woolf's closely observed moth, the narrator returns the body to its "narrow tomb" and turns on the radio in its own "dark-brown Bakelite case" (*Aus*, 232). Like the jars a material container of immaterial spirits, the radio channels the nocturnal voices of female announcers and performers from far-flung European cities whose enumeration (Monte Ceneri, Rome, Ljubljana, Stockholm, Beromünster, Hilversum) culminates in Prague. Anticipated by the (Woolfian) description of the moth wings that "might have been woven of some immaterial fabric," the nighttime female voices transmitted through the airwaves, "drifting in the air from a great distance" (as the narrator puts it) or "weaving their erratic way far out in the air" (as Austerlitz puts it the following morning), compose a sonic elegiac web that reaches from London to Prague (234). As the voices of the narrator and Austerlitz mingle, Woolf's voice is interwoven with the voices of the Holocaust dead through the ethereal crossings of multiple voices "moving through the air after the onset of darkness" with "a life of their own, like bats" (or moths) that "shunned the light of day." Rather than an integrated announcer or performer, the radio transmits a disembodied chorus that fades in and out of audibility and mingles with "two careful hands moving . . . over the keyboard" in a performance of Bach's *Well-Tempered Clavier* (234). Interwoven and purged of identity, like the moths that had arrived to Woolf unbidden on the waves of Leonard's gramophone, this plural insubstantial female voice, accompanied by Bach's intricate reworkings of recurrent musical motifs, blends individual and collective mourning in a wordless female elegy that inscribes the memories of Agáta in a distilled, depersonalized choral form inflected with the historical trajectory implicit in "The Death of the Moth." The aerial female voices channeled at night through the radio-tomb weave together the moths that travel literally from the Jewish cemetery next door and literarily from Woolf's essay into a collective elegiac form. Relinquishing *Orlando*'s aspiration to transcend temporality,

Austerlitz embraces the historically freighted death of the moth *and* its transfiguration into elegy.

The night in Austerlitz's modest house in London's East End reprises the descent from the Royal Observatory that evokes Orlando's time-defying estate, but rather than focalizing the implications of that descent in the mechanical Moths that accompany the men, Sebald taps Woolf's minor story-essay to render moths that have crossed the barriers dividing outside from inside, death from life, history from literature, Europe from England. By drawing from disparate Woolfian texts and thereby drawing them into a new relation, Sebald offers a novel reading of Woolf while recruiting her to an increasingly permeable and plural iteration of elegy whose transmedial analogy modulates from architecture to music.

[AFTERWORD]

Vibrations and Visibility

> The traveling frequencies of literary texts [are] received and amplified across time, moving farther and farther from their points of origin, causing unexpected vibrations in unexpected places.
>
> Wai Chee Dimock, "A Theory of Resonance"

From the earlier side of the Second World War, Woolf anticipated Sebald's turn to communal choral modes. Her final novel, *Between the Acts*, published posthumously in 1941, experimented with the genre of the village pageant that gained popularity in Britain in the late 1930s. In *A Shrinking Island: Modernism and National Culture in England*, Jed Esty reads the novel and the cultural traditions it revives as an illustration of England's midcentury Anglocentric retreat from the high modernist cosmopolitanism that had been buttressed by its imperial position earlier in the century. By affiliating Woolf with a cluster of English writers from Browne to Auden, Sebald both gestures toward this national turn and complicates it by intermingling her voice with an international chorus. Woolf's late interest in communal choral forms affords a final crossing between the arc of her career and that of the long modernism brought into focus by her evanescent presence.

Set in the garden of a country house that hosts the community pageant organized by Miss La Trobe, *Between the Acts* deliberately breaks with the conventions that divide audience from actors, art from nature, and human from animal. The goal is to create an inclusive chorus that might bridge the divisions being enacted dramatically on the international stage. Wary of sentimentalizing community at a time of such fractured global existence, Woolf scripts the pageant to include a scene in which the local children race onto the stage holding fragments of mirrors that both reflect the disaggregated members of the audience and incorporate them into a larger (but far from cohesive) whole. The failure to integrate the human "scraps, orts, and fragments" is given auditory form by a malfunctioning gramophone and interruptions from the animal world.[1] By giving the statement of the pageant's message to the questionable figure of the Reverend Streatfield, who tentatively offers it as "We act different parts; but are the same," Woolf manages to affirm an underlying unity while withholding authorial consent (*BTA*, 192).

Although this dramatized exploration of an underlying unity is more ironic than Sebald's sonic web, a more lyrical version emerges in Woolf's two late unfinished essays. In "Anon" and "The Reader," she looks back from the fractured social world of the early years of the Second World War to the communal origins of cultural expression in order to reaffirm the collective sources of English literature that emanate from "the world beneath our consciousness; the anonymous world to which we can still return."[2] From this vantage point, the "reservoir of common belief," a metaphor that recalls "The Fascination of the Pool," takes the form primarily of song (*Anon*, 384). The anonymity that Woolf personifies in the figure of "Anon" is "the common voice singing outdoors. . . . A simple singer, lifting a song or a story from other peoples lips and letting the audience join in the chorus" (*Anon*, 382). This anonymous chorus, whose technologically mediated global iteration Sebald also embraced, measures the distance traveled from Woolf's high modernist version of anonymity as impersonal design, but it also allows us to reflect back on the dynamics of her shadow genealogy.

From their complementary positions before and after the full force of the Second World War, Woolf and Sebald celebrate the echoing voices at the center of the concept of resonance. For Wai Chee Dimock, who both builds on and diverges from Stephen Greenblatt's essay "Resonance and Wonder," resonance is the defining attribute of literature's existence as "a relation, a form of engagement, between a changing object and a changing recipient, between a tonal presence and the way it is differently heard over time."[3] For both theorists, resonance derives from an auditory register that is both internal to a text and a mode of its extension (and potential dissolution) over time. Both also contrast the dispersive auditory character of resonance to the centripetal visual operation of wonder, but rather than accepting Greenblatt's tethering of wonder to modes of looking, Dimock argues for an aural experience of wonder that responds to "the work of time, the feat of motion that keeps a text vibrating" as it travels further and further from its point of origin, "causing unexpected vibrations in unexpected places."[4] As an occasion for wonder rather than an impediment to it, resonance offers an alternative to the awe-inspired, "rapturous gaze" that is both a cause and effect of iconicity, indeed a cause and effect of the "Virginia Woolf icon" that has sutured this writer's arresting face to the body of her writing.[5]

By embracing versions of resonance rather than iconicity, Woolf and Sebald articulate the principles that have guided *Odd Affinities*. This map of Woolf's shadowy genealogies has displaced her from the singular object of an enchanted gaze to a participant in a chorus of murmuring voices within and across the texts involved. To characterize this genealogy as shadowy may seem to introduce an incongruous visual term, but the visual and the auditory are more reciprocal than they may at first appear. Complementing Dimock's proposal of an aural version of wonder is a visual analogue of resonance that Woolf and Sebald share.

Dimock's central figure of vibration—whether as the meshing of "apparently interfering but effectively enhancing vibrations" or as the "persistence of sound not originating in texts but vibrating in response to them"—opens a pathway to the visual, for vibrations can be perceptible as well as audible.[6] An additional step takes place through Dimock's exposition of W. V. Quine's mathematical concept of "twilight half-entities," designed to challenge the assumption that all objects are individuated and solidly located in space.[7] By evoking a liminal space between day and night that complements these conceptual objects' indeterminate position, the metaphor of twilight carries abstraction to the verge of visibility. Woolf and Sebald take a further step by evoking the vibrating wings of moths. Neither stable enough to constitute a solid entity nor entirely immaterial, hovering at the borders between darkness and light, their moths render conceptual vibrations visible. Most vividly evoked in *Jacob's Room*, in which the figure of the moth joins the vibrating mind of the reader to that of the elusive protagonist over whom we "hum vibrating, like the hawk moth, at the mouth of the cavern of mystery," the figure of the moth reverberates through Woolf's and Sebald's texts in the interstices between singular and plural, death and life, stasis and motion, music and vision, tea and dinner (*JR*, 73).

The vibrations of the moth gain full visibility—indeed, become the figure of a mode of visibility—in the work of Georges Didi-Huberman. In the collection of essays he titles *Phalènes: Essais sur l'apparition*, 2 (2013), he unravels the implications of his central term: *phalènes* (the French term for moths) or butterflies of the night that appear with the onset of darkness and whose fluttering wings enable us to glimpse the fluctuations of the visible: *battements d'ailes, battements du visible et battements du temps*.[8] Reminding us that *imago* is the term for the mature (winged) stage of the moth's development, Didi-Huberman takes the flickering wings of these nocturnal butterflies as the emblem of the unstable ontology of the image, an emblem that makes us repeatedly return to the question of the image. As the vibrations that are the medium of resonance evolve into an emblem of the image, the oscillation between the auditory and the visual becomes a powerful instance of the code switching indexed by the fluttering of moth wings.

Perhaps this is why, despite their fleeting mention in a text replete with vivid images, moths emerge in one of Sebald's final interviews as the most resonant trope of *Austerlitz*. In this 2001 interview, Michael Silverblatt notes that the horror of the camps is "the invisible subject as one reads the book [*Austerlitz*] and one watches moths dying or many of the images. It is almost as if this has become a poem of an invisible subject, all of whose images refer back to it, a metaphor that has no statement of its ground, only of its vehicle."[9] Silverblatt's intuition that dying moths (which we actually see dying only in Woolf's essay rather than Sebald's novel) are the text's signal figure of its "invisible subject," and Sebald's immediate turn in response to the "wonderful example" of "The Death of the Moth," enact a relay through which Woolf becomes another of *Austerlitz*'s "invisible subjects." She is not invisible in the manner of the indescribable camps, but intermittently and elusively visible—here in a phrase, there in an image, elsewhere in an avatar or formal disposition. She is visible, that is, in the manner of the moths whose flickering along the borders of visibility and invisibility makes them both a signal figure and locus of resonance in *Austerlitz*.

This may explain how a minor trope comes to register as pivotal, how it can transmit a strong signal from Woolf to Sebald and Silverblatt despite its understatement and infrequency. Woolf's resonance across these writers and others in this study may illustrate the process through which "certain overtones are taken as significant overtones, certain echoes as significant echoes."[10] Intermittency can be a source of resonance, even of endurance. Unlike the imprimatur of a fixed iconic presence, Woolf's wayward, recessive, intermittent evocation in the works of her odd heirs enacts what Dimock calls a "nonintegral survival, marked not by the text's endurance as a sealed package but by its tendency to fall apart, to pick up noise, to break out in a riot of tongues."[11]

This mode of survival suggests a way we might discern the traces of a precursor amid the "heterogeneous materials" Sebald recommends for our attention in the conversation with Joseph Cuomo that offers an epigraph to this book. If instead of looking for "the things that are like the things" that typically structure literary inheritance along the lines of gender, genre, race, or nationality, we attended to partial, minor, unexpected echoes, we might find a shadowy genealogy as evanescent as the moths that came to Woolf unbidden on the sounds of Leonard's gramophone and proceeded to assume unheralded forms across the century.

List of Abbreviations

AC	*Another Country*
ANON	"Anon"
AROO	*A Room of One's Own*
AUS	*Austerlitz*
BTA	*Between the Acts*
CE	*Collected Essays* (James Baldwin)
CL	*Camera Lucida*
DM	"The Death of the Moth"
GR	*Giovanni's Room*
JR	*Jacob's Room*
L	"Longtemps, je me suis couché de bonne heure . . . "
MD	*Mrs. Dalloway*
MDY	*Mourning Diary*
MM	"Mourning and Melancholia"
ND	"The New Dress"
O	*Orlando*
P	*Passing*
SF	*Slaves to Fashion*
SKETCH	"A Sketch of the Past"
SS	*Second Skin*
SW	"The Light of the South West"
TTL	*To the Lighthouse*

Notes

INTRODUCTION

1. Virginia Woolf, *Mrs. Dalloway* (New York: Harvest/HBJ, 1981), 9; abbreviated in the text as *MD*.

2. On the talismanic nature of *Mrs. Dalloway*, see Monica Latham's comprehensive study of the novel's many rewritings in *A Poetics of Postmodernism and Neomodernism: Rewriting Mrs. Dalloway* (Nancy: Université de Lorraine, 2015) and "Clarissa Dalloway's Global Itinerary: From London to Paris and Sydney," in *The Edinburgh Companion to Virginia Woolf and Contemporary Global Literature*, ed. Jeanne Dubino, Paulina Pająk, Catherine W. Hollis, Celiese Lypka, and Vara Neverow (Edinburgh: Edinburgh University Press, 2021), 354–70. James Schiff examines the novel's invitation to rewriting in "Rewriting Woolf's *Mrs. Dalloway:* Homage, Sexual Identity, and the Single-Day Novel by Cunningham, Lippincott, and Lanchester," *Critique* 45, no. 4 (Summer 2004): 363–80. As Katie Roiphe puts it in "Who's Afraid of Virginia Woolf: What Critics Didn't Say about Ian McEwan's Saturday," *Slate*, March 30, 2005, https://slate.com/culture/2005/03/ian-mcewan-s-mrs-dalloway.html, "It is as if something in *Mrs. Dalloway* calls out to be transported to other places and times, to be shared and updated and rethought." Michael Cunningham, who responded to *Mrs. Dalloway*'s call with its most widely read revision, similarly asserts, "I don't think there's anyone who's inspired this level of devotion and fascination and adulation"; see James Schiff, "An Interview with Michael Cunningham," *BOMB* 66 (Winter 1999): 77. For Cunningham's most recent tribute to Woolf, see "How Virginia Woolf Revolutionized the Novel," *New York Times*, December 27, 2020, Sunday Book Review, 14.

3. In "A Sketch of the Past," Woolf characterizes her mother's infusion of the familial atmosphere as an "invisible presence." *Moments of Being: Unpublished Autobiographical Writings*, ed. Jeanne Schulkind (New York: Harcourt Brace Jovanovich, 1985), 80; abbreviated in the text as Sketch.

4. "Reading at Random" was the title Woolf gave the history of English literature on which she was working shortly before her death. She voices her critique of "fixed labels and settled hierarchies" in "Phases of Fiction" (1929), in *Granite and Rainbow: Essays by Virginia Woolf* (New York: Harcourt Brace Jovanovich, 1975), 94.

5. Susan Stanford Friedman, "Migration, Encounter, and Indigenisation: New Ways of Thinking about Intertextuality in Women's Writing," in *European Intertexts: Women's Writing in a European Context*, ed. Patsy Stoneman and Ana María Sánchez-Arce with

Angela Leighton (Bern: Peter Lang, 2005), 234. Even the recent, monumental *Edinburgh Companion to Virginia Woolf and Contemporary Global Literature* (2021), which analyzes "Woolf's worldwide impact, as well as the planetary and global responses her work has provoked," focuses primarily on the response of women writers (2).

6. On the ramifications of Mr. Dalloway's name in *Brick Lane*, see Susan Stanford Friedman, "Migratory Modernisms: Novel Homelands in Monica Ali's *Brick Lane*," *Asiatic* 11, no. 1 (June 2017): 102–18.

7. This account of Woolfian adaptations and commodities briefly paraphrases Brenda Silver's pathbreaking *Virginia Woolf Icon* (Chicago: University of Chicago Press, 1999), which introduced and charted the field of Woolf's contemporary "versionings."

8. Michel Foucault, "Nietzsche, Genealogy, History," in *The Foucault Reader*, ed. Paul Rabinow (New York: Pantheon, 1984), 76–100. I am paraphrasing David Herman's helpful summary in "Histories of Narrative Theory (1): A Genealogy of Early Developments," in *A Companion to Narrative Theory*, ed. James Phelan and Peter J. Rabinowitz (Malden, MA: Blackwell, 2005), 20.

9. M. M. Bakhtin, *The Dialogic Imagination*, ed. Michael Holquist, trans. Caryl Emerson and Michael Holquist (Austin: University of Texas Press, 1981), 358. Bakhtin's significance for theorizing Woolfian revisions and adaptations is compellingly explored by Susan Stanford Friedman in "Migration, Encounter, and Indigenisation," 215–71. The examples she investigates of women's international engagements with *A Room of One's Own* make a case for both intentional and unintentional modes of intertextuality.

10. Wai Chee Dimock, "A Theory of Resonance," *PMLA* 112, no. 5 (October 1997): 1060–71. We will revisit Dimock's theory in the afterword.

11. October 29, 1933, *The Diary of Virginia Woolf*, vol. 4, *1931–1935*, ed. Anne Olivier Bell, assisted by Andrew McNeillie (New York: Harcourt Brace Jovanovich, 1982), 186. See also an earlier entry in which she rejoices in receiving criticism of her story "In the Orchard": "At once I feel refreshed. I become anonymous, a person who writes for the love of it. . . . I feel as if I slipped off all my ball dresses & stood naked—which as I remember was a very pleasant thing to do." June 19, 1923, *The Diary of Virginia Woolf*, vol. 2, *1920–1924*, ed. Anne Olivier Bell, assisted by Andrew McNeillie (New York: Harcourt Brace Jovanovich, 1978), 248.

12. Virginia Woolf, "Professions for Women" (1931), in *The Death of the Moth and Other Essays* (New York: Harcourt Brace Jovanovich, 1970), 240. Woolf introduces the image as the opening scene in *A Room of One's Own*.

13. Virginia Woolf, "The Fascination of the Pool," in *The Complete Shorter Fiction of Virginia Woolf*, ed. Susan Dick (New York: Harvest/Harcourt, 1989), 226. This reading was inspired by Christine Reynier's "Woolf's Radical Theory of Recycling," in *Recycling Virginia Woolf in Contemporary Art and Literature*, ed. Monica Latham, Caroline Marie, and Anne-Laure Rigeade (London: Routledge, 2022), 23–35.

14. The papers from the international conference at the Université de Lorraine, Nancy, France, June 27–29, 2019, have been expanded into the collection *Recycling Virginia Woolf*. For a more general account of literary recycling, see Christian Moraru, *Rewritings: Postmodern Narrative and Cultural Critique in the Age of Cloning* (Albany: SUNY Press, 2001). For a broad ecocritical framework on modernism in general and Woolf in particular, see Peter Adkins, *The Modernist Anthropocene: Nonhuman Life and*

Planetary Change in James Joyce, Virginia Woolf, and Djuna Barnes (Edinburgh: Edinburgh University Press, 2022) and Peter Adkins, ed., *Virginia Woolf and the Anthropocene* (Edinburgh: Edinburgh University Press, 2024).

15. For Kabe Wilson's account of the relation between Woolf's text and his recycled version, see Kabe Wilson and Susan Stanford Friedman, "Of Words, Worlds, and Woolf: Recycling *A Room of One's Own* into *Of One Woman or So*," in Latham et al., *Recycling Virginia Woolf*, 55–85. For illuminating analyses of Wilson's project, see Valérie Favre, "Recycling/Upcycling the Iconic Woolf: Negotiating Virginia Woolf as a Literary and Feminist Icon in Kabe Wilson's *Of One Woman or So, by Olivia N'Gowfri*," in *Recycling Virginia Woolf*, 86–99; and Susan Stanford Friedman, "Recycling Revolution: Re-Mixing *A Room of One's Own* and Black Power in Kabe Wilson's Performance, Installation, and Narrative Art," in *Contemporary Revolutions: Turning Back to the Future in 21st-Century Literature and Art*, ed. Susan Stanford Friedman (London: Bloomsbury Academic, 2019), 21–50.

16. *Looking for Virginia: An Artist's Journey through 100 Archives* is the product of Kabe Wilson's 2023 residency at the Centre for Modernist Studies Artist in Residence program at the University of Sussex. It can be viewed at https://www.sussex.ac.uk/research/centres/centre-for-modernist-studies/artist-in-residence. Wilson borrows the term "compost" from Supriya Chaudhury's essay, "Virginia Woolf and Compost" (in *Recycling Virginia Woolf*, 36–52), and describes his project of transforming *A Room of One's Own* from icon into compost in Wilson and Friedman, "Of Words," 64–65.

17. "Dalloway Day," June 15, 2022, British Library, https://www.bl.uk/british-library-player/videos/dalloway-day-2022.

18. See "'Anon' and 'The Reader': Virginia Woolf's Last Essays," ed. Brenda R. Silver, *Twentieth Century Literature* 25, no. 3/4, Virginia Woolf issue (Autumn–Winter 1979): 356–441, esp. 384–85.

19. Virginia Woolf, *A Room of One's Own*, annotated by Susan Gubar (New York: Harcourt/Harvest, 2005), 26; abbreviated in the text as *AROO*.

20. "Minor" was famously redefined and reclaimed by Gilles Deleuze and Félix Guattari that "there is nothing that is major or revolutionary except the minor" (*Kafka: Toward a Minor Literature*, trans. Dana Polan [Minneapolis: University of Minnesota Press, 1986], 26). In "Genet's Genealogy: European Minorities and the Ends of the Canon," *Cultural Critique* 6 (Spring 1987): 161–85, David Lloyd provides a concise summary of Deleuze and Guattari's characterization of a "minor literature" as involving "the questioning or destruction of the concepts of identity and identification, the rejection of representations of developing autonomy and authenticity, if not the very concept of development itself" (173). "Minor" is also a feature of the amateur critical mode that Melanie Micir and Aartie Vadde elaborate as a Woolfian legacy in "Obliterature: Toward an Amateur Criticism," *Modernism/modernity* 25, no. 3 (September 2018): 517–49.

21. David Denby discusses this historical dismissal in *Great Books: My Adventures with Homer, Rousseau, Woolf, and Other Indestructible Writers of the Western World* (New York: Simon & Schuster, 1996), 444–45.

22. Wai Chee Dimock, "Weak Theory: Henry James, Colm Tóibín, and W. B. Yeats," *Critical Inquiry* 39 (Summer 2013): 737.

23. Monica Latham offers the term "woolfalators," modeled on George Bernard Shaw's "Bardolators," in *A Poetics of Postmodernism*, 1. She introduces the phrase

"commemorative novel" in "Clarissa Dalloway's Global Itinerary," 368, and refers to "updating" throughout both texts.

24. Woolf's dismissal as a "minor" writer was launched by M. C. Bradbrook's "Notes on the Style of Mrs. Woolf" in the inaugural issue of *Scrutiny* 1, no. 1 (1932): 33–38; sustained in that journal through the 1930s by the diatribes of Q. D. Leavis; and consolidated by the New York School through the 1960s, until a major feminist revision in the 1970s–80s finally laid them to rest. "Provincial" was often deployed as a cognate term, as in Hugh Kenner's notorious dismissal of Woolf as a "provincial writer" who "pertains to the English province" in "The Making of the Modernist Canon," *Chicago Review* 34, no. 2 (Spring 1984): 57.

25. David Damrosch, "World Literature in a Postcanonical, Hypercanonical Age," in *Comparative Literature in an Age of Globalization*, ed. H. Saussy (Baltimore: Johns Hopkins University Press, 2006), 43–53.

26. "Old dead girl" is from Lidia Yuknavitch, *The Small Backs of Children* (New York: Harper Perennial, 2015), 7. In "The Woolf Girl: A Mother-Daughter Story with Virginia Woolf and Lidia Yuknavitch," in Dubino et al., *The Edinburgh Companion to Virginia Woolf*, Catherine W. Hollis complicates this blanket repudiation by eliciting both writers' subtle negotiations of the figures of the writing woman and the wounded girl (412–27). Spearheaded by Jane Marcus in "A Very Fine Negress," in *Hearts of Darkness: White Women Write Race* (New Brunswick, NJ: Rutgers University Press, 2004), 24–58, diverse critiques of Woolf's hold on women's literary production have been marshaled by Gloria Anzaldúa, "Speaking in Tongues: A Letter to Third World Women Writers," in *The Gloria Anzaldúa Reader*, ed. Ana Louise Keating (Durham, NC: Duke University Press, 2009), 26–35; and Michelle Cliff, "Virginia Woolf and the Imperial Gaze: A Glance Askance," in *Virginia Woolf: Emerging Perspectives; Selected Papers from the Third Annual Conference on Virginia Woolf*, ed. Mark Hussey and Vara Neverow (New York: Pace University Press, 1994), 91–102.

27. For a detailed and perceptive reading of Pamela Mordecai's "The Angel in the House," in which Woolf is derided as "safe / inside this 'room for just / she-one,'" (251), see Friedman, "Migration, Encounter, and Indigenisation," 239–51. Gloria Anzaldúa issues her directive in "Speaking in Tongues," 26–35.

28. Chimamanda Ngozi Adichie, "The Arrangements," *New York Times*, July 3, 2016, Sunday Book Review, 1. In the accompanying article "Adichie on Mrs. Trump," Adichie explains that *Mrs. Dalloway* "both criticizes, and is also complicit in, a certain kind of conservative class-privileged England and . . . this story has the same general spirit" (Sunday Book Review, 4).

29. Examples include Maggie Gee, *Virginia Woolf in Manhattan* (London: Telegram, 2014); Susan Sellers, *Vanessa and Virginia* (London: Ravens, 2008); Priya Parmar, *Vanessa and Her Sister* (New York: Ballantine, 2014); Kyo Maclear and Isabelle Arsenault, *Virginia Wolf* (Toronto: Kids Can Press, 2012); Norah Vincent, *Adeline: A Novel of Virginia Woolf* (New York: Houghton Mifflin, 2015); and Maggie Humm, *Talland House* (Berkeley, CA: She Writes Press, 2020). For critical studies of Woolf's salience as a subject of biofiction, see Monica Latham, "'Serv[ing] under Two Masters': Virginia Woolf's Afterlives in Contemporary Biofictions," *a/b: Auto/Biographical Studies* 27, no. 2 (Winter 2012): 354–73; Bethany Layne, "Great Poets Do Not Die: Maggie Gee's *Virginia Woolf in Manhattan* (2014) as Metaphor for Contemporary Biofiction,"

in Dubino et al., *The Edinburgh Companion to Virginia Woolf*, 399–411; and Laura Cernat, "Life as Legacy: Truth, Fiction, and Fidelity of Representation in Biographical Novels Featuring Virginia Woolf," in *Virginia Woolf and Heritage*, ed. Jane de Gay, Tom Breckin, and Anne Reus (Clemson, SC: Clemson University Press, 2017), 208–16.

30. Harold Bloom, *The Anxiety of Influence* (New York: Oxford, 1973).

31. Michael Cunningham, "First Love," in *The Mrs. Dalloway Reader*, ed. Francine Prose (New York: Harvest/Harcourt, 2003), 136–37. Cunningham's own account, of course, is more benign.

32. Ian McEwan, *Atonement* (London: Jonathan Cape, 2001), 296. McEwan has good reason to be concerned about Woolf's influence. The echoes of her voice and narrative structures in *Atonement* and *Saturday* testify to her informing presence in his fiction. For a probing study of this ambivalence, see David James, *Modernist Futures: Innovation and Inheritance in the Contemporary Novel* (Cambridge: Cambridge University Press, 2012), 135–60, which points out, among other things, that the two references to "Mrs. Woolf" in *Atonement* constitute the only example of a modernist novelist identified by name in a work of contemporary fiction. For another reading of McEwan's ambivalence toward Woolf, see Laura Marcus, "The Legacies of Modernism," in *The Cambridge Companion to the Modernist Novel*, ed. Morag Shiach (Cambridge: Cambridge University Press, 2007), 82–98.

33. Paulina Pająk, Jeanne Dubino, and Catherine W. Hollis, "Introduction: Planetary Woolf," in Dubino et al., *The Edinburgh Companion to Virginia Woolf*, 2. This ambitious undertaking traces Woolf's planetary dissemination in terms of both "trees" (distinct national cultures) and "waves" (common vision): metaphors drawn from Franco Moretti's "Conjectures on World Literature," *New Left Review* 1 (2001): 54–68, but especially well-suited to Woolf's own genealogical metaphors.

34. In their introduction to *The Edinburgh Companion*, the editors parse some of the implications of the terms *transnational, international, cosmopolitan, global*, and *planetary*. For a defense of *international*, see Aarthi Vadde, *Chimeras of Form: Modernist Internationalism beyond Europe, 1914–2016* (New York: Columbia University Press, 2017); for *global*, see Eric Hayot and Rebecca L. Walkowitz, eds., *A New Vocabulary for Global Modernism* (New York: Columbia University Press, 2016); and Mark Wollaeger, with Matt Eatough, *The Oxford Handbook of Global Modernisms* (Oxford: Oxford University Press, 2012); for *transnational*, see Jessica Berman, *Modernist Commitments: Ethics, Politics, and Transnational Modernism* (New York: Columbia University Press, 2011); for *planetary*, see Susan Stanford Friedman, *Planetary Modernisms: Provocations on Modernity across Time* (New York: Columbia University Press, 2015); for *cosmopolitan*, see Rebecca L. Walkowitz, *Cosmopolitan Style: Modernism beyond the Nation* (New York: Columbia University Press, 2006), 79–106.

35. Eve Kosofsky Sedgwick, *Tendencies* (Durham, NC: Duke University Press, 1993), xii. In keeping with Sedgwick's etymology, I have tried to reserve the term *queer* for skewed trajectories and counternormative sites and desires, while using *gay* in consonance with particular historical moments and movements. On the complexity of *queer*'s usage, especially in relation to Baldwin, see Matt Brim, *James Baldwin and the Queer Imagination* (Ann Arbor: University of Michigan Press, 2014).

36. Although Amy Hungerford proposes the term "long modernism" in passing in her essay, "On the Period Formerly Known as Contemporary," *American Literary*

History 20, nos. 1–2 (Spring/Summer 2008): 418, it has since been widely adopted as a useful moniker for the persistence of modernist aesthetics. In their influential essay, "The New Modernist Studies," *PMLA* 123, no. 3 (2008): 737–48, Douglas Mao and Rebecca L. Walkowitz summarize the shifts in modernist literary scholarship through the single word *expansion*. See also Peter Brooker, Andrzej Gąsiorek, Deborah Longworth, and Andrew Thacker, "Introduction," in Brooker et al., *The Oxford Handbook of Modernisms* (Oxford: Oxford University Press, 2010), 1–13.

37. The classic text on "Black Paris" is Tyler Stovall, *Paris Noir: African-Americans in the City of Light* (New York: Houghton Mifflin, 1996).

38. In *Modernist Futures*, David James proclaims: "It is thanks to the postmodern, then, that modernism has any future at all" (10). In "Introduction: Modernism after Postmodernity," *New German Critique* 99 (Fall 2006), Andreas Huyssen similarly attributes the "remarkable comeback" of the "discourses of modernism and modernity" to the advent of postmodernism that "has largely disappeared from critical discourse today" (2). See also Douglas Mao and Rebecca L. Walkowitz, "Introduction: Modernisms Bad and New," in *Bad Modernisms*, ed. Douglas Mao and Rebecca L. Walkowitz (Durham, NC: Duke University Press, 2006), 1–17.

39. For example, Zadie Smith has returned to E. M. Forster; Colm Tóibín, Alan Hollinghurst, and David Lodge to Henry James; Salman Rushdie to James Joyce; Chinua Achebe, V. S. Naipaul, Tayeb Salih, and Arundhati Roy to Joseph Conrad; and Jeanette Winterson to Gertrude Stein. For a fuller account, see Marcus, "The Legacies of Modernism," 82–98.

40. Monica Latham glosses some of this terminology in *A Poetics of Postmodernism*, where she differentiates explicit and playful postmodern versioning from more subtly "neomodern" rewritings in which Woolf remains a "hovering presence" (7). Following the work of Billy Childish and Charles Thompson, Ann Marie Adams adds "remodernism" to the mix in "Mr. McEwan and Mrs. Woolf: How a Saturday in February Follows 'This Moment of June,'" *Contemporary Literature* 53, no. 3 (Fall 2012): 548–72. Timotheus Vermeluen and Robin van den Akker add "metamodernism" in "Notes on Metamodernism," *Journal of Aesthetics & Culture* 2 (2010): 1–14. Along with David James in *Modernist Futures*, I have chosen the term "late modernism" despite its ambiguous chronological referent because the perception of belatedness is a feature of the works I examine.

41. Michaela Bronstein, *Out of Context: The Uses of Modernist Fiction* (Oxford: Oxford University Press, 2016), 7, 10.

42. Bronstein, *Out of Context*, 9.

43. Mark Wollaeger and Kevin Dettmar, "Series Editors' Foreword" to Bronstein, *Out of Context*, x. Conceptions of form vary, however. Some studies of long modernism, such as David James's compelling analysis in *Modernist Futures* of contemporary global Anglophone fiction's recruitment of modernist form, affirm its classic definition as organic, autonomous, integrated, and disinterested. Others, such as Aarthi Vadde's *Chimeras of Form*, explore strained, hybrid, and politically engaged alternatives. See also Walkowitz, *Cosmopolitan Style*.

44. Woolf is one of three "metics" (or resident aliens) that constitute the modernist catalyst for late twentieth-century expressions of grief in Madelyn Detloff's *The*

Persistence of Modernism: Loss and Mourning in the Twentieth Century (Cambridge: Cambridge University Press, 2009). In *Cosmopolitan Style*, for example, Rebecca L. Walkowitz positions Woolf along with Conrad and Joyce as representatives of a "cosmopolitan modernism" that evolves into the "modernist cosmopolitanism" of three late-century diversely British (but not necessarily Anglophone or England-residing) writers: Kazuo Ishiguro, Salman Rushdie, and W. G. Sebald (whom she affiliates with Conrad rather than Woolf, whose traces she locates in Ishiguro and Rushdie).

45. Caroline Levine, *Forms: Whole, Rhythm, Hierarchy, Network* (Princeton, NJ: Princeton University Press, 2015), xi. See also Marjorie Levinson, "What Is New Formalism?," *PMLA* 122, no. 2 (March 2007): 558–69; Susan J. Wolfson, "Reading for Form," *MLQ* 61, no. 1 (March 2000): 1–16; and Samuel Otter, "An Aesthetics in All Things," *Representations* 104, no. 1 (Fall 2008): 116–25.

46. The classic locus is the narrator's notorious observation in *A Room of One's Own* about white English women's ability to "pass even a very fine negress without wishing to make an Englishwoman of her" (50). For the genealogy and complexity of references to "good" and "bad" modernisms, see Mao and Walkowitz, *Bad Modernisms*.

47. Initially presented in *Modernism and the Harlem Renaissance* (Chicago: University of Chicago Press, 1987), Houston A. Baker Jr.'s call was reissued and reframed in the special issue "The Harlem Renaissance and the New Modernist Studies," *Modernism/modernity* 20, no. 3 (September 2013): 433–35.

48. Kristin Czarnecki, "Comparative Modernism: The Bloomsbury Group and the Harlem Renaissance," in *Virginia Woolf's Bloomsbury: Aesthetic Theory and Literary Practice*, vol. 1, ed. Lisa Shahriari and Gina Potts (London: Palgrave Macmillan, 2010), 135. See also Jeannette McVicker, "Dislocating the Discourses of Modernism: The Example of Woolf and Hurston," in Hussey and Neverow, *Virginia Woolf: Emerging Perspectives*, 313–18; and Kristina Deffenbacher, "Woolf, Hurston, and the House of the Self," in *Herspace: Women, Writing, and Solitude*, ed. Jo Malin and Victoria Boynton (Philadelphia: The Haworth Press, 2003), 105–22. The most productive of the comparative essays is Adrienne Brown, "Hard Romping: Zora Neale Hurston, White Women, and the Right to Play," *Twentieth Century Literature*, 64, no. 3 (September 2018), which contrasts Woolf's emphasis on a room of one's own as a "form of private property insulated from intrusions both domestic and public" to Hurston's insistence on the value of "continually making herself public" (296).

49. Ann duCille, *The Coupling Convention: Sex, Text, and Tradition in Black Women's Fiction* (Oxford: Oxford University Press, 1993).

50. "Loophole of retreat" is the title of chapter 21 of Harriet A. Jacob's *Incidents in the Life of a Slave Girl*, ed. Jean Fagan Yellin (Cambridge, MA: Harvard University Press, 1978), 114. For some readings of this and similar spaces, see Valerie Smith, *Self-Discovery and Authority in Afro-American Narrative* (Cambridge, MA: Harvard University Press, 1987); and Adrienne Brown, "'My Hole Is Warm and Full of Light': The Sub-urban Real Estate of Invisible Man," in *Race and Real Estate*, ed. Adrienne Brown and Valerie Smith (Oxford: Oxford University Press, 2015), 177–94.

51. August 30, 1923, *The Diary of Virginia Woolf*, 2:263.

52. Virginia Woolf, "Mr. Bennett and Mrs. Brown," in *The Captain's Death Bed and Other Essays* (New York: Harcourt Brace Jovanovich, 1950), 105.

53. In her diary entry for June 19, 1923, Woolf noted about Septimus, "Of course the mad part tries me so much, makes my mind squint so badly that I can hardly face spending the next weeks at it." *The Diary of Virginia Woolf*, 2:248. In her "Introduction to *Mrs. Dalloway*," she characterizes Septimus as Clarissa's double. *The Mrs. Dalloway Reader*, 11.

54. For other accounts of the connections between Woolf's Septimus and Morrison's Shadrack, see Eileen Barrett, "'For Books Continue Each Other . . .': Toni Morrison and Virginia Woolf," in Hussey and Neverow, *Virginia Woolf: Emerging Perspectives*, 26–33; and Barbara Christian's more expansive "Layered Rhythms: Virginia Woolf and Toni Morrison," *Modern Fiction Studies* 39, nos. 3&4 (Fall/Winter 1993): 483–500. On Septimus as precursor in a literary genealogy of "madness," see Nicolas Boileau, *The Function of Symptoms in British Literature since Modernism, from Virginia Woolf to Ali Smith* (London: Palgrave Macmillan, 2023).

55. Paul K. Saint-Amour deftly characterizes this affective temporality in *Tense Future: Modernism, Total War, Encyclopedic Form* (Oxford: Oxford University Press, 2015).

56. Virginia Woolf, *To the Lighthouse* (New York: Harcourt/Harvest, 1981), 133–34; abbreviated in the text as *TTL*.

57. The most comprehensive account is offered by Sandra M. Gilbert in her magisterial *Death's Door: Modern Dying and the Ways We Grieve* (New York: Norton, 2006).

58. Serge Lebovici and Daniel Widlocher provide a succinct account of the evolution of psychoanalysis in France in "Psychoanalytic Publications in France," *Psychoanalysis in France*, ed. Lebovici and Widlocher (New York: International Universities Press, 1980), vii–xiv. Their edited volume also reproduces Nicolas Abraham and Maria Torok, "Introjection—Incorporation: Mourning or Melancholia" (3–16). The first extensive discussion of Freud's essay occurs in Jacques Lacan's seminars "Desire and the Interpretation of Desire in *Hamlet*," trans. James Hulbert, ed. Jacques-Alain Miller, *Yale French Studies* 55/56 (1977): 11–52.

59. Robert Castel, "Images and Phantasms," trans. Peter France, Tamar Jacoby, and Chris Baxter, *Le nouvel observateur/New York Review of Books*, "Special Photo," no. 4 (December 1978): 16. Castel's essay was published in both French and English. The English translation was published in an additional supplement by the *New York Review of Books*. A French translation of Benjamin's full essay had appeared in 1971; the excerpted version appears in the special series as (a title drawn from the end of Benjamin's essay) Walter Benjamin, "Les analphabètes de l'avenir," trans. Maurice de Gandillac, *Le nouvel observateur*, "Special Photo," no. 2 (November 1977): 6–25.

60. This is inevitably an oversimplification of a multifaceted phenomenon with diverse representations in different mediums and national cultures. In American popular culture, for example, there was a spate of Hollywood films about returning World War II veterans.

61. Jesse Matz, *Modernist Time Ecology* (Baltimore: Johns Hopkins University Press, 2018), 96.

62. The critique could be summarized by Julia Kristeva's complaint that "Virginia Woolf describes suspended states, subtle sensations and, above all, colors—green, blue—but she does not dissect language as Joyce does." "Oscillation du 'pouvoir' au

'refus'" ["Oscillation between 'power' and 'denial'"], interview by Xavière Gauthier, *Tel Quel* (Summer 1974); reprinted in *New French Feminisms*, ed. Elaine Marks and Isabelle de Courtivron (Amherst: University of Massachusetts Press, 1980), 166. For accounts of Woolf's reception in France, see the essays by Pierre-Eric Villeneuve, Carole Rodier, Francoise Pellan, and Mary Ann Caws in *The Reception of Virginia Woolf in Europe*, ed. Mary Ann Caws and Nicola Luckhurst (London: Continuum, 2002), 19–67. The most recent and nuanced account, which focuses on Woolf's reception by French women writers, is Anne-Laure Rigeade, "Virginia Woolf and French Writers: Contemporaneity, Idolisation, Iconisation," in Dubino et al., *The Edinburgh Companion to Virginia Woolf*, 371–86.

63. Gilles Deleuze and Félix Guattari, *A Thousand Plateaus: Capitalism and Schizophrenia*, trans. Brian Massumi (Minneapolis: University of Minnesota Press, 1987); Jacques Rancière and Davide Panagia, "Dissenting Words: A Conversation with Jacques Rancière," *diacritics* 30, no. 2 (Summer 2000): 113–26; quote from Rancière, 121. See also Jacques Rancière, "From Politics to Aesthetics?," *Paragraph* 8, no. 1 (January 2008): 13–25, and "The Thread of the Novel," *Novel: A Forum on Fiction* 47, no. 2 (Summer 2014): 196–209.

64. Arthur Lubow, "Crossing Boundaries," in *The Emergence of Memory: Conversations with W. G. Sebald*, ed. Lynne Sharon Schwartz (New York: Seven Stories Press, 2007), 161.

65. On the Anglocentric turn of late British modernism, which we will revisit in the afterword, see Jed Esty, *A Shrinking Island: Modernism and National Culture in England* (Princeton, NJ: Princeton University Press, 2004).

CHAPTER ONE

1. Nella Larsen, *Quicksand and Passing* (New Brunswick, NJ: Rutgers University Press, 1986), 222; abbreviated in the text as *P*.

2. Cherene Sherrad-Johnson, "Questionnaire Responses," *Modernism/modernity* 20, no. 3 (September 2013): 456. This issue of *Modernism/modernity* is devoted to exploring temporal and spatial expansions of the Harlem Renaissance.

3. In addition to the "blues geographies" that Houston A. Baker Jr. explores in his foundational *Modernism and the Harlem Renaissance*, see Henry Louis Gates Jr., *The Signifying Monkey: A Theory of African American Literary Criticism* (Oxford: Oxford University Press, 1988); Michael North, *The Dialect of Modernism: Race, Language, and Twentieth-Century Literature* (Oxford: Oxford University Press, 1994); Geoffrey Jacques, *A Change in the Weather: Modernist Imagination, African American Imaginary* (Amherst: University of Massachusetts Press, 2009); and Mae G. Henderson, *Speaking in Tongues and Dancing Diaspora: Black Women Writing and Performing* (Oxford: Oxford University Press, 2014). In *Slaves to Fashion: Black Dandyism and the Styling of Black Diasporic Identity* (Durham, NC: Duke University Press, 2009), Monica L. Miller reappropriates the derogatory term "mulatto modernism" and defines its representative figure, the Black dandy, as the signifier of a provocative syncretism.

4. Adam McKible and Suzanne W. Churchill, "Introduction: In Conversation; The Harlem Renaissance and the New Modernist Studies," *Modernism/modernity* 20, no. 3 (September 2013): 430. Respondents to the "Questionnaire" in this issue of *Modernism/*

modernity frequently mention gender and sexuality as areas to be developed in Harlem Renaissance scholarship.

5. Maureen Honey, "Questionnaire Responses," *Modernism/modernity* 20, no. 3 (September 2013): 443.

6. Deborah E. McDowell initiated the lesbian reframing of *Passing* in her introduction to the 1986 Rutgers University Press edition of *Quicksand* and *Passing* (ix-xxxvii). See also Judith Butler, "Passing, Queering: Nella Larsen's Psychoanalytic Challenge," in *Bodies That Matter: On the Discursive Limits of "Sex"* (New York and London: Routledge, 1993), 167–86; David L. Blackmore, "'That Unreasonable Restless Feeling': The Homosexual Subtexts of Nella Larsen's *Passing*," *African American Review* 26, no. 3 (Autumn 1992): 475–84; and Brian Carr, "Paranoid Interpretation: Desire's Nonobject and Nella Larsen's *Passing*," *PMLA* 119, no. 2 (March 2004): 282–95. See Nella Larsen, *Passing: Authoritative Text, Backgrounds and Contexts, Criticism*, ed. Carla Kaplan (New York: W.W. Norton, 2007), for the social and literary history of racial passing.

7. Barbara Hochman, "Filling in the Blanks: Nella Larsen's Application to Library School," *PMLA* 133, no. 5 (October 2018): 1181; Anna Brickhouse, "Nella Larsen and the Intertextual Geography of *Quicksand*," *African American Review* 35, no. 4 (2001): 533–60. See also Barbara Hochman, "Love and Theft: Plagiarism, Blackface, and Nella Larsen's 'Sanctuary,'" *American Literature* 88, no. 3 (2016): 509–40.

8. James Weldon Johnson, "Harlem: The Culture Capital," in *The New Negro: Voices of the Harlem Renaissance*, ed. Alain Locke (New York: Atheneum, 1925), 301–11; reprinted with an introduction by Arnold Rampersad (New York: Simon & Schuster, 1992). The title of the original 1925 *Survey Graphic* issue was "Harlem: Mecca of the New Negro."

9. Richard Hughes, "A Day in London Life," *Saturday Review of Literature* 1, no. 42 (May 16, 1925): 755.

10. Thadious M. Davis, *Nella Larsen: Novelist of the Harlem Renaissance; A Woman's Life Unveiled* (Baton Rouge: Louisiana State University Press, 1994), 328–29. Elsewhere, Davis cites Conrad and Joyce as modernist echoes in *Passing* (310–11). In "Beautiful White Girlhood? Daisy Buchanan in Nella Larsen's *Passing*," *African American Review* 47, no. 1 (Spring 2014): 37–49, Sinéad Moynihan argues that *Passing* "blackens" Fitzgerald's *Great Gatsby* by rewriting Daisy Buchanan as Clare Kendry.

11. Letter to Dorothy Peterson, July 19, 1927, Dorothy Peterson Collection, Yale Collection of American Literature, Beinecke Rare Book and Manuscript Library, Yale University; reprinted in Larsen, *Passing: Authoritative Text*, ed. Kaplan, 164.

12. For the impact of Baker's performance on the Parisian audience, see Phyllis Rose, *Jazz Cleopatra: Josephine Baker in Her Time* (New York: Doubleday, 1989), 9, 18–27. According to Anne Anlin Cheng, a transnational cultural elite including e. e. cummings, Jean Cocteau, Fernand Léger, and Janet Flanner attended the performance. *Second Skin: Josephine Baker and the Modern Surface* (Oxford: Oxford University Press, 2011), 184.

13. According to Sianne Ngai, Baker was "the most famous transatlantic cabaret performer of not only her own time but arguably all time" who "knew how to specularize herself better and in more mediums than any other entertainer of her time, or even ours." "Black Venus, *Blonde Venus*," in *Bad Modernisms*, ed. Douglas Mao and Rebecca L.

Walkowitz (Durham, NC: Duke University Press, 2006), 153. Baker's image circulated throughout Europe in the 1920s on commercial products and in high art forms from poetry to painting, sculpture, and architecture. In her breakthrough study, *Second Skin*, Anne Anlin Cheng cites the international modernist architect Le Corbusier's claim that Baker "lives all over the world" (92).

14. Ngai, "Black Venus, *Blonde Venus*," 172.

15. In "Nella Larsen's *Passing* and the Fading Subject," *African American Review* 32, no. 3 (1998): 373–86, Nell Sullivan introduces the phrase "twin" protagonists and interprets Irene's fascination with Clare via Lacan's concept of the mirror stage. Helena Michie offers a similar reading of Clare's necessity and challenge to the self-concept of Irene, who "can neither keep Clare in the place of difference nor in the place of sameness." *Sororophobia: Differences among Women in Literature and Culture* (New York: Oxford, 1992), 154. On the ways that Clare does and does not conform to the figure of the tragic mulatta, see the depictions of the tragic mulatto/a collected in Larsen, *Passing: Authoritative Text*, ed. Kaplan, 171–221; Cheryl A. Wall, "Passing for What? Aspects of Identity in Nella Larsen's Novels," *Black American Literature Forum* 20, no. 1/2 (Spring-Summer 1986): 99–111; and Mae G. Henderson, "Nella Larsen's *Passing*: Passing, Performance, and (Post)modernism," in *Speaking in Tongues and Dancing Diaspora: Black Women Writing and Performing* (New York: Oxford University Press, 2014), 52–75. See also Claudia Tate, "Nella Larsen's *Passing*: A Problem of Interpretation," *Black American Literature Forum* 14, no. 4 (Winter 1980): 142–46.

16. Samuel Richardson, "Preface," *Clarissa* (Oxford: Shakespeare Head, 1930); cited by Ian Watt, *The Rise of the Novel: Studies in Defoe, Richardson, and Fielding* (Berkeley and Los Angeles: University of California Press, 1967), 192, emphasis in original; Virginia Woolf, "Modern Fiction," in *The Common Reader* (1925; New York: Harcourt Brace, 1953), 155; *Mrs. Dalloway* (1925; New York: Harcourt Brace, 1981), 124–25. Watt traces Richardson's lineage to D. H. Lawrence and James Joyce, but references Woolf only occasionally, and exclusively as a critic rather than a novelist. By contrast, Nancy Armstrong's claim in *Desire and Domestic Fiction: A Political History of the Novel* (Oxford: Oxford University Press, 1987) that "the modern individual was first and foremost a woman" finds its logical culmination in Virginia Woolf (8). See also Watt's claim that the epistolary form enabled Richardson a "short-cut . . . to the heart" (195).

17. Miller, *Slaves to Fashion*, 37; abbreviated in the text as *SF*.

18. Lisa Freeman, *Character's Theater: Genre and Identity on the Eighteenth-Century Stage* (Philadelphia: University of Pennsylvania Press, 2001), 16; cited by Miller, *Slaves to Fashion*, 35.

19. Elisa Tamarkin, *Anglophilia: Deference, Devotion, and Antebellum America* (Chicago: University of Chicago Press, 2007).

20. Melville Herskovitz, "The Color Line," *American Mercury*, October 1925, reported in the *Chicago Defender*, October 1925; reproduced in Larsen, *Passing: Authoritative Text*, ed. Kaplan, 107.

21. Nella Larsen to Carl Van Vechten, March 14, 1927, in *Nella Larsen's Letters: 1917–1935*, ed. M. Giulia Fabi and Jacquelyn Y. McLendon (Città di Castello: Emil, 2022), 93.

22. In "American Literature and the American Language," T. S. Eliot accused the book of "issuing a kind of linguistic Declaration of Independence, an act of

emancipation of American from English." *To Criticize the Critic* (New York: Farrar, Straus & Giroux, 1965); cited by Michael North, *The Dialect of Modernism: Race, Language, and Twentieth-Century Literature* (New York: Oxford University Press, 1994), 128.

23. On the African American investment in American cultural nationalism, see George Hutchinson, *The Harlem Renaissance in Black and White* (Cambridge, MA: Harvard University Press, 1995). On the white modernist appropriation of the Black vernacular, see North, *The Dialect of Modernism*.

24. Langston Hughes, "Our Wonderful Society: Washington," *Opportunity* 5, no. 8 (August 1927): 226–27; reprinted in *The Collected Works of Langston Hughes: Essays on Art, Race, Politics, and World Affairs*, vol. 9, ed. and intro. Christopher C. De Santis (Columbia: University of Missouri Press, 2002), 227.

25. See Alain Locke's "The New Negro," in Locke, *The New Negro: Voices of the Harlem Renaissance*, 3–16.

26. Donald Brace to Leonard Woolf, December 16, 1924; cited by Hermione Lee, *Virginia Woolf* (New York: Vintage Books, 1999), 550–51.

27. C.V.D., "Without Stage Directions," *Century Magazine*, October 1925, 768.

28. Louis Kronenberger, "Virginia Woolf Explores an English Country Home," *New York Times*, May 8, 1927, http://www.nytimes.com/books/97/06/08reviews/woolf-lighthouse.html; Edwin Clark, "Six Months in the Field of Fiction," *New York Times*, June 26, 1927, 20. Reviewing her status in 1939, Carl Van Doren and his illustrious brother Mark noted that "there are those who put her [Woolf's] achievement above that of any living English novelist." *American and British Literature since 1890*, rev. ed. (New York: D. Appleton-Century Company, 1939), 238.

29. In "The Transatlantic Virginia Woolf: Essaying an American Audience," *Virginia Woolf Miscellany* 76 (Fall–Winter 2009): 9–11, Beth Daugherty attributes America's greater receptivity to Woolf's feminism and pacifism to the relatively broader distribution of her essays across a range of American periodicals and foregrounds the nineteen essays that appeared only in the United States.

30. Virginia Woolf, "American Fiction," reprinted from the *Saturday Review of Literature* (1925) in *The Moment and Other Essays* (New York: Harcourt Brace, 1948), 116.

31. Woolf, "American Fiction," 116. The richest account of Woolf's conflicted attitude toward American literature is Andrew McNeillie, "Virginia Woolf's America," *Dublin Review* 5 (Winter 2001–2002), https://thedublinreview.com/article/virginia-woolfs-america/.

32. Sam Roberts, "Recalling a 'Writers' Paper' as a Name Fades," *New York Times*, March 6, 2013, City Room (blog), https://cityroom.blogs.nytimes.com/2013/03/06/fondly-recalling-a-paper-that-punched-the-times-in-the-nose/.

33. Woolf experienced Irita Van Doren's investment in her work as a form of bondage as well as gratification, writing in a September 2, 1927, letter to Vita Sackville-West: "I'm a sold soul. . . . The soul to Mrs Van Doren. Here am I bound hand and foot to write an article on the works of a man called Hemingway. There are 3 more to follow. For this I shall be paid £120." *The Letters of Virginia Woolf*, vol. 3, *1923–1928*, ed. Nigel Nicolson and Joanne Trautmann (New York: Harcourt, 1977), 416. See also Woolf's diary entry for April 13, 1929, in which she notes that she has "just agreed to do another

4 articles for Mrs. Van Doren because she has raised her price to 50 pounds an article." *The Diary of Virginia Woolf*, vol. 3, *1925–1930*, ed. Anne Olivier Bell (New York: Harcourt Brace, 1981), 221.

34. Barbara Hochman, "Filling in Blanks," *PMLA* 133, no. 5 (October 2018): 1172–90. Larsen also listed *The Bookman*, the *Literary Digest*, and *The Nation*.

35. Charles S. Johnson to Walter White, August 5, 1926; cited by Davis, *Nella Larsen*, 163.

36. Thadious M. Davis cites Walter F. White's impression of Larsen's books from his letter to Samuel Craig, September 25, 1928, in *Nella Larsen* (163–64). Larsen was the first African American accepted to the library school of the New York Public Library. On the nuances of Larsen's ambivalent relationship to the vocation of librarian, see Barbara Hochman, "Filling in Blanks"; and Karin Roffman, "Nella Larsen, Librarian at 135th Street," *Modern Fiction Studies* 53, no. 4 (Winter 2007): 752–87. Roffman notes that Larsen rebelled against the prevailing mission of the library to embrace and enhance the local culture of Harlem.

37. Nella Larsen to Dorothy Peterson, July 12, 1927, and July 19, 1927, *Nella Larsen's Letters*, 66, 68. Although the references to Katherine Mansfield that relay a message from Larsen's husband, Elmer Ives, are typically taken as a cautionary note derived from a common involvement with the writings of Gurdjieff, the fact that Larsen was familiar with Mansfield increases the likelihood that she was familiar with Woolf as well.

38. Hochman, "Filling in the Blanks," 1176.

39. Nella Larsen to Gertrude Stein, February 1, 192[9] and January 26, 1931, *Nella Larsen's Letters*, 74–76.

40. Nella Larsen to Charles S. Johnson, 1926, *Nella Larsen's Letters*, 57. Larsen was especially eager to differentiate herself from Wharton, with whom, as Emily J. Orlando has argued, she conducted a complicated "careerlong" conversation. See Emily J. Orlando, "Irreverent Intimacy: Nella Larsen's Revisions of Edith Wharton," *Twentieth Century Literature* 61, no. 1 (March 2015): 32–62.

41. Woolf chronicled the exchange in her letters to Vita Sackville-West on December 30, 1926; January 31, 1927; and February 28, 1927; and her letter to Vanessa, February 9, 1927. *The Letters of Virginia Woolf*, 3:313, 320, 328, 338.

42. Nella Larsen to Carl Van Vechten, June 15, 1929, *Nella Larsen's Letters*, 105.

43. On the celebratory tea party, see George Hutchinson, *In Search of Nella Larsen: A Biography of the Color Line* (Cambridge, MA: Harvard University Press, 2006), 327. On Blanche Knopf's pioneering role in publishing, see Laura Claridge, *The Lady with the Borzoi: Blanche Knopf, Literary Tastemaker Extraordinaire* (New York: Farrar, Straus & Giroux, 2016). Since their correspondence reveals that Woolf twice invited Van Doren to visit her in London, a visit in the opposite direction might have occurred at any time until their correspondence ceased in 1934. See Irita Van Doren's responses in her letters of November 16, 1927, and December 2, 1929, Irita Taylor Van Doren Papers, 1920–1967, MSS43844, Box 13, Folder 1, Library of Congress.

44. On "mongrel Manhattan," see Ann Douglas, *Terrible Honesty: Mongrel Manhattan in the 1920s* (New York: Farrar, Straus & Giroux, 1995). The discourse of a "mongrel" or "mongrelized" modernism also appears in North, *The Dialect of Modernism*; Sarah Wilson, *Melting-Pot Modernism* (Ithaca, NY: Cornell University Press, 2010); and Rita

Keresztesi, *Strangers at Home: American Ethnic Modernism between the World Wars* (Lincoln: University of Nebraska Press, 2005).

45. Laura Doyle, "Transnational History at Our Backs: A Long View of Larsen, Woolf, and Queer Racial Subjectivity in Atlantic Modernism," *Modernism/modernity* 13, no. 3 (2006): 531–59.

46. Daniel Hack, *Reaping Something New: African American Transformations of Victorian Literature* (Princeton, NJ: Princeton University Press, 2017), 2.

47. Clive Bell defined "significant form" as the way that "lines and colours combined in a particular way, certain forms and relations of forms, stir our aesthetic emotions," in *Art* (1914; New York: Capricorn Books, 1958), 17. Victoria Rosner discusses the "visual abstraction" of Bloomsbury's taste for white-washed rooms in *Modernism and the Architecture of Modern Life* (New York: Columbia University Press, 2005), 157. See Virginia Woolf, "Modern Fiction," in *The Common Reader* (New York: Harcourt Brace, 1953), 153–54.

48. Virginia Woolf, "The Art of Fiction" (1927), in *The Moment and Other Essays* (New York: Harcourt Brace, 1948), 109, 111. The essay appeared at a critical juncture in Larsen's career. As Thadious M. Davis notes in *Nella Larsen*, Knopf's acceptance of the manuscript for Larsen's first novel, *Quicksand*, in 1927 and the informal offer of a contract for a new novel inspired Larsen to begin working on a second novel during the summer of 1927, since she now "considered herself a novelist—not merely a writer of fiction" (226).

49. See, for example, Ralph Friedman, *The Lyrical Novel: Studies in Herman Hesse, Andre Gide, and Virginia Woolf* (Princeton, NJ: Princeton University Press, 1963).

50. *The Diary of Virginia Woolf*, vol. 2, *1920–1924*, ed. Anne Olivier Bell, assisted by Andrew McNeillie (New York: Harcourt Brace, 1978), 249.

51. Caroline Levine, *Forms: Whole, Rhythm, Hierarchy, Network* (Princeton, NJ: Princeton University Press, 2015), 13–14. It is striking in this regard that several reviewers of *Passing* noted its formal as well as thematic transcendence of race. Writing in the *Saturday Review*, for example, W. B. Seabrook claimed, in "Touch of the Tar-brush," that "Negro writers seldom posses [*sic*] a sense of form comparable to that of Miss Nella Larsen," who "has produced a work so fine, sensitive, and distinguished that it rises above race categories." *Saturday Review of Literature*, May 18, 1929, 1017–18; cited in Larsen, *Passing: Authoritative Text*, ed. Kaplan, 91–93.

52. Gates, *The Signifying Monkey*, esp. 44–60.

53. Nella Larsen to Carl Van Vechten, March 19, 1928, *Nella Larsen's Letters*, 99.

54. To Carl Van Vechten, March 19, 1928, *Nella Larsen's Letters*, 102. On October 19, 1928, she informs Van Vechten that Knopf will publish "Nig" (still the title of the novel) on April 19, 1929.

55. Pamela L. Caughie, "'The Best People': The Making of the Black Bourgeoisie in Writings of the Negro Renaissance," *Modernism/modernity* 20, no. 3 (September 2013): 527.

56. Samuel Richardson, *Correspondence*, 3:253; quoted in Watt, *The Rise of the Novel*, 188.

57. August 30, 1923, *The Diary of Virginia Woolf*, 2:263.

58. October 15, 1923, *The Diary of Virginia Woolf*, 2:272.

59. In her introduction to the 1986 republication of *Quicksand* and *Passing* by Rutgers University Press, Deborah E. McDowell famously analogizes the figure of the envelope to a "metaphoric vagina" (xxvi), initiating a tradition of lesbian readings of the novel.

60. In "Filling in Blanks," Barbara Hochman details Larsen's general "habit of inscribing her reading into her writing" without acknowledgment (1181).

61. April 27, 1925, *The Diary of Virginia Woolf*, 3:12–13. See also Woolf's comment a couple of weeks later: "My love of clothes interests me profoundly: only it is not love; & what it is I must discover" (May 14, 1925, 3:21). The portrait from April 27, 1925, appeared in an issue of *Vogue* in early May 1926; an earlier photograph had appeared in *Vogue*'s "We Nominate for the Hall of Fame" section in late May 1924, and can be found in Quentin Bell, *Virginia Woolf: A Biography* (New York: Harcourt Brace, 1972), vol. 2, plate 6a. For other Woolf citations and commentary that reveal her ambivalence about clothing, see Lisa Cohen, "'Frock Consciousness': Virginia Woolf, the Open Secret, and the Language of Fashion," *Fashion Theory* 3, no. 2 (1999): 149–74; Jane Garrity, "Virginia Woolf and Fashion," in *The Edinburgh Companion to Virginia Woolf and the Arts*, ed. Maggie Humm (Edinburgh: Edinburgh University Press, 2010), 195–211; Claire Nicholson, "But Woolf Was a Sophisticated Observer of Fashion . . . : Virginia Woolf, Clothing, and Contradiction," in *Contradictory Woolf*, ed. Derek Ryan and Stella Bolaki (Clemson, SC: Clemson University Press, 2012), 129–45; and Catherine Gregg, *Virginia Woolf and "Dress Mania": The Eternal & Insoluble Question of Clothes* (London: Cecil Woolf Publishing, 2010).

62. Woolf, "Modern Fiction," 154.

63. "Negro metropolis" is from James Weldon Johnson, *Black Manhattan*; cited in Miller, *Slaves to Fashion*, 181–82, 191, 195–200. "Cosmopolite self-concept" is a phrase Miller borrows from Johnson's biographer, Eugene Levy, *James Weldon Johnson: Black Leader, Black Voice* (Chicago: University of Chicago Press, 1973); quoted by Miller, 191.

64. On the long-standing association between European decadence and orientalism, see Cheng, *Second Skin*, 152 (abbreviated in the text as *SS*); for the Victorian fascination with Japan, see Grace Lavery, *Quaint, Exquisite: Victorian Aesthetics and the Idea of Japan* (Princeton, NJ: Princeton University Press, 2019).

65. Oscar Wilde, *The Picture of Dorian Gray and Other Writings*, ed. Richard Ellmann (New York: Bantam, 1982), 17, 21.

66. For a different account of the modern surface as a derivative of plastics, especially cellophane "as pure surface" with the "glassy sheen" that "arrests the gaze at its glittering surface," see Judith Brown, "Cellophane Glamour," *Modernism/modernity* 15, no. 4 (November 2008): 605–26; quote 608–9.

67. The first interview is paraphrased from Phyllis Rose's account in *Jazz Cleopatra* of Baker's interview with Georges Schmitt, "Joséphine Baker passant à Paris nous dit. . . . ," *Volonté*, April 9, 1929. The passage is from Pierre Lazareff, "Joséphine Baker sage est revenue à Paris," *Paris-Midi*, April 20, 1929; cited by Evelyne Cohen, *Paris dans l'imaginaire nationale de l'entre-deux-guerres* (Paris: Publications de la Sorbonne, 1999), 106.

68. Hoyningen-Huene was a Russian American émigré who worked in Paris and the United States. The two book covers, Cheng's *Second Skin* and Rose's *Jazz Cleopatra*,

offer a marked contrast to the banana skirt images that appear on popular commodities, such as postcards and coffee mugs.

69. On the aesthetics of Black sheen, see Krista Thompson, "The Sound of Light: Reflections on Art History in the Visual Culture of Hip-Hop," *Art Bulletin* 91, no. 4 (2009): 481–505.

70. Charles Baudelaire, "The Dandy," in "The Painter of Modern Life" (1863), *The Painter of Modern Life and Other Essays*, trans. and ed. Jonathan Mayne (New York: Phaidon, 1970), 26–29.

71. Baudelaire, "The Dandy," 27–29.

72. Amber Medland details Larsen's attention to sartorial nuance in "They Roared with Laughter," *London Review of Books*, May 6, 2021, 33.

73. See Sianne Ngai's brilliant reading of irritation as Larsen's narrative and affective alternative to aestheticization in *Quicksand*. Ngai, *Ugly Feelings* (Cambridge, MA: Harvard University Press, 2005), 174–208. I am grateful to Merve Emre for reminding me of Ngai's parallel but differently weighted argument.

74. The distinction between a *gown* and a *frock* is drawn subtly but clearly in a March 1923 essay in *Vanity Fair* titled "Every Evening Occasion Has Its Appropriate Style of Dress," in which the author admonishes: "It is in just as bad taste to wear too elaborate a gown to a public restaurant as it is to wear too informal a frock to the opera" (8). For the complexities of women's evening gowns in the early twentieth century, see Celia Marshik, *At the Mercy of Their Clothes: Modernism, the Middlebrow, and British Garment Culture* (New York: Columbia University Press, 2017), especially chapter 1, "What Do Women Want? At the Mercy of the Evening Gown" (25-65). Marshik cites the passage from *Vanity Fair* on page 28, and discusses Woolf's ambivalent relation to the evening gown on pages 44-47.

75. Virginia Woolf, "The New Dress," in *The Mrs. Dalloway Reader*, ed. Francine Prose (New York: Harcourt, 2003), 49, emphasis in original; abbreviated in the text as ND.

76. Virginia Woolf, "The New Dress," *Forum* 77, no. 5 (May 1927): 704–11.

77. The disputed boundaries between plagiarism, adaptation, intertextuality, and allusion have generated a lively critical debate about these texts. In a letter to the editors of *Forum*, Larsen denied the charge of plagiarism, claiming that the constitutive elements of her story were part of African American folklore and pointing out that if she had intended to plagiarize, she would have altered more features of the story (such as urbanizing the rural setting). See "The Author's Explanation," *Forum* Supplement 4, no. 83 (April 1930): 41–42, reprinted in Larsen, *Passing: Authoritative Text*, ed. Kaplan, 156–58. Although the journal editors accepted her account, most critics remain unpersuaded. For a range of ambivalent defenses, see Barbara Hochman, "Love and Theft: Plagiarism, Blackface, and Nella Larsen's 'Sanctuary,'" *American Literature* 88, no. 3 (September 2016), 509–40; Hildegard Hoeller, "Race, Modernism, and Plagiarism: The Case of Nella Larsen's 'Sanctuary,'" *African American Review* 40, no. 3 (2006): 421–37; Kelli A. Larsen, "Surviving the Taint of Plagiarism: Nella Larsen's 'Sanctuary' and Sheila Kaye-Smith's 'Mrs. Adis,'" *Journal of Modern Literature* 30, no. 4 (2007): 82–104; and Davis, *Nella Larsen*. More generally, the striking echoes between a story set in rural England and one in the rural American South suggest habits of assimilative

reading that reinforce the larger case for Larsen's absorption and transposition of *Mrs. Dalloway* in *Passing*.

78. In "'Structure Would Equal Meaning': Blues and Jazz Aesthetics in the Fiction of Nella Larsen," *Tulsa Studies in Women's Literature* 28, no. 2 (Fall 2009), 269–71, Lori Harrison-Kahan argues that although Larsen's novels "share a tendency with high modernism to probe characters' interior consciousness—the realm of the unsaid—through free indirect discourse," these novels "also employ the expressive forms of Black oral tradition" to constitute a distinctive version of the "blues aesthetic" audible in the novel's division into three sections, each subdivided into four chapters, which "mimics the form of the classic blues, which consists of twelve bars, spread across three lines with four measures to each line." This measurement seems accurate but somewhat mechanical and detached from the movements of memory and desire that give form to these sections, at the same time that the three-part structure has multiple sources in the history of Western philosophy and theater.

79. Butler, "Passing, Queering," 172.

80. According to the "Introduction," published in December 1928, "In the first version Septimus, who later is intended to be her double, had no existence; and . . . Mrs. Dalloway was originally to kill herself, or perhaps merely to die at the end of the party." Virginia Woolf, "An Introduction to *Mrs. Dalloway*," in Prose, *The Mrs. Dalloway Reader*, 11. Although Larsen wouldn't have read Woolf's "Introduction" before completing *Passing*, she seems to have intuited the significance of Septimus.

81. Larsen, *Passing: Authoritative Text*, ed. Kaplan, 82. On the unresolved question of the novel's two endings, see Mark J. Madigan, "'Then Everything Was Dark': The Two Endings of Nella Larsen's *Passing*," *Papers of the Bibliographical Society of America* 83, no. 4 (December 1989): 521–23. It is impossible to know why the second ending was dropped from the third printing (and several subsequent reprintings) of the novel or what Larsen's intentions were. In "The Recurring Conditions of Nella Larsen's *Passing: Authoritative Text*" (in Larsen, *Passing*, ed. Kaplan, 463–85), Kate Baldwin interprets the undecidability of the two endings as a productive facet of the indeterminacy of "passing" between races and across the boundary between life and death.

82. The afterlife of the masculine Black dandy has been well charted in the final chapter of Miller's *Slaves to Fashion*, 219–90.

83. On the complex relation between paranoid interpretation in and of the text, see Brian Carr, "Paranoid Interpretation, Desire's Nonobject, and Nella Larsen's *Passing*," *PMLA* 119, no. 2 (March 2004): 282–95.

84. Woolf, "The Art of Fiction," 109.

85. On the ritual's historical and cultural insistence, see Julie E. Fromer, *A Necessary Luxury: Tea in Victorian England* (Athens: Ohio University Press, 2008).

86. Hochman, "Fill the Blanks," 1175, 1178.

87. Hochman, "Fill the Blanks," 1184.

CHAPTER TWO

1. James Baldwin, "Fifth Avenue, Uptown: A Letter from Harlem," in *Collected Essays*, ed. Toni Morrison (New York: The Library of America, 1998), 174; "The Harlem Ghetto," *Collected Essays*, 42; abbreviated in the text as *CE*. In one of his few references

to what he calls the Negro Renaissance, which he notes was "going on" while he was "coming into the world," Baldwin makes clear his disdain: "This Negro Renaissance is an elegant term which means that white people had then discovered that Negroes could act and write as well as sing and dance and this Renaissance was not destined to last very long." "Notes for a Hypothetical Novel: An Address," *CE*, 223.

2. Virginia Woolf, "Modern Fiction" (1925), in *The Common Reader* (New York: Harcourt Brace, 1953), 156–57.

3. On his deathbed, Baldwin instructed his brother David and his friend and biographer David Leeming to arrange for his papers (minus "some of the more personal letters") to be deposited at the Schomburg Center for Research in Black Culture. See David Leeming, *James Baldwin: A Biography* (New York: Arcade Publishing, 2015), 382. My account of the missing journals is based on correspondence with David Leeming (March 19, 2017 and February 15, 2018); Mary F. Yearwood, Director of Collections and Information Services, Schomburg Center for Research in Black Culture (March 2, 2018); and Eileen Ahearn, the literary executor of the James Baldwin Estate at that time (February 20–22, 2018).

4. Leeming, *James Baldwin*, 130.

5. According to David Leeming, "Suicide was a subject that obsessed [Baldwin] throughout his life. He lost several close friends by that route and attempted it himself at least four times" (*James Baldwin*, 12). And again, "Suicide was a clear tendency in Baldwin's personality. It grew out of an essential loneliness that was in turn related to his sexuality and his mission" (132). Harmony Holiday reiterates this point in "Preface to James Baldwin's Unwritten Suicide Note," https://www.poetryfoundation.org/harriet-books/2018/08/preface-to-james-baldwins-unwritten-suicide-note#.

6. James Baldwin to Mary Painter, October 10, 1956, JWJ MSS 107, Box 2, Folder 4, Walter O. Evans Collection of James Baldwin, Beinecke Rare Book and Manuscript Library, Yale University. The African American musician with whom Baldwin was involved at this time has been identified only by his first name, Arnold.

7. In "Notes on a Native Son," *Soul on Ice* (New York: Dell Press, 1992), 96–107, Eldridge Cleaver elaborates the interrelations among whiteness, suicide, and homosexuality. For a later generation of Black writers, Woolf became an icon of self-indulgent white suicide. Speaking through the persona of Richard Pryor's (imaginary) sister, Hilton Als nominates her "Suicide Bitch" and holds her "at least partially responsible for the mealy-mouthed nonthink that permeates contemporary women's writing" since "everything she wrote was infused with special pleading for her genius, her madness, her Leonard." See Hilton Als, *White Girls* (San Francisco: McSweeney's, 2014), 271–73. More recently, Als has written movingly about Baldwin's struggles to transpose his own experiences of race and sexuality in *Giovanni's Room*. Hilton Als, "Song of Himself," *T: The New York Times Style Magazine*, September 8, 2019, 98–107.

8. See, for example, Baldwin's description of his first experience of near drowning at Coney Island: a kind of primal scene of death from which he is rescued by his half brother Sam, in "Take Me to the Water," *No Name in the Street*, *CE*, 356–57. See also the end of "Nothing Personal," in which Baldwin writes: "The sea rises, the light fails, . . . the sea engulfs us and the light goes out" (*CE*, 706). The metaphor recurs frequently, as in Baldwin's description of the dangers of living in Greenwich Village in the 1950s,

when the Village "was an alabaster maze perched above a boiling sea. To lose oneself in the maze was to fall into the sea"; "The Price of the Ticket," *CE*, 832.

9. Baldwin's transgender identifications began with the childhood fascination with white female movie stars he describes in *The Devil Finds Work* (*CE*, 479–85). These transgender and transracial identifications have led Marquis Bey to insist on Baldwin's pervasively anti-identitarian "*trans*-ness" in "'The Song Required of Captivity: *Just Above My Head* and the *Trans*-ness of James Baldwin," *Palimpsest: A Journal on Women, Gender, and the Black International* 5, no. 1 (2016): 42–58. For other accounts of Baldwin's crossings, see Matt Brim's careful parsing of *gay* and *queer* in *James Baldwin and the Queer Imagination* (Ann Arbor: University of Michigan Press, 2014); Cora Kaplan and Bill Schwarz, eds., *James Baldwin: America and Beyond* (Ann Arbor: University of Michigan, 2011); and Dwight A. McBride, ed., *James Baldwin Now* (New York: New York University Press, 1999).

10. Quoted by Randall Kenan, *James Baldwin* (New York: Chelsea House, 1994), 56.

11. In *Empty Houses: Theatrical Failure and the Novel* (Princeton, NJ: Princeton University Press, 2012), David Kurnick asserts that "Baldwin's debt to Henry James (a writer he called 'my master') is evident in the shape of his sentences, in the plots of his major novels, and in the title of his most famous essay, "Notes of a Native Son"—which references both Richard Wright's *Native Son* and James' *Notes of a Son and Brother*" (192).

12. In the April 15, 1920, initiation of the Holograph edition of *Jacob's Room*, Woolf writes, "I think the main point is that it should be free. Yet what about form? Let us suppose that the Room will hold it together." *Virginia Woolf's "Jacob's Room": The Holograph Draft*, transcribed and edited by Edward L. Bishop (New York: Pace University Press, 1998), 1.

13. Baldwin describes the literary benefits and emotional discomfort of the room trope in a letter to Sam from Paris, 1955, Box 16, Folder 4, James Baldwin Papers, The Schomburg Center for Research in Black Culture.

14. Taken for granted as the sui generis foundation of a queer Black literary tradition that takes off from *Giovanni's Room*, Baldwin himself had few precursors. For his status as a standard-bearer for queer culture, see Brim, *James Baldwin and the Queer Imagination*.

15. On reproductive futurism, see Lee Edelman, *No Future: Queer Theory and the Death Drive* (Durham, NC: Duke University Press, 2004). For debates about the antisocial thesis, see "The Antisocial Thesis in Queer Theory," based on a panel at the 2005 MLA Convention, in *PMLA* 121, no. 3 (May 2006): 819–28.

16. Carolyn Dinshaw, *Getting Medieval: Sexualities and Communities, Pre- and Postmodern* (Durham, NC: Duke University Press, 1999), 35, 39. Dinshaw is primarily interested in historical differences, but the argument applies as well to racial, national, or gender differences.

17. David Leeming, "An Interview with James Baldwin on Henry James," *Henry James Review* 8, no. 1 (Fall 1986): 55–56.

18. See "James Baldwin, The Art of Fiction No. 78," interview by Jordan Elgrably and George Plimpton, *Paris Review* 91 (Spring 1984); reprinted in *Conversations with James Baldwin*, ed. Fred L. Standley and Louis H. Pratt (Jackson: University Press of

Mississippi, 1989), 238. For some of Baldwin's other overt expressions of indebtedness to James, see Leeming, *James Baldwin*, 253–58.

19. Baldwin's affiliation with James featured in white appreciations from early on. See, for example, Elizabeth Hardwick's description of Baldwin as "a Negro writer who has modeled himself on Henry James" in "The New Books," *Harper's Magazine*, January 1962, 94. David Leeming was an early and strong proponent of Baldwin's indebtedness to James. In addition to his biography of Baldwin, see Leeming, "An Interview with James Baldwin on Henry James," 47–56. Other examples include Kevin Birmingham, "No Name in the South: James Baldwin and the Monuments of Identity," *African American Review* 44, nos. 1–2 (Spring/Summer 2011): 221–34; Charles Newman, "The Lesson of the Master: Henry James and James Baldwin," in *James Baldwin: A Collection of Critical Essays*, ed. Kenneth Kinnamon (Englewood Cliffs, NJ: Prentice Hall, 1974), 45–59; Lyall H. Powers, "Henry James and James Baldwin: The Complex Figure," *Modern Fiction Studies* 30 (1984): 651–67; and Kurnick, *Empty Houses*, chap. 3.

20. See Colm Tóibín's introduction to *Giovanni's Room* (New York: Knopf, 2016), x–xii; "Baldwin and 'the American Confusion,'" in Kaplan and Schwarz, *James Baldwin: America and Beyond*, 55–56; and "The Henry James of Harlem: James Baldwin's Struggles," *London Review of Books*, September 14, 2001, https://www.theguardian.com/books/2001/sep/14/jamesbaldwin.

21. Colm Tóibín, "Baldwin and 'the American Confusion,'" 62. Baldwin's reference to "the private life" is from "A Word from Writer Directly to Reader," in James Baldwin, *The Cross of Redemption: Uncollected Writings*, ed. Randall Kenan (New York: Pantheon, 2010), 8. Tóibín is by no means unusual in his assumption that James holds a singular place in Baldwin's literary pantheon. In his otherwise excellent study *Empty Houses*, for example, David Kurnick identifies James's *The Golden Bowl* as the model for the "collective fictional subject" of Baldwin's *Another Country*, overlooking the much closer model of Woolf's "play poem" *The Waves*. Kurnick, *Empty Houses*, 198; November 7, 1928, *The Diary of Virginia Woolf*, vol. 3, *1925–1930*, ed. Anne Olivier Bell (New York: Harvest/HBJ, 1981), 203.

22. According to the store's website, www.shakespeareandcompany.com/pate/32/history. In *Exiled in Paris: Richard Wright, James Baldwin, Samuel Beckett, and Others on the Left Bank* (New York: Scribner, 1995), James Campbell notes that the bookstore served as "The Left Bank Arts Center" and lending library, offering about 10,000 books that could be borrowed for a few francs, a reading room on the first floor, and frequent open houses. Campbell also notes the existence of other English-language bookstores and meeting places in Paris, such as the English Bookshop at 42, rue de Seine, which "served as talking shops for the young literati" (72).

23. On what was probably that occasion, Baldwin inscribed a photograph of himself in the bookstore to "the old curiosity shop," suggesting that he imagined a British cultural lineage for the store. See Krista Halverson, *Shakespeare & Co., Paris: A History of the Rag and Bone Shop of the Heart* (Paris: Shakespeare and Company Paris Press, 2016), 103. Halverson claims that Baldwin sold his personal library to the bookstore, but according to James Campbell in *Exiled in Paris*, Baldwin sold only some of his own books to the bookstore when he was hard up, gaining a few hundred francs for them.

24. See especially Virginia Woolf, "The Art of Fiction" (a title Woolf borrows from James) and "On Re-reading Novels," in *The Moment and Other Essays* (New York: Harcourt Brace Jovanovich, 1948), 106–12 and 155–66.

25. Woolf, "The Art of Fiction" (1927), 109. Woolf offers her fullest assessment of Percy Lubbock in "On Re-reading Novels" (1922), 155–66.

26. Virginia Woolf, *Three Guineas* (New York: Harcourt Brace, 1966), 14; Baldwin, "Autobiographical Notes," *CE*, 7.

27. Baldwin, "Autobiographical Notes," *CE*, 8; Virginia Woolf, *A Room of One's Own* (New York: Harcourt, Brace & World, 1957), 26–27.

28. Baldwin, *No Name in the Street, CE*, 380; Woolf, *A Room of One's Own*, 86.

29. Baldwin, "The Discovery of What It Means to Be an American," *CE*, 137.

30. James Baldwin, "Introduction to *Notes of a Native Son,*" *CE*, 810. Baldwin and Woolf both use the metaphor of the open sky to represent the escape from racial and gender categories. For the narrator of *A Room of One's Own*, her aunt's legacy unveiled "a view of the open sky" (39). For Baldwin's American in Europe, "it is as though he suddenly came out of a dark tunnel and found himself beneath the open sky" (*CE*, 140).

31. Woolf, *A Room of One's Own*, 108. Baldwin expresses this view, in part through a quotation from the Irish writer Sean O'Faolain, in "Must Negro Novelists Write Negro Novels?," an undated typescript for a lecture. Box 57, Folder 1, James Baldwin Papers.

32. Woolf, *A Room of One's Own*, 112; "Modern Fiction," 153.

33. Baldwin, "What It Means to Be an American," *CE*, 142. In the typescript for "Mass Culture and the Creative Artist: Some Personal Notes" (1959), Baldwin claims that the writer's challenge is to communicate "something intangible" through observable phenomena. Box 42, Folder 9, p. 2, James Baldwin Papers.

34. Baldwin, "Words of a Native Son," *CE*, 708.

35. Baldwin, "Nothing Personal," *CE*, 701.

36. Baldwin, "Words of a Native Son," *CE*, 708.

37. Woolf, "Modern Fiction," 156; Baldwin, "Nothing Personal," *CE*, 705.

38. Cited by David Leeming as a conversation with Baldwin in *James Baldwin*, 119. Note also Baldwin's account of the universe shrinking to "the prison of the self" in "Nothing Personal," *CE*, 701, and his emphasis in "The Male Prison" on the need to escape "the tyranny of one's own personality," *CE*, 235; January 26, 1920, *The Diary of Virginia Woolf*, vol. 2, *1920–1924*, ed. Anne Olivier Bell, assisted by Andrew McNeillie (New York: Harcourt Brace, 1978), 14.

39. Baldwin, typescript for "American Experience and the Novel," Box 42, Folder 9, p. 2, James Baldwin Papers; Woolf, "Women and Fiction" (1929), in *Granite and Rainbow: Essays by Virginia Woolf* (New York: Harcourt Brace Jovanovich, 1975), 76–84. See, for example, Woolf's claim that the "greater impersonality of women's lives" makes it possible for women to "look beyond the personal and political relationships to the wider questions which the poet tries to solve—of our destiny and the meaning of life" (83).

40. Baldwin, "'This Nettle, Danger . . . ,'" *CE*, 691; Woolf, *A Room of One's Own*, 112.

41. Virginia Woolf, "'Anon' and 'The Reader,'" in "'Anon' and 'The Reader': Virginia Woolf's Last Essays," ed. Brenda R. Silver, *Twentieth Century Literature* 25, no. 3/4

(Autumn–Winter 1979): 356–441; James Baldwin, untitled contribution to a catalogue produced for an exhibit by The Center for African Arts, *Perspectives: Angles on African Art* (New York: The Center for African Art, 1987), 118.

42. Baldwin makes this claim in his March 1956 letter to his friend and editor Sol Stein explaining why he couldn't write a preface to a book entitled *The Negro in America*. Box 3b, Folder 16, James Baldwin Papers.

43. Baldwin, "Everybody's Protest Novel," *CE*, 13.

44. Baldwin, "Notes of a Native Son," *CE*, 84; Woolf, *A Room of One's Own*, 60–61, 69.

45. Baldwin's regrets and qualifications in the three essays written the year after Wright's death in 1960 are enumerated in the essay "Alas, Poor Richard," *CE*, 247–68.

46. Baldwin, "The Male Prison," *CE*, 232.

47. Baldwin, "Freaks and the American Ideal of Manhood" (previously titled "Here Be Dragons"), *CE*, 827.

48. "Freaks and the American Ideal of Manhood," *CE*, 823. For astute analyses of the sociopolitical costs and complications of Baldwin's feminine identifications, see Marlon B. Ross, "Baldwin's Sissy Heroics," *African American Review* 46, no. 4 (Winter 2013): 633–51, and "White Fantasies of Desire: Baldwin and the Racial Identities of Sexuality," in McBride, *James Baldwin Now*, 13–55.

49. Baldwin, "Freaks and the American Ideal of Manhood," *CE*, 815.

50. Baldwin describes these identifications in his unpublished "Early Personal Essay" (untitled, undated), Box 1, Folder 4, James Baldwin Papers; and in an undated fragment in Box 43, Folder 11, James Baldwin Papers. In a letter to a friend in Turkey in December 1961, he noted that he was probably undergoing a version of the postpartum blues writers often experience after finishing a book (Box 43, Folder 11, James Baldwin Papers). Note the resonance with Woolf's comment upon completing *The Years*: "I wonder if anyone has ever suffered so much from a book. Once out I will never look at it again. It's like a long childbirth." November 10, 1936, *The Diary of Virginia Woolf*, vol. 5, *1936–1941*, ed. Anne Olivier Bell, assisted by Andrew McNeillie (New York: Harcourt Brace, 1984), 31.

51. See Baldwin's typescript plan edits for "The Only Pretty Ring Time," February 13, 1954, Box 47, Folder 4, p. 2, James Baldwin Papers.

52. Baldwin, "Freaks and the American Ideal of Manhood," *CE*, 815.

53. Baldwin, "Freaks and the American Ideal of Manhood," *CE*, 814.

54. Baldwin, "Freaks and the American Ideal of Manhood," *CE*, 828.

55. Baldwin, typed notes to parts of an essay on Richard Wright on verso, Box 47, Folder 5, p. 1, James Baldwin Papers.

56. Baldwin, typed notes to parts of an essay on Richard Wright on verso.

57. Baldwin, typescript outline edits, (Shanks Village) Summer 1948, Box 47, Folder 3, p. 1, James Baldwin Papers.

58. Baldwin, typed notes to parts of an essay on Richard Wright on verso, p. 1.

59. Baldwin, typescript outline edits, p. 3. It was not capricious (or perhaps surprising) for Baldwin to have focused on Lonergan's sexuality, since the murder trial apparently "sparked an ongoing, if reductive and damning, public conversation about

homosexuality and bisexuality," according to Naben Ruthnum, "Footnotes to a Murder," *Hazlitt*, November 30, 2015, https://hazlitt.net/feature/footnotes-murder.

60. Baldwin, typed notes to parts of an essay on Richard Wright on verso, p. 2.

61. Baldwin, typed notes to parts of an essay on Richard Wright on verso, p. 2.

62. Baldwin, typed notes to parts of an essay on Richard Wright on verso, p. 2; "Everybody's Protest Novel," *CE*, 17.

63. Baldwin, "Many Thousands Gone," *CE*, 34.

64. Baldwin, "Many Thousands Gone," *CE*, 22. For a queer reading of James's novella, see Eve Kosofsky Sedgwick, "The Beast in the Closet: James and the Writing of Homosexual Panic," in *Epistemology of the Closet* (Berkeley: University of California Press, 1990), 182–212.

65. Baldwin, typescript outline edits, p. 2.

66. "So Long at the Fair (First Part)," Box 47, Folder 8, James Baldwin Papers. It is difficult to date this draft with certainty, but the fact that the title, a variant of which was subsequently rejected in favor of "The Only Pretty Ring Time," is also used for a different draft dated Shanks Village, 1948 (Box 47, Folder 7, James Baldwin Papers) suggests that "So Long at the Fair (First Part)" was roughly contemporaneous with the typescript outline edits. In yet another early undated draft titled "One" (Box 47, Folder 2), references to racial unrest are associated with a larger breakdown of the social order that culminates in World War II.

67. Baldwin, typed notes to parts of an essay on Richard Wright on verso.

68. Baldwin, "Two," Box 47, Folder 11, p. 30, James Baldwin Papers.

69. Baldwin, "One," p. 11.

70. Virginia Woolf, *To the Lighthouse* (New York: Harcourt/Harvest, 1981), 132–33, 127.

71. Woolf, *To the Lighthouse*, 128; Baldwin, "Two," 30.

72. Baldwin, "Two," 34.

73. Baldwin, "Two," 30.

74. Baldwin, "Two," 31.

75. Baldwin, "Two," 36–37; Woolf, *Mrs. Dalloway*, 14. Richard Wright renders the trial of Bigger Thomas, by contrast, almost entirely through the speeches of the defense and prosecuting lawyers. When Bigger's own feelings are represented, it is via narrative summary (e.g., Bigger's "feeling that it was all a wild and intense dream that must end soon, somehow,") rather than an attempt to capture the rhythms of his thought. Richard Wright, *Native Son: And How Bigger Was Born* (New York: Harper Perennial, 1993), 432.

76. Baldwin, "Autobiographical Notes," *CE*, 6.

77. Baldwin, "Two," 34.

78. Baldwin, "Two," 35.

79. Baldwin, "Words of a Native Son," *CE*, 711–12, emphasis in original.

80. Baldwin, "Words of a Native Son," *CE*, 712, emphasis added.

81. Baldwin, "Words of a Native Son," *CE*, 712.

82. Baldwin, "Notes for a Hypothetical Novel," *CE*, 224.

83. Baldwin, "Notes for a Hypothetical Novel," *CE*, 225.

84. James Baldwin, "The New Lost Generation," *CE*, 659. In "Preface to James Baldwin's Unwritten Suicide Note," Harmony Holiday powerfully renders the lifelong impact of this suicide: "Eugene Worth became both muse and demon, voice of reason and madman, inspiration to live and temptation to die, hero and antagonist in Baldwin's psychic life. . . . A taunting intimacy on the other side of time"; https://www.poetryfoundation.org/harriet-books/2018/08/preface-to-james-baldwins-unwritten-suicide-note#.

85. Baldwin, "The Price of the Ticket," *CE*, 833.

86. Baldwin, *No Name in the Street, CE*, 426.

87. Baldwin, "Take Me to the Water," *CE*, 365.

88. Baldwin, 33-page typescript, 1954, Box 14, Folder 4, James Baldwin Papers. On the first page, under the title *Giovanni's Room*, Baldwin refers to his text as a "story"; on the title page he calls it a "novella," which is crossed out with "novel" written next to it in pencil. This is clearly a text in transition, for which Baldwin radically condensed the structure and scope of his narrative, and then expanded it within these more compact terms.

89. Baldwin, 33-page typescript, 1954.

90. Baldwin, 33-page typescript, 1954.

91. Baldwin, 33-page typescript, 1954; *MD*, 149.

92. Baldwin, 33-page typescript, 1954, emphasis added.

93. Baldwin, "The Long Farewell," typescript dated July 29, 1949, Box 18, Folder 2, James Baldwin Papers. Although Baldwin notes that his draft is only an outline, it is worth observing that the structure he outlines bears a strong resemblance to Woolf's "play poem" *The Waves*, which is similarly structured around six speakers whose voices culminate in Bernard's retrospective summary. There are even distinct textual echoes in an undated 65-page typescript of *Another Country* for the William Morris Agency, in which the narrator's reference to "a many-sided crisis" composed of his six friends Cass, Richard, Eric, Yves, Daniel, and Ida echoes Bernard's figure of the "six-sided flower; made of six lives" that crystallizes the narrative framework of *The Waves*. The narrator's reference also echoes Bernard's self-description: "I am many people; I do not altogether know who I am—Jinny, Susan, Neville, Rhoda, or Louis." Box 18, Folder 4, James Baldwin Papers; Virginia Woolf, *The Waves* (New York: Harvest, 1959), 229, 276. It is also worth pointing out Baldwin's note that the character he calls Cass is a nickname for Clarissa, who is married to a character named Richard.

94. Leeming, *James Baldwin*, 131. In an interview with Jordan Elgrably and George Plimpton, Baldwin explains that Rufus "was the last person to arrive" in *Another Country*, a kind of afterthought that made the "entire action," and especially the psychology of the central character Ida, come into focus. "James Baldwin, The Art of Fiction No. 78," 243–44.

95. James Baldwin, *Another Country* (New York: Dell Press, 1963), 77; abbreviated in the text as *AC*.

96. Virginia Woolf, "An Introduction to *Mrs. Dalloway*," in *The Mrs. Dalloway Reader*, ed. Francine Prose (New York: Harvest, 2004), 11.

97. Baldwin, "Words of a Native Son," *CE*, 709.

98. Baldwin, "Words of a Native Son," *CE*, 709.

99. A similar figure (with a more optimistic message) occurs in *To the Lighthouse* when Paul and Minta are returning from the beach after getting engaged: "And as they came out on the hill and saw the lights of the town beneath them, the lights coming out suddenly one by one seemed like things that were going to happen to him—his marriage, his children, his house." *To the Lighthouse*, 77–78.

100. Eldridge Cleaver, "Notes on a Native Son," in *Soul on Ice* (New York: Dell Press, 1992), 103. Cleaver was the most outspoken proponent of a certain strain of Black Nationalist homophobia during the late 1960s–1970s. Other proponents included Amiri Baraka, Nathan Hare, Robert Staples, Molefi Asante, and Louis Farrakhan. However, as Marlon B. Ross makes clear in "White Fantasies of Desire," 13–55, Cleaver's version of homophobia (which he subsequently tempered) emerged in the context of intramural struggles within and between Black Power movements. A different perspective was propounded by Huey Newton, whose collected speeches reveal a complex understanding of the relations between the women's, gay, and Black liberation movements.

101. Baldwin, "Two."

102. Virginia Woolf, *Jacob's Room*, annotated and introduced by Vara Neverow (New York: Harcourt/Harvest, 2008), 4, 3; abbreviated in the text as *JR*.

103. Christopher Nealon, *Foundlings: Lesbian and Gay Historical Emotion before Stonewall* (Durham, NC: Duke University Press, 2001). In his typescript for his unpublished lecture "Must Negro Novelists Write Negro Novels?," Baldwin notes Randall Jarrell's definition of style as being as much about what the writer can't say as about what he can. Box 57, Folder 1, James Baldwin Papers. Baldwin seems to have heard what Woolf could not say in *Jacob's Room* several decades before literary critics began to hear the novel's queer subtexts. For some recent examples, see Vara Neverow, "Virginia Woolf's Editorial Self-Censorship and Risk-Taking in *Jacob's Room*," in *Virginia Woolf and the Literary Marketplace*, ed. Jeanne Dubino (New York: Palgrave 2010), 57–71, and "Desiring Statues and Ambiguous Sexualities in *Jacob's Room*," in *Interdisciplinary/Multidisciplinary Woolf*, ed. Ann Martin and Kathryn Holland (Clemson, SC: Clemson University Press, 2013), 27–34; Eileen Barrett, "Indecency: *Jacob's Room*, Modernist Homosexuality, and the Culture of War," in *Virginia Woolf: Twenty-First-Century Approaches*, ed. Jeanne Dubino, Gill Lowe, Vara Neverow, and Kathryn Simpson (Edinburgh: Edinburgh University Press, 2015), 169–86; and Susan C. Harris, "The Ethics of Indecency: Censorship, Sexuality, and the Voice of the Academy in the Narration of *Jacob's Room*," *Twentieth Century Literature* 43, no. 4 (Winter 1997): 420–38.

104. Dinshaw, *Getting Medieval*, 34.

105. Baldwin, "One." All citations in this paragraph are from this source; the call for Jon is underlined in the original.

106. Baldwin, "One." For the death drive's imbrication with queerness, see Leo Bersani, "Is the Rectum a Grave?," *October* 43 (1987): 197–222; and Lee Edelman, *No Future: Queer Theory and the Death Drive* (Durham, NC: Duke University Press, 2004).

107. On Baldwin's childhood experience of strangeness, see *The Devil Finds Work*, *CE*, 483.

108. Baldwin, typescript plan edits for "The Only Pretty Ring Time."

109. Kathryn Bond Stockton beautifully unfolds the shadowy sideways path of the queer child in *The Queer Child, Or Growing Sideways in the Twentieth Century* (Durham, NC: Duke University Press, 2009).

110. The itinerary of the room offers a queer inflection of the resistance to the Bildungsroman plot that numerous critics of the novel have noted. See especially Judith Little, "*Jacob's Room* as Comedy: Woolf's Parodic *Bildungsroman*," and Alex Zwerdling, "*Jacob's Room*: Woolf's Satiric Elegy," both in *Jacob's Room*, ed. Suzanne Raitt (New York: Norton, 2007), 229–63.

111. Julie Anne Taddeo provides a rich account in *Lytton Strachey and the Search for Modern Sexual Identity: The Last Eminent Victorian* (New York and London: The Haworth Press, 2002), esp. chap. 1, "Brotherly Love: The Cambridge Apostles and the Pursuit of the Higher Sodomy," 15–50. See also Julie Anne Taddeo, "Plato's Apostles: Edwardian Cambridge and the 'New Style of Love,'" *Journal of the History of Sexuality* 8, no. 2 (October 1997): 196–228. The most detailed and astute reading of the classical Greek support for the queer undercurrents of *Jacob's Room* is Eileen Barrett, "Indecency: *Jacob's Room*, Modernist Homosexuality, and the Culture of War," in Dubino et al., *Virginia Woolf: Twenty-First-Century Approaches*, 169–86. See also the essays collected in *Queer Bloomsbury*, ed. Brenda Helt and Madelyn Detloff (Edinburgh: Edinburgh University Press, 2016).

112. Linda Dowling, *Hellenism and Homosexuality in Victorian Oxford* (Ithaca, NY: Cornell University Press, 1994).

113. Virginia Woolf, "Old Bloomsbury," in *Moments of Being*, ed. Jeanne Schulkind (New York and London: Harcourt Brace Jovanovich, 1985), 179–201.

114. Plato offers the term "spiritual procreancy" in the *Symposium* for the intellectual benefits of pederasty (209a). The maternal tenderness of Woolf's narrative gesture is consistent with the Apostolic idealization of the mother-son relationship that Julie Ann Taddeo describes in "Plato's Apostles," 220–21.

115. In "Queer Entomology: Virginia Woolf's Butterflies," *Modernism/modernity* 24, no. 4 (November 2017): 723–50, Benjamin Bagocius explores how "the queer promise of unstable bodies figured by the butterfly accompanies Jacob to Cambridge" (742). Unlike the heteronormative hum that Woolf imagines beneath the spoken words at luncheons before the war in *A Room of One's Own*, the queer hum her narrator hears in Simeon's room takes an immediate sonic form rather than being mediated through the poetry of Tennyson and Rossetti.

116. Woolf, "Old Bloomsbury," 195. "Old Bloomsbury" was written very close in time to *Jacob's Room*. Vara Neverow unpacks the resonance between semen and Simeon in "Contrasting Urban and Rural Transgressive Sexualities in *Jacob's Room*," in *Virginia Woolf and the City: Selected Papers from the Nineteenth Annual Conference on Virginia Woolf*, ed. E. F. Evans and S. E. Cornish (Clemson, SC: Clemson University Digital Press, 2010), 154–60.

117. Bersani, "Is the Rectum a Grave?," 197–222. See also Cora Kaplan, "'A Cavern Opened in my Mind': The Poetics of Homosexuality and the Politics of Masculinity in James Baldwin," in *Representing Black Men*, ed. Marcellus Blount and George P. Cunningham (New York: Routledge, 1996), 27–54.

118. Lytton Strachey to Leonard Woolf, April 1905; cited by Taddeo, "Plato's Apostles," 228. As Taddeo further explains, "Within their private rooms at Cambridge the Apostles continued to invoke Dorianism, read Walt Whitman's poetry, and view their relations as anti-Victorian, but outside this protective atmosphere, they realized that any degree of intimacy between men called into question their respectability and masculinity" (200).

119. Taddeo, *Lytton Strachey and the Search for Modern Sexual Identity*, 23.

120. In a powerful chapter in *Beautiful Bottom, Beautiful Shame: Where "Black" Meets "Queer"* (Durham, NC: Duke University Press, 2006), Katheryn Bond Stockton homes in on the figure of the corpse as the source of what she calls "decomposition as narrative form" in *Giovanni's Room* (153). To her association of the corpse with the mangled body of Emmett Till and the soon-to-be-corpse of Giovanni, I add David's vivid imagination of his mother's corpse.

121. "Saint-Germain-des-Prés, capitale du non-conformisme," *Futur* 1 (October 1952): 2; quoted by Georges Sidéris, "*Folles*, Swells, Effeminates, and Homophiles in Saint-Germain-des-Prés of the 1950s," *Journal of Homosexuality* 41, nos. 3–4 (2002): 220. There was also a critique launched primarily by André Baudry, who founded the homophile magazine *Arcadie* in 1954. Differentiating homophiles from *folles*, Baudry wanted homosexuals to "blend in with others, without singularities, without eccentricities." Baudry, "La Faute," *Arcadie*, April 1959, 206; cited in Sidéris, "*Folles*, Swells, Effeminates, and Homophiles," 223. As Sidéris points out, a new journal, *Joventus*, appeared in 1959 with the motto "Virility, Health, Truth," which promoted a new virile model and scapegoated Saint-Germain for the harassment of homosexuals.

122. Sidéris, "*Folles*, Swells, Effeminates, and Homophiles," 220. Sidéris does an excellent job of mapping the historical evolution and debates surrounding the midcentury homosexual culture of Saint-Germain-des-Prés, which Baldwin frequented from 1948 through the mid-1950s.

123. In *Exiled in Paris*, James Campbell reads *Giovanni's Room* as puritanically repudiating the gay scene in Saint-Germain-des-Prés and differentiating itself as much as possible from Genet. While agreeing about Baldwin's ultimate repudiation of the scene, I think he also grants it an important role in David's trajectory toward Giovanni's room.

124. According to Julie Anne Taddeo, the Higher Sodomists considered copulation (in the words of Lytton Strachey) "the act of beasts." Taddeo, *Lytton Strachey and the Search for Modern Sexual Identity*, 23. Taddeo is citing a poem by Lytton Strachey entitled "Ménage à Trois."

125. Eve Kosofsky Sedgwick, *Between Men: English Literature and Male Homosocial Desire* (New York: Columbia University Press, 1985), 208.

126. See, among others, Brim, *James Baldwin and the Queer Imagination*, 55–91; Mae G. Henderson, "James Baldwin's *Giovanni's Room*: Expatriation, 'Racial Drag,' and Homosexual Panic," in *Black Queer Studies: A Critical Anthology*, ed. E. Patrick Johnson and Mae G. Henderson (Durham, NC: Duke University Press, 2005), 298–322; and Ross, "Baldwin's Sissy Heroics."

127. E. B. Saunders, "Reformers' Choice: Marriage License or Just License?," *One* 1, no. 8 (August 1953): 10; the letters are reprinted in *One* 1, no. 10 (October 1953). Titled as an homage to Thomas Carlyle's assertion that "a mystic bond of brotherhood makes

all men one," *One* was the first gay rights organization in the United States to have its own office and to publish a monthly periodical. Baldwin would have had access to the periodical during his visit to the United States in 1954, as well as in Paris, where it advertised in and could be subscribed to via the journal *Arcadie*.

128. Critics occasionally view Giovanni's room as more of a womb. For example, Charlotte Alexander characterizes the male couple as "enwombed" in "a comfortable, floating, prenatal state" in "The 'Stink' of Reality," in Kinnamon, *James Baldwin: A Collection of Critical Essays*, 80. My view is closer to Mae G. Henderson's glossing of abjection in "James Baldwin's *Giovanni's Room*, 'Racial Drag,' and Homosexual Panic," in Johnson and Henderson, *Black Queer Studies*, 298–322.

129. Baldwin, "The Preservation of Innocence," *CE*, 595. The description of the "smashed flower of light" in Giovanni's room seems to be written with foreknowledge of AIDS, but as Jeff Nunokawa argues in "'All the Sad Young Men': AIDS and the Work of Mourning," *Yale Journal of Criticism* 4, no. 2 (Spring 1991): 1–12, the tradition of representing gay men's blighted future precedes the AIDS epidemic. Thanks to Sylvie Thode for calling Nunokawa's article to my attention.

130. José Esteban Muñoz, *Cruising Utopia: The Then and There of Queer Futurity* (New York: New York University Press, 2009), 1.

131. Muñoz, *Cruising Utopia*, 1.

132. Muñoz, *Cruising Utopia*, 5.

133. *The Diary of Virginia Woolf*, 2:249.

134. Muñoz, *Cruising Utopia*, 16.

135. Box 14, Folder 1, James Baldwin Papers. In his unpublished essay on James and Dos Passos, "Le Mâle et la Femelle d'une Espèce: Deux Buffonneries," Baldwin uses the phrase "antechambers of consciousness" in relation to Winterbourne, an American Anglicized enough to mediate between American innocence and European decadence. Box 42, Folder 17, James Baldwin Papers.

136. See Magdalena J. Zamborowska on the "sprawling stone Provencal house" as a creative transnational Black queer space. *Me and My House: James Baldwin's Last Decade in France* (Durham, NC: Duke University Press, 2006), 17.

137. Virginia Woolf, "American Fiction" (1925), in *The Moment and Other Essays*, 126.

138. See Marilyn R. Chandler, *Dwelling in the Text: Houses in American Fiction* (Berkeley and Los Angeles: University of California Press, 1991).

139. James Baldwin, "Every Good-Bye Ain't Gone" (1977), *CE*, 779, emphasis in original.

140. "Sitting in the House" is the title of part 1 of *Nobody Knows My Name*. As Cora Kaplan and Bill Schwarz point out in their "Introduction: America and Beyond," in *James Baldwin: America and Beyond*, the figure of the American house recurs throughout Baldwin's oeuvre. Blake Morrison characterizes the British country house as a "national literary obsession": "Of all the great things that the English have invented and made part of the credit of the national character, the most perfect, the most characteristic, the only one they have mastered completely in all its details, so that it becomes a compendious illustration of their social genius and their manners, is the well-appointed,

well-administered, well-filled country house." Morrison, "The Country House and the English Novel," *The Guardian*, June 11, 2011, https://www.theguardian.com/books/2011/jun/11/country-house-novels-blake-morrison.

141. Woolf, "An Introduction to *Mrs. Dalloway*," 12.

142. Baldwin, "Typescript plan edits for 'The Only Pretty Ring Time.'"

143. Jacob Stockinger, "Homotextuality," in *The Gay Academic*, ed. Louie Crew (Palm Springs, CA: ETC Publications, 1978); cited by Mae G. Henderson, "James Baldwin: Expatriation, Homosexual Panic, and Man's Estate," *Callaloo* 23, no. 2 (2000): 319.

144. Baldwin, "Every Good-Bye Ain't Gone," *CE*, 778.

145. Woolf, *To the Lighthouse*, 192, 28; November 28, 1928, *The Diary of Virginia Woolf*, 3:209.

CHAPTER THREE

1. Roland Barthes, "Longtemps, je me suis couché de bonne heure . . . ," delivered at the Collège de France a few weeks before the first session of "La préparation du roman." The essay is presented in translation but under the French title in Roland Barthes, *The Rustle of Language*, trans. Richard Howard (New York: Farrar, Straus & Giroux, 1986), 277–90; abbreviated in the text as L.

2. Barthes, "Longtemps," 286; Roland Barthes, entry for November 30, 1977, *Mourning Diary*, trans. Richard Howard (New York: Hill and Wang, 2010), 74. Barthes preferred the Latin version of *Vita Nova* to Dante's *Vita Nuova*.

3. Barthes does associate Woolf and Proust once: in his seminar of 1973–74, where he refers to "les romans à réseaux de langages désirants (James, Virginia Woolf, Proust)." *Le lexique de l'auteur: Seminaire à l'École pratique des hautes études 1973–74* (Paris: Seuil, 2010), 55–56.

4. Letter to Vanessa Bell, April 21, 1927, *The Letters of Virginia Woolf*, vol. 3, *1923–1928*, ed. Nigel Nicolson and Joanne Trautmann (New York: Harcourt Brace Jovanovich, 1977), 365. Woolf was introduced to Proust's work by Roger Fry, one of his earliest British fans, in 1918–19.

5. Letter to Roger Fry, May 6, 1922, *The Letters of Virginia Woolf*, vol. 2, *1912–1922*, ed. Nigel Nicolson and Joanne Trautmann (New York: Harcourt Brace Jovanovich, 1978), 525, emphasis in original. See also the letter to Fry, October 3, 1922, *The Letters of Virginia Woolf*, 2:565–66; and the diary entry April 8, 1925, in *The Diary of Virginia Woolf*, vol. 3, *1925–1930*, ed. Anne Olivier Bell (New York: Harcourt Brace, 1981), 7.

6. November 28, 1928, *The Diary of Virginia Woolf*, 3:209.

7. In "A Sketch of the Past," Woolf called these "moments of being," the title given her posthumously published autobiographical pieces, which appeared in France as *Instants de vie* in 1977. The phrase also appears, in English, in an influential essay by Maurice Blanchot, "L'echec du démon: La vocation," in *Le livre à venir* (Paris: Éditions Gallimard, 1959), occasioned by the publication of *A Writer's Diary* (*Journal d'un écrivain*) in France in 1958.

8. In her diary entry of June 27, 1925, Woolf muses, "I have an idea that I will invent a new name for my books to supplant 'novel'. A new —— by Virginia Woolf. But what? Elegy?" *The Diary of Virginia Woolf*, 3:34. Critics usually note the mutability of elegy as it

has evolved over centuries from the classical prototypes governed by different metrical norms and generic distinctions from contemporary versions. With the disappearance of meter as an essential attribute, the genre's defining features have centered on a meditative stance toward a tragic circumstance. I am following the broad usage of "elegy" as a question of mournful affect and lyric mode rather than specific metrical conventions. For a broader account of Woolfian elegy, see Christine Froule, *Virginia Woolf and the Bloomsbury Avant-Garde: War, Civilization, Modernity* (New York: Columbia University Press, 2005), esp. chap. 4. Regarding Barthes, Elissa Marder contends that "any reader of *La chambre claire* knows" that his reflections on photography "ultimately take the form of an autobiographical elegy to his dead mother." "Nothing to Say: Fragments on the Mother in the Age of Mechanical Reproduction," *L'esprit créature* 40, no. 1 (Spring 2000): 6.

9. Roland Barthes, *The Preparation of the Novel: Lecture Courses and Seminars at the Collège de France (1978–1979)*, trans. Kate Briggs, ed. Nathalie Léger (New York: Columbia University Press, 2011), 172.

10. Virginia Woolf, "Mr. Bennett and Mrs. Brown," in *The Captain's Death Bed and Other Essays* (New York: Harcourt Brace Jovanovich, 1950), 117. The reference to Queen Victoria is to Strachey's biography of the queen.

11. Woolf, "Mr. Bennett and Mrs. Brown," 119.

12. Roland Barthes, *Roland Barthes by Roland Barthes*, trans. Richard Howard (New York: Hill and Wang, 1977), epigraph; Virginia Woolf, *A Room of One's Own*, 4.

13. This version of the photograph differs from the more famous one in the National Galleries of Scotland, popularized by the film *Mrs. Brown*. In this case, the collodion plate has been scratched to efface the background of trees, making the photograph look like a studio portrait (somewhat implausibly, given the horse).

14. Roland Barthes, *Camera Lucida: Reflections on Photography*, trans. Richard Howard (1981; New York: Hill and Wang, 2010), 56. At the bottom of the page in the French edition and in the list of illustrations at its end, the photograph is identified in French as "La Reine Victoria 1863," heightening the contrast to the untranslated caption from Woolf. Given the liberal sprinkling of Latin phrases (and the more modest sprinkling of Greek) in *Camera Lucida*, it is striking that Woolf's voice is the sole citation in English. *Camera Lucida* is abbreviated in the text as *CL*.

15. A French translation of Benjamin's full essay had appeared in 1971; the excerpted version appeared under the title (drawn from Benjamin's essay) "Les analphabètes de l'avenir" in *Le nouvel observateur*, November 1977, one of six special issues on photography that the journal published between June 1977 and June 1979, evidence of the surge of interest in photography in France in the late 1970s.

16. Roland Barthes, "Délibération," *Tel Quel* 82 (1979): 8–18.

17. December 27, 1930, *The Diary of Virginia Woolf*, 3:341.

18. Woolf's synopsis of the Victorian era in *Orlando: A Biography*—"Love, birth, and death were all swaddled in a variety of fine phrases"—anticipates Barthes's and was included in the excerpt from *Orlando* that introduces *Virginia Woolf par elle-même* (Paris: Éditions du Seuil, 1956), 9, where it reinforces the contrast to Queen Victoria that facilitated Woolf's entrée into France. *Orlando* (New York: Harcourt, 2006), 167.

19. Roland Barthes, *La chambre claire: Note sur la photographie* (Paris: Gallimard, Le Seuil, 1980), 91. Ironically, if Barthes had attended more to the *studium*, an

inattention for which he has often been criticized, he might have noted the imputation of horseplay within the scene itself. The groom, whose social position Barthes dismisses as uninteresting, is the queen's personal attendant John Brown, whose close relationship to Victoria after Prince Albert's death aroused the speculation that gave rise to the derisive name for the queen, "Mrs. Brown." Perhaps that Mrs. Brown gave her name to Woolf's imaginary character in "Mr. Bennett and Mrs. Brown," whose elusive everydayness is the antithesis of the self-recording queen. For criticism of Barthes's dismissal of the *studium*, see Shawn Michelle Smith, "Race and Reproduction in *Camera Lucida*," in *Photography Degree Zero: Reflections on Roland Barthes's "Camera Lucida*," ed. Geoffrey Batchen (Cambridge, MA: MIT Press, 2009), 243–58; and Fred Moten, "Black Mo'nin'," in *Loss: The Politics of Mourning*, ed. David Eng and David Kazanijian (Berkeley: University of California Press, 2002), 59–76.

20. In his forthcoming book, *The Barthes Fantastic: Literature, Criticism, and the Practice of Language*, John Lurz insightfully characterizes the blind field as "a kind of (fantastic) reserve in which unactivated alternatives and other potential meanings are secreted."

21. Lynne Vallone, *Becoming Victoria* (New Haven, CT: Yale University Press, 2001), xv; cited by Carol Mavor, *Reading Boyishly: Roland Barthes, J. M. Barrie, Jacques Henri Lartigue, Marcel Proust, and D. W. Winnicott* (Durham, NC: Duke University Press, 2007), 208.

22. November 30, 1977, *Mourning Diary*, 73, emphasis in original. The fact that Barthes titled his reflections *Journal de deuil* (*Mourning Diary*)—that is, that he used the French word for "mourning" despite his critique of the term—reveals the linguistic challenge of speaking about mourning in the aftermath of psychoanalysis. Interestingly, Richard Howard translates Barthes's alternative word *chagrin* as "grief" in *Camera Lucida* and as "suffering" in *Mourning Diary*.

23. December 15, 1978, *Mourning Diary*, 216, brackets and emphasis in original. Barthes offers the dates of composition at the end of *Camera Lucida* as April 15–June 3, 1979, a rate at which he would have written one of the text's forty-eight sections per day.

24. Woolf, "A Sketch of the Past," in *Moments of Being*, 79; Roland Barthes, "The Light of the South West," in *Incidents*, trans. Teresa Lavender Fagan (Calcutta: Seagull Books, 2010), 16. Although Barthes traveled back and forth between the South West and Paris with his mother, he associates her imaginatively with the Land of Childhood. Similarly, Woolf traveled with her family between London and St. Ives, but splits these locations imaginatively between paternal and maternal environments.

25. Peter M. Sacks, *The English Elegy: Studies in the Genre from Spenser to Yeats* (Baltimore: Johns Hopkins University Press, 1985), xiii.

26. Marcel Proust, *Remembrance of Things Past*, trans. C. K. Scott Moncrieff (New York: Random House, 1927), 6:741.

27. For a critique of the reflexive privileging of melancholy over mourning, see Slavoj Žižek, "Melancholy and the Act," *Critical Inquiry* 26, no. 4 (Summer 2000): 657–81; and Giorgio Agamben, *Stanzas: Word and Phantasm in Western Culture*, trans. Ronald L. Martinez (Minneapolis: University of Minnesota Press, 1993), esp. chaps. 3–5. See also R. Clifton Spargo, *The Ethics of Mourning: Grief and Responsibility in Elegiac Literature* (Baltimore: John Hopkins University Press, 2004), on the "melancholic

potential in all mourning" as an expression of allegiance to the dead (11). See also Eng and Kazanjian, *Loss: The Politics of Mourning*.

28. Jonathan Flatley, *Affective Mapping: Melancholia and the Politics of Modernism* (Cambridge, MA: Harvard University Press, 2008), 2–3.

29. Flatley, *Affective Mapping*, 42. See Lauren Berlant, *Cruel Optimism* (Durham, NC: Duke University Press, 2011); Ann Cvetkovich, *Depression: A Public Feeling* (Durham, NC: Duke University Press, 2012); Anne Anlin Cheng, *The Melancholy of Race: Psychoanalysis, Assimilation, and Hidden Grief* (Oxford: Oxford University Press, 2000); Wendy Brown on "left melancholia" in *Politics out of History* (Princeton, NJ: Princeton University Press, 2001); Seth Moglen, *Mourning Modernity: Literary Modernism and the Injuries of American Capitalism* (Stanford, CA: Stanford University Press, 2007); Lecia Rosenthal, *Mourning Modernism: Literature, Catastrophe, and the Politics of Consolation* (New York: Fordham University Press, 2011); and Peter Schwenger, *The Tears of Things: Melancholy and Physical Objects* (Minneapolis: University of Minnesota, 2006).

30. See, for example, the description of the thyrsis and flute as "symbolic purveyors of a patriarchal lineage" in Jahan Ramazani, *The Poetry of Mourning: The Modern Elegy from Hardy to Heaney* (Chicago: University of Chicago Press, 1994), 302. In *The English Elegy*, Peter M. Sacks also notes that "so many traditional elegies perform a multiple exclusion or occlusion of figures representing the mother" (321).

31. See Celeste M. Schenk, "Feminism and Deconstruction: Re-Constructing the Elegy," *Tulsa Studies in Women's Literature* 5, no. 1 (Spring 1986): 13–27.

32. "Monsters of Elegy" is the title Sandra M. Gilbert gives to the penultimate chapter of *Death's Door: Modern Dying and the Ways We Grieve* (New York: Norton, 2006), 398–438. See especially her readings of maternal elegies by Robert Lowell, Allen Ginsberg, and Adrienne Rich.

33. "Le lieu le plus sombre est toujours sous la lampe." Roland Barthes, "A quoi sert un intellectual?," interview by Bernard-Henri Lévy, *Le nouvel observateur*, January 10, 1977.

34. Note the resemblance to Lacan's description of light that "is refracted, diffused, it floods, it fills—the eye is a sort of bowl." Jacques Lacan, "Of the Gaze as an *Objet Petit a*," in *The Four Fundamental Concepts of Psycho-Analysis*, trans. Alan Sheridan, ed. Jacques-Alain Miller (New York: W.W. Norton, 1978), 94.

35. Virginia Woolf, "Modern Fiction," in *The Common Reader* (New York: Harcourt Brace, 1953), 154. Woolf explores the hazards of puckering in a subsequent memory of the face of an old woman selling gradually puckering air-balls at the Gloucester Gate of Kensington Park (Sketch, 75–76). On the pervasiveness and porousness of skin as a medium throughout Woolf's oeuvre, and the anxiety about its hardening with age, see Maureen F. Curtin, *Out of Touch: Skin Tropes and Identities in Woolf, Ellison, Pynchon, and Acker* (New York: Routledge, 2003), 15–40.

36. We could take as a brief summation of the post-Impressionist aesthetic Roger Fry's description of the painterly desire "to make images which by the clearness of their logical structure, and by the closely-knit unity of texture, shall appeal to our disinterested and contemplative imagination." Roger Fry, "The French Post-Impressionists," in *Vision and Design* (Cleveland: World Publishing Company, 1966), 239. The Gare

Saint-Lazarre was painted by both Monet and Manet. Closer to home, the ferrovitre-
ous architecture of London's railroad stations, conservatories, and exhibition halls,
as Isobel Armstrong demonstrates in *Victorian Glassworlds: Glass Culture and the
Imagination, 1830–1880* (New York: Oxford University Press, 2008), epitomized a conspicuous new aesthetic of glass. Ruskin, echoing Shelley, offers a particularly germane
description of the "variegated crystal" of the station roofs that put "all London under
one blazing dome of many colours." *Illustrated London News*, May 3, 1851; cited by
Armstrong, 147.

37. On memory, trauma, and photography, see Sigmund Freud, *Beyond the
Pleasure Principle* (1920); Ulrich Baer, *Spectral Evidence: The Photography of Trauma*
(Cambridge, MA: MIT Press, 2002); Geoffrey Batchen, *Burning with Desire: The
Conception of Photography* (Cambridge, MA: MIT Press, 1997); Sarah Kofman,
Camera Obscura: Of Ideology, trans. Will Straw (Ithaca, NY: Cornell University Press,
1990); and Kaja Silverman, *World Spectators* (Stanford, CA: Stanford University
Press, 2000).

38. For a full account of Virginia's and Vanessa's artistic competition and collaboration, see Diane Filby Gillespie, *The Sisters' Arts: The Writing and Painting of Virginia
Woolf and Vanessa Bell* (Syracuse, NY: Syracuse University Press, 1988).

39. For similar evocations of photography, see Woolf's description of the mind as
the receptacle of "a myriad impressions—trivial, fantastic, evanescent, or engraved
with the sharpness of steel. . . . an incessant shower of innumerable atoms" in "Modern
Fiction," 154; and her letter to Ethel Smyth (April 22, 1940), in which she asks, "How
then do I transfer these images to my sensitive paper brain?" *The Letters of Virginia
Woolf*, vol. 6, *1936–1941*, ed. Nigel Nicolson and Joanne Trautmann (New York: Harcourt Brace Jovanovich, 1980), 393.

40. Virginia Woolf, *The Waves* (1931; New York: Harcourt Brace Jovanovich, 1959),
287. In "The Cameraless Optic: Anna Atkins and Virginia Woolf," *English Language
Notes* 44, no. 2 (Fall/Winter 2006): 87–100, Louise Hornby characterizes this as a
"photographic epistemology of objectivity, precision and material fact" (88). For other
accounts of the modernist investment in photography's depersonalizing effects, see
Ann Banfield, "L'imparfait de l'objectif: The Imperfect of the Object Glass," *Camera
Obscura: A Journal of Feminism and Film Theory* 8 (1990): 64–87; and Dora Zhang, "A
Lens for an Eye: Proust and Photography," *Representations* 118 (Spring 2012): 103–25.

41. William Henry Fox Talbot, "Introductory Remarks," in *The Pencil of Nature*
(1844; New York: Hans P. Kraus, Jr., 1989), 1–2. Similarly, Dominique Francois Arago
describes Daguerre's early images as "drawn by nature's most subtle pencil, the light
ray"; see "Report to the Commission of the Chamber of Deputies" (July 3, 1839), in
Classic Essays on Photography, ed. Alan Trachtenberg (New Haven, CT: Yale University
Press, 1980), 18.

42. Roger Fry, "Mrs. Cameron's Photographs," in *Victorian Photographs of Famous
Men and Fair Women by Julia Margaret Cameron* (London: Hogarth Press, 1926; Boston: David R. Godine, 1973), 27–28. Cameron's account of her autobiography as an endeavor to "clothe my little history with light, as with a garment" reiterates the centrality of light to her aesthetic. See *Annals of My Glass House: Photographs by Julia Margaret
Cameron*, text by Violet Hamilton (Seattle: University of Washington Press, 1996), 11.
Maggie Humm offers a more nuanced reading of post-Impressionism's antagonism to

photography in *Modernist Women and Visual Cultures: Virginia Woolf, Vanessa Bell, Photography, and Cinema* (Edinburgh: Edinburgh University Press, 2002).

43. Carol Armstrong, "Cupid's Pencil of Light: Julia Margaret Cameron and the Maternalization of Photography," *October* 76 (Spring 1996): 117. The focus on maternal light is compatible with (if less traumatic and fractured than) Bracha Lichtenberg Ettinger's notion of the "matrixial borderspace," which Maggie Humm invokes in *Modernist Women and Visual Cultures* to theorize the recurring motifs of Woolf's family photo albums; see Bracha Ettinger, *The Matricial Borderspace* (Minneapolis: University of Minnesota Press, 2005). By associating Woolf via Cameron with a Victorian aesthetic of tactile maternal light, rather than (or in addition to) a modernist aesthetic of impersonal, object-disclosing light, I am also, with Armstrong, anticipating that Woolf's stance will be compatible with the late twentieth-century aesthetic of Roland Barthes. Woolf's legacy of light differentiates her relation to photography from that of the modernists who emphasize the "writing" component of "light-writing." See Michael North, *Camera Works: Photography and the Twentieth-Century Word* (Oxford: Oxford University Press, 2005). For the spectrum of Woolf's affiliations with Victorian, modernist, and postmodern aesthetics, see the essays included in *The Edinburgh Companion to Virginia Woolf and the Arts*, ed. Maggie Humm (Edinburgh: Edinburgh University Press, 2010).

44. For Proust's critique of snapshot compilations as the product and analogue of voluntary memory, see Suzanne Guerlac, "Visual Dust: On Time, Memory, and Photography in Proust," *Contemporary French and Francophone Studies* 13, no. 4 (September 2009): 397–404. For a more positive view of Bloomsbury's family albums as a "practice of coded resonances" that engage the viewer in the active construction of memory, see Humm, *Modernist Women and Visual Cultures*, 21. See also Maggie Humm, *Snapshots of Bloomsbury: The Private Lives of Virginia Woolf and Vanessa Bell* (New Brunswick, NJ: Rutgers University Press, 2006); and "Virginia Woolf and Photography," *Études britanniques contemporaines: Revue de la Société d'études anglaises contemporaines* 53 (2017), https://doi.org/10.4000/ebc.3957. The other essays in that journal's special issue on "Bare Lives/Virginia Woolf: Becoming Photographic" – Adèle Cassigneul, "Giving something to be seen: Virginia Woolf and Photography"; Floriane Reviron-Piégay, "Virginia Woolf's 'raids across boundaries': Biography vs Photography"; and Hélène Orain, "Julia Margaret Cameron: l'ambivalence victorienne" – explore diverse facets of Woolf's photographic practice and inheritance. On the class associations of family photographs, see Emily Dalgarno, *Virginia Woolf and the Visible World* (Cambridge: Cambridge University Press, 2001), 151–54.

45. Fry, "Mrs. Cameron's Photographs," 26; Woolf argues similarly in her essay that Cameron's goal was to diminish realism by loosening the precision of her focus. Woolf makes her disdain for snapshots produced by the recent popular Kodak technology explicit on several occasions. She disparages it in *Three Guineas* as "simply a crude statement of fact directed to the eye"; she satirizes it in *Jacob's Room* via Madame Lucien Grave's Kodak pointed at Jacob on the Acropolis; and she derides it via North's complaint in *The Years* that "these little snapshot pictures of people left much to be desired, these little surface pictures that one made, like a fly crawling over a face." Virginia Woolf, *Three Guineas* (New York: Harcourt/Harvest, 1966), 11; *The Years*, (New York: Harcourt/Harvest, 1965), 317.

46. In "Virginia Woolf and Photography," in Humm, *The Edinburgh Companion to Virginia Woolf and the Arts*, 375–91, Colin Dickey argues along different lines that Woolf frequently associates the formal photographic portrait, in contrast to casual snapshots, with patriarchy's memorializing practices. For a more extended account of memorialization and Bloomsbury photography, see Humm, *Modernist Women and Visual Cultures* and *Snapshots of Bloomsbury*.

47. Barthes, "The Light of the South West"; abbreviated in the text as SW.

48. Roland Barthes, *A Lover's Discourse: Fragments*, trans. Richard Howard (New York: Hill and Wang, 1979), 168. Barthes was reading and referencing Winnicott throughout this period. The conceptual framework of his final essay, "One Always Fails in Speaking of What One Loves" (1980), is drawn from Winnicott's writings on the scribble. See *The Rustle of Language*, trans. Richard Howard (New York: Farrar, Straus & Giroux, 1986), 296–305.

49. August 13, 1979, *Mourning Diary*, 238.

50. Roland Barthes, *Roland Barthes by Roland Barthes*, trans. Richard Howard (New York: Hill and Wang, 1977), 175–76, emphasis in original.

51. Eduardo Cadava and Paola Cortés-Rocca, "Notes on Love and Photography," in Batchen, *Photography Degree Zero*, 127; Marder, "Nothing to Say," 26, 32. In W. J. T. Mitchell's evocative reading of Robert Frank's photographs "My Family" and *U.S. 90, En Route to Del Rio, Texas*, the camera is a mouth that "thirsts for [the] pure white, milky light" manifested in the single exposed breast of Frank's wife nursing their infant and in the headlight of the family car. "The Ends of American Photography: Robert Frank as National Medium," in *What Do Pictures Want: The Lives and Loves of Images* (Chicago: University of Chicago Press, 2005), 290.

52. Castel's essay, "Images et phantasmes," "Images and Phantasms," was published in both French and English; the citation appears in English in *Le nouvel observateur*, December 1978, 16. The crosscurrents between psychoanalysis and cultural theory in France may have made it possible for a text like "Mourning and Melancholia" to cross over from the clinical to the cultural domain. For a helpful account, see Serge Lebovici and Daniel Widlocher, eds., "Introduction," in *Psychoanalysis in France* (New York: International Universities Press, 1980), vii–xiv. Nicolas Abraham and Maria Torok's essay "Introjection—Incorporation: Mourning or Melancholia" (1972) offers evidence that Freud's "Mourning and Melancholia" was emerging as a subject of inquiry within the French psychoanalytic community, but Barthes and Castel were the first to translate its more technical psychoanalytic discourse into broader cultural terms.

53. Sigmund Freud, "Mourning and Melancholia" (1917), in *The Standard Edition of the Complete Psychological Works of Sigmund Freud*, vol. 14 (1914–1916), trans. James Strachey (London: Hogarth Press, Institute of Psychoanalysis, 1961), 249; abbreviated in the text as MM. Barthes's entries for November 14, 1977, and June 16, 1978, *Mourning Diary*, 50, 148.

54. The photograph is the second in *Roland Barthes by Roland Barthes*. See D. A. Miller, *Bringing Out Roland Barthes* (Berkeley: University of California Press, 1992), on the long legs as the outward sign of a prolonged maternal attachment. Barthes is Carol Mavor's preeminent example of prolonged childhood in *Reading Boyishly*.

55. Barthes makes this most explicit in his explanation of the split between the introductory photographs and the written text of his mock autobiography, *Roland Barthes by Roland Barthes*: "I don't recount anything about my youth: this youth, I have put in photographs, because it's properly the age, the time of memory: images. And for the rest, on the contrary, I say nothing in images because I have no more, and everything passes through writing" (n.p.).

56. Barthes, *Roland Barthes by Roland Barthes*, 21.

57. Carol Armstrong, *Scenes in a Library: Reading the Photograph in the Book, 1843–1875* (Cambridge, MA: MIT Press, 1998), 16.

58. For some compelling analyses of the racialization of "desirable or detestable bodies" in *Camera Lucida*, see Shawn Michelle Smith, "Race and Reproduction in *Camera Lucida*," and Margaret Olin, "Roland Barthes's 'Mistaken Identification,'" in Olin, *Touching Photographs* (Chicago: University of Chicago Press, 2012), 51–69.

59. Jean-Paul Sartre, *The Imaginary: A Phenomenological Psychology of the Imagination*, trans. Jonathan Webber, ed. Arlette Elkaïm-Sartre (1940; New York: Routledge, 2004), 183.

60. Sartre, *The Imaginary*, 133, 16.

61. Laura Wexler, "The Purloined Image," in *Photography and the Optical Unconscious*, ed. Shawn Michelle Smith and Sharon Sliwinski (Durham, NC: Duke University Press, 2017), 267. Wexler is deliberately referencing the title of Shawn Michelle Smith's book, *At the Edge of Sight: Photography and the Unseen* (Durham, NC: Duke University Press, 2013).

62. Barthes, "Loving Schumann," in *The Responsibility of Forms: Critical Essays on Music, Art, and Representation*, trans. Richard Howard (Berkeley: University of California Press, 1991), 298.

63. Choosing the phrase as his title, Christopher Bollas redefines the shadow more positively as a transformational object that embraces the nascent subject, in *The Shadow of the Object: Psychoanalysis of the Unthought Known* (New York: Columbia University Press, 1987). In "'The Shadow of the Object': Photography and Realism," *Textual Practice* 10, no. 1 (1996): 145–63, Sarah Kember develops Bollas's reading in relation to photography.

64. Flatley, *Affective Mapping*, 47, 46, emphasis in original. Shrewdly parsing the differences between the figure of the shadow and the precipitate of abandoned object choices that constitute the ego, Flatley proposes that Freud's theory harbors two versions of melancholia: a depressive one (figured by the shadow) and a dialectical one (figured by the precipitate).

65. Sigmund Freud, *The Ego and the Id* (1923), in *Standard Edition*, vol. 19 (1923–25), 26.

66. Sigmund Freud, *Inhibitions, Symptoms and Anxiety* (1926), in *Standard Edition*, vol. 20 (1925–26), 171.

67. Freud concludes "Mourning and Melancholia" by acknowledging the incompleteness of his investigation into mania. Karl Abraham concurs that Freud "has penetrated so much more deeply into the nature of the depressive states than into that of the manic ones." See Abraham, "A Short Study of the Development of the Libido, Viewed in the Light of Mental Disorders" (1924), in *Selected Papers of Karl Abraham*,

trans. Douglas Bryan and Alix Strachey, ed. Ernest Jones (London: Hogarth Press, 1955), 470.

68. Karl Abraham, "Notes on the Psycho-Analytical Investigation and Treatment of Manic-Depressive Insanity and Allied Conditions," in Jones, *Selected Papers of Karl Abraham*, 150.

69. The father is the prototypically melancholic object for Freud, since the death of the father, the object of the (male) child's earliest identification, is "the most important event, the most poignant loss, of a man's life." Preface to the second edition of *The Interpretation of Dreams* (1908), in *Standard Edition*, vol. 4 (1900) (London: Hogarth Press, Institute of Psychoanalysis, 1953), xxvi. Because the father is irreplaceable, he is internalized rather than relinquished, which in turn provokes or exacerbates one of the defining attributes of melancholia: ambivalence, which Freud claims was probably "acquired by the human race in connection with their father-complex." "Totem and Taboo" (1913), in *Standard Edition*, vol. 13 (1913–14) (London: Hogarth Press, Institute of Psychoanalysis, 1953), 157; in a footnote, Freud amends the father-complex as, "more correctly, their parental complex." For Abraham and Klein, the primary staging ground of mania is the process of weaning that elicits reactive fantasies of incorporating the breast.

70. Abraham, "A Short Study of the Development of the Libido," 441–42, emphasis added.

71. Melanie Klein, "A Contribution to the Psychogenesis of Manic-Depressive States" (1935), in *Love, Guilt, and Reparation & Other Works, 1921–1945* (New York: Dell/Delta Press, 1977), 277, emphasis in original. Arguably most significant for its elaboration of the depressive position, Klein's essay also crystallizes an influential account of a manic subject that both controls and disparages the objects it incorporates.

72. Melanie Klein, "Mourning and Its Relation to Manic-Depressive States," in *Love, Guilt, and Reparation*, 355.

73. According to Phyllis Grosskurth in *Melanie Klein: Her World and Her Work* (Cambridge, MA: Harvard University Press, 1987), Mrs. A in this essay is "quite obviously" Klein herself, who had lost her son in 1934 (251).

74. "The Empty Space" is the title of an essay by Karin Michaelis about the painter Ruth Kjär that Klein analyzes in "Infantile Anxiety-Situations Reflected in a Work of Art and in the Creative Impulse" (1929), in *Love, Guilt, and Reparation*, 210–18.

75. Klein, "Mourning and Its Relation to Manic-Depressive States," 362. Despite the emphasis on transitional spaces and implicitly tactile transitional objects in the work of D. W. Winnicott, Klein's most influential and independent supervisee, his focus is less on the child's sensory experience than on the mother-child negotiations of an intermediate zone. For the reparative function of sensory symbiosis in the clinical context, see Peter Goldberg, "Active Perception and the Search for Sensory Symbiosis," *Journal of the American Psychoanalytic Association* 60, no. 4 (2012): 791–812.

76. March 1, 1978, *The Diary of Virginia Woolf*, vol. 5, *1936–1941*, ed. Anne Olivier Bell, assisted by Andrew McNeillie (New York: Harcourt Brace, 1984), 63.

77. Some powerful examples of this expanding archive include Kay Redfield Jamison, *Touched with Fire: Manic Depressive Illness and the Artistic Temperament* (New York: Free Press, 1993) and *An Unquiet Mind: A Memoir of Moods and Madness* (New

York: Vintage, 1995); Terri Cheney, *Manic: A Memoir* (New York: Harper Collins, 2008); Ellen Foney, *Marbles: Mania, Depression, Michelangelo, and Me; A Graphic Memoir* (New York: Penguin, 2012); and a founding text that places Woolf at the center of a neurochemical understanding of manic depression, Thomas C. Caramagno, *The Flight of the Mind: Virginia Woolf and Manic-Depressive Illness* (Berkeley: University of California Press, 1992).

78. Caramagno, *The Flight of the Mind*, 2. Caramagno also cites Kay Redfield Jamison's claim in *Touched with Fire* that Woolf was "a classical case of manic-depressive illness" (347) and Sherman C. Feinstein's assertion that Woolf's case history "fulfills every criterion for manic-depressive illness" in "Why They Were Afraid of Virginia Woolf: Perspectives on Juvenile Manic-Depressive Illness," in *Adolescent Psychiatry: Developmental and Clinical Studies*, Annals of the American Society for Adolescent Psychiatry 8 (Chicago: University of Chicago Press, 1980), 339.

79. *The Diary of Virginia Woolf*, vol. 2, *1920–1924*, ed. Anne Olivier Bell, assisted by Andrew McNeillie (New York: Harcourt Brace Jovanovich, 1978), 283.

80. Freud both hints at and sidesteps this paradox in his brief contemporaneous essay "On Transience," in which he attempts to think through the "great riddle" of mourning primarily in terms of grief's uncertain termination, but also gestures toward the riddle of mourning's onset, "since the mind instinctively recoils from anything that is painful." *Standard Edition*, vol. 14 (1914–16), 306.

81. Didier Anzieu, *The Skin Ego*, trans Chris Turner (New Haven, CT: Yale University Press, 1989), 105. See also Didier Anzieu, ed., *Psychic Envelopes*, trans. Daphne Briggs (London: Karnac Press, 1990).

82. Kathleen Woodward, "Freud and Barthes: Theorizing Mourning, Sustaining Grief," *Discourse* 13, no. 1 (Fall–Winter 1990–91): 99. See also Kathleen Woodward, "Grief Work in Contemporary American Cultural Criticism," *Discourse* 15, no. 2 (Winter 1992–93): 94–112; James Krasner, *Home Bodies: Tactile Experience in Domestic Space* (Columbus: University of Ohio Press, 2010); and Laura E. Tanner, *Lost Bodies: Inhabiting the Borders of Life and Death* (Ithaca, NY: Cornell University Press, 2006). An earlier generation of psychoanalytic theorists such as D. W. Winnicott and Heinz Kohut stressed the importance of an empathic environment as a condition of mourning but as an interpersonal rather than sensorial surround.

83. Barthes, "Le neutre—The Neutral," in *Roland Barthes by Roland Barthes*, 132–33.

84. Barthes, "The Third Meaning," in *The Responsibility of Forms*, 54.

CHAPTER FOUR

1. W. G. Sebald, *Austerlitz*, trans. Anthea Bell (London: Penguin, 2002), 5; abbreviated in the text as *Aus*.

2. The German citation is from W. G. Sebald, *Austerlitz* (Munich: Carl Hanser Verlagen, 2001), 263. Ostensibly a model internment camp, Terezín deported most of its inmates to Auschwitz, where Austerlitz's mother presumably died.

3. D. W. Winnicott, "Mirror-Role of Mother and Family in Child Development," in *Playing and Reality* (Harmondsworth: Penguin, 1974), 130–38.

4. Sebald was adamant about what he called the "conspiracy of silence" surrounding the war crimes committed by both sides during World War II. See, for example,

Charles Simic, "Conspiracy of Silence," and Eleanor Wachtel, "Ghost Hunter," both in *The Emergence of Memory: Conversations with W. G. Sebald*, ed. Lynne Sharon Schwartz (New York: Seven Stories Press, 2007), 145–58, 37–62. According to Sebald's biographer Carole Angier, the Holocaust was "the catastrophe for which he [Sebald] would spend the rest of his life atoning." *Speak, Silence: In Search of W. G. Sebald* (London: Bloomsbury Circus, 2021), 249.

5. For a discussion of Sebald's use of the Xerox machine, see the "Proceedings of the Associates of the Institute of Cultural Inquiry," in *Searching for Sebald: Photography after W. G. Sebald*, ed. Lise Patt (Los Angeles: The Institute of Cultural Inquiry, 2007), 506–7. See also Lise Patt, "Introduction: Searching for Sebald; What I Know for Sure," in *Searching for Sebald*, for an incisive account of Sebald's photographs as the "mimesis of a mimesis" that resemble one another more than the external world (73).

6. W. G. Sebald, quoted in a conversation with Eleanor Wachtel in "Ghost Hunter," *The Emergence of Memory*, 40.

7. For readings of these pairs of eyes as two owls, see Andrea Kőhler, "Penetrating the Dark," in W. G. Sebald and Jan Peter Tripp, *Unrecounted*, trans. Michael Hamburger (New York: New Directions, 2007), 97–102; for readings of them as a bat and an owl, see Ross Posnock, "'Don't Think, but Look!' W. G. Sebald, Wittgenstein, and Cosmopolitan Poverty," *Representations* 112, no. 1 (Fall 2010): 118.

8. A collection of thirty-three of these lithographs comprises Tripp's contribution to his collaborative volume with Sebald, *Unrecounted*. All four of the lithographs in *Austerlitz*, not just the bottom pair, were produced by Tripp. For Wittgenstein's role as the basis of Sebald's character Paul Bereyter in *The Emigrants*, see Angier, *Speak, Silence*, 163, 168, 227. For a powerful reading of Sebald's collaboration with Tripp and of the motif of eyes in Sebald's work, see Andrea Kohler, "Penetrating the Dark," in Sebald and Tripp, *Unrecounted*, 97–102.

9. The formal parallel between the two pages is especially clear in the German text. In the tenth anniversary version of the English translation, the two pairs of eyes are divided between two pages. Sebald offers a pointed commentary on the gaze in his essay on Kafka and cinema, in which he explains that the more obscure or enticing the object, the larger the eyes and more insistent the gaze, until "nothing is left but looking." "Kafka Goes to the Movies," in *Campo Santo*, trans. Anthea Bell (New York: Modern Library, 2005), 157.

10. Walter Benjamin, "Theses on the Philosophy of History," in *Illuminations*, ed. Hannah Arendt, trans. Harry Zohn (New York: Schocken, 1969), 257–58.

11. W. G. Sebald, *The Rings of Saturn*, trans. Michael Hulse (New York: New Directions, 1999), 295.

12. Sigmund Freud, "The 'Uncanny'" (1919), in *The Standard Edition of the Complete Psychological Works of Sigmund Freud*, ed. James Strachey, Anna Freud, Alix Strachey, and Alan Tyson, vol. 17, *1917–1919* (London: The Hogarth Press; The Institute of Psycho-Analysis, 1955), 245. In their introduction to *W. G. Sebald: A Critical Companion* (Seattle: University of Washington Press, 2004), editors J. J. Long and Anne Whitehead note that "Sebald's work is steeped in psychoanalysis and he consciously integrates Freudian terms into his writing . . . he focuses overwhelmingly on 'The Uncanny' and *Beyond the Pleasure Principle*" (8). They proceed to claim that Sebald's investment in the uncanny culminates in *Austerlitz*, which "underlines the significance

of Freud's concept as a figure for contemporary haunting" (12). Sebald's investment in Freudian theory is explicit and sustained in *Unheimliche Heimat: Essays zur
österreichischen Literatur* (1991).

13. Freud, "The 'Uncanny,'" 227.

14. Freud, "The 'Uncanny,'" 233.

15. Freud, "The 'Uncanny,'" 252. In "Lost and Found: Disorientation, Nostalgia, and
Holocaust Melodrama in Sebald's *Austerlitz*," *Modern Language Notes* 121 (2006): 681,
John Zilcosky differentiates the disorientation of Sebald's characters from desperately
lost postmodern urban nomads, arguing that "like Freud, Kafka, and Thomas Mann,
Sebald viewed modern travel as primarily uncanny." In "Against the Irreversible: On
Jean Améry," Sebald quotes Améry's claim that "home is the land of one's childhood
and youth. Whoever has lost it remains lost himself, even if he has learned not to
stumble about in the foreign country as if he were drunk." *On the Natural History of
Destruction*, trans. Anthea Bell (New York: Random House, 2003), 160–61.

16. In *Speak, Silence*, Carole Angier describes Adorno as Sebald's "substitute father"
and characterizes *Minima Moralia* as one of Sebald's favorite books since 1966 and
"a work of immediate post-war despair that would inform Max's [Sebald's] historical
pessimism for ever" (257, 243). Angier also details Adorno's influence on Sebald's 1968
dissertation, in whose foreword Sebald references personal letters that he claimed
showed Adorno's endorsement of his argument. Although Sebald cites two such letters
from Adorno, apparently only one exists (Angier, 248–49).

17. Theodor Adorno, *Minima Moralia: Reflections from a Damaged Life* (1951), trans.
E. F. M. Jephcott (Verso: London and New York, 2005), 39.

18. An offhand reference to a performance of *Les contes d'Hoffmann* at the falsely
idealized Terezín, putatively gleaned from Adler's monumental study of the camp,
further underlines the opera's implication in the obfuscation of political reality.

19. W. G. Sebald, "The Last Word," interview by Maya Jaggi, *The Guardian*, December 21, 2001, https://www.theguardian.com/education/2001/dec/21/artsandhuman-
ities.highereducation. Sebald's figuration of Agáta as a psychological, if not a biological,
threat may have been suggested by, but lacks the positive cast of, the Frankfurt School's
evocation of Medusa to suggest the revolutionary possibilities of freezing certain moments (out) of history. On these possibilities in Benjamin's philosophy of history, see
Eduardo Cadava, *Words of Light: Theses on the Photography of History* (Princeton, NJ:
Princeton University Press, 1997), 59–63; and Akbar Abbas, "On Fascination: Walter
Benjamin's Images," *New German Critique* 48 (Fall 1989): 43–62.

20. Clive Scott, "Sebald's Photographic Annotations," in *Saturn's Moons: W. G.
Sebald—A Handbook*, ed. Jo Catling and Richard Hibbitt (London: Legenda: Modern
Humanities Research Association and Maney Publishing, 2011), 223.

21. Roland Barthes, "Longtemps, je me suis couché de bonne heure . . . ," in Roland
Barthes, *The Rustle of Language*, trans. Richard Howard (New York: Farrar, Straus &
Giroux, 1986), 279.

22. Joseph Cuomo, "A Conversation with W. G. Sebald," in Schwartz, *The Emergence of Memory*, 98–99. In *Speak, Silence*, Carole Angier calls into question Sebald's
account of the timing of his literary turn, which she locates much earlier during his
participation in the Group 64 in Freiburg in 1964. According to Angier, Sebald's

narrative of his belated coming to writing was "one of his tallest tales; one of his biggest lies" (193).

23. Christian Scholz, "'But the Written Word Is Not a True Document': A Conversation with W. G. Sebald on Literature and Photography," in Patt, *Searching for Sebald*, 105.

24. Scholz, "'But the Written Word Is Not a True Document,'" 107. Sebald goes on to say that "sometimes it's the most minor things in an image that contain the secret," a claim clearly indebted to Barthes's notion of the *punctum*.

25. Into the "pedagogies of social life" implicit in the genre of the school photo that "Ernest" evokes, the unnamed girl introduces a "disobedient gaze" that invites a critical reframing. For a brilliant analysis of these terms in relation to the seemingly conventional genre of the school photo, see Marianne Hirsch and Leo Spitzer, *School Photos in Liquid Time: Reframing Difference* (Seattle: University of Washington Press, 2020); terms cited are on pp. 27 and 20.

26. On Wittgenstein's phrase, see Posnock, "'Don't Think but Look!,'" 112–39. For Wittgenstein's general influence on Sebald, especially on the construction of the character Paul Bereyter in *The Emigrants*, see Angier, *Speak, Silence*. In *Austerlitz*, the narrator prepares us to recognize Wittgenstein in the protagonist through the two figures' attachment to their rucksacks and the "horror-stricken expressions on both their faces" that lead the narrator to feel as if Austerlitz is gazing at him through photographs of Wittgenstein and vice versa (55–56).

27. Included in Box 1, plate 38h, in Sir Leslie Stephen's Photograph Album in Smith College's Special Collections Northampton, Massachusetts. As Maggie Humm points out in *Modernist Women: Virginia Woolf, Vanessa Bell, Photography and Cinema*, this is one of two versions of this key photograph, which she argues persuasively must have been taken by Vanessa Stephen. Virginia includes the other version, cropped somewhat differently and dated 1892, as a frontispiece to her own Monk's House album 3. Testifying to its resonance for the entire family, the photograph also shows up in the photo albums of Vanessa Stephen and Stella Duckworth as well as Leslie Stephen (Humm, 19–24). In his own comments on the photograph, to which he was especially attached, Leslie Stephen initially notes "Virginia in the background" only in passing, but adds in a postscript to his memoir in 1897 that "Virginia has been out of sorts, nervous and overgrown, too" and "devouring books, almost faster than I like," as if he were anticipating how she would outgrow her place in the background to reconstruct the scene from her own perspective. Leslie Stephen's comments can be found on the Smith College Special Collections website: https://www.smith.edu/libraries/libs/rarebook/exhibitions/stephen.

28. The critical study is *Virginia Woolf mit Selbstzeugnissen und Bilddokumenten* (Hamburg: Rowohlt, 1983) by Werner Waldmann, who tellingly captions the photograph "Virginia im Hintergrund, um 1892." Sebald's library also includes *A Room of One's Own* in English. Sebald obviously read more of Woolf, whose works would have been very available in the University of East Anglia library, which he used regularly. The "archive that gathers dust behind the lid of an eye" is the phrase used by the Associates of the Institute of Cultural Inquiry to characterize the "multitude of images" that every optical event catalyzed in Sebald's imagination. See the "Proceedings of the Associates of the Institute of Cultural Inquiry," in Patt, *Searching for Sebald*, 507.

29. Eric Homberger, "W. G. Sebald," *The Guardian*, December 17, 2001, 2, www.guardian.co.uk/news/2001/ded/17/guardianobituaries.book. See also Arthur Lubow, "Crossing Boundaries," in *The Emergence of Memory*, 159–73; and Michiko Kakutani's review of *Austerlitz* in the *New York Times*, October. 26, 2001, Section E, 42.

30. W. G. Sebald, *After Nature*, trans. Michael Hamburger (New York: Random House, 2002), 6. For accounts of Sebald's kindred writers, see the obituary by Eric Homberger in *The Guardian*, December 17, 2001, which notes that Sebald has been compared to "Borges, Calvino, Thomas Bernhard, Nabokov, and Kafka." Other proposed members of the fraternal band have included Stendhal, Rousseau, Canetti, Primo Levi, and more proximate German precursors such as Adelbert Stifter, Gottfried Keller, Johann Peter Hebel, Heinrich von Kleist, Paul Richter, Jean Paul, Hugo von Hoffmannstal, Robert Walser, and Thomas Bernhard. For the German lineage, see Susan Sontag, *Where the Stress Falls* (New York: Farrar, Straus & Giroux, 2001), 46–47.

31. See, for example, Richard Eder's review of *Austerlitz*, which notes that "Proust must be mentioned not to suggest a ranking—though a certain equivalence is not out of the question—but as contrast. Sebald's writing is similarly woven of fine detail and subtle ricochets, but his madeleine is poisoned." The review proceeds immediately to reference "another name-drop. *Sebald* stands with Primo Levi as the prime speaker of the Holocaust and, with him, the prime contradiction of Adorno's dictum that after it, there can be no art." "Excavating a Life," *New York Times*, October 28, 2001, https://www.nytimes.com/2001/10/28/books/excavating-a-life.html.

32. Hugh Kenner, "The Making of the Modernist Canon," *Chicago Review* 34, no. 2 (Spring 1984): 57.

33. W. G. Sebald, "An Attempt at Restitution," in *Campo Santo*, 205.

34. Zilcosky, "Lost and Found," 685. For critics who agree that *Austerlitz* is Sebald's "first 'real'" or "one true" novel, see Andreas Huyssen, *Present Pasts: Urban Palimpsests and the Politics of Memory* (Palo Alto, CA: Stanford University Press, 2003), 177n40; and Simic, "Conspiracy of Silence," 149.

35. Sebald's comments on *Vertigo* are from Cuomo, "A Conversation with W. G. Sebald," 103; his comments on *The Emigrants* are from "Ghost Hunter," interview by Eleanor Wachtel, 37.

36. Sebald, "An Attempt at Restitution," 205.

37. Sebald's comments are reported in Maya Jaggi, "Recovered Memories," in *The Guardian Profile: W. G. Sebald*, 5–6, www.theguardian.com/books/2001/sep/22/artsandhumanities. His claim to Sigrid Löffler in 1993 (i.e., several years before the composition of *Austerlitz*) that his "medium is prose, not the novel," by which he seems to mean the traditional novel, is cited by Sven Meyer in his "Editorial Note" to *Campo Santo*, ix; for a similar claim, see his interview with Malcolm Jones in "Books: Outside the Box," *Newsweek*, October 21, 2001, www.newsweek.com/2001/10/24/books-outside-the-box.print.html. Sebald's critique of the traditional novel has fostered his characterization as an "antinovelist," which Ross Posnock proposes as a link between Sebald and Wittgenstein as an "antiphilospher." "'Don't Think but Look!,'" 113. Posnock goes on to cite Sebald's disdain for the "clumsy machinery" of "heavily plotted novels" (attributed to Sebald, although without direct citation, by Eric Homberger,

"W. G. Sebald," *The Guardian*, December 17, 2001). That this disdain might not apply to minimally plotted modernist novels seems not to occur to any of these critics.

38. November 28, 1928, *The Diary of Virginia Woolf*, vol. 3, *1925–1930*, ed. Anne Olivier Bell (New York: Harcourt Brace, 1981), 209. Other realist conventions that Woolf and Sebald both eschew are vernacular language and dialogue.

39. Sebald describes the "periscopic method" in his interview with Eleanor Wachtel, "Ghost Hunter," 37. In "Architecture and Cinema: The Representation of Memory in W. G. Sebald's *Austerlitz*," in Long and Whitehead, *W. G. Sebald: A Critical Companion*, 140–54, Russell J. A. Kilbourn argues that *Austerlitz* tracks a course from a spatialized architectural model of memory, inherited from classical mnemonic traditions and practices, to a modern unreliable cinematic model that is epitomized by the Nazi film *The Fuhrer Gives a City to the Jews*. I contend, by contrast, that the architectural model persists as (among other things) a formal analogue to *Austerlitz*'s narrative structure.

40. Sebald invokes the metaphor of pockets in an interview with Joseph Cuomo to describe the circumscribed persistence of ancient forests (and thus of an unchanged ancient era) in modern Corsica. In his very next comment, he characterizes *Austerlitz* as an elegy. The association between these comments (and the application of the figure of pockets to the novel) is only implicit, but these are precisely the type of unplanned associations Sebald endorses throughout the interview. Cuomo, "A Conversation with W. G. Sebald," 102–3. The references in this and the following sentence in the text to redemption and time are from "Ghost Hunter," 41–42.

41. Cuomo, "A Conversation with W. G. Sebald," 103, emphasis added.

42. Virginia Woolf, "A Sketch of the Past," in *Moments of Being: Unpublished Autobiographical Writings*, ed. Jeanne Schulkind (New York: Harcourt Brace Jovanovich, 1985), 79.

43. Henry James, "Preface to 'The Portrait of a Lady,'" in *The Art of the Novel: Critical Prefaces*, ed. Richard P. Blackmur (New York and London: Charles Scribner's Sons, 1962), 46.

44. For the debate about Sebald's modernist versus postmodern affiliations, see Zilcosky, "Lost and Found," 685.

45. W. G. Sebald, in an interview with Michael Silverblatt titled "A Poem of an Invisible Subject," in Schwartz, *The Emergence of Memory*, 86.

46. On the mythology of rural England, see Raymond Williams, *The Country and The City* (New York: Oxford University Press, 1973); and Jed Esty, *A Shrinking Island: Modernism and National Culture in England* (Princeton, NJ: Princeton University Press, 2004).

47. On these strategies, see Jesse Matz, "Introduction," in *Modernist Time Ecology* (Baltimore: Johns Hopkins University Press, 2018), 11–12.

48. W. G. Sebald, "Against the Irreversible: On Jean Améry," in *On the Natural History of Destruction*, 150.

49. In *Knole and the Sackvilles* (New York: George H. Doran, 1922), Vita Sackville-West explains that the number of courts "is supposed to correspond to the days in the week; and in pursuance of this conceit there are in the house fifty-two staircases, corresponding to the weeks in the year, and three hundred and sixty-five rooms,

corresponding to the days. I cannot truthfully pretend that I have ever verified these counts, and it may be that their accuracy is accepted solely on the strength of the legend; but if this is so, then it has been a very persistent legend" (4).

50. Sackville-West, *Knole and the Sackvilles*, 2, 18. On the celebration of Englishness by the genre of the country house poem that developed in the seventeenth century, see Hugh Jenkins, *Feigned Commonwealths: The Country-House Poem and the Fashioning of the Ideal Community* (Pittsburgh: University of Pittsburgh Press, 1998); and Alastair Fowler, *The Country House Poem: A Cabinet of Seventeenth-Century Estate Poems and Related Items* (Edinburgh: Edinburgh University Press, 1994). Expanding on her claim that Knole is one of the five largest houses in England, Kate Ravilious explains: "There are only a few places like Knole, from the ancient paths that still crisscross the estate to the hidden stories behind its walls, where history accretes, layer upon layer, generation upon generation." "The Many Lives of an English Manor House," *Archaeology* 69, no. 1 (January/February 2016): 44–49.

51. The translation loses some of the spatializing thrust of the original, in which *nebeneinander* means literally "next to one another" rather than "simultaneously."

52. Psychotherapy, according to Winnicott, who famously got down on the floor and played with his clients, "takes place in the overlap of two areas of playing, that of the patient and that of the therapist. Psychotherapy has to do with two people playing together." D. W. Winnicott, "Playing: A Theoretical Statement," in *Playing and Reality*, 44. Virginia Woolf's geographic and imaginative proximity to Winnicott has elicited more than one attempt to parse their relation. See especially Alison Bechdel, *Are You My Mother? A Comic Drama* (New York: Houghton Mifflin, 2012), 24–26; and Elizabeth Abel, *Virginia Woolf and the Fictions of Psychoanalysis* (Chicago: University of Chicago Press, 1980), chap. 4.

53. D. W. Winnicott, "Transitional Objects and Transitional Phenomena," in *Playing and Reality*, 26. The likelihood that Sebald knew this case study is strengthened by the similarity between Winnicott's account of one of this patient's strategies for dealing with her separation from her parents—sudden flashes in which she would see her otherwise forgotten toy dog Toby, supplemented by Winnicott's comment that "there is a picture in the family album of herself with Toby" (28)—and the Welsh family album in which Austerlitz at around age eleven finds a photograph of a girl holding a dog on her lap, the name Toby transposed to the dog who sits by Gerald's side (73).

54. Sebald has greatly elaborated on Vera's prototype in his source for this portion of the text, Saul Friedlander's memoir of his return to Prague in search of a lost childhood: *When Memory Comes*, trans. Helen R. Lane (Madison: University of Wisconsin Press, 1979). In Friedlander's narrative, a character named Vlasta is merely a nanny with a quotidian name and only a room of her own in the parental home rather than a separate apartment.

55. D. W. Winnicott introduces the concept of the good-enough mother in "Transitional Objects and Transitional Phenomena," first formulated in 1951, and subsequently expanded with clinical material to become a core concept of the collected papers published as *Playing and Reality*.

56. The most egregious example occurs in Richard Eder's otherwise luminous review of *Austerlitz*, in which he refers to Vera in passing as "an old woman who knew his

[Austerlitz's] parents." "Excavating a Life," *New York Times*, October 28, 2001, https://www.nytimes.com/2001/10/28/books/excavating-a-life.html.

57. For a fuller account of the perseverating A's of *Austerlitz*, see Angier, *Speak, Silence*, 415–16.

58. In an interview with Christian Scholz, Sebald claimed to have been haunted by this photograph "like something lying on the floor and accumulating dust, you know, where these clumps of dust get caught, [and] it steadily becomes a bigger ball. Eventually you can pull out strings." "'But the Written Word Is Not a True Document': A Conversation with W. G. Sebald on Literature and Photography," trans. Markus Zisselsberger, in Patt, *Searching for Sebald*, 109.

59. Marianne Hirsch, *Family Frames: Photography, Narrative, and Postmemory* (Cambridge, MA: Harvard University Press, 1997), 165.

60. W. G. Sebald, "The Undiscover'd Country: The Death Motif in Kafka's Castle," *Journal of European Studies* 2, no. 1 (March 1972): 22–34. See also "Kafka Goes to the Movies," in which Sebald describes Kafka's attitude toward photography as a mirror image of his own, and "To the Brothel by Way of Switzerland: On Kafka's Travel Diaries," in which he perceives himself as traveling in Kafka's footsteps. Both essays are in *Campo Santo*, 151–68 and 135–40. Sebald also describes his perception of Kafka as a double in "Dr K. Takes the Waters at Riva," *Vertigo*, trans. Michael Hulse (New York: New Directions, 2000), 139–68.

61. Scholz, "'But the Written Word Is Not a True Document,'" 108.

62. Sebald, "The Undiscover'd Country," 22.

63. Walter Benjamin, "A Short History of Photography," in *Classic Essays on Photography*, ed. Alan Trachtenberg (New Haven, CT: Leete's Island Books, 1980), 207, 206.

64. Walter Benjamin, *Berlin Childhood around 1900*, trans. Howard Eiland (Cambridge, MA: Harvard University Press, 2006), 132. Since Sebald owned Benjamin's collected works and refers to them repeatedly, it is likely that Benjamin's account of Kafka's photograph was familiar to him. For a thorough and thoughtful analysis of the triangulation among Sebald, Benjamin, and Kafka, see Markus Zisselsberger, "Melancholy Longings: Sebald, Benjamin, and the Image of Kafka," in Patt, *Searching for Sebald*, 280–301.

65. Benjamin, "A Short History of Photography," 206.

66. See Cadava, *Words of Light*, esp. 106–27, for a powerful account of Benjamin's reading of Kafka's childhood photograph as an exchange of petrifying Medusan gazes between a mother who has presumably arranged for the photo session and the child who petrifies her in turn through his verbal redescription. In the "final" edition of *Berlin Childhood*, Benjamin sidesteps the mother's implication in this circuit of toxic mimicry, proceeding to other modes and instances of his childhood transformations into the world around him.

67. The passage closely follows Hugo von Hofmannsthal's *Andreas*, to which Sebald had devoted a chapter of *Die Beschreibung des Unglücks* (Frankfurt: S. Fischer Verlag, 1985). Sebald's psychoanalytic reading of *Andreas* substantiates the reading of the shoe he borrows from it as a fetish that defends against maternal lack.

68. Proust offers the most extreme recollection of the tranquility his mother bestowed when she "bent her loving face down over my bed, and held it out to [him] like a Host, for an act of Communion in which [his] lips might drink deeply the sense of her real presence, and with it the power to sleep." Marcel Proust, *Swann's Way*, trans. C. K. Scott Moncrieff (New York: Modern Library, 1928), 14. Similar scenes can be found in Woolf, "A Sketch of the Past" and *To the Lighthouse*, and Benjamin, *Berlin Childhood*.

69. Cited by Maya Barzilai, "Facing the Past and the Female Spectre in W. G. Sebald's *The Emigrants*," in Long and Whitehead, *W. G. Sebald: A Critical Companion*, 208.

70. July 20, 1925, *The Diary of Virginia Woolf*, 3:36.

71. For Winnicott, transitional space is situated developmentally in the place in which "*continuity* is giving way to *contiguity*" and culturally in the liminal zone between subjective and objective worlds. "The Location of Cultural Experience," in *Playing and Reality*, 119, emphasis in original.

72. Virginia Woolf, "Modern Fiction," in *The Common Reader* (New York: Harcourt Brace, 1953), 154.

73. On Woolf's lifelong interest in entomology in the context of Victorian attitudes toward science and gender, see Christina Alt, *Virginia Woolf and the Study of Nature* (Cambridge: Cambridge University Press, 2010), esp. chap. 3; and Holly Henry, *Virginia Woolf and the Discourse of Science: The Aesthetics of Astronomy* (Cambridge: Cambridge University Press, 2003). Drawing from Georges Didi-Huberman's *Phalènes: Essai sur l'apparition* 2 (Paris: Minuit, 2013), Catherine Lanone analyzes the moth as a figure of the image in "An Entomology of Literature: Male Taxonomies and Female Antennae from Mrs. Gaskell to Virginia Woolf," in *Beyond the Victorian/Modernist Divide: Remapping the Turn-of-the-Century Break in Literature, Culture, and the Visual Arts*, ed. Anne-Florence Gillard-Estrada and Anne Besnault-Levita (New York: Routledge, 2018), 181–96.

74. Vanessa Bell to Virginia Woolf, May 3, 1927; cited by Quentin Bell, *Virginia Woolf: A Biography* (New York: Harcourt Brace Jovanovich, 1972), 2:126.

75. Virginia Woolf to Vanessa Bell, May 8, 1927, *The Letters of Virginia Woolf*, vol. 3, *1923–1928*, ed. Nigel Nicolson and Joanne Trautmann (New York: Harcourt, 1977), 372.

76. November 28, 1928, *The Diary of Virginia Woolf*, 3:209.

77. November 28, 1928, *The Diary of Virginia Woolf*, 3:209.

78. In her diary entry for September 16, 1929, Woolf notes: "Moths, I suddenly remember, don't fly by day." *The Diary of Virginia Woolf*, 3:254.

79. May 28, 1929, *The Diary of Virginia Woolf*, 3:229.

80. Although we don't know exactly when Woolf wrote "The Death of the Moth," the evidence of the letters and diaries suggests it was in the late 1920s.

81. Virginia Woolf, "The Death of the Moth," in *The Death of the Moth and Other Essays* (New York: Harcourt/Harvest, 1974), 4.

82. Sarah Kafatou, "An Interview with W. G. Sebald," *Harvard Review* 15 (Fall 1998): 34–35.

83. Sebald, interview by Michael Silverblatt, 80–81.

84. In "'Against you I will fling myself, unvanquished and unyielding, O Death!':

Vanessa Bell's *Death of the Moth* Dust Jacket as Monument to Virginia Woolf," Hana Leaper uncovers the deliberation with which Vanessa Bell arrived at the seemingly casual cover design, which "paints an association between title and author; between the deaths of the eponymous moth and Woolf." In *Virginia Woolf and Heritage*, ed. Jane de Gay, Tom Breckin, and Anne Reus (Liverpool: Liverpool University Press; Clemson, SC: Clemson University Press, 2017), 82. Leaper also points out that Leonard Woolf's choice of the essay's title for the entire collection suggests that "he saw it as the most important work in the collection, and as setting the tone for the rest" (82). In addition, Leaper notes that the V-shape design in the lower right-hand corner links the shape of the moth with Virginia's first name: a form of iconographic allusion that Sebald would deploy in his inscription of the letter A in *Austerlitz*.

85. W. G. Sebald, *The Emigrants*, trans. Michael Hulse (New York: New Directions, 1997). See, for example, pp. 104, 115, 174, 214. There has been much discussion of the significance of Nabokov's spectral appearances in *The Emigrants*. See especially Adrian Curtin and Maxim D. Shrayer, "Netting the Butterfly Man: The Significance of Vladimir Nabokov in W. G. Sebald's *The Emigrants*," *Religion and the Arts* 9, nos. 3–4 (2005): 258–83; Leland de la Durantaye, "The Facts of Fiction, or the Figure of Vladimir Nabokov in W. G. Sebald," *Comparative Literature Studies* 45, no. 4 (2008): 425–45; and Karen Jacobs, "Sebald's Apparitional Nabokov," *Twentieth Century Literature* 61, no. 2 (Summer 2014): 137–68. Despite their different emphases, these critics agree about Sebald's fundamentally appreciative stance toward Nabokov in *The Emigrants*.

86. W. G. Sebald, "Dream Textures: A Brief Note on Nabokov," in *Campo Santo*, 141–50.

87. In an interview with Herbert Gold in the *Paris Review* (Summer–Fall 1967), Nabokov claimed: "The pleasures and rewards of literary inspiration are nothing beside the rapture of discovering a new organ under the microscope or an undescribed species on a mountainside in Iran or Peru. It is not improbable that had there been no revolution in Russia, I would have devoted myself entirely to lepidopterology and never written any novels at all" (41). For an appraisal of Nabokov's contribution as an entomologist, see Stephen Jay Gould, "No Science without Fancy, No Art without Facts: The Lepidoptery of Vladimir Nabokov," in *I Have Landed: The End of a Beginning in Natural History* (Cambridge, MA: Harvard University Press, 2011), 29–53. See also Nancy Pick, "Vladimir Nabokov's Genitalia Cabinet & Other Miscellany," in *The Rarest of the Rare: Stories behind the Treasures at the Harvard Museum of Natural History* (Cambridge, MA: Harvard University Press, 2004), 142–62.

88. Vladimir Nabokov, *Speak, Memory* (New York: Vintage, 1989), 119.

89. Lynn L. Wolff identifies the photograph in "Untangling Fact from Fiction: Sebald's Extratextual Materials," in *W. G. Sebald's Hybrid Poetics: Literature as Historiography*, Interdisciplinary German Cultural Studies 14 (Hawthorne, NY: De Gruyter, 2014), 130. According to the photographer Arwed Messmer in a personal communication (July 11, 2022), the photograph shows a display box from the Museum of Natural History in Petersburg rather than Nabokov's personal collection. Its inclusion in a special issue of the Swiss magazine *Du* on Nabokov has fostered the assumption that the display box belonged to Nabokov. On the literary ramifications of Nabokov's avocation as a lepidopterist, see Bryan Boyd and Robert Michael Pyle, eds., *Nabokov's Butterflies: Unpublished and Uncollected Writings* (Boston: Beacon Press, 2000).

90. Virginia Woolf, "Reading," in *The Captain's Death Bed and Other Essays* (New York: Harcourt Brace Jovanovich, 1978), 167–68. A similar passage occurs in *Jacob's Room*, annotated and introduced by Vara Neverow (New York: Harcourt/Harvest, 2008), 30–31.

91. Woolf, "Reading," 174.

92. Sebald, interview by Sarah Kafatou, 34; Woolf, "The Death of the Moth," 6.

93. In *Touching Photographs* (Chicago: University of Chicago Press, 2012), Margaret Olin also makes the connection of this passage to "The Death of a Moth" but reads the photograph of the moth exclusively in terms of her inquiry into photography's truth value, arguing that the moth "has shriveled unnoticed on a bright wall, until it is a dry, empty exoskeleton . . . as though photographs are but the dead exoskeleton of the truth" (97). She doesn't comment on the fact that the moth has not been pinned and typologized in a specimen box but is shown alone against an illuminated backdrop and could be either, as Olin says, dead or flying upward in the light: the troubling of distinctions that characterizes moths in this text.

94. W. G. Sebald, *The Rings of Saturn*, trans. Michael Hulse (New York: New Directions, 1999), 9. Virginia Woolf, "The Elizabethan Lumber Room," in *The Common Reader*, 47–48; Sebald, *The Rings of Saturn*, 19–20. Note too how the claim of Sebald's Browne that "it seems a miracle that we should last so much as a single day" echoes Clarissa's belief that "it was very, very dangerous to live even one day" (*The Rings of Saturn*, 24; *Mrs. Dalloway*, 8). Woolf's recommendation of Browne's *The Garden of Cyrus*, especially "the heart of the quincunx" in chapter 3, may have inspired Sebald's elaboration of Browne's quincunx in *The Rings of Saturn*, 283.

95. The critical role of Sir Thomas Browne in *The Rings of Saturn*, Sebald's reflections on his walking tour along the coast of Surrey, which opens with a scenario at a hospital window in Norwich, home of Sir Thomas Browne, son of a silk merchant, and concludes with a history of sericulture that foregrounds the brutalization of human and insect workers required to produce the "truly fabulous variety" and "quite indescribable beauty" of silk, further reveals how the trope of the moth affiliates Sebald, Browne, and Woolf. *The Rings of Saturn*, 283. In *Speak, Silence*, Carole Angier describes Thomas Browne as "the hero of Sebald's most metaphysical book, *The Rings of Saturn*" (428).

96. Woolf, "The Elizabethan Lumber Room," 48, 47.

97. Woolf seems to have invented this painting, since it is not mentioned in the catalogue of art at Knole House.

98. See, for example, Max Bluestone, "The Iconographic Sources of Auden's 'Musée des Beaux Arts,'" *Modern Language Notes* 76, no. 4 (April, 1961): 331–36; and Marcel Sarot, "Transformative Poetry: A Case Study of W. H. Auden's *Musée des Beaux Arts* and General Conclusions," *Perichoresis* 14, no. 2 (2016): 81–97.

99. Sebald's poem alludes to "Icarus, / sailing in the midst of / the currents of light . . . , if he falls / down into the lake, / will then, as in Bruegel's / picture, the beautiful ship, / the ploughing peasant, the whole / of nature somehow turn away / from the son's misfortune?" (*After Nature*, 105–6). Carole Angier reproduces the image on Sebald's office door in "Who Is W. G. Sebald?," *Jewish Quarterly*, Winter 1996/97, 10–14.

100. The conjunction between Auden and Woolf receives some bibliographic support from the poem's initial appearance in John Lehmann's magazine, *New Writing*, which had been published by the Hogarth Press since 1938, when Lehmann replaced Virginia Woolf (with her consent) as co-editor of the press. For Woolf's complex relation with the Auden generation, see Hermione Lee, *Virginia Woolf* (New York: Vintage Books, 1999), esp. chaps. 33 and 38.

101. Paul K. Saint-Amour, *Tense Future: Modernism, Total War, Encyclopedic Form* (New York: Oxford University Press, 2015).

AFTERWORD

1. Virginia Woolf, *Between the Acts* (New York: Harcourt/Harvest, 1969), 188; abbreviated in the text as *BTA*.

2. "Anon" in "'Anon' and 'The Reader': Virginia Woolf's Last Essays," ed. Brenda R. Silver, *Twentieth Century Literature* 25, no. 3/4 (Autumn–Winter 1979): 385. For an illuminating reading of the figure and force of Anon in Woolf's late work, see Maria DiBattista, *Virginia Woolf's Major Novels: The Fables of Anon* (New Haven, CT: Yale University Press, 1980), 235–45. For a more philosophical analysis of late Woolfian anonymity as one manifestation of a posthuman or inhuman comedy, see Rasheed Tazudeen, "Hearing beyond Extinction: The Inhuman Comedy of *Between the Acts*," in *Virginia Woolf and the Anthropocene*, ed. Peter Adkins (Edinburgh: Edinburgh University Press, 2024).

3. Wai Chee Dimock, "A Theory of Resonance," *PMLA* 112, no. 5 (October 1997): 1064; Stephen Greenblatt, "Resonance and Wonder," in *Exhibition Cultures: The Poetics and Politics of Museum Display*, ed. Ivan Karp and Steven D. Lavine (Washington, D.C.: Smithsonian Institute, 1991), 42–56.

4. Dimock, "A Theory of Resonance," 1062–63, 1061.

5. Dimock, "A Theory of Resonance," 1062. The reference to "Virginia Woolf icon" is, of course, to the title of Brenda Silver's influential book *Virginia Woolf Icon* (Chicago: University of Chicago Press, 1999).

6. Dimock, "A Theory of Resonance," 1063, 1067.

7. Dimock, "A Theory of Resonance," 1064.

8. Georges Didi-Huberman, *Phalènes: Essai sur l'apparition 2* (Paris: Minuit, 2013). In "An Entomology of Literature: Male Taxonomies and Female Antennae from Mrs. Gaskell to Virginia Woolf," in *Beyond the Victorian/Modernist Divide: Remapping the Turn-of-the-Century Break in Literature, Culture, and the Visual Arts*, ed. Anne-Florence Gillard-Estrada and Anne Besnault-Levita (New York: Routledge, 2018), Catherine Lanone deftly summarizes Didi-Huberman's version of the *phalène* as "not simply the recurrent representation of the moth, but the flickering process of the image per se, blending presence and absence, emerging and oscillating" (193).

9. W.G. Sebald, interview by Michael Silverblatt, *Bookworm*, December 6, 2001; reprinted in *The Emergence of Memory: Conversations with W. G. Sebald*, ed. Lynne Sharon Schwartz (New York: Seven Stories Press, 2007), 80–81.

10. Dimock, "A Theory of Resonance," 1066.

11. Dimock, "A Theory of Resonance," 1064.

Index

Page numbers in *italics* refer to figures.

Dimock, Wai Chee, 3, 5, 223–26; "A
Theory of Resonance," 223
Dinshaw, Carolyn, 66; *Getting Medieval*,
247n16
domesticity: as feminine, 27, 64; and
psychoanalysis, 188; as queer, 27, 105,
107, 109–10
Dowling, Linda, 94
Doyle, Laura, 35
Du Bois, W. E. B., *Dark Princess*, 28
Duval, Jeanne, 47–48

ecocriticism, and Woolf, 4, 230n14
Edelman, Lee, 108; *No Future*, 109,
247n15
Eden, 97–98, 103, 105–6, 108
Edinburgh Companion to Virginia Woolf,
8, 230n5
effeminacy, 101–2, 105. *See also*
femininity; masculinity
elegy: and affect, 130; and closure, 17;
generic conventions of, 130–31,
133–34; maternal, 19, 123, 133, 138; and
the mourning/melancholia binary,
132, 136; mutability of, 257n8; tone of,
19; traditions of, 19, 122–23. See also
Camera Lucida (*La chambre claire*;
Barthes); *To the Lighthouse* (Woolf)
Englishness, 31, 58–59, 272n50. *See also*
Anglophilia
entomology, 202–3, 254n115, 274n73,
275n87. *See also* Browne, Thomas;
Didi-Huberman, George; moths;
Nabokov, Vladimir
Entomology Society, 202–3
envelopes, 27, 37, 39–42, 47, 49, 51, 53,
58, 95, 154, 165, 199, 243n59. *See also*
epistolary novel; letters
epistolary novel, 27, 29, 36–37, 40,
239n16. *See also* Richardson, Samuel,
Clarissa; Watt, Ian
Esty, Jed, *A Shrinking Island*, 223, 237n65
European modernism, 15, 18–19, 117.
See also modernism
existentialism, 102. *See also*
phenomenology; Sartre, Jean-Paul,
L'imaginaire

fashion, 28, 40, 46, 53, 195, 243n61.
See also Black dandy; frock
consciousness; frocks; gowns
femininity: and the Black dandy, 28–29,
48; and childhood, 153, 177; and
Christianity, 113; and domesticity,
27, 64; and fashion, 51–52; and
the literary canon, 7, 24, 27; and
masculinity, 72, 104; and Paris,
100–102. *See also* effeminacy; gender;
masculinity
feminism: and literary culture, 32–33;
perceptions of, 2; and protest, 71;
second-wave, 6, 72
Flatley, Jonathan, 132, 160
formalist aesthetic, 54–56
Forster, E. M., *Aspects of the Novel*, 35–36,
68
Forum (magazine), 32, 52–54, 244n77
Foucault, Michel, 3
Frankfurt School, 132, 172, 268n19
French language, 16, 50, 67, 102, 111,
123–24, 127, 134, 149, 169, 198, 225,
236n59, 258nn14–15
Freud, Sigmund: on mania, 161–62; on
mourning, 15, 131–32, 149–51, 160–61;
and philosophical pessimism, 19; and
Queen Victoria, 129; and shock, 138;
on the uncanny, 171–73, 197. *See also*
psychoanalysis
Freud, Sigmund, works of: *The Ego and
the Id*, 160; *Inhibitions, Symptoms
and Anxiety*, 160; "Medusa's Head,"
171; "Mourning and Melancholia," 15,
131–32, 149, 160–61, 263n52, 264n67;
"On Transience," 266n80
Friedman, Susan Stanford, 2, 230n6,
230n9
frock consciousness, 40, 48, 51, 53, 243n61
frocks, 43, 50–52, 57, 244n74. *See also*
fashion; gowns
Froule, Christine, 258n8
Fry, Roger, 141, 260n36, 261n42

Gates, Henry Louis, Jr., 36, 237n3
gaze: and the audience, 46; and
photography, 146, 170, 193; shifting

Mapplethorpe, Robert, "Young Man with Arm Extended," 128
Marcus, Jane, 232n26
masculinity, 10–11, 28, 48, 56, 71–72, 92, 94–96, 98, 101–2, 104, 131. *See also* femininity; gender
masks, 42–43, 46
maternal: and the body, 150–51, 173; and death, 15–17, 120–22, 131, 134–35, 138, 148, 151, 153, 161–62, 164; and eroticism, 141; gaze, 193; kiss, 199, 274n68; light, 145, 152; as precursor, 7; veil, 137. *See also* elegy; mania; mourning; photography
McDowell, Deborah E., 238n6, 243n59
McEwan, Ian, *Atonement*, 7, 233n32
melancholia, 15–17, 19, 120, 131–34, 149, 151–52, 161–62, 164–66, 260n29, 265n69. *See also* depression; mania; mourning
memory: and childhood, 196–97; and death, 1, 85; layers of, 38–39, 176; persistence of, 81–82, 167, 173; and photography, 140, 143–44, 147–49; recollection of, 134–36; and spatialization, 182–83; and temporality, 23. *See also* cave of memory; tunneling process
Mencken, H. L., "The American Language," 30
Messmer, Arwed, *209*, 275n89
Miller, Monica L., 27–29; *Slaves to Fashion*, 72, 237n3
minor: as disparaging term, 5–7; genealogy, 17; reclamation of, 8, 20, 231n20. *See also* anonymity; queerness
mirrors, 38–39, 49, 113, 145, 168–69, 189, 239n15
Mitscherlich, Alexander and Margarete, *The Inability to Mourn*, 15–16
modernism: and childhood, 190–91, 200; contending modes of, 26, 34, 36, 53, 56; and gender, 10–11, 29; good vs. bad, 10; identification with, 33–34; and implicit straightness, 8; and interiority, 37–38, 61; linear trajectory of, 5–6, 13–14; markers of, 1–2, 13–14, 32, 47–49, 51, 57–58,

182, 235n44; and melancholia, 132; and polished surfaces, 43–44, 47; and the room trope, 11–12, 247n13; and temporality, 9, 17, 20, 198–99. *See also* African American modernism; Anglo-American modernism; European modernism; long modernism; mulatta modernism; postmodernism
Mordecai, Pamela, "The Angel in the House," 6, 232n27
Morrison, Toni, 6, 13, 236n54
moths, 20, 202–5, 207–12, 218, 220–22, 225–26, 276n93. *See also* butterflies; vibrations
mourning: failures of, 15–16; and mania, 165; modes of, 17, 128–29, 219; in the postwar era, 10, 15; and psychoanalysis, 129, 148–50; queering the binaries of, 120; and temporality, 142. *See also* melancholia; psychoanalysis
Mrs. Dalloway (Woolf): and African American modernism, 20; and boundary trespass, 82; cover design of, 40, *41*; and death, 63, 87; drafting of, 138; and heteronormative social sphere, 54–55; influences of, 2–3, 6, 23–24; narrative form of, 10, 36, 38, 110, 114; reception of, 31–32, 36–37, 229n2; as representative of modernism, 1–2; and the room trope, 11–13; and temporality, 14, 17, 184. *See also* cave of memory
mulatta modernism, 23–24, 29, 60. *See also* modernism
Munich Agreement, 172, 217. *See also* World War II
Muñoz, José Esteban, 109–10, 114

Nabokov, Vladimir, 168, 204, 208, 275n87; "Christmas," 210–11
narrative mode: and interiority, 31, 39; and long modernism, 9–10; and omniscience, 77, 181; and ordinary life, 68; periscopic narration, 188–89; and structure, 57; and temporality, 12–14, 37, 110